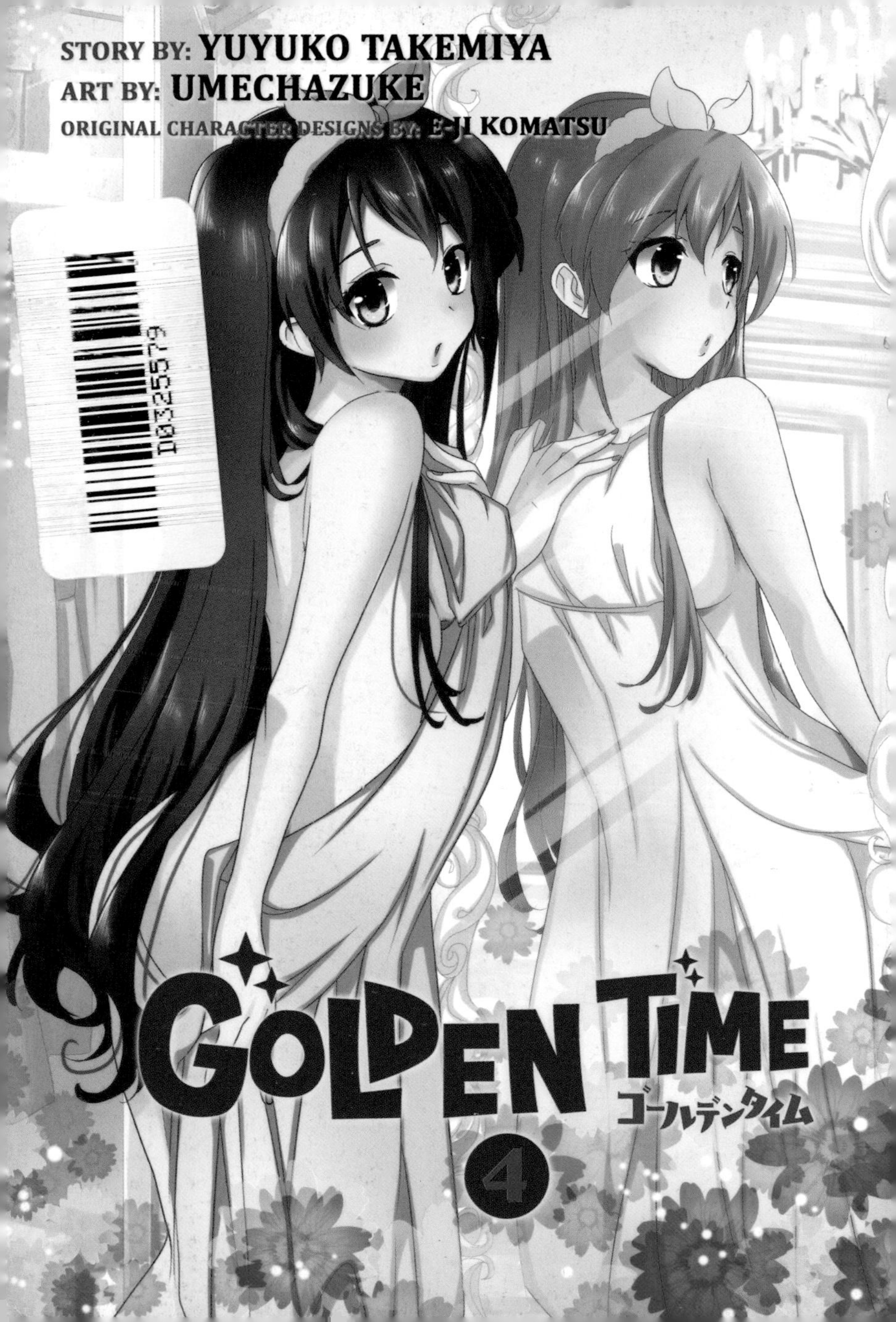
STORY BY: YUYUKO TAKEMIYA
ART BY: UMECHAZUKE
ORIGINAL CHARACTER DESIGNS BY: E-JI KOMATSU
GOLDEN TIME
ゴールデンタイム
4

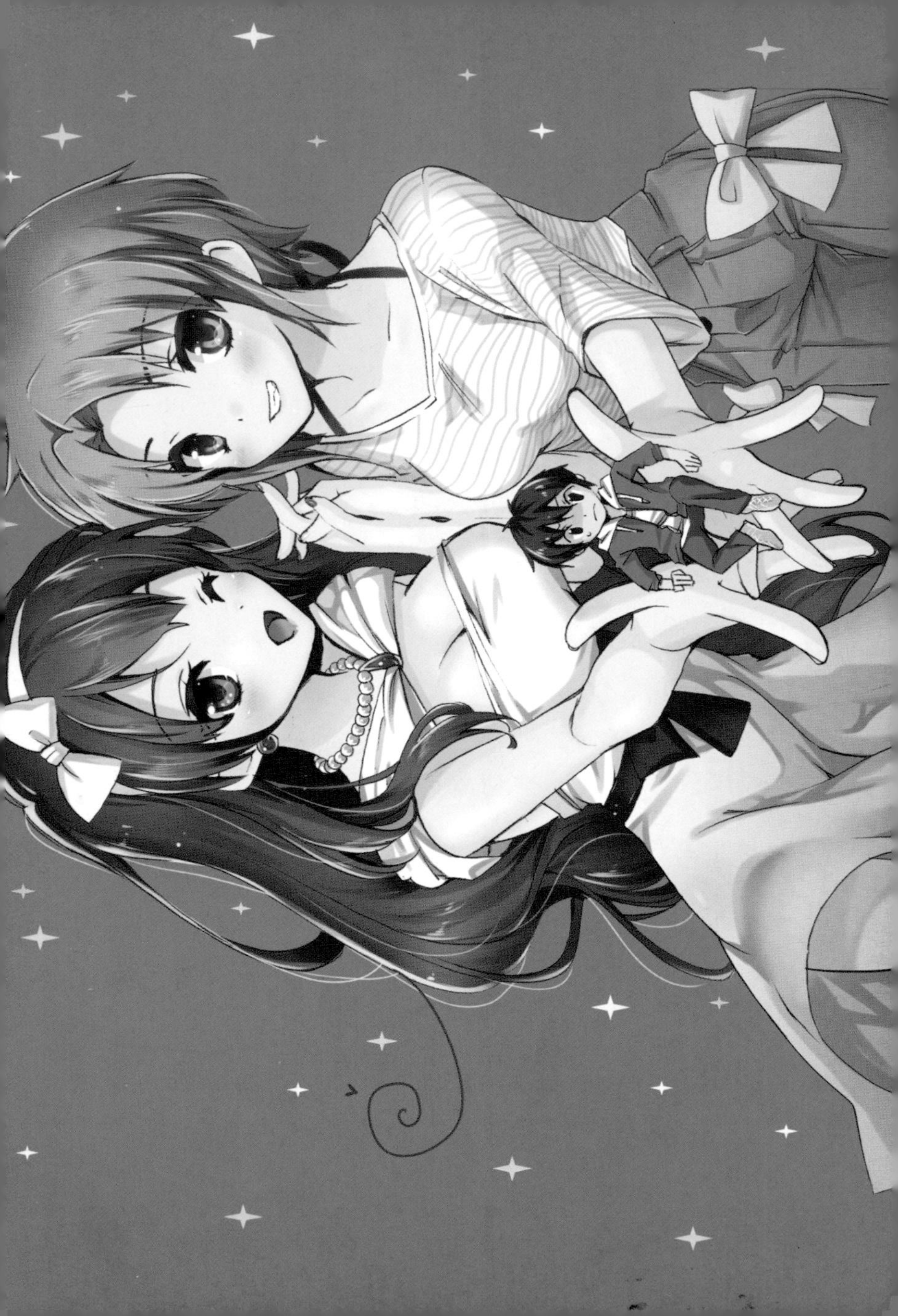

CHAPTER 18

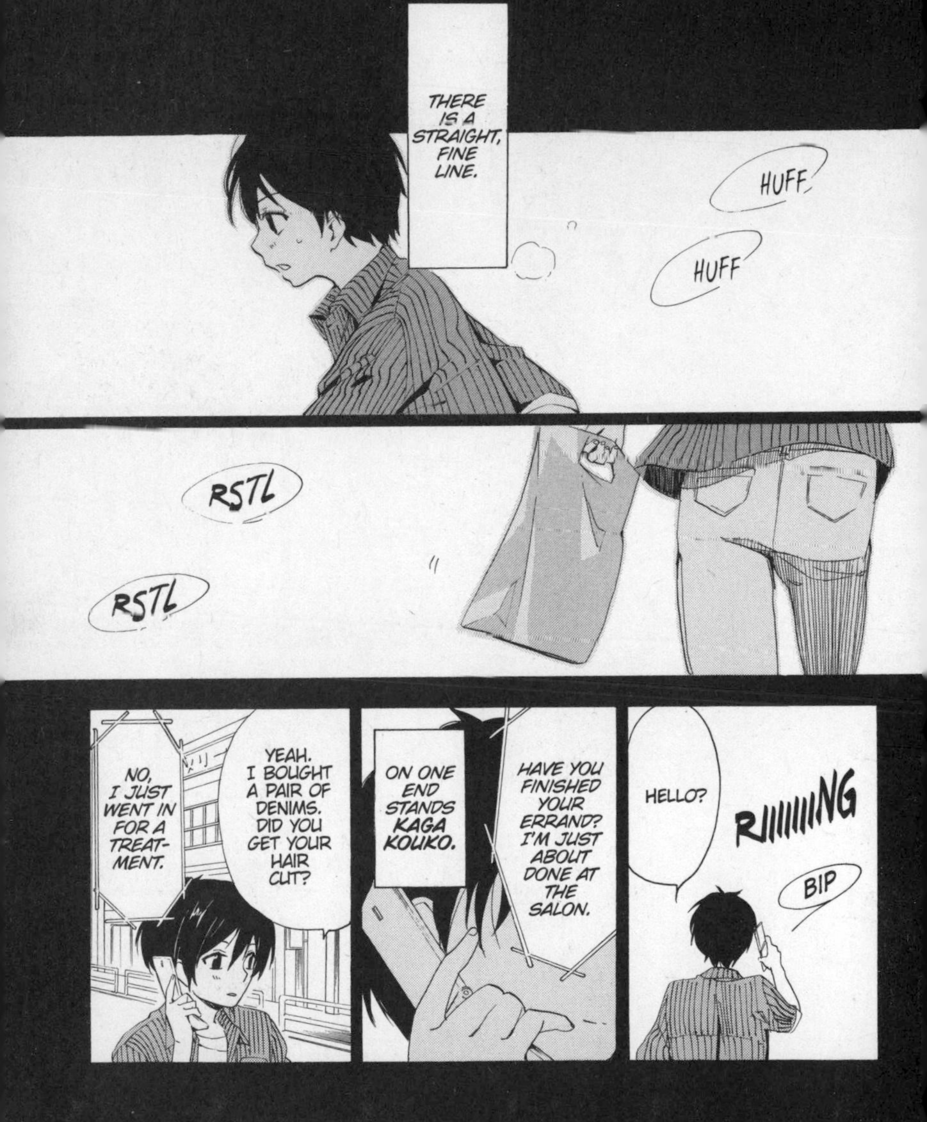
THERE IS A STRAIGHT, FINE LINE.
HUFF
HUFF
RSTL
RSTL
RIIIIIIIING
BIP
HELLO?
HAVE YOU FINISHED YOUR ERRAND? I'M JUST ABOUT DONE AT THE SALON.
ON ONE END STANDS KAGA KOUKO.
YEAH. I BOUGHT A PAIR OF DENIMS. DID YOU GET YOUR HAIR CUT?
NO, I JUST WENT IN FOR A TREATMENT.

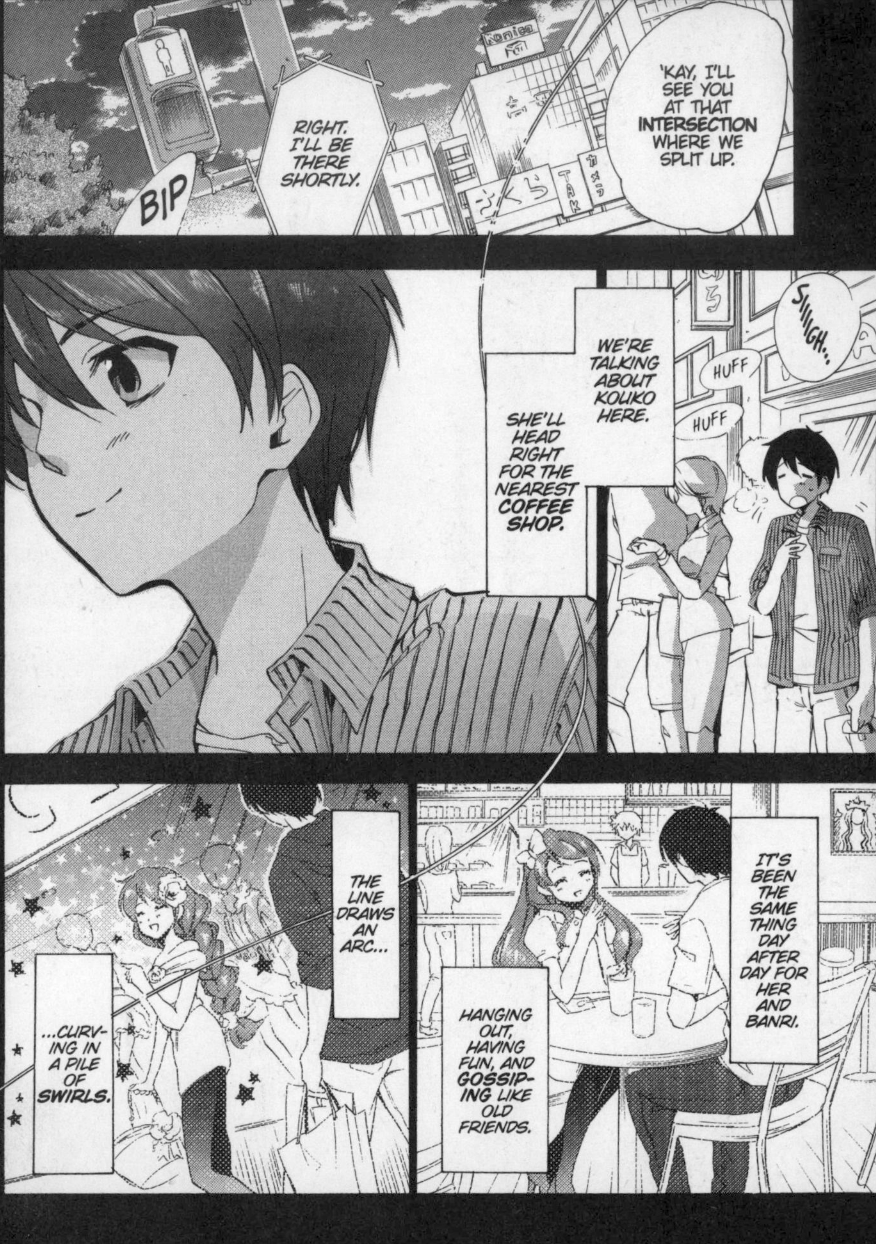
'KAY, I'LL SEE YOU AT THAT INTERSECTION WHERE WE SPLIT UP.
RIGHT. I'LL BE THERE SHORTLY.
BIP
SIIIGH...
HUFF
HUFF
WE'RE TALKING ABOUT KOUKO HERE.
SHE'LL HEAD RIGHT FOR THE NEAREST COFFEE SHOP.
IT'S BEEN THE SAME THING DAY AFTER DAY FOR HER AND BANRI.
HANGING OUT, HAVING FUN, AND GOSSIPING LIKE OLD FRIENDS.
THE LINE DRAWS AN ARC...
...CURVING IN A PILE OF SWIRLS.

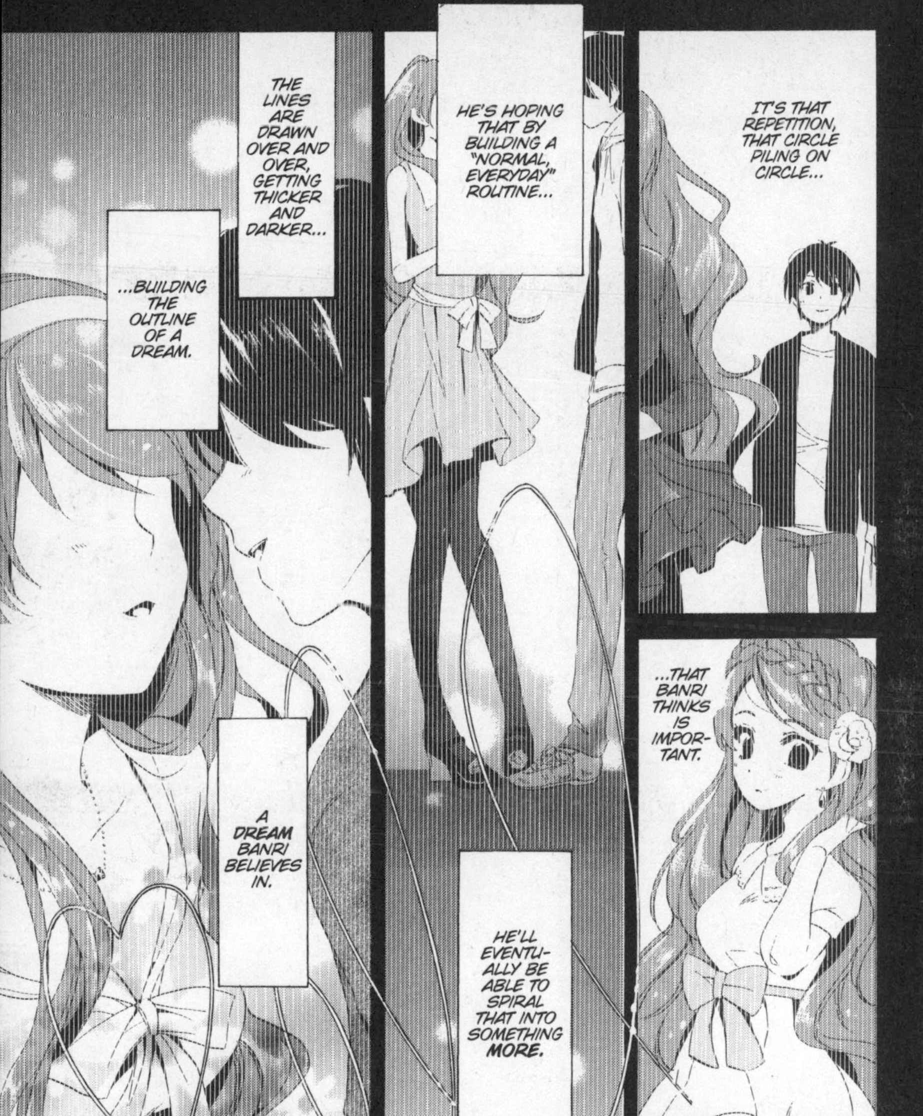
IT'S THAT REPETITION, THAT CIRCLE PILING ON CIRCLE...
...THAT BANRI THINKS IS IMPORTANT.
HE'S HOPING THAT BY BUILDING A "NORMAL, EVERYDAY" ROUTINE...
HE'LL EVENTUALLY BE ABLE TO SPIRAL THAT INTO SOMETHING MORE.
THE LINES ARE DRAWN OVER AND OVER, GETTING THICKER AND DARKER...
...BUILDING THE OUTLINE OF A DREAM.
A DREAM BANRI BELIEVES IN.

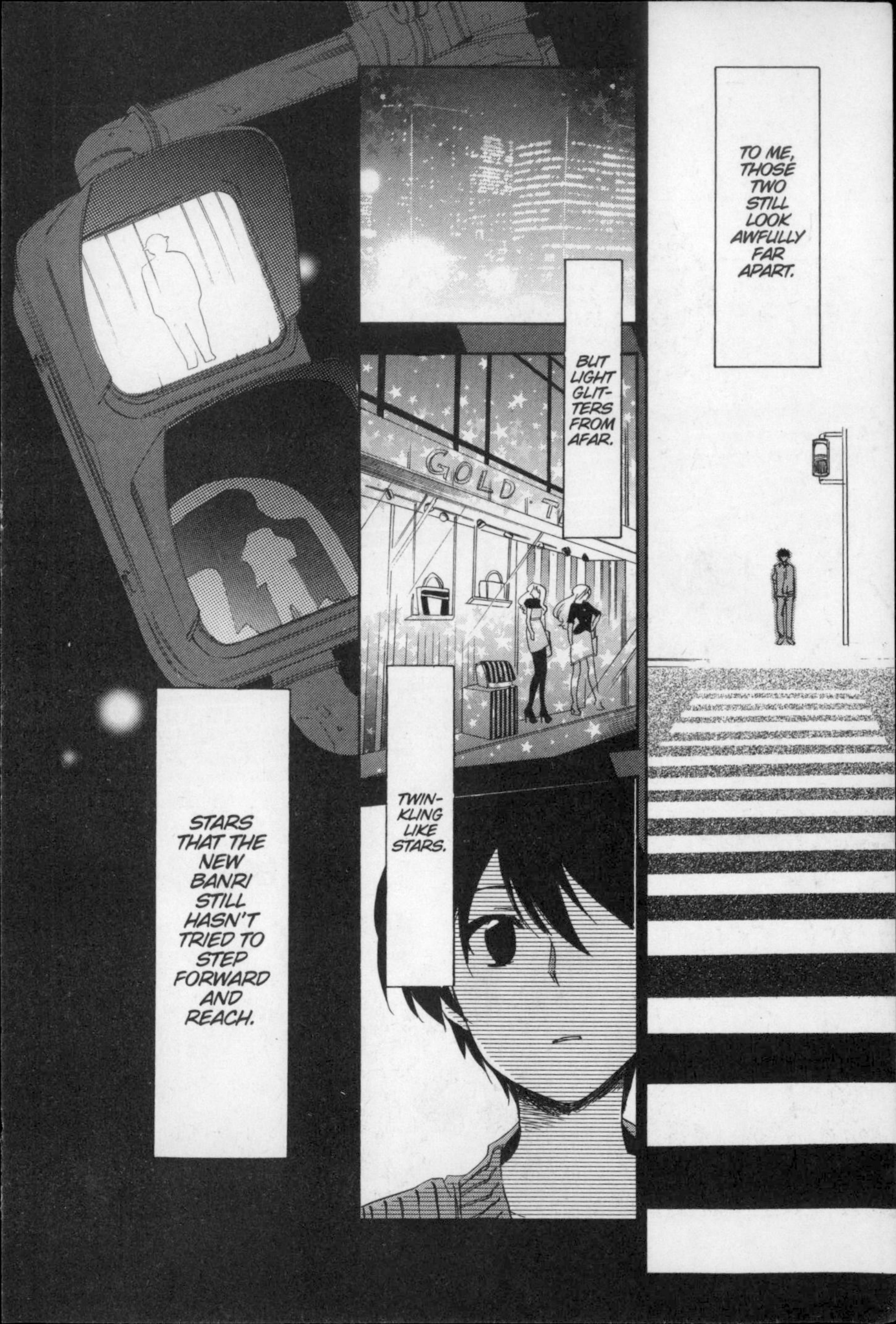
TO ME, THOSE TWO STILL LOOK AWFULLY FAR APART.
BUT LIGHT GLITTERS FROM AFAR.
GOLD
TWINKLING LIKE STARS.
STARS THAT THE NEW BANRI STILL HASN'T TRIED TO STEP FORWARD AND REACH.

CHAPTER 18: Here & There

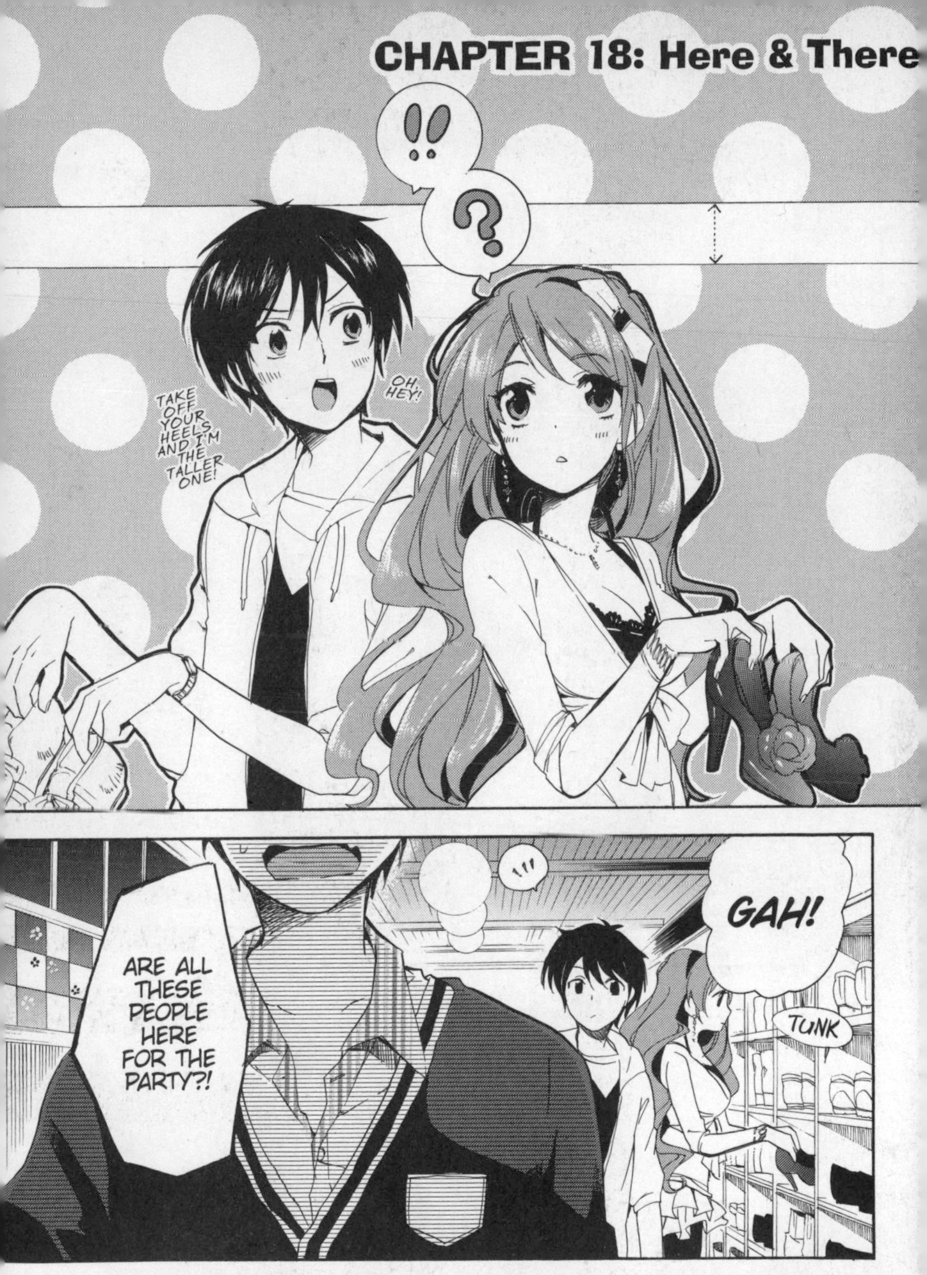
!!
?
OH, HEY!
TAKE OFF YOUR HEELS AND I'M THE TALLER ONE!
GAH!
TUNK
ARE ALL THESE PEOPLE HERE FOR THE PARTY?!

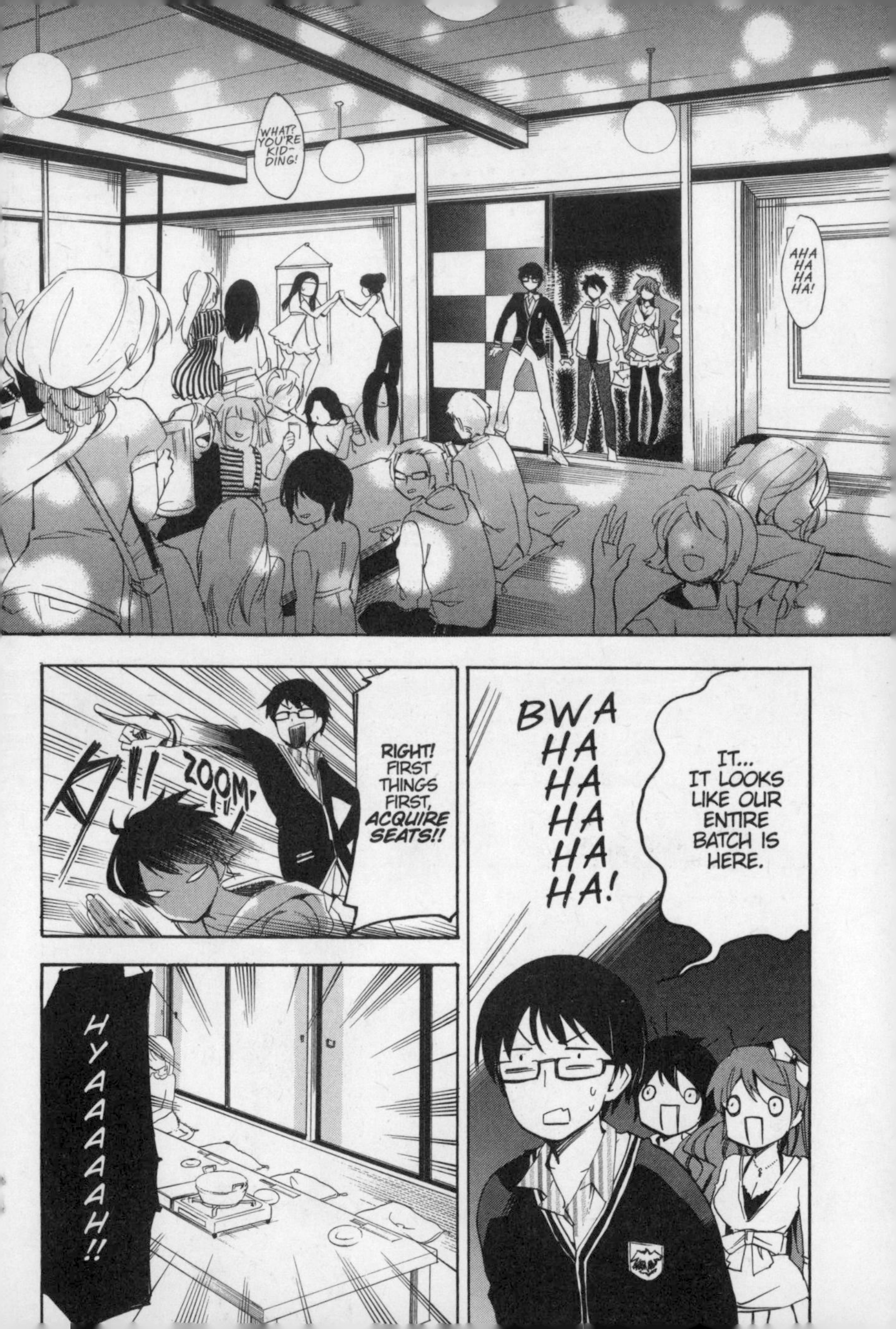
AHA HA HA HA!
WHAT? YOU'RE KID-DING!
IT... IT LOOKS LIKE OUR ENTIRE BATCH IS HERE.
BWA HA HA HA HA HA HA!
RIGHT! FIRST THINGS FIRST, ACQUIRE SEATS!!
ZOOM
HYAAAAAAH!!

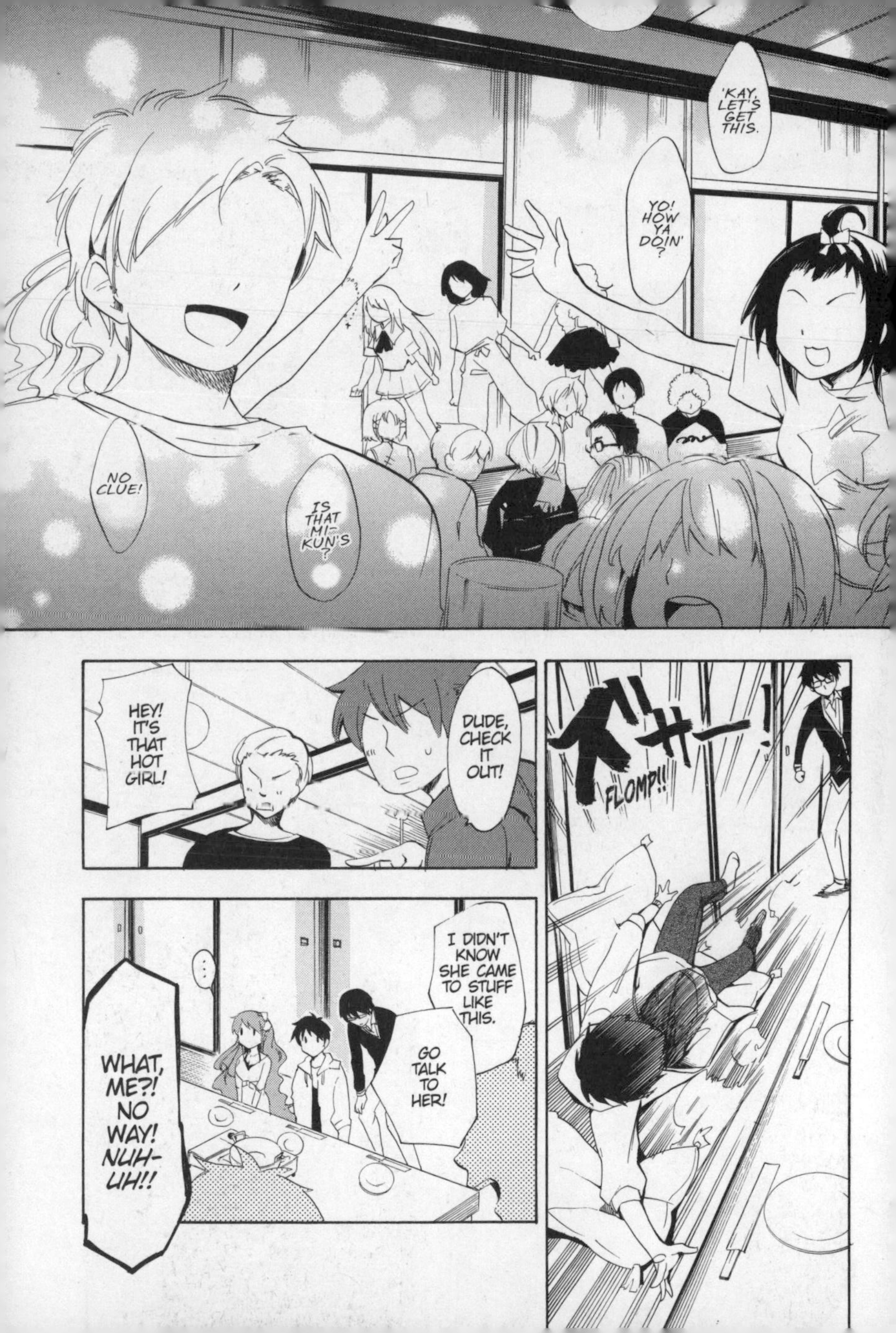
'KAY, LET'S GET THIS.
YO! HOW YA DOIN'?
IS THAT MI-KUN'S?
NO CLUE!
FLOMP!!
DUDE, CHECK IT OUT!
HEY! IT'S THAT HOT GIRL!
I DIDN'T KNOW SHE CAME TO STUFF LIKE THIS.
GO TALK TO HER!
...
WHAT, ME?! NO WAY! NUH-UH!!

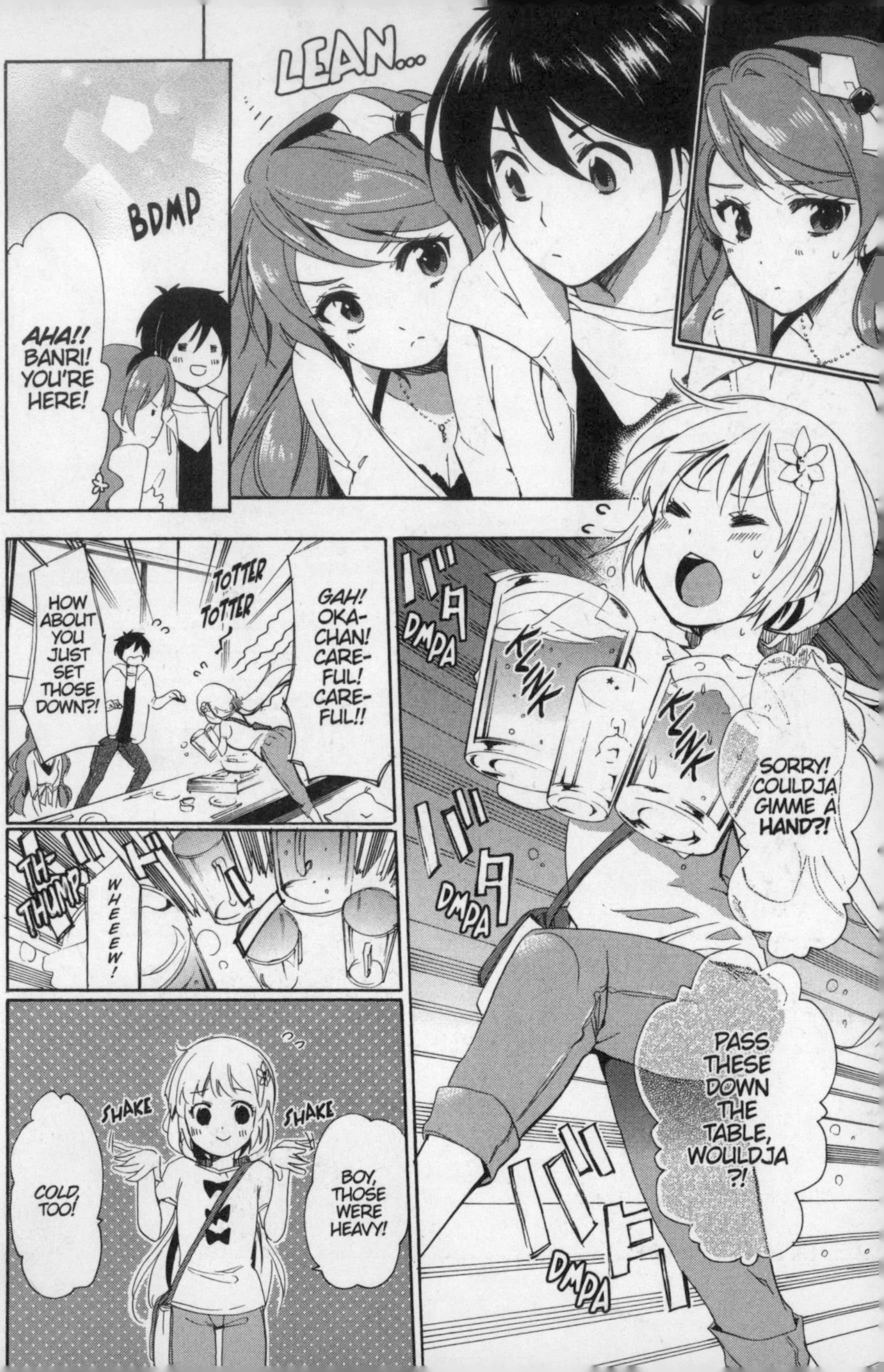
LEAN...
BDMP
AHA!! BANRI! YOU'RE HERE!
DMPA
KLINK
KLINK
SORRY! COULDJA GIMME A HAND?!
DMPA
PASS THESE DOWN THE TABLE, WOULDJA?!
DMPA
GAH! OKA-CHAN! CARE-FUL! CARE-FUL!!
TOTTER TOTTER
HOW ABOUT YOU JUST SET THOSE DOWN?!
WHEEEEW!
TH-THUMP
SHAKE
SHAKE
BOY, THOSE WERE HEAVY!
COLD, TOO!

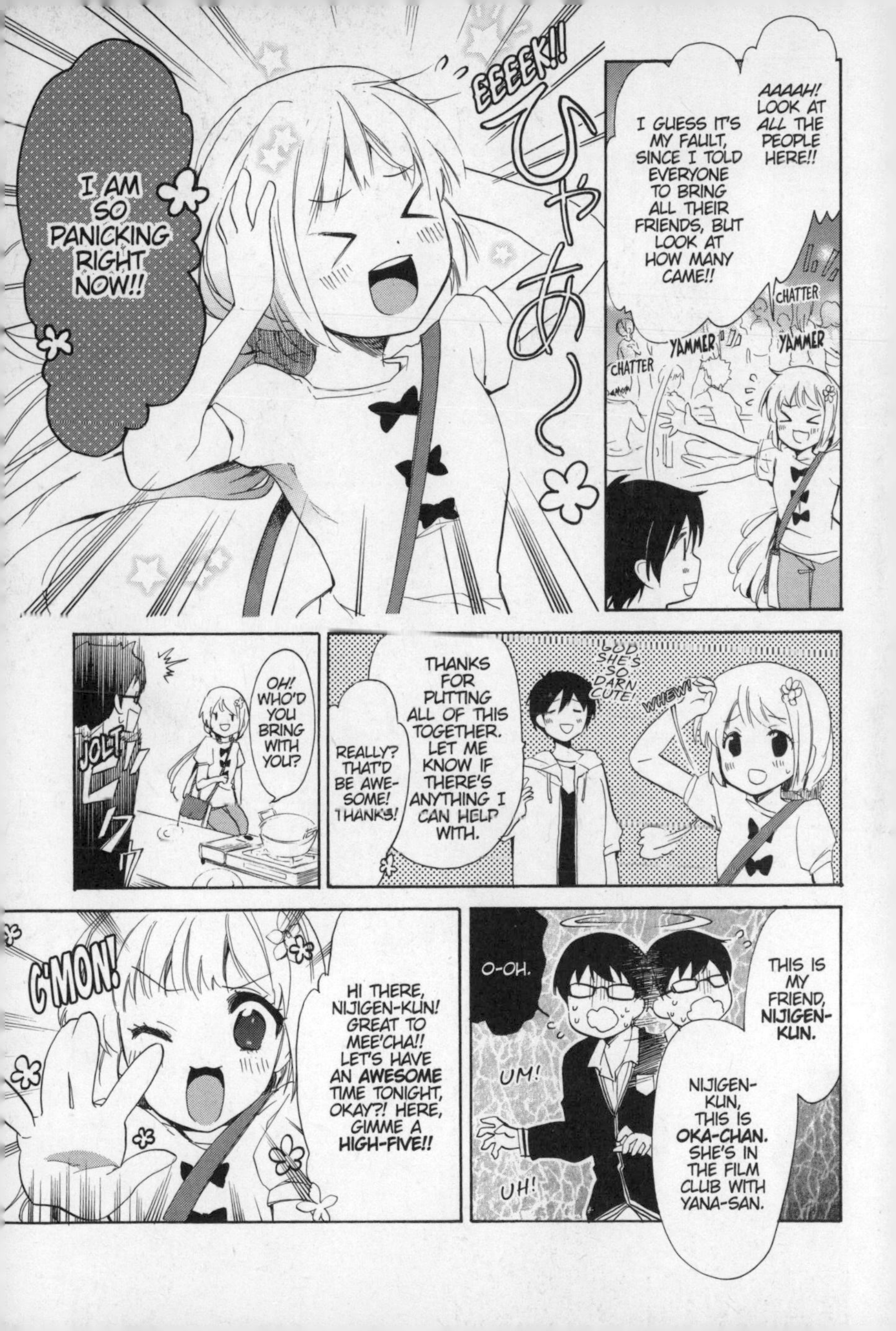
AAAAH! LOOK AT ALL THE PEOPLE HERE!!
I GUESS IT'S MY FAULT, SINCE I TOLD EVERYONE TO BRING ALL THEIR FRIENDS, BUT LOOK AT HOW MANY CAME!!
CHATTER
YAMMER
YAMMER
CHATTER
EEEEK!!
ひゃあ〜
I AM SO PANICKING RIGHT NOW!!
GOD SHE'S SO DARN CUTE!
WHEW!
THANKS FOR PUTTING ALL OF THIS TOGETHER. LET ME KNOW IF THERE'S ANYTHING I CAN HELP WITH.
REALLY? THAT'D BE AWESOME! THANKS!
OH! WHO'D YOU BRING WITH YOU?
JOLT
THIS IS MY FRIEND, NIJIGEN-KUN.
NIJIGEN-KUN, THIS IS OKA-CHAN. SHE'S IN THE FILM CLUB WITH YANA-SAN.
O-OH.
UM!
UH!
C'MON!
HI THERE, NIJIGEN-KUN! GREAT TO MEE'CHA!! LET'S HAVE AN AWESOME TIME TONIGHT, OKAY?! HERE, GIMME A HIGH-FIVE!!

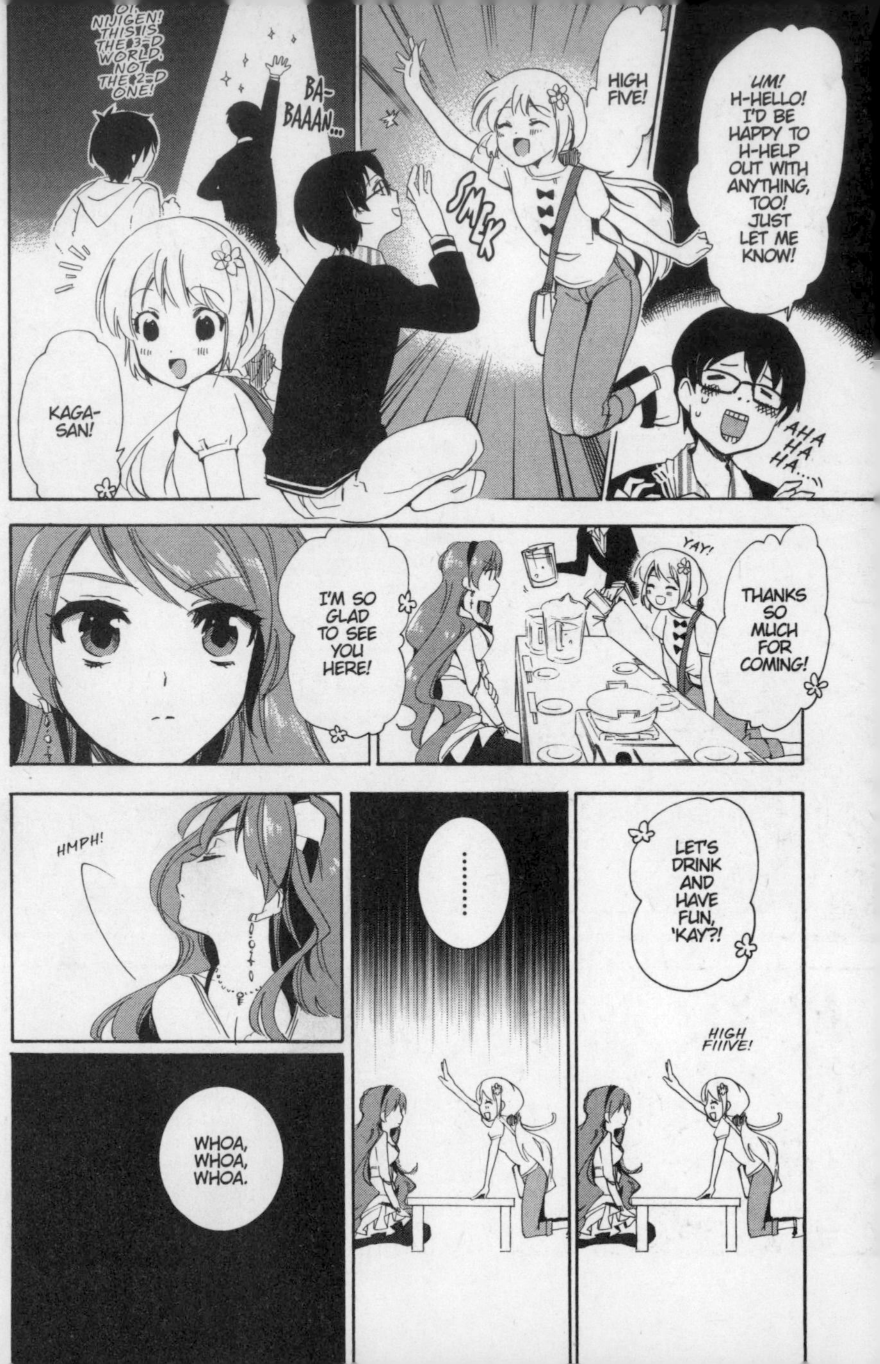
UM! H-HELLO! I'D BE HAPPY TO H-HELP OUT WITH ANYTHING, TOO! JUST LET ME KNOW!
HIGH FIVE!
SMEK
BA-BAAAN...
OI, NIJIGEN! THIS IS THE 3-D WORLD, NOT THE 2-D ONE!
AHA HA HA...
KAGA-SAN!
YAY!
THANKS SO MUCH FOR COMING!
I'M SO GLAD TO SEE YOU HERE!
LET'S DRINK AND HAVE FUN, 'KAY?!
......
HMPH!
HIGH FIIIVE!
WHOA, WHOA, WHOA.

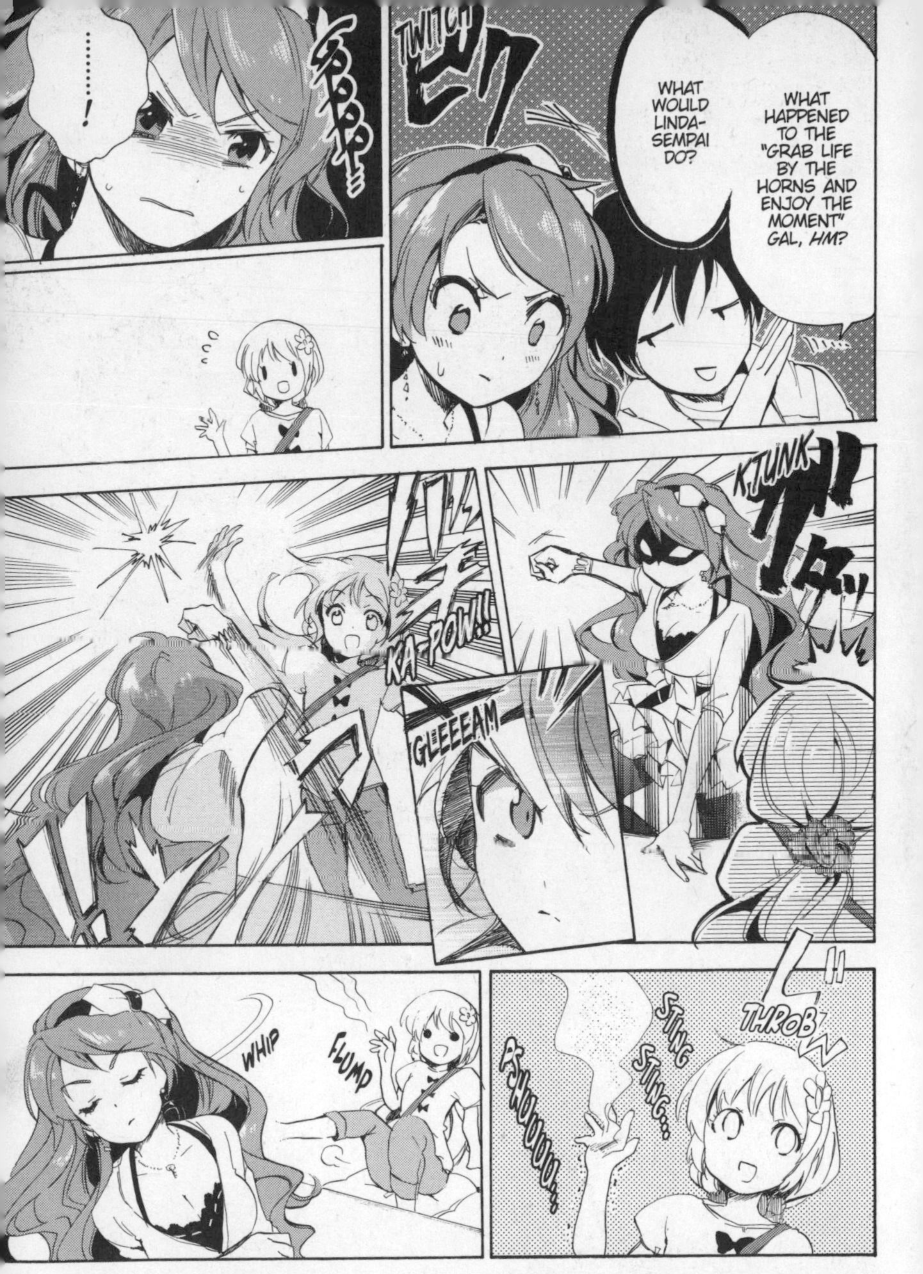
WHAT HAPPENED TO THE "GRAB LIFE BY THE HORNS AND ENJOY THE MOMENT" GAL, HM?
WHAT WOULD LINDA-SEMPAI DO?
TWITCH
......!
KJUNK
GLEEEAM
KA-POW!!
THROB
STING STING...
PSHUUUUU...
FLUMP
WHIP

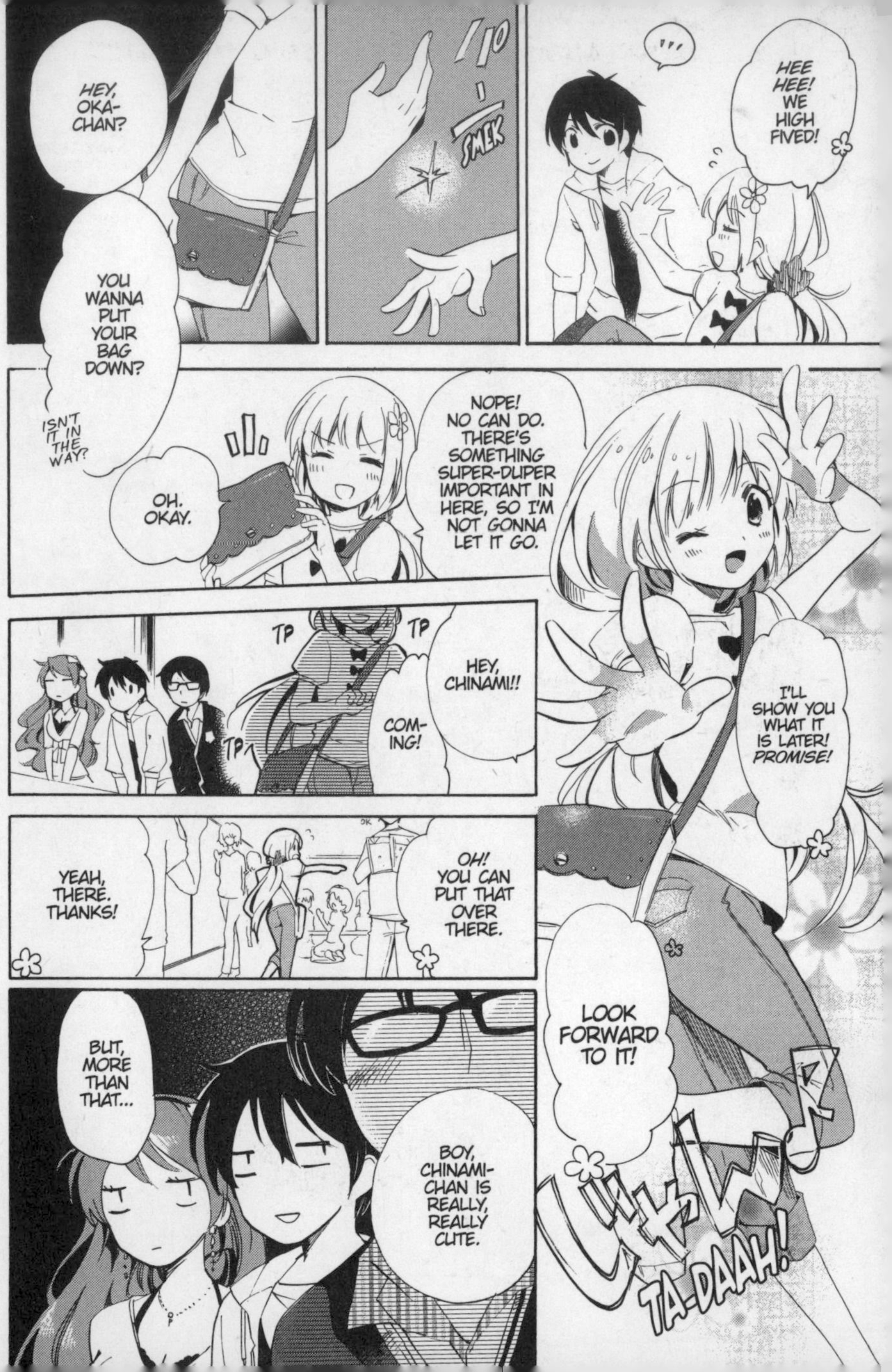
...!
HEE HEE! WE HIGH FIVED!
SMEK
HEY, OKA-CHAN?
YOU WANNA PUT YOUR BAG DOWN?
ISN'T IT IN THE WAY?
I'LL SHOW YOU WHAT IT IS LATER! PROMISE!
LOOK FORWARD TO IT!
TA-DAAH!
NOPE! NO CAN DO. THERE'S SOMETHING SUPER-DUPER IMPORTANT IN HERE, SO I'M NOT GONNA LET IT GO.
OH. OKAY.
TP
TP
HEY, CHINAMI!!
COMING!
TP
OK
OH! YOU CAN PUT THAT OVER THERE.
YEAH, THERE. THANKS!
BUT, MORE THAN THAT...
BOY, CHINAMI-CHAN IS REALLY, REALLY CUTE.

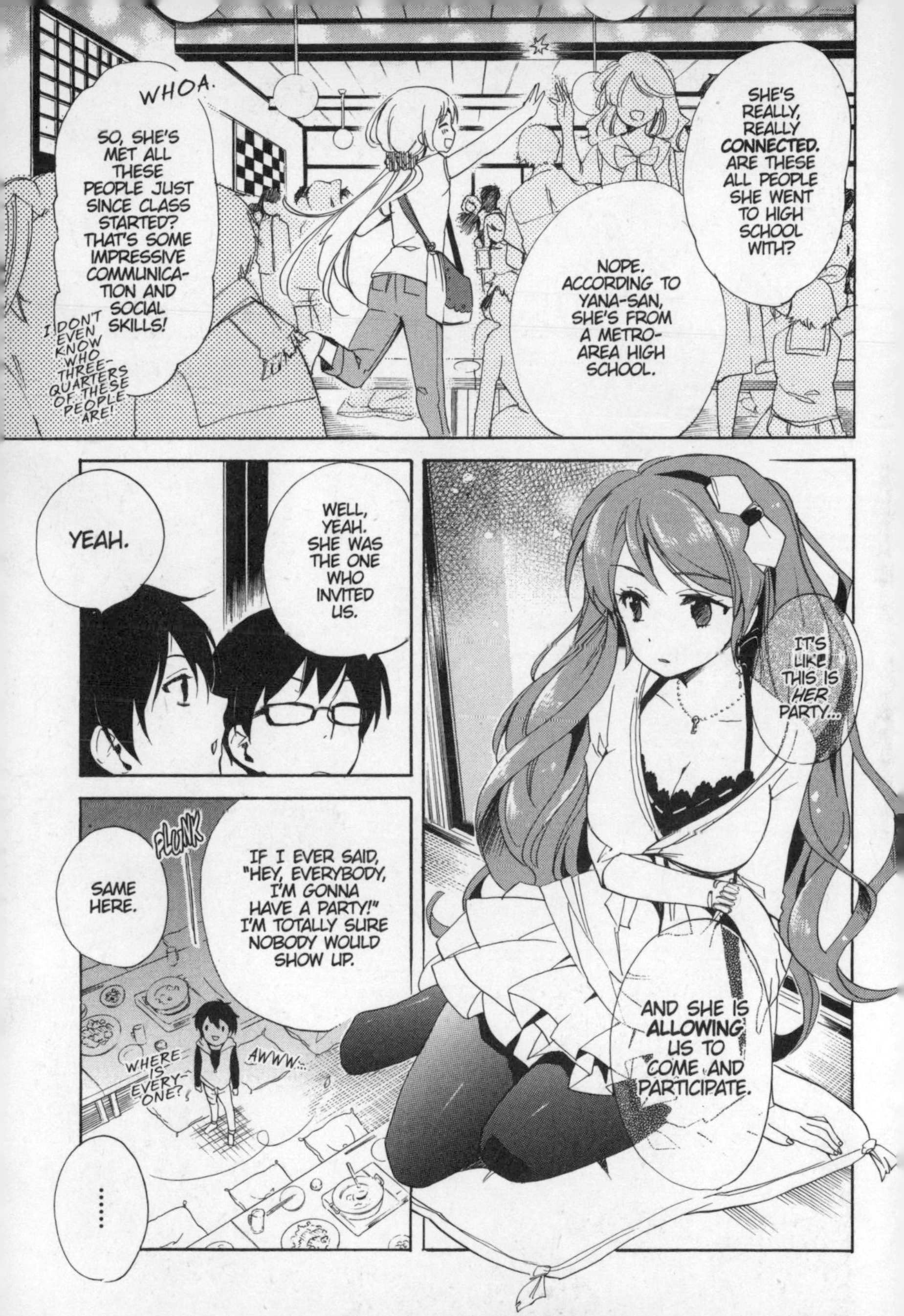
SHE'S REALLY, REALLY **CONNECTED.** ARE THESE ALL PEOPLE SHE WENT TO HIGH SCHOOL WITH?
NOPE. ACCORDING TO YANA-SAN, SHE'S FROM A METRO-AREA HIGH SCHOOL.
WHOA.
SO, SHE'S MET ALL THESE PEOPLE JUST SINCE CLASS STARTED? THAT'S SOME IMPRESSIVE COMMUNICATION AND SOCIAL SKILLS!
I DON'T EVEN KNOW WHO THREE-QUARTERS OF THESE PEOPLE ARE!
IT'S LIKE THIS IS *HER* PARTY...
AND SHE IS **ALLOWING** US TO COME AND PARTICIPATE.
WELL, YEAH. SHE WAS THE ONE WHO INVITED US.
YEAH.
IF I EVER SAID, "HEY, EVERYBODY, I'M GONNA HAVE A PARTY!" I'M TOTALLY SURE NOBODY WOULD SHOW UP.
PLUNK
SAME HERE.
AWWW...
WHERE IS EVERY-ONE?
......

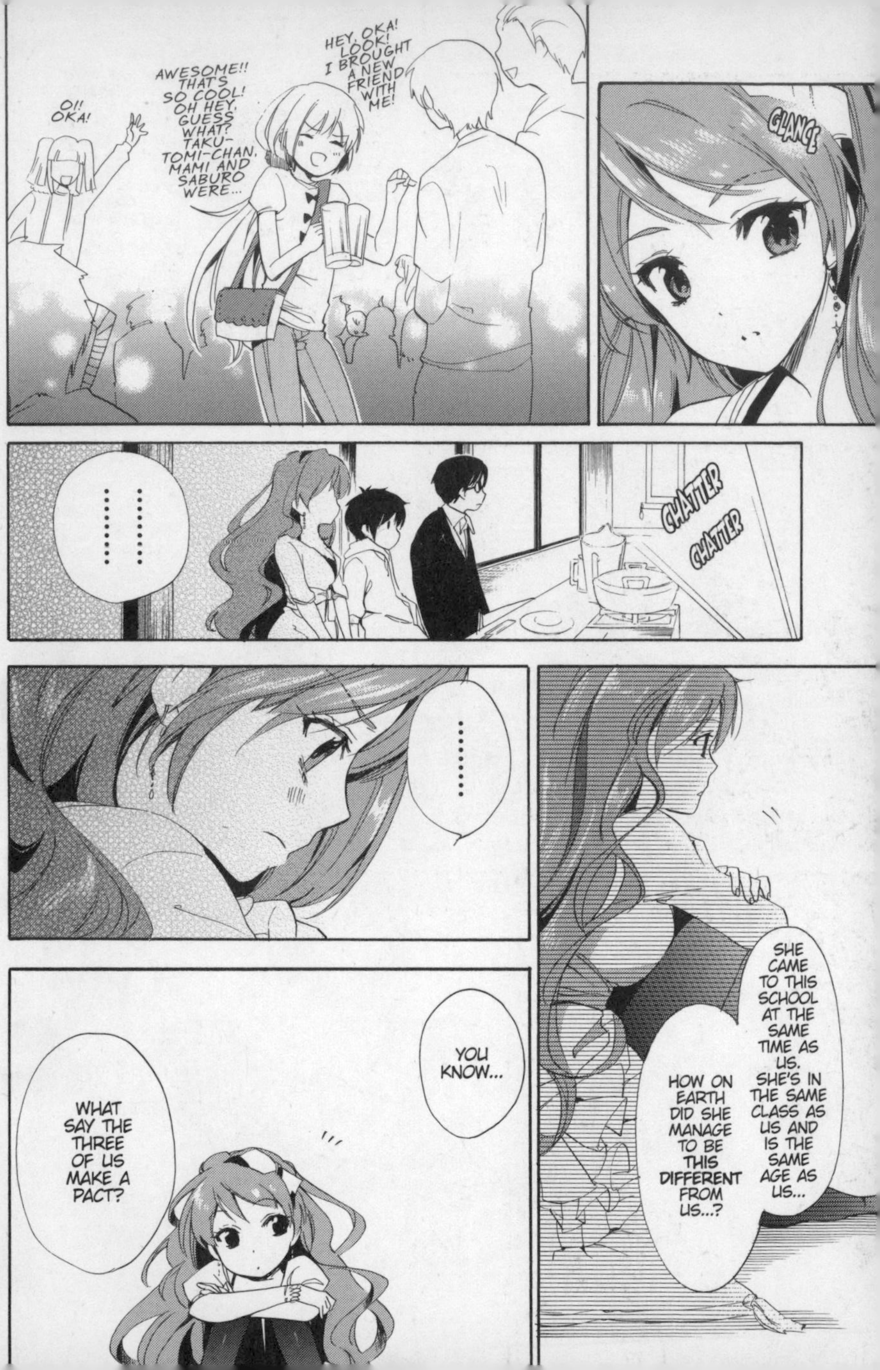
GLANCE
HEY, OKA! LOOK! I BROUGHT A NEW FRIEND WITH ME!
AWESOME!! THAT'S SO COOL! OH HEY, GUESS WHAT? TAKU-TOMI-CHAN, MAMI AND SABURO WERE...
OI! OKA!
CHATTER
CHATTER
......
......
SHE CAME TO THIS SCHOOL AT THE SAME TIME AS US. SHE'S IN THE SAME CLASS AS US AND IS THE SAME AGE AS US...
HOW ON EARTH DID SHE MANAGE TO BE THIS DIFFERENT FROM US...?
......
YOU KNOW...
WHAT SAY THE THREE OF US MAKE A PACT?

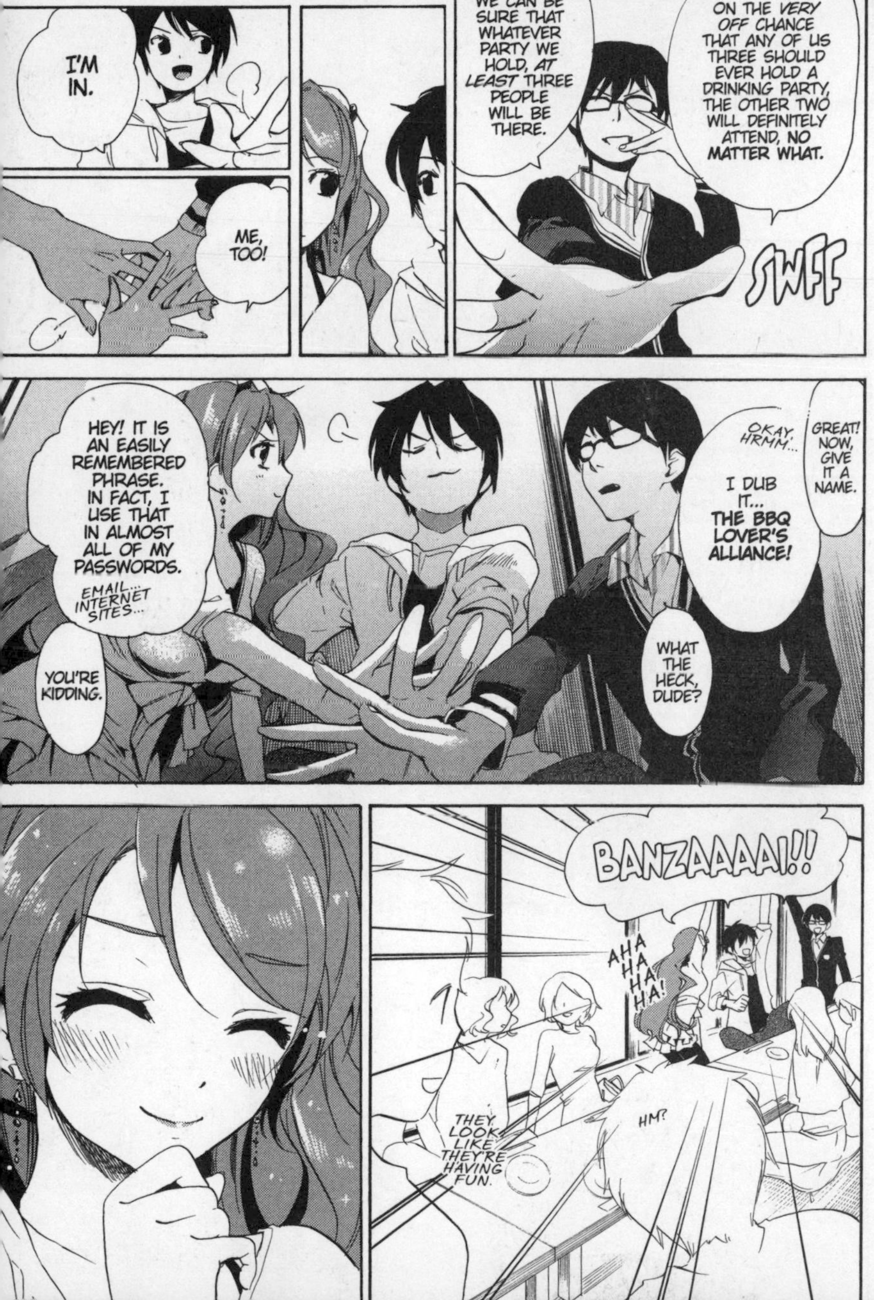
ON THE VERY OFF CHANCE THAT ANY OF US THREE SHOULD EVER HOLD A DRINKING PARTY, THE OTHER TWO WILL DEFINITELY ATTEND, NO MATTER WHAT.
THAT WAY, WE CAN BE SURE THAT WHATEVER PARTY WE HOLD, AT LEAST THREE PEOPLE WILL BE THERE.
SWFF
I'M IN.
ME, TOO!
GREAT! NOW, GIVE IT A NAME.
OKAY, HRMM...
I DUB IT... THE BBQ LOVER'S ALLIANCE!
WHAT THE HECK, DUDE?
HEY! IT IS AN EASILY REMEMBERED PHRASE. IN FACT, I USE THAT IN ALMOST ALL OF MY PASSWORDS.
EMAIL... INTERNET SITES...
YOU'RE KIDDING.
BANZAAAAAI!!
AHAHAHAHA!
HM?
THEY LOOK LIKE THEY'RE HAVING FUN.

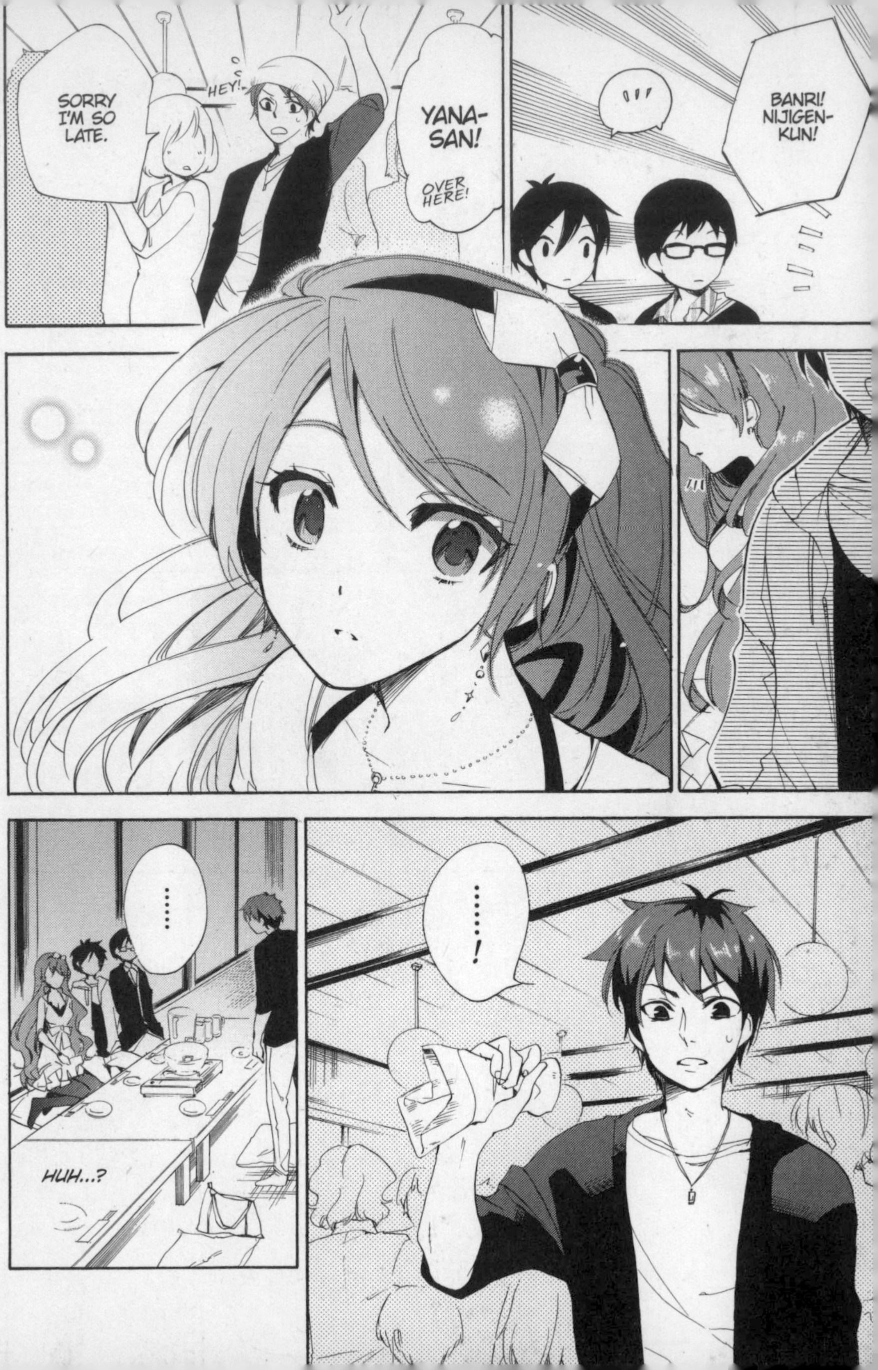
BANRI! NIJIGEN-KUN!
YANA-SAN!
OVER HERE!
HEY!
SORRY I'M SO LATE.
......!
......
HUH...?

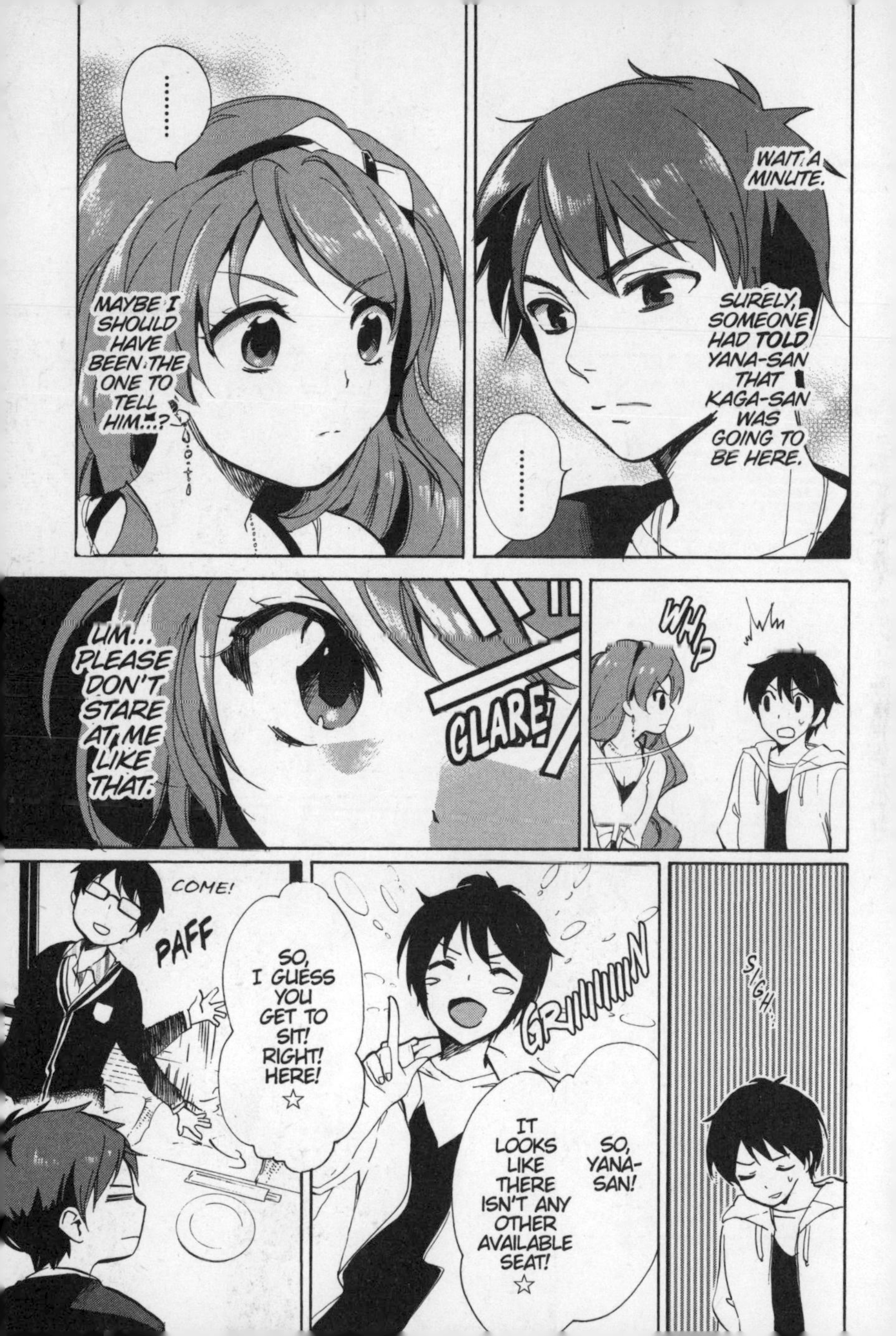
WAIT A MINUTE.
SURELY, SOMEONE HAD TOLD YANA-SAN THAT KAGA-SAN WAS GOING TO BE HERE.
......
......
MAYBE I SHOULD HAVE BEEN THE ONE TO TELL HIM...?
WHIP
GLARE
UM... PLEASE DON'T STARE AT ME LIKE THAT.
SIGH...
GRIIIIIIIN
SO, YANA-SAN!
IT LOOKS LIKE THERE ISN'T ANY OTHER AVAILABLE SEAT! ☆
SO, I GUESS YOU GET TO SIT! RIGHT! HERE! ☆
COME!
PAFF

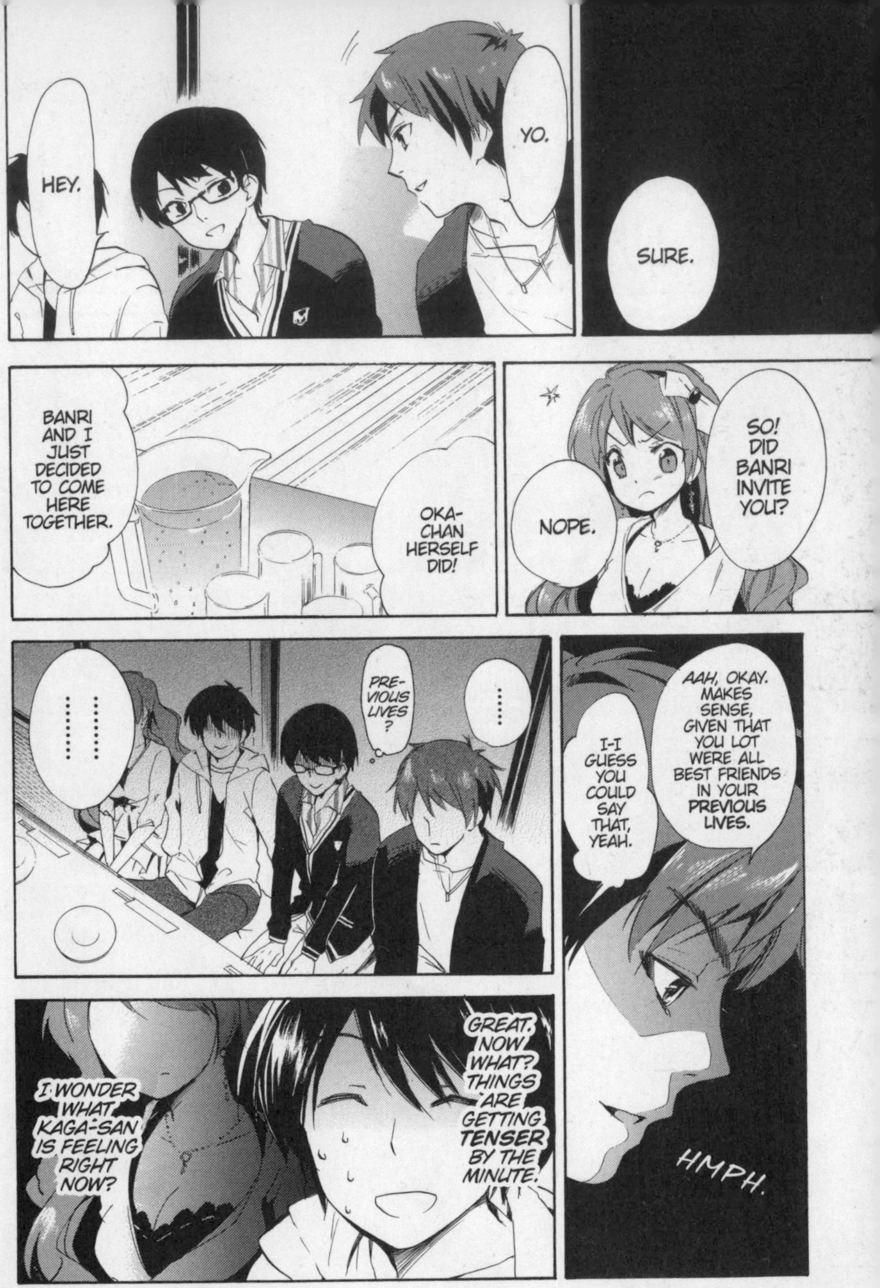
SURE.
YO.
HEY.
SO! DID BANRI INVITE YOU?
NOPE.
OKA-CHAN HERSELF DID!
BANRI AND I JUST DECIDED TO COME HERE TOGETHER.
AAH, OKAY. MAKES SENSE, GIVEN THAT YOU LOT WERE ALL BEST FRIENDS IN YOUR PREVIOUS LIVES.
I-I GUESS YOU COULD SAY THAT, YEAH.
HMPH.
......
PRE-VIOUS LIVES?
......
GREAT. NOW WHAT? THINGS ARE GETTING TENSER BY THE MINUTE.
I WONDER WHAT KAGA-SAN IS FEELING RIGHT NOW?

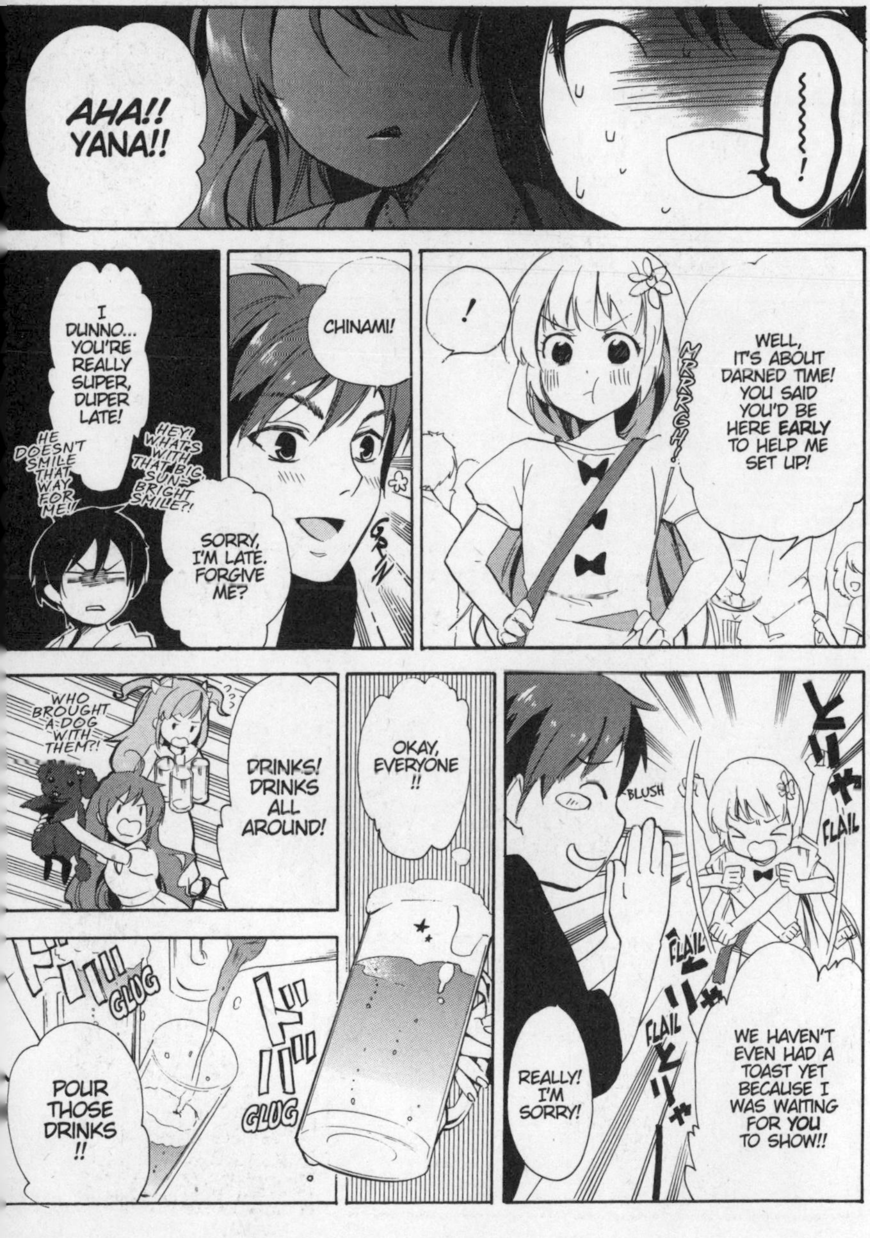

AHA!! YANA!!
!
MRRRGH!
WELL, IT'S ABOUT DARNED TIME! YOU SAID YOU'D BE HERE EARLY TO HELP ME SET UP!
CHINAMI!
GRIN
SORRY, I'M LATE. FORGIVE ME?
I DUNNO... YOU'RE REALLY SUPER, DUPER LATE!
HEY! WHAT'S WITH THAT BIG, SUN-BRIGHT SMILE?!
HE DOESN'T SMILE THAT WAY FOR ME!!
BLUSH
FLAIL
FLAIL
FLAIL
WE HAVEN'T EVEN HAD A TOAST YET BECAUSE I WAS WAITING FOR YOU TO SHOW!!
REALLY! I'M SORRY!
OKAY, EVERYONE!!
GLUG
DRINKS! DRINKS ALL AROUND!
WHO BROUGHT A DOG WITH THEM?!
GLUG
POUR THOSE DRINKS!!

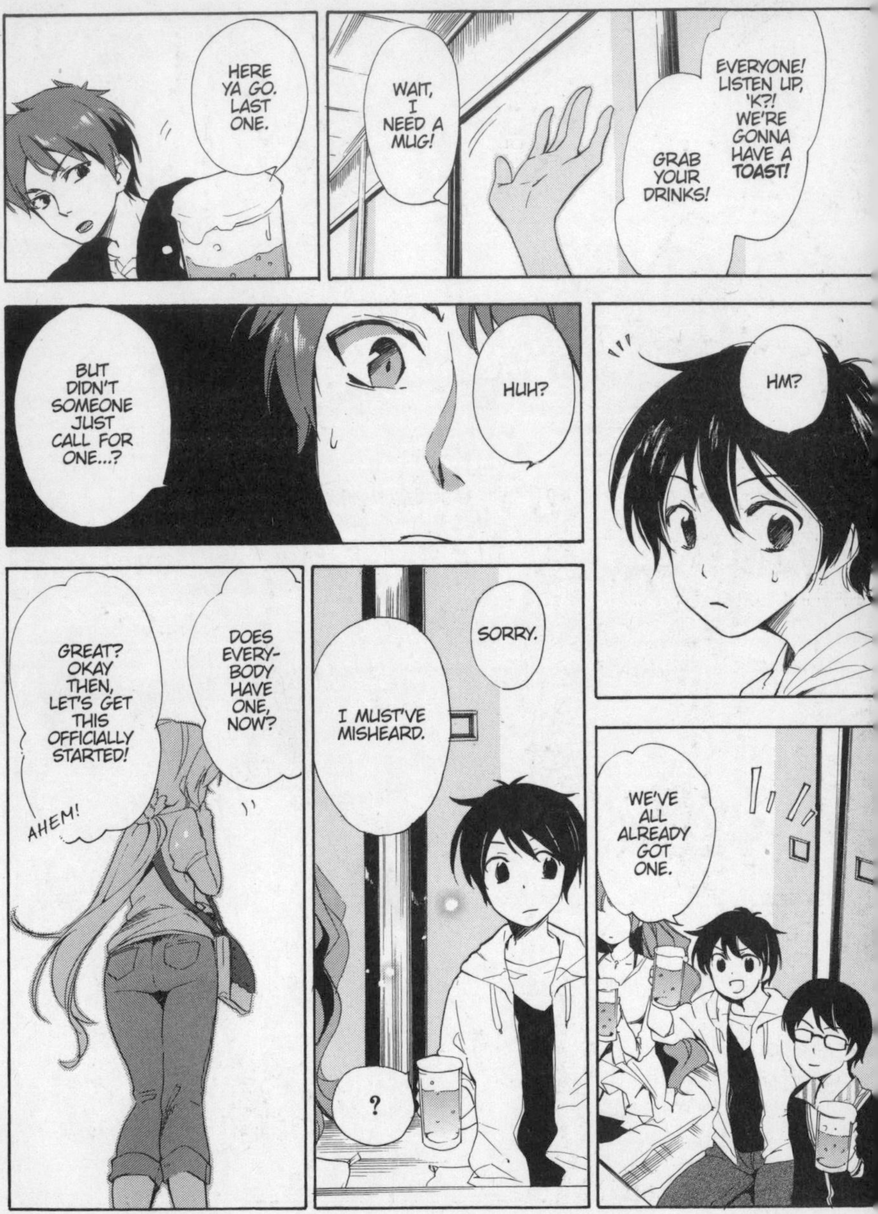
EVERYONE! LISTEN UP, 'K?! WE'RE GONNA HAVE A TOAST!
GRAB YOUR DRINKS!
WAIT, I NEED A MUG!
HERE YA GO. LAST ONE.
HM?
HUH?
BUT DIDN'T SOMEONE JUST CALL FOR ONE...?
WE'VE ALL ALREADY GOT ONE.
SORRY.
I MUST'VE MISHEARD.
?
DOES EVERY-BODY HAVE ONE, NOW?
GREAT? OKAY THEN, LET'S GET THIS OFFICIALLY STARTED!
AHEM!

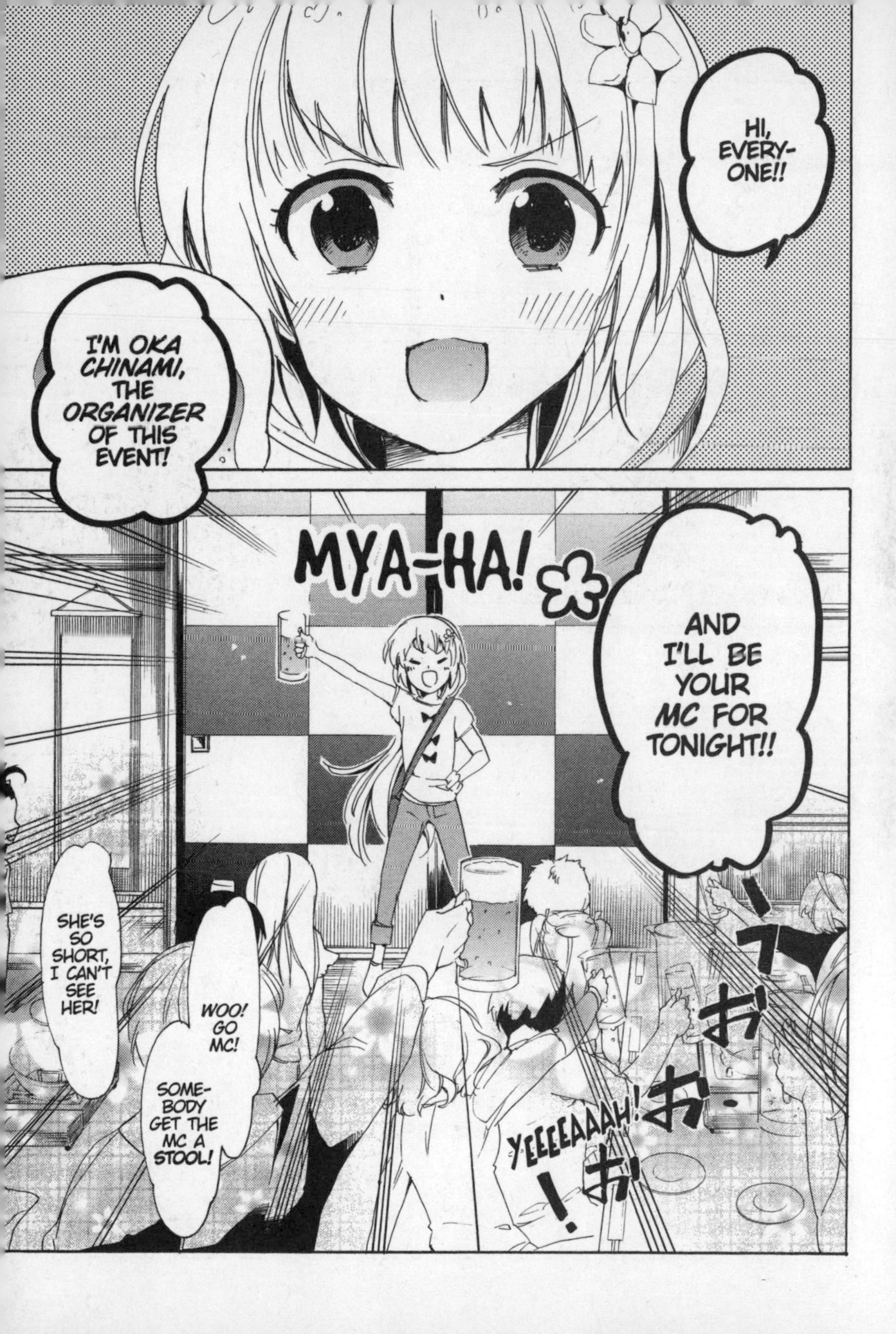
HI, EVERY-ONE!!
I'M OKA CHINAMI, THE ORGANIZER OF THIS EVENT!
AND I'LL BE YOUR MC FOR TONIGHT!!
MYA-HA!
うおおお！
YEEEEAAAH!
SOME-BODY GET THE MC A STOOL!
WOO! GO MC!
SHE'S SO SHORT, I CAN'T SEE HER!

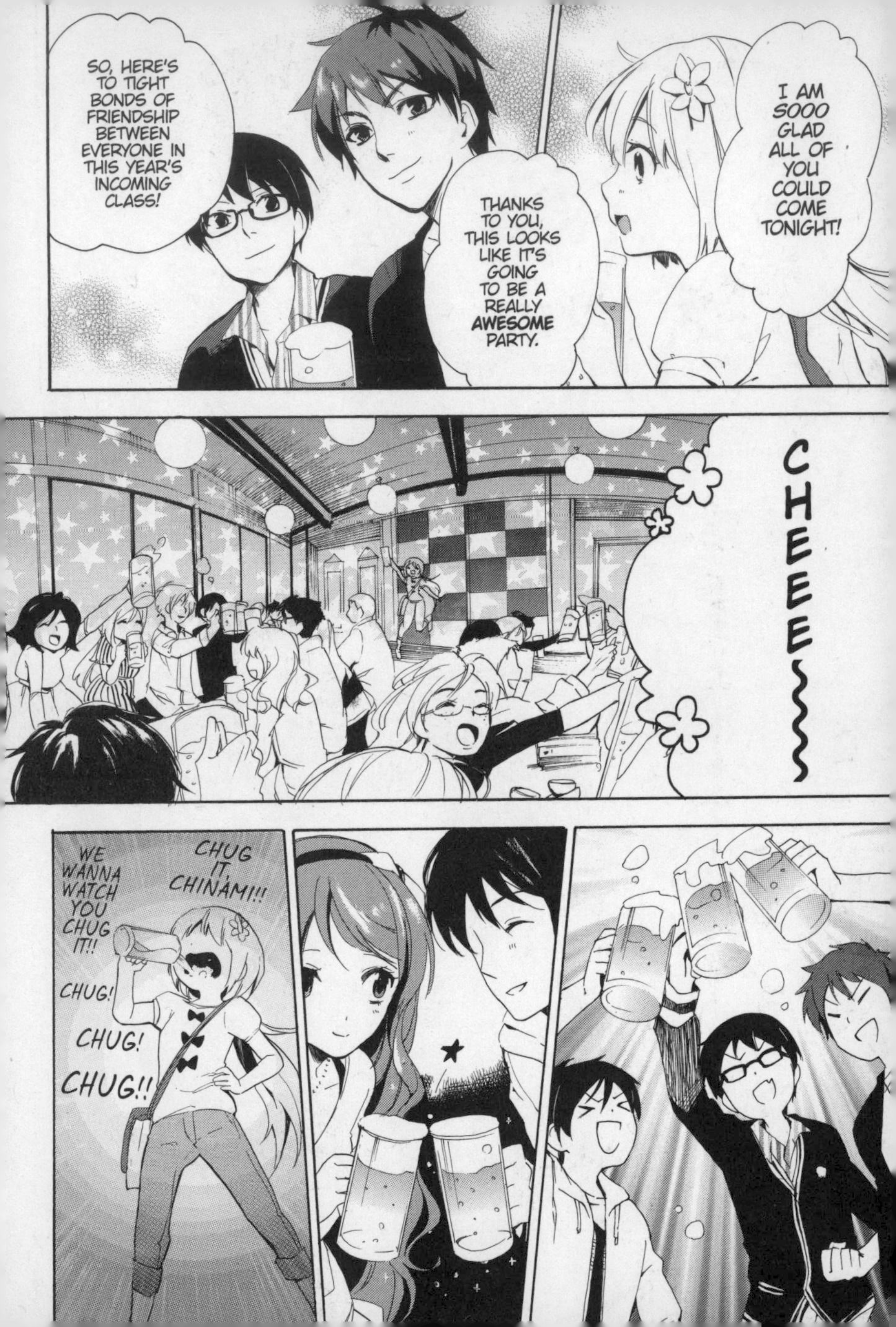
I AM SOOO GLAD ALL OF YOU COULD COME TONIGHT!
THANKS TO YOU, THIS LOOKS LIKE IT'S GOING TO BE A REALLY **AWESOME** PARTY.
SO, HERE'S TO TIGHT BONDS OF FRIENDSHIP BETWEEN EVERYONE IN THIS YEAR'S INCOMING CLASS!
CHEEE~~~
CHUG IT, CHINAMI!!
WE WANNA WATCH YOU CHUG IT!!
CHUG!
CHUG!
CHUG!!

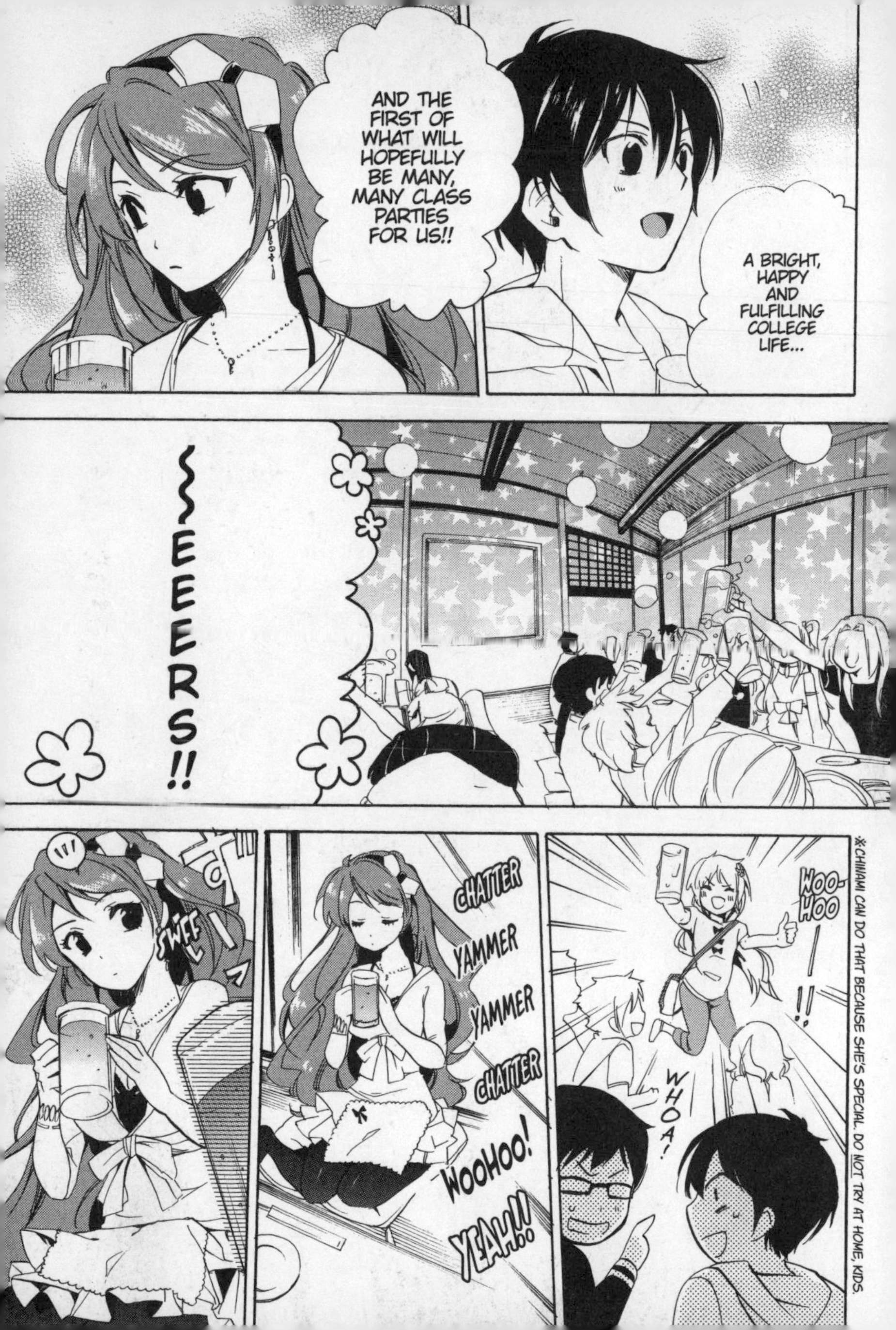
A BRIGHT, HAPPY AND FULFILLING COLLEGE LIFE...
AND THE FIRST OF WHAT WILL HOPEFULLY BE MANY, MANY CLASS PARTIES FOR US!!
EEERS!!
※CHINAMI CAN DO THAT BECAUSE SHE'S SPECIAL. DO NOT TRY AT HOME, KIDS.
WOO-HOO!!
WHOA!
CHATTER
YAMMER
YAMMER
CHATTER
WOOHOO!
YEAH!!!
SWFF

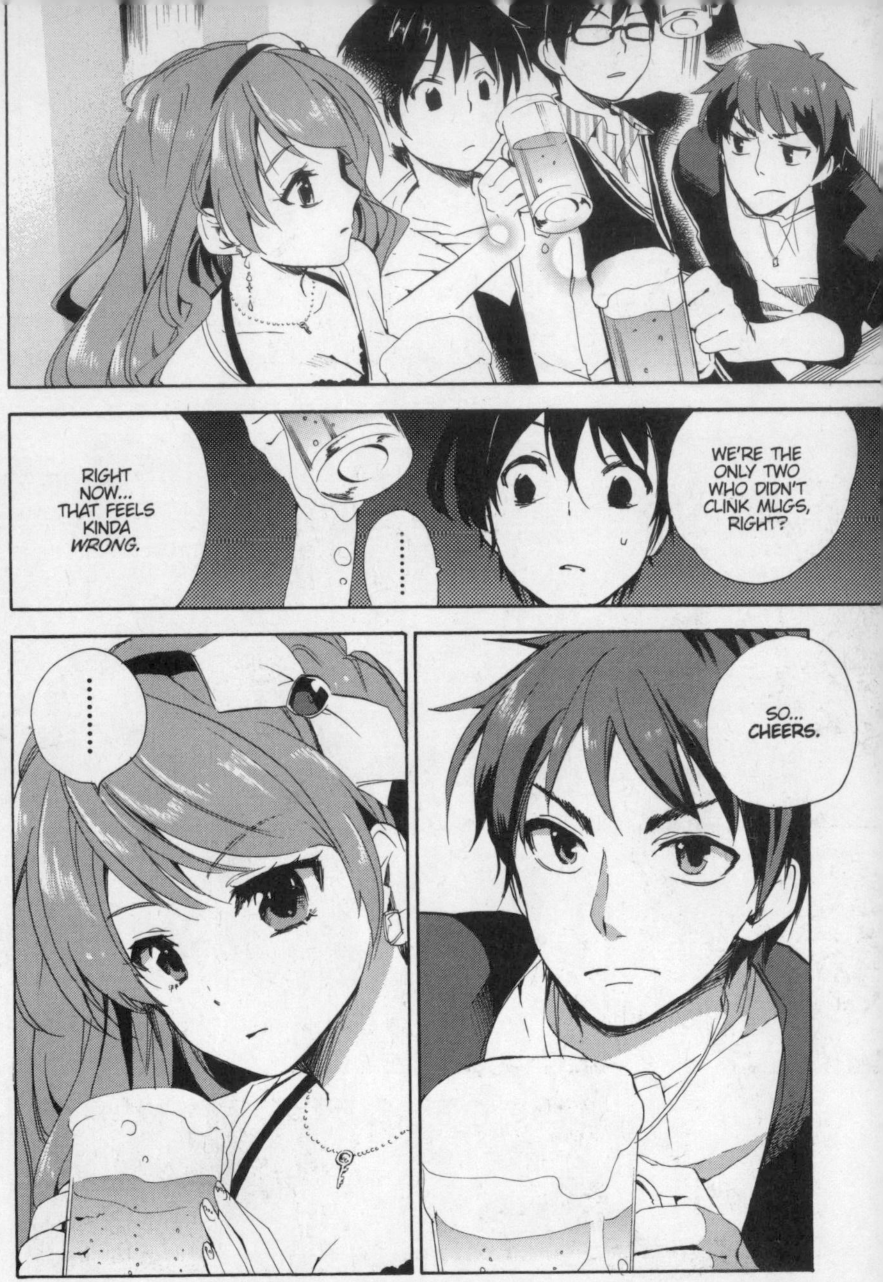
WE'RE THE ONLY TWO WHO DIDN'T CLINK MUGS, RIGHT?
......
RIGHT NOW... THAT FEELS KINDA *WRONG.*
SO... CHEERS.
......

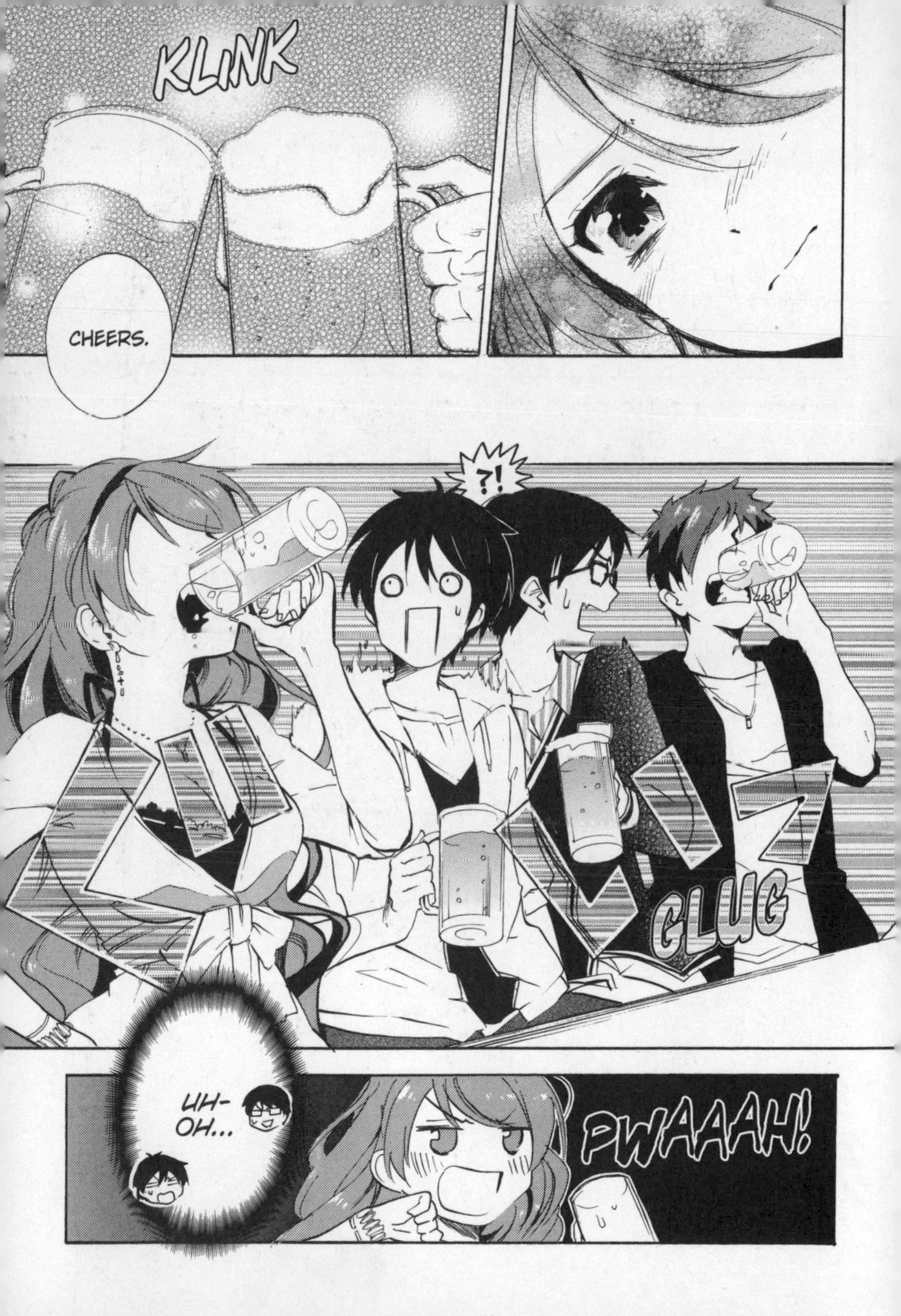
KLINK
CHEERS.
?!
CLUG
PWAAAH!
UH-OH...

GOLDEN TIME
ゴールデンタイム

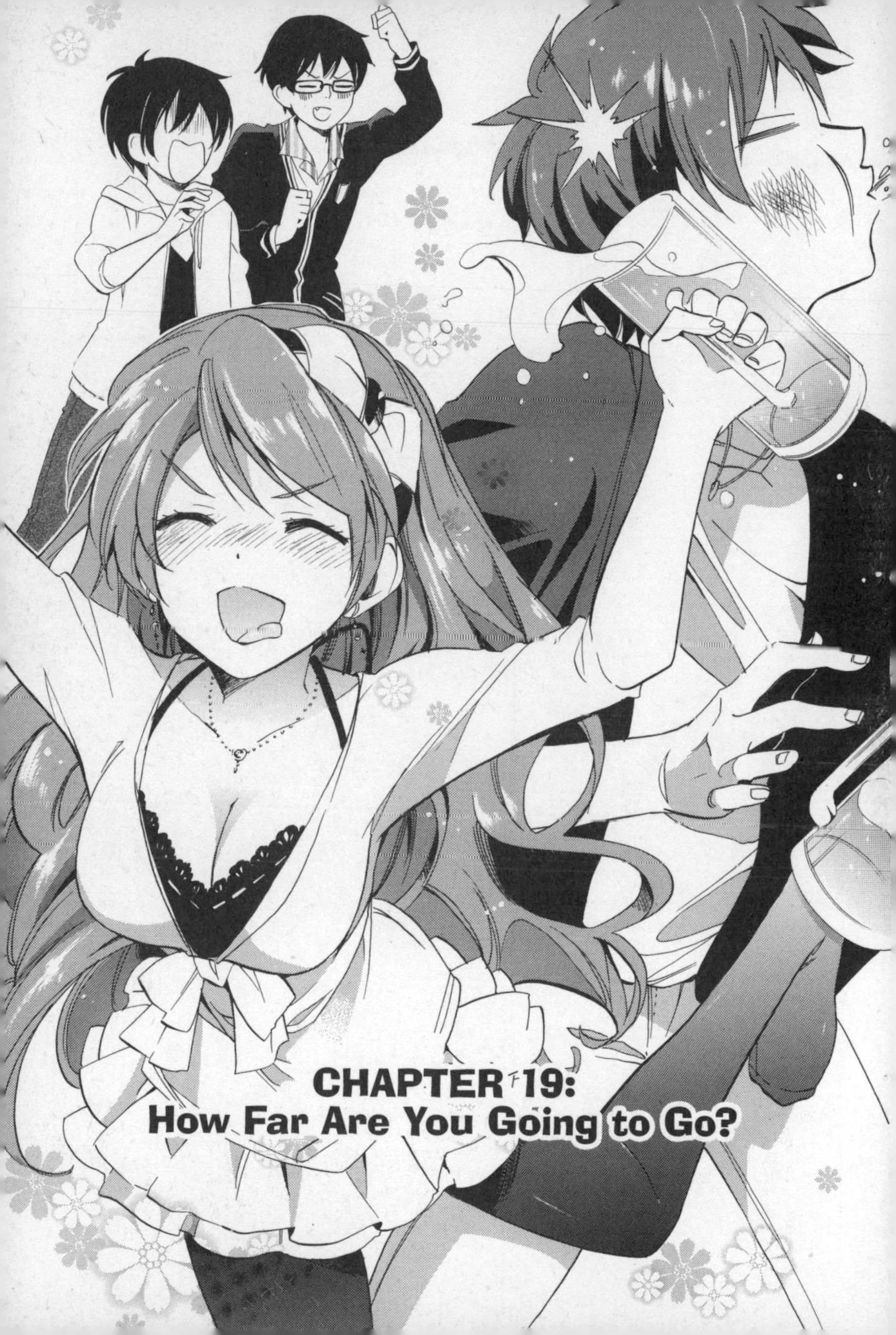
CHAPTER 19:
How Far Are You Going to Go?

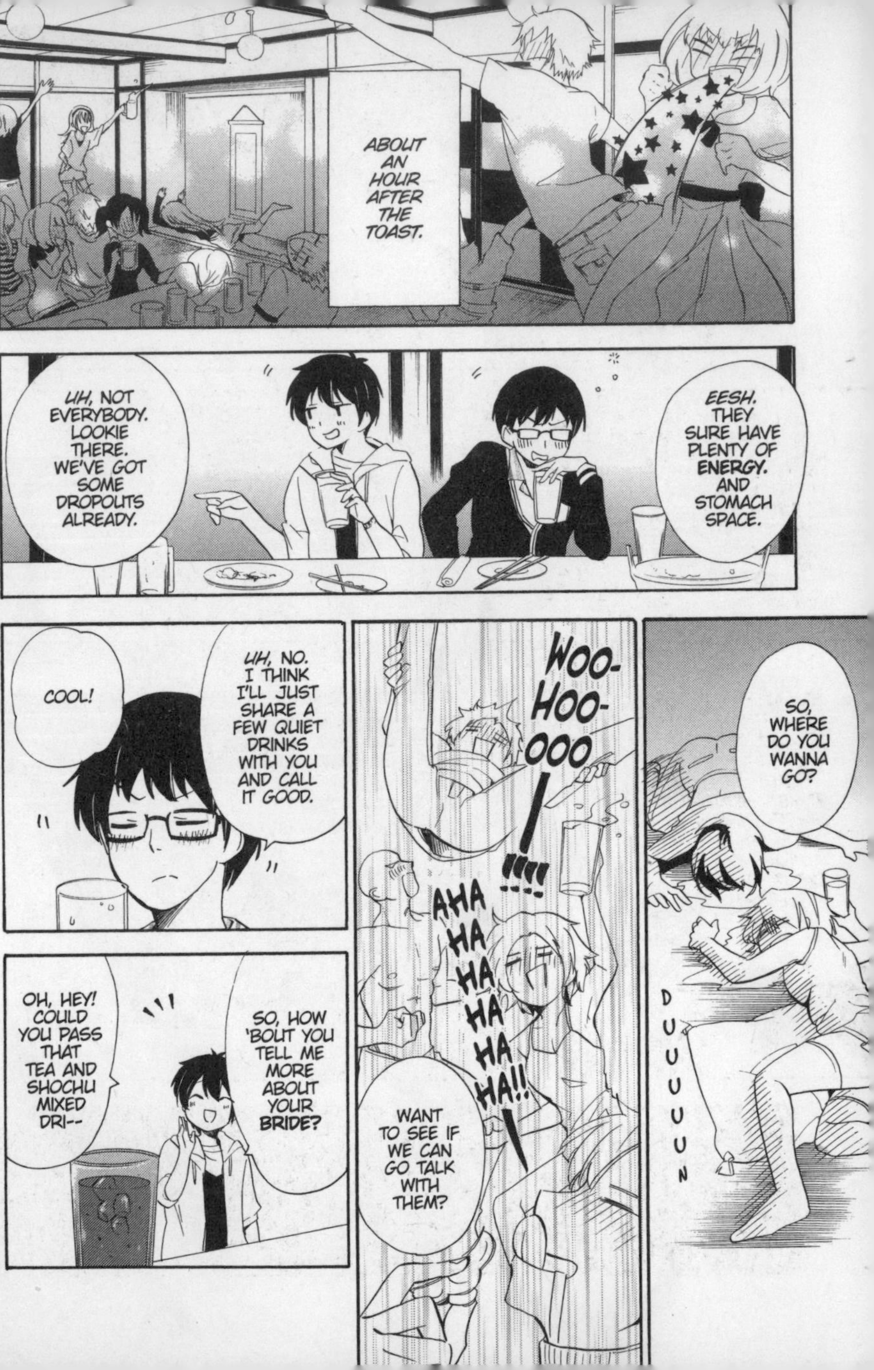
ABOUT AN HOUR AFTER THE TOAST.
EESH. THEY SURE HAVE PLENTY OF ENERGY. AND STOMACH SPACE.
UH, NOT EVERYBODY. LOOKIE THERE. WE'VE GOT SOME DROPOUTS ALREADY.
SO, WHERE DO YOU WANNA GO?
DUUUUUN
WOO-HOO-OOO-!!!!
AHAHAHAHAHAHA!!
WANT TO SEE IF WE CAN GO TALK WITH THEM?
UH, NO. I THINK I'LL JUST SHARE A FEW QUIET DRINKS WITH YOU AND CALL IT GOOD.
COOL!
SO, HOW 'BOUT YOU TELL ME MORE ABOUT YOUR BRIDE?
OH, HEY! COULD YOU PASS THAT TEA AND SHOCHU MIXED DRI--

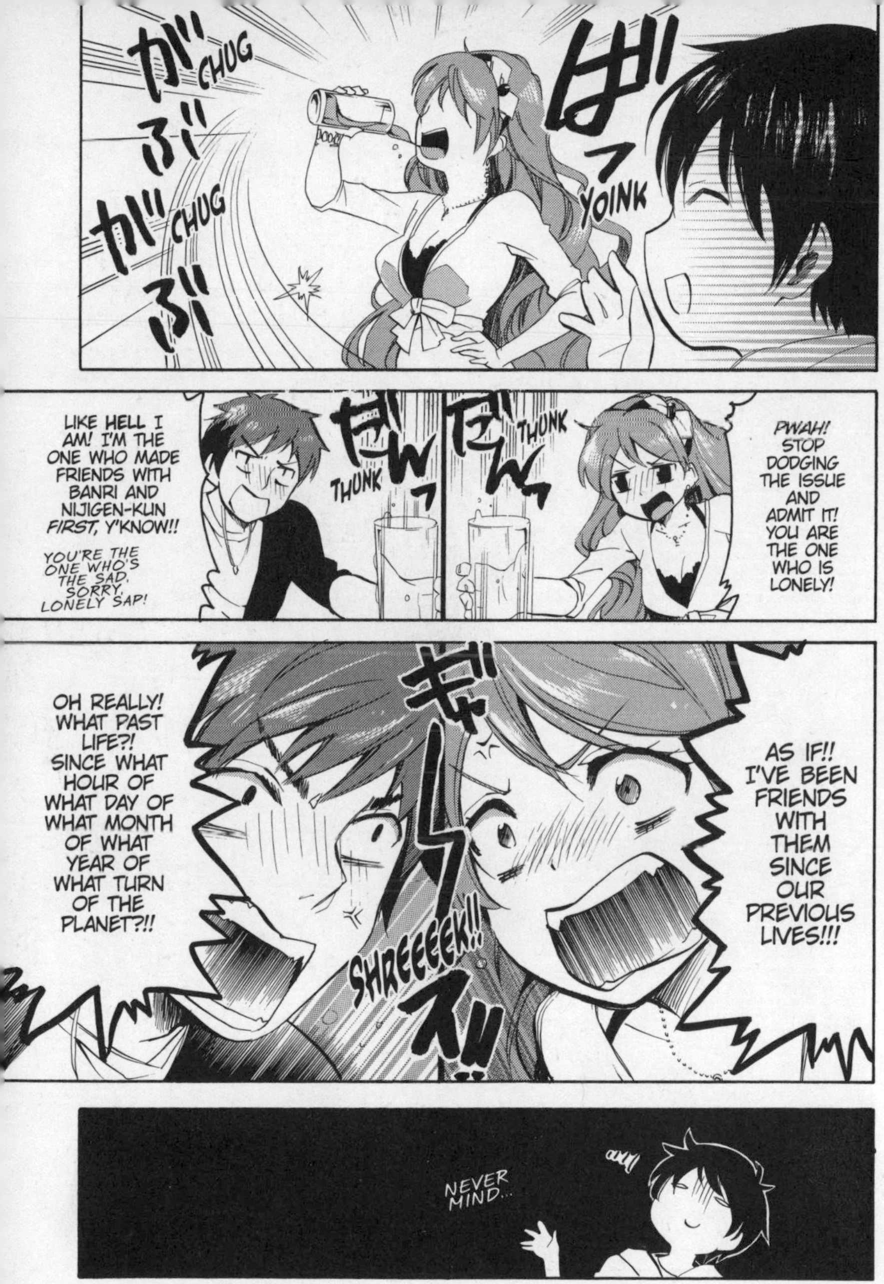
ばっ
YOINK
がぶ
CHUG
がぶ
CHUG
だんっ
THUNK
PWAH! STOP DODGING THE ISSUE AND ADMIT IT! YOU ARE THE ONE WHO IS LONELY!
だんっ
THUNK
LIKE HELL I AM! I'M THE ONE WHO MADE FRIENDS WITH BANRI AND NIJIGEN-KUN *FIRST*, Y'KNOW!!
YOU'RE THE ONE WHO'S THE SAD, SORRY, LONELY SAP!
AS IF!! I'VE BEEN FRIENDS WITH THEM SINCE OUR PREVIOUS LIVES!!!
SHREEEEK!!
OH REALLY! WHAT PAST LIFE?! SINCE WHAT HOUR OF WHAT DAY OF WHAT MONTH OF WHAT YEAR OF WHAT TURN OF THE PLANET?!!
NEVER MIND...

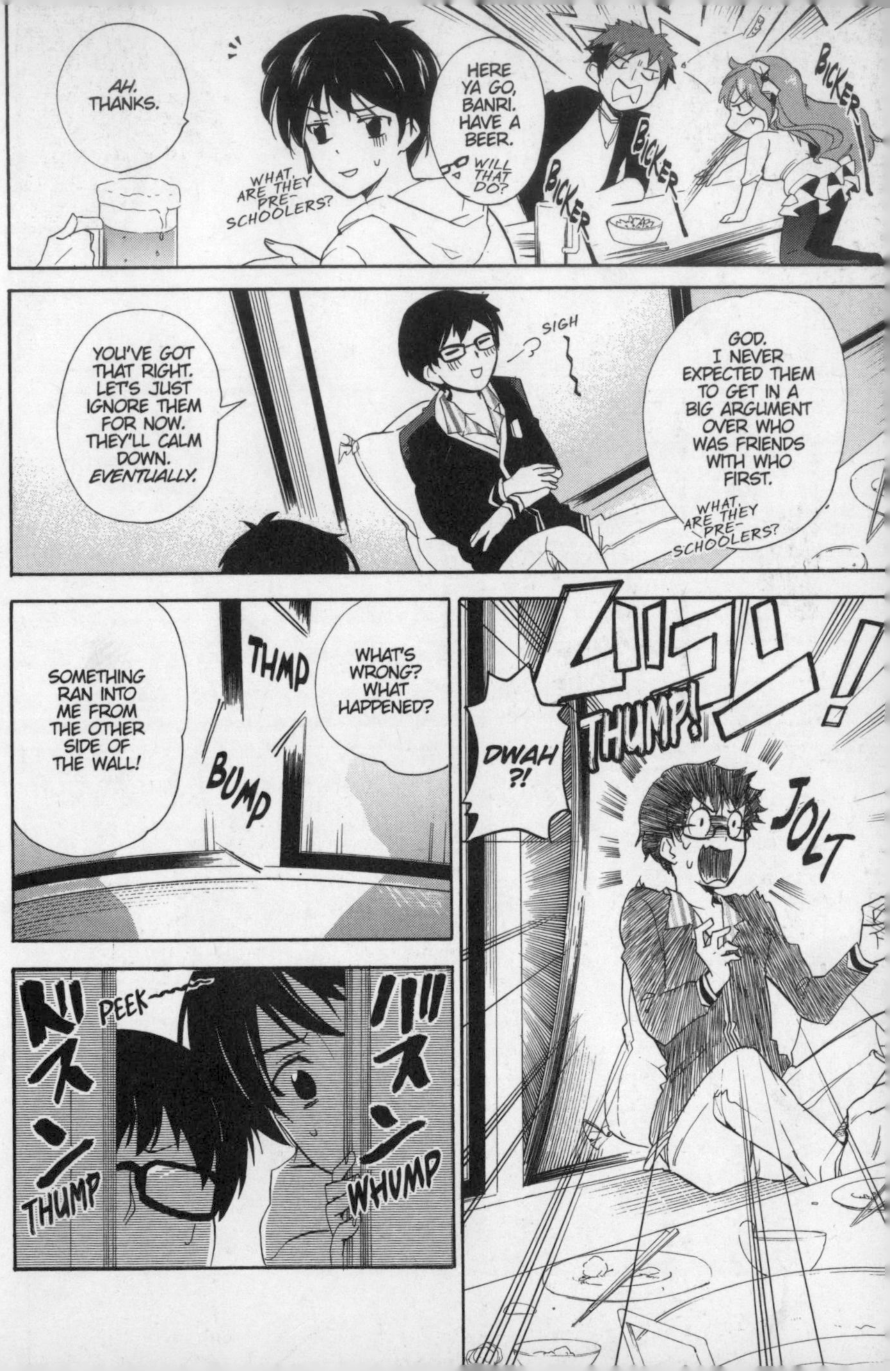
BICKER
BICKER-ER
BICKER
HERE YA GO, BANRI. HAVE A BEER.
WILL THAT DO?
WHAT, ARE THEY PRE-SCHOOLERS?
AH. THANKS.
GOD. I NEVER EXPECTED THEM TO GET IN A BIG ARGUMENT OVER WHO WAS FRIENDS WITH WHO FIRST.
WHAT, ARE THEY PRE-SCHOOLERS?
SIGH
YOU'VE GOT THAT RIGHT. LET'S JUST IGNORE THEM FOR NOW. THEY'LL CALM DOWN. *EVENTUALLY.*
THUMP!
JOLT
DWAH ?!
WHAT'S WRONG? WHAT HAPPENED?
THMP
BUMP
SOMETHING RAN INTO ME FROM THE OTHER SIDE OF THE WALL!
バスン
WHUMP
PEEK
ドスン
THUMP

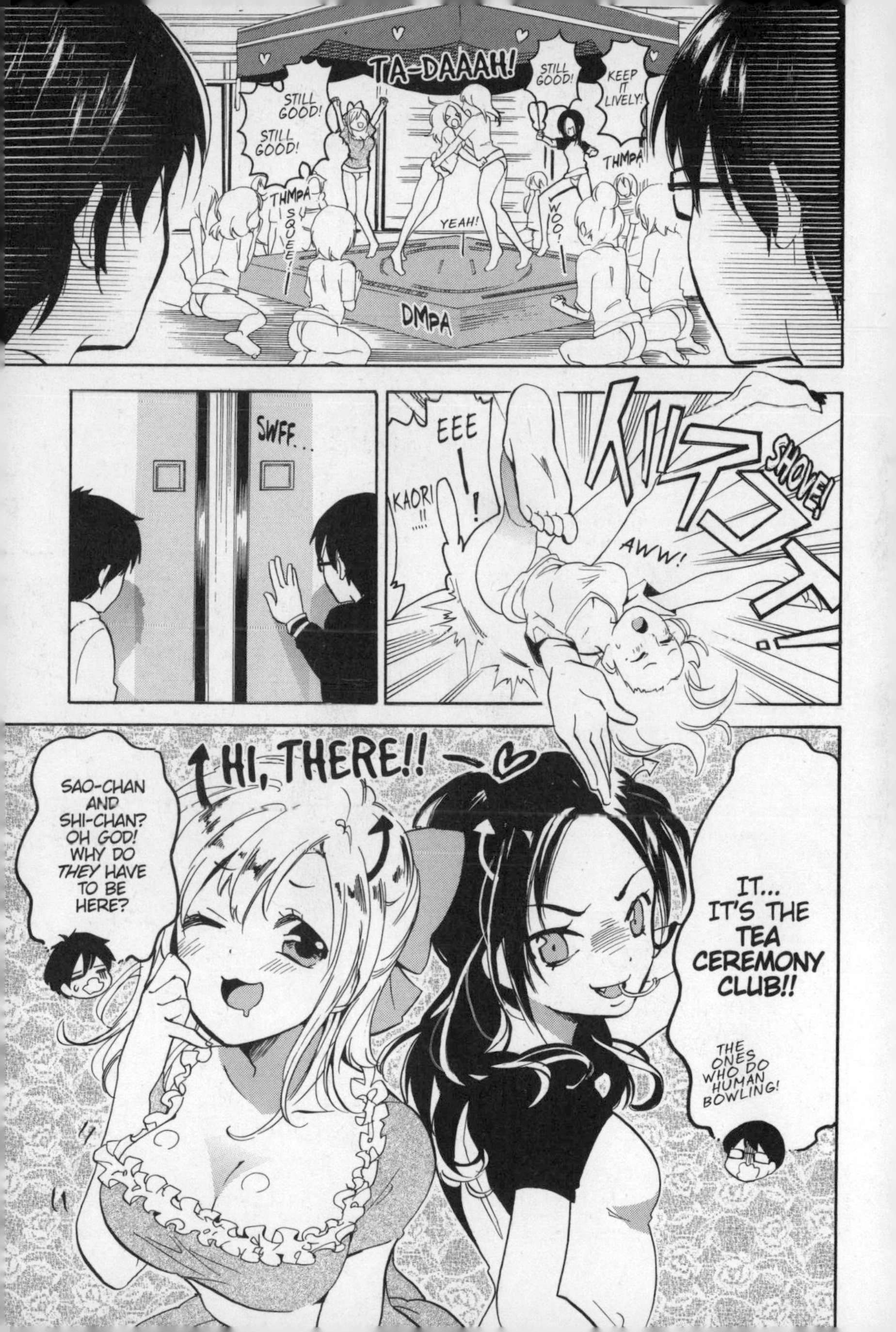
KEEP IT LIVELY!
STILL GOOD!
TA-DAAAH!
STILL GOOD!
STILL GOOD!
THMPA
WOO!
YEAH!
THMPA
SQUEEE!
DMPA
SHOVE!
AWW!
EEE!!
KAORI!!
SWFF...
IT... IT'S THE TEA CEREMONY CLUB!!
THE ONES WHO DO HUMAN BOWLING!
HI, THERE!!
SAO-CHAN AND SHI-CHAN? OH GOD! WHY DO THEY HAVE TO BE HERE?

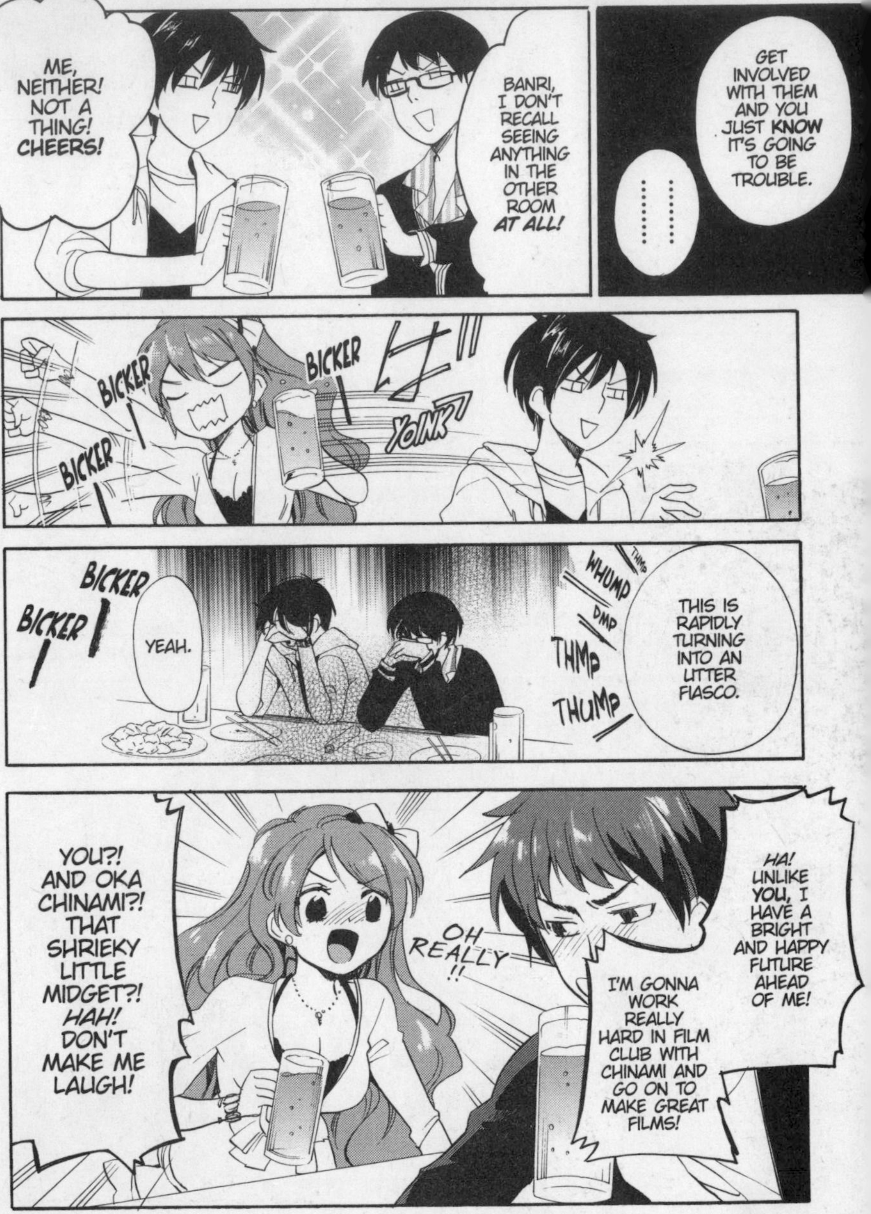
GET INVOLVED WITH THEM AND YOU JUST KNOW IT'S GOING TO BE TROUBLE.
......
BANRI, I DON'T RECALL SEEING ANYTHING IN THE OTHER ROOM AT ALL!
ME, NEITHER! NOT A THING! CHEERS!
YOINK
BICKER
BICKER
BICKER
THMP
WHUMP
THIS IS RAPIDLY TURNING INTO AN UTTER FIASCO.
DMP
THMP
THUMP
YEAH.
BICKER
BICKER
HA! UNLIKE YOU, I HAVE A BRIGHT AND HAPPY FUTURE AHEAD OF ME!
I'M GONNA WORK REALLY HARD IN FILM CLUB WITH CHINAMI AND GO ON TO MAKE GREAT FILMS!
OH REALLY!!
YOU?! AND OKA CHINAMI?! THAT SHRIEKY LITTLE MIDGET?! HAH! DON'T MAKE ME LAUGH!

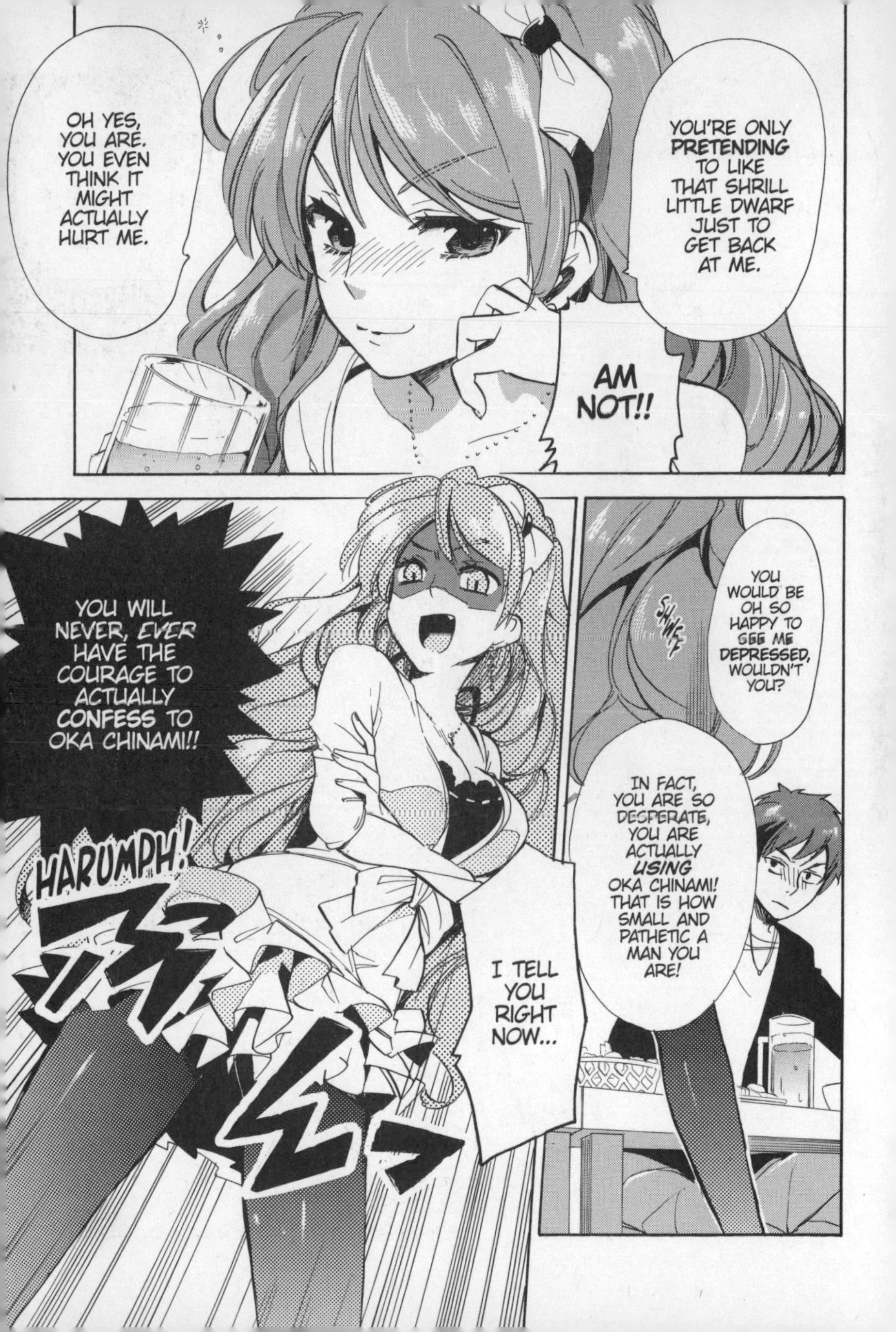
YOU'RE ONLY PRETENDING TO LIKE THAT SHRILL LITTLE DWARF JUST TO GET BACK AT ME.
AM NOT!!
OH YES, YOU ARE. YOU EVEN THINK IT MIGHT ACTUALLY HURT ME.
YOU WOULD BE OH SO HAPPY TO SEE ME DEPRESSED, WOULDN'T YOU?
IN FACT, YOU ARE SO DESPERATE, YOU ARE ACTUALLY USING OKA CHINAMI! THAT IS HOW SMALL AND PATHETIC A MAN YOU ARE!
I TELL YOU RIGHT NOW...
YOU WILL NEVER, EVER HAVE THE COURAGE TO ACTUALLY CONFESS TO OKA CHINAMI!!
HARUMPH!

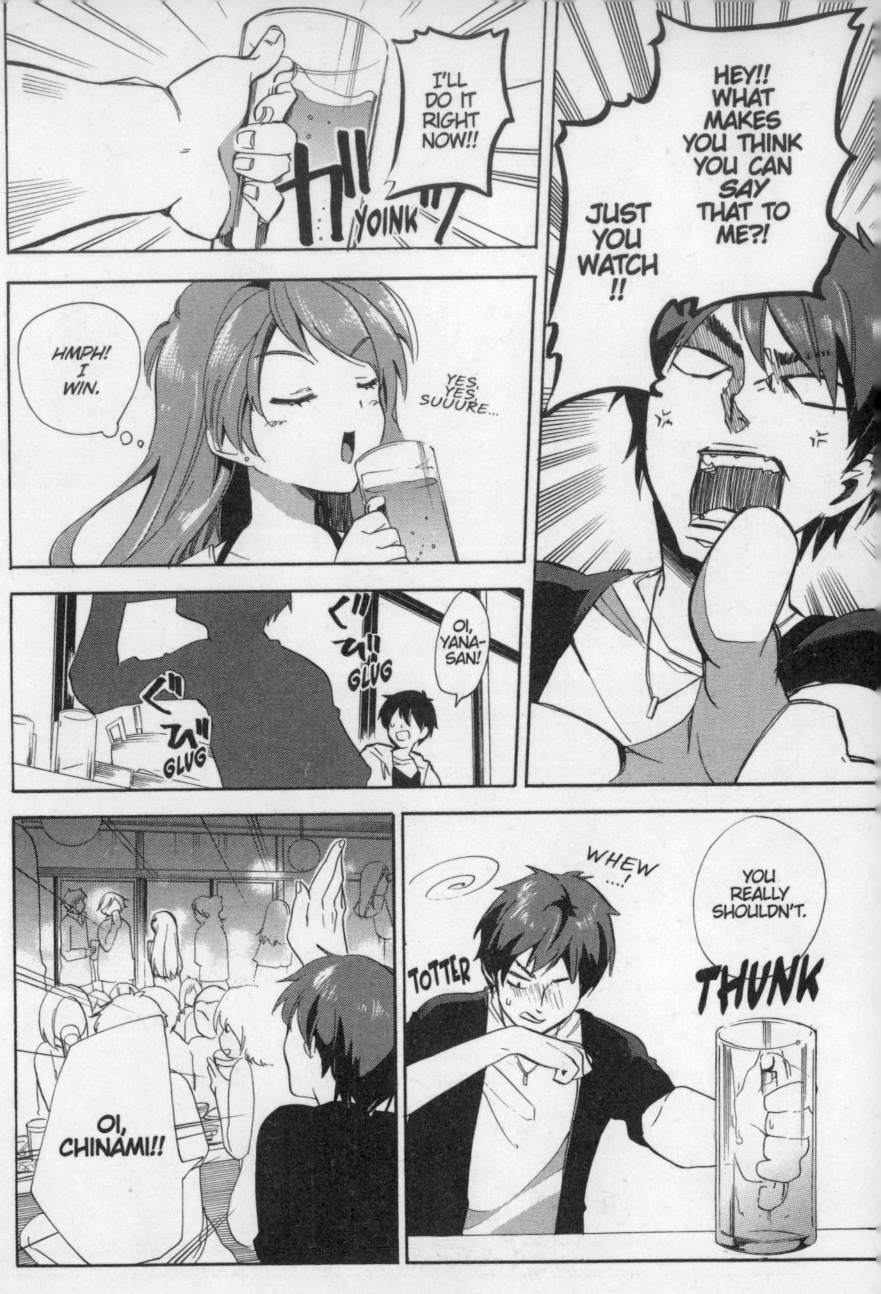
HEY!! WHAT MAKES YOU THINK YOU CAN SAY THAT TO ME?!
JUST YOU WATCH!!
I'LL DO IT RIGHT NOW!!
YOINK
YES, YES, SUUURE...
HMPH! I WIN.
OI, YANA-SAN!
GLUG
GLUG
YOU REALLY SHOULDN'T.
WHEW...!
THUNK
TOTTER
OI, CHINAMI!!

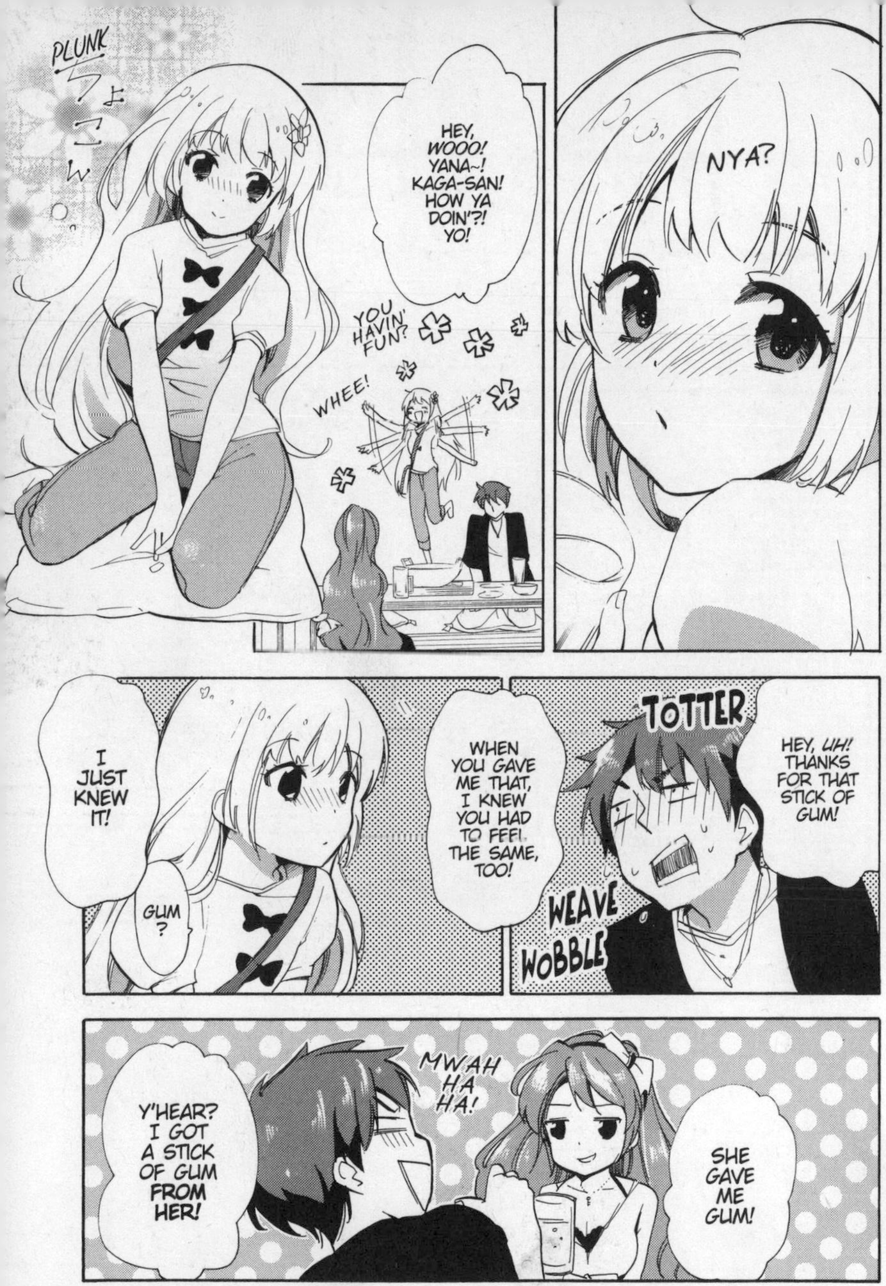
NYA?
HEY, WOOO! YANA~! KAGA-SAN! HOW YA DOIN'?! YO!
YOU HAVIN' FUN?
WHEE!
PLUNK
TOTTER
HEY, UH! THANKS FOR THAT STICK OF GUM!
WEAVE
WOBBLE
WHEN YOU GAVE ME THAT, I KNEW YOU HAD TO FEEL THE SAME, TOO!
I JUST KNEW IT!
GUM?
SHE GAVE ME GUM!
MWAH HA HA!
Y'HEAR? I GOT A STICK OF GUM FROM HER!

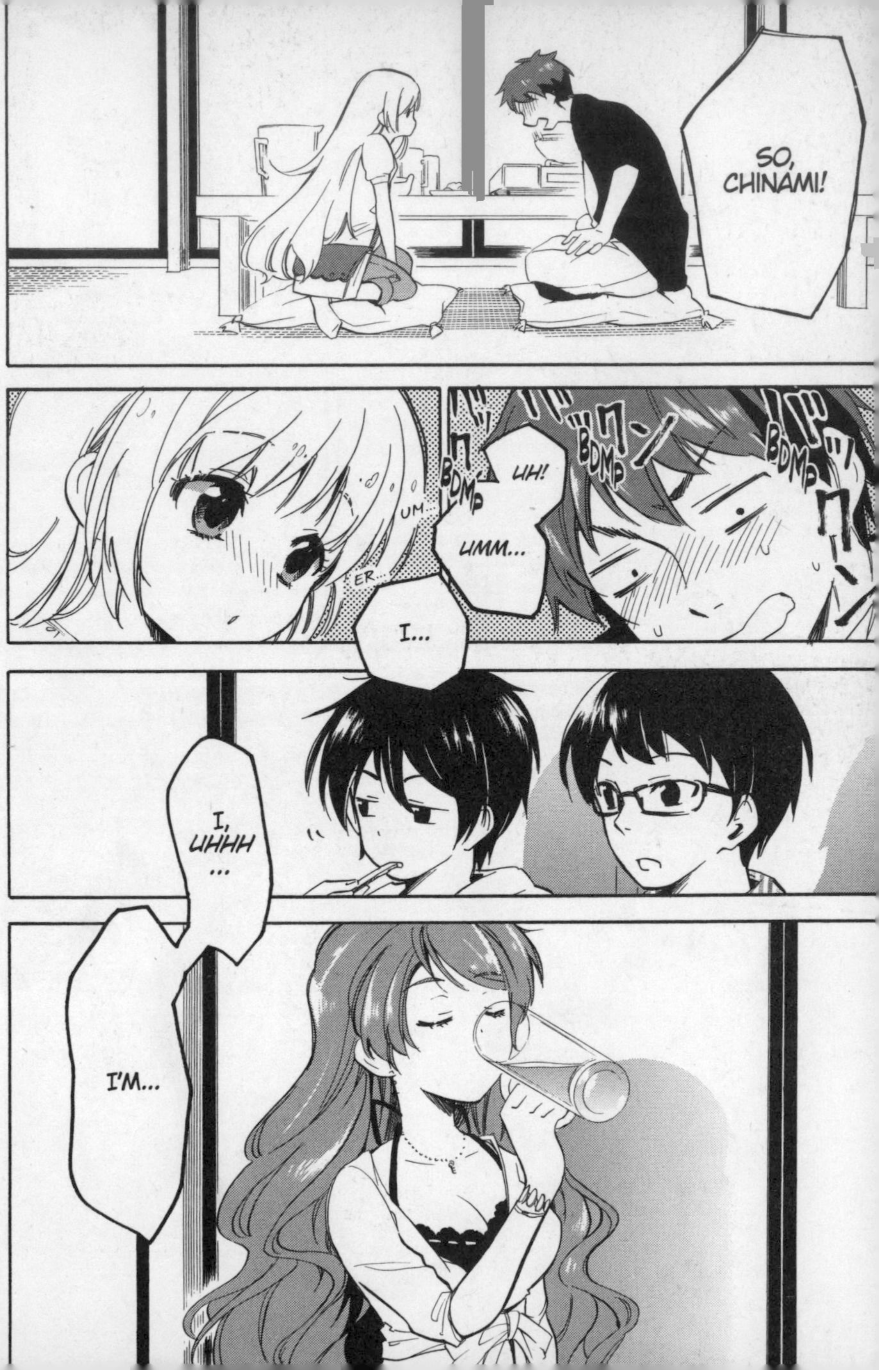
SO, CHINAMI!
BDMP
BDMP
BDMP
UH!
UMM...
UM...
ER...
I...
I, UHHH ...
I'M...

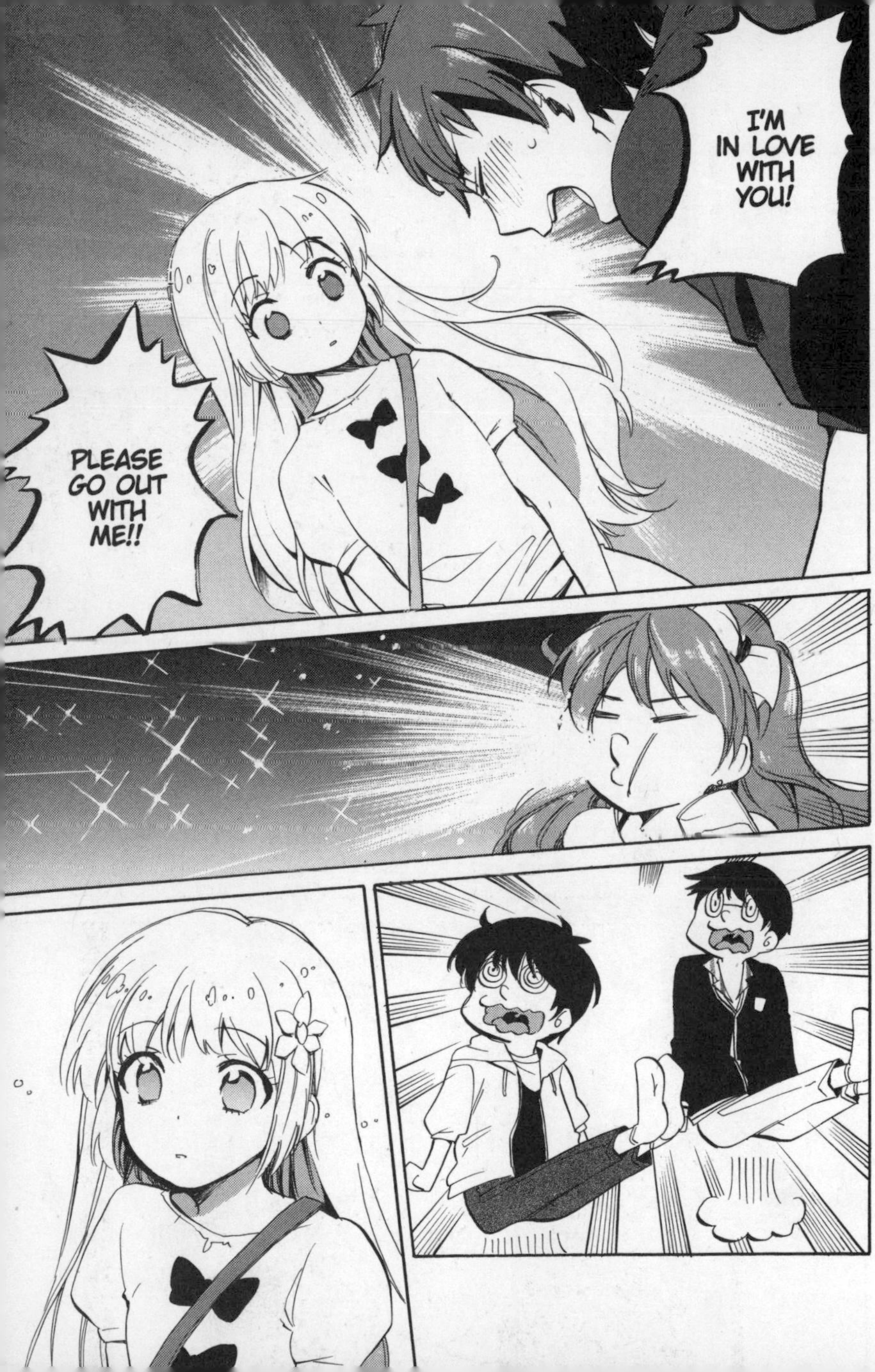
I'M IN LOVE WITH YOU!
PLEASE GO OUT WITH ME!!

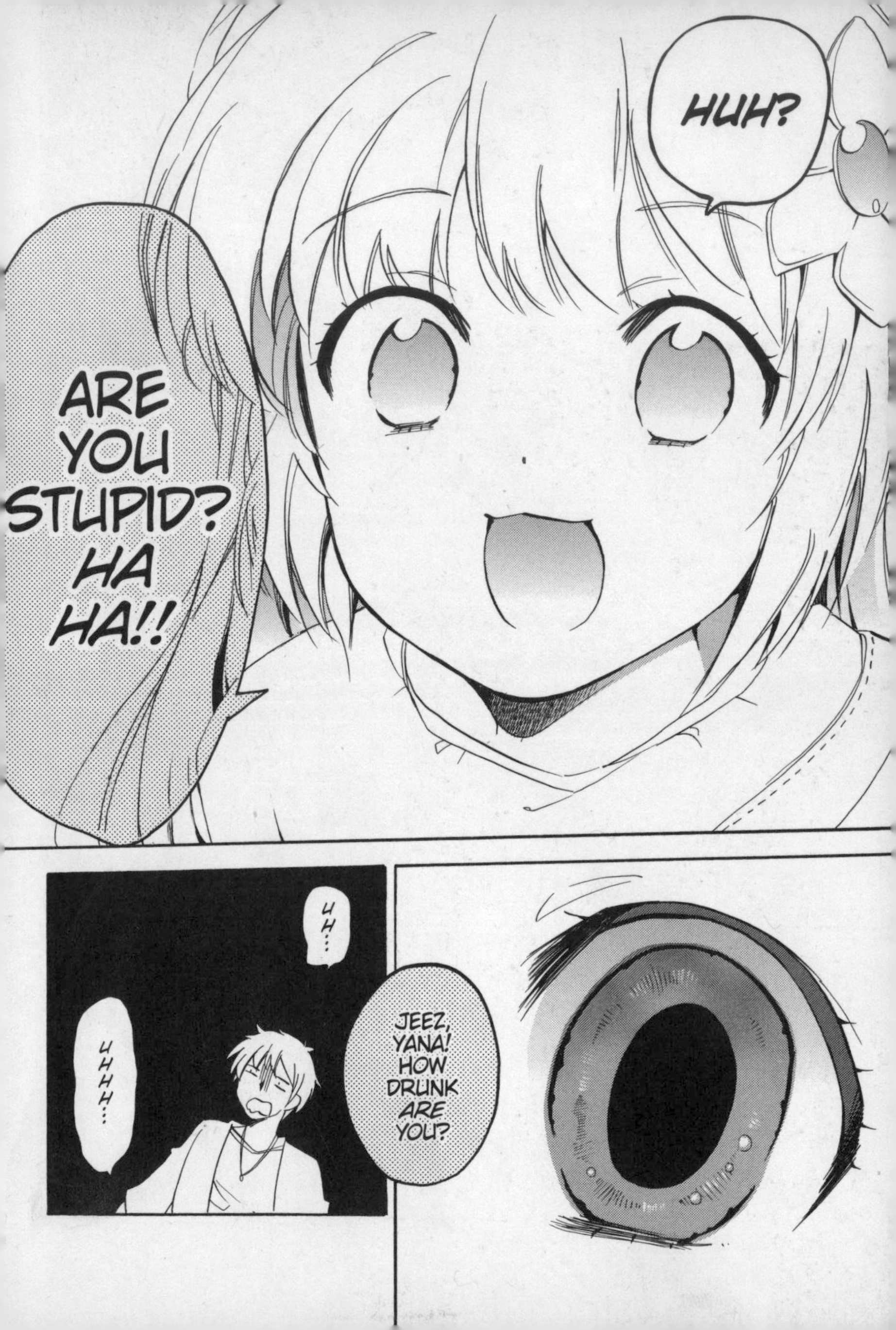
HUH?
ARE YOU STUPID? HA HA!!
JEEZ, YANA! HOW DRUNK ARE YOU?
UH...
UHHH...

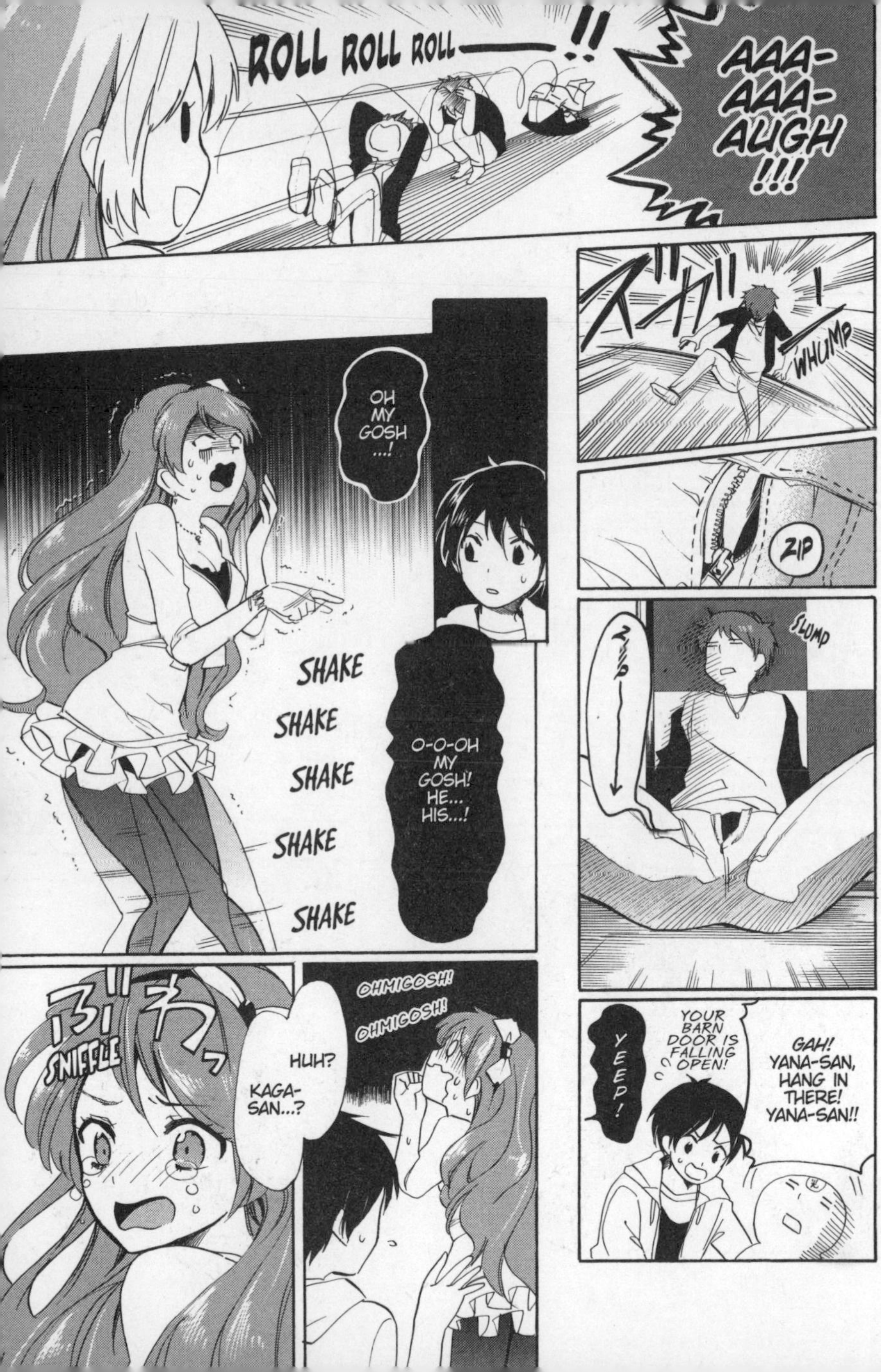
AAA-AAA-AUGH!!!
ROLL ROLL ROLL——!!
ズガーッ
WHUMP
ZIP
ZIIP
SLUMP
OH MY GOSH...!
SHAKE
SHAKE
SHAKE
SHAKE
SHAKE
O-O-OH MY GOSH! HE... HIS...!
YOUR BARN DOOR IS FALLING OPEN!
YEEP!
GAH! YANA-SAN, HANG IN THERE! YANA-SAN!!
OHMIGOSH!
OHMIGOSH!
HUH? KAGA-SAN...?
ぶわっ
SNIFFLE

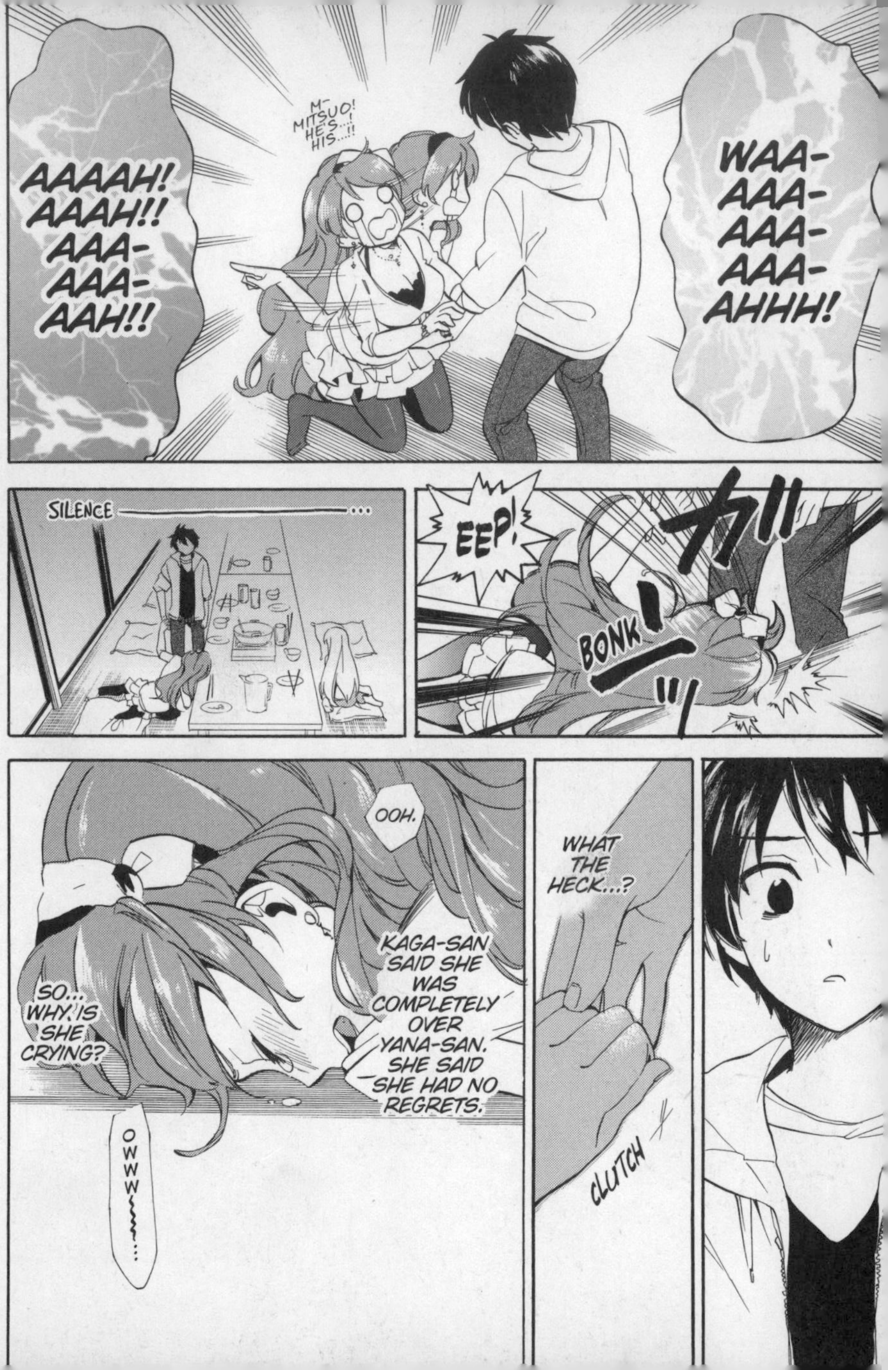
WAA-AAA-AAA-AAA-AHHH!
M-MITSUO! HE'S...! HIS...!!
AAAAH! AAAH!! AAA-AAA-AAH!!
EEP!
BONK
SILENCE———...
WHAT THE HECK...?
CLUTCH
OOH.
KAGA-SAN SAID SHE WAS COMPLETELY OVER YANA-SAN. SHE SAID SHE HAD NO REGRETS.
SO... WHY IS SHE CRYING?
OWWW...

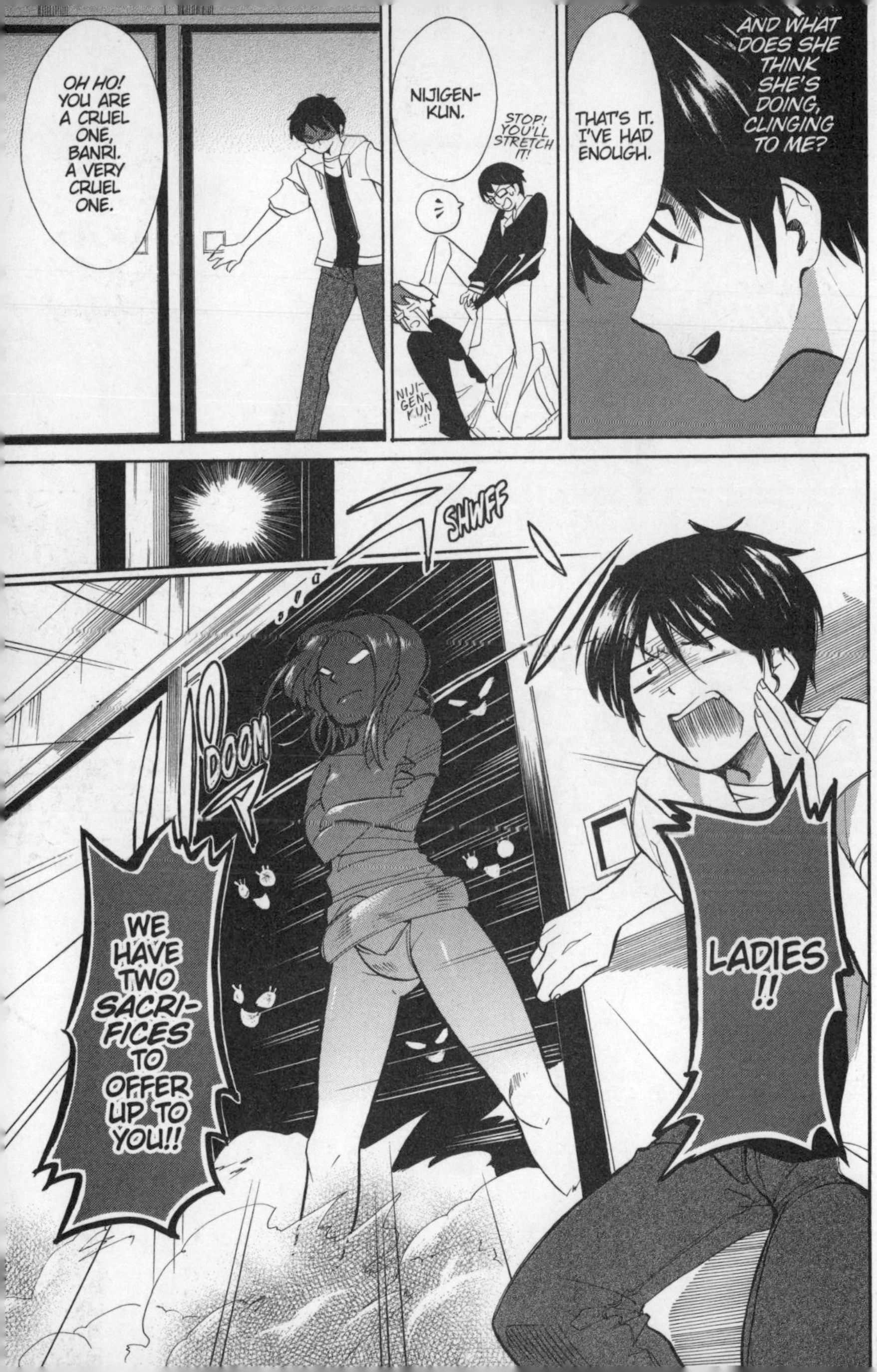
AND WHAT DOES SHE THINK SHE'S DOING, CLINGING TO ME?
THAT'S IT. I'VE HAD ENOUGH.
NIJIGEN-KUN.
STOP! YOU'LL STRETCH IT!
NIJI-GEN-KUN...!!
OH HO! YOU ARE A CRUEL ONE, BANRI. A VERY CRUEL ONE.
SHWFF
LADIES!!
DOOM
WE HAVE TWO SACRI-FICES TO OFFER UP TO YOU!!

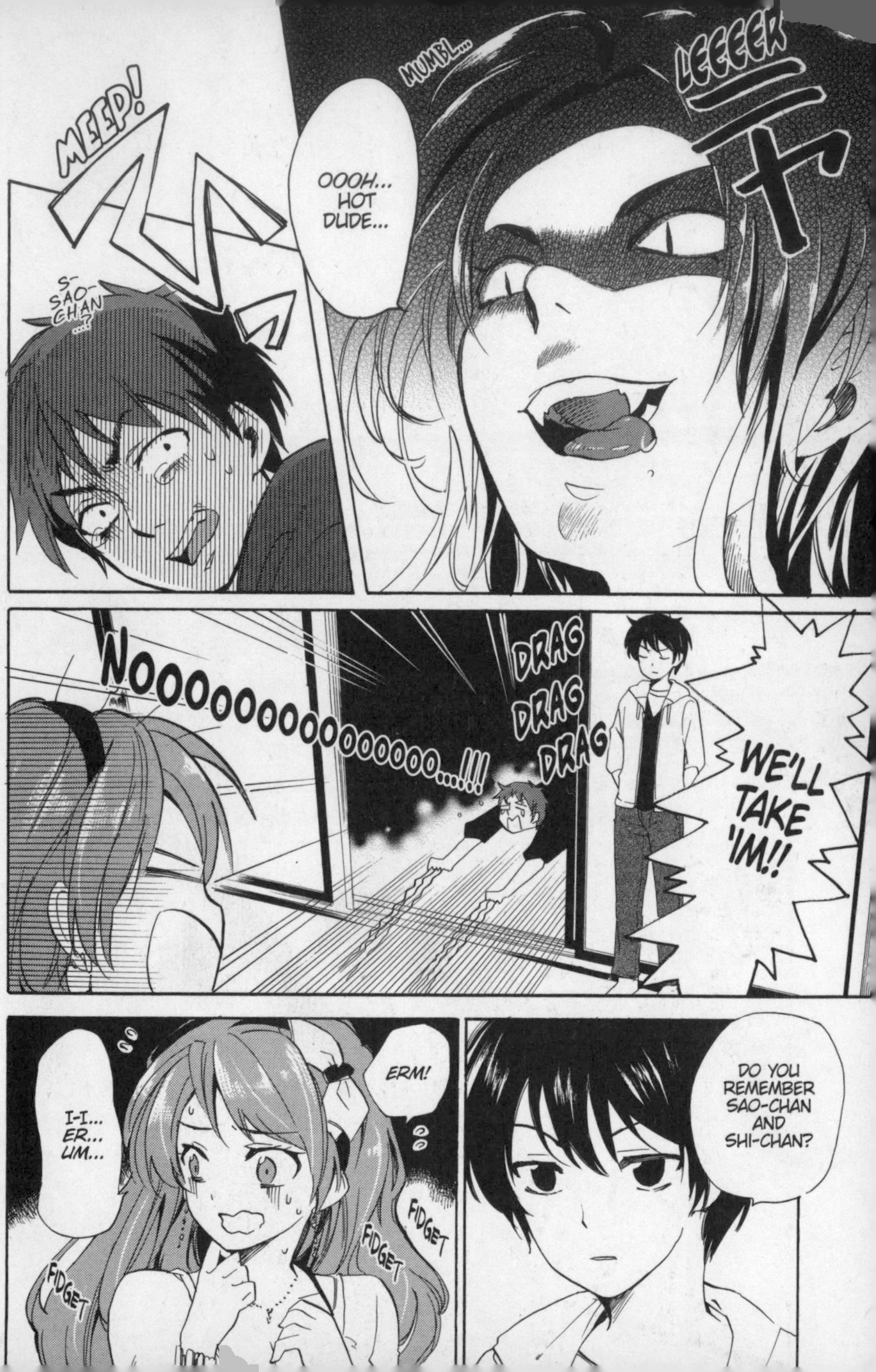
LEEEER
MUMBL...
OOOH... HOT DUDE...
MEEP!
S-SAO-CHAN...?
WE'LL TAKE 'IM!!
DRAG DRAG DRAG
NOOOOOOOOOOOOOOOOOO...!!!
DO YOU REMEMBER SAO-CHAN AND SHI-CHAN?
ERM!
I-I... ER... UM...
FIDGET
FIDGET
FIDGET

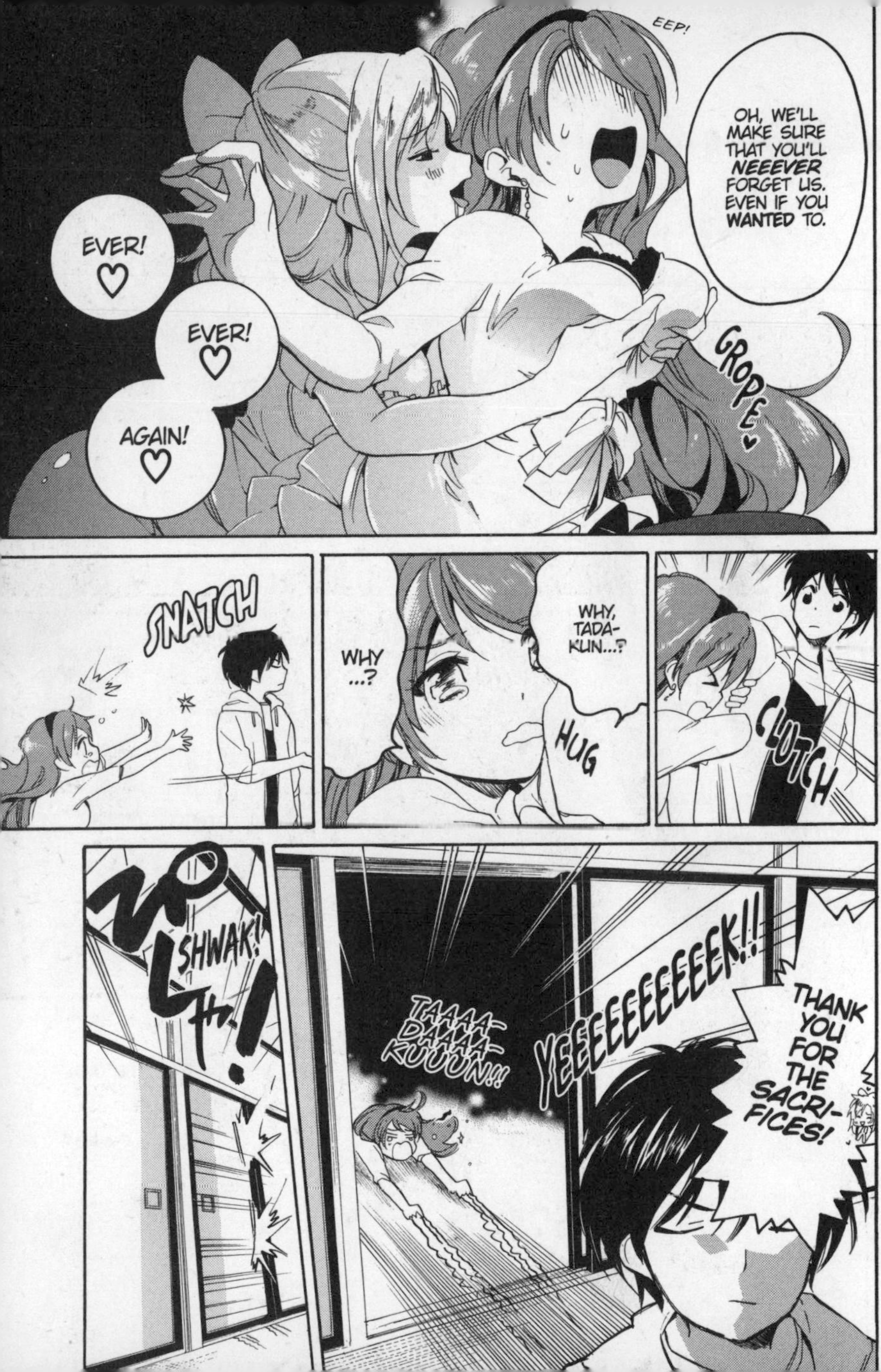
EEP!
OH, WE'LL MAKE SURE THAT YOU'LL NEEEVER FORGET US. EVEN IF YOU WANTED TO.
GROPE♥
EVER! ♥
EVER! ♥
AGAIN! ♥
CLUTCH
WHY, TADA-KUN...?
WHY ...?
HUG
SNATCH
THANK YOU FOR THE SACRIFICES!
YEEEEEEEEEEK!!
TAAAA-DAAAA-KUUUN!!
SHWAK!

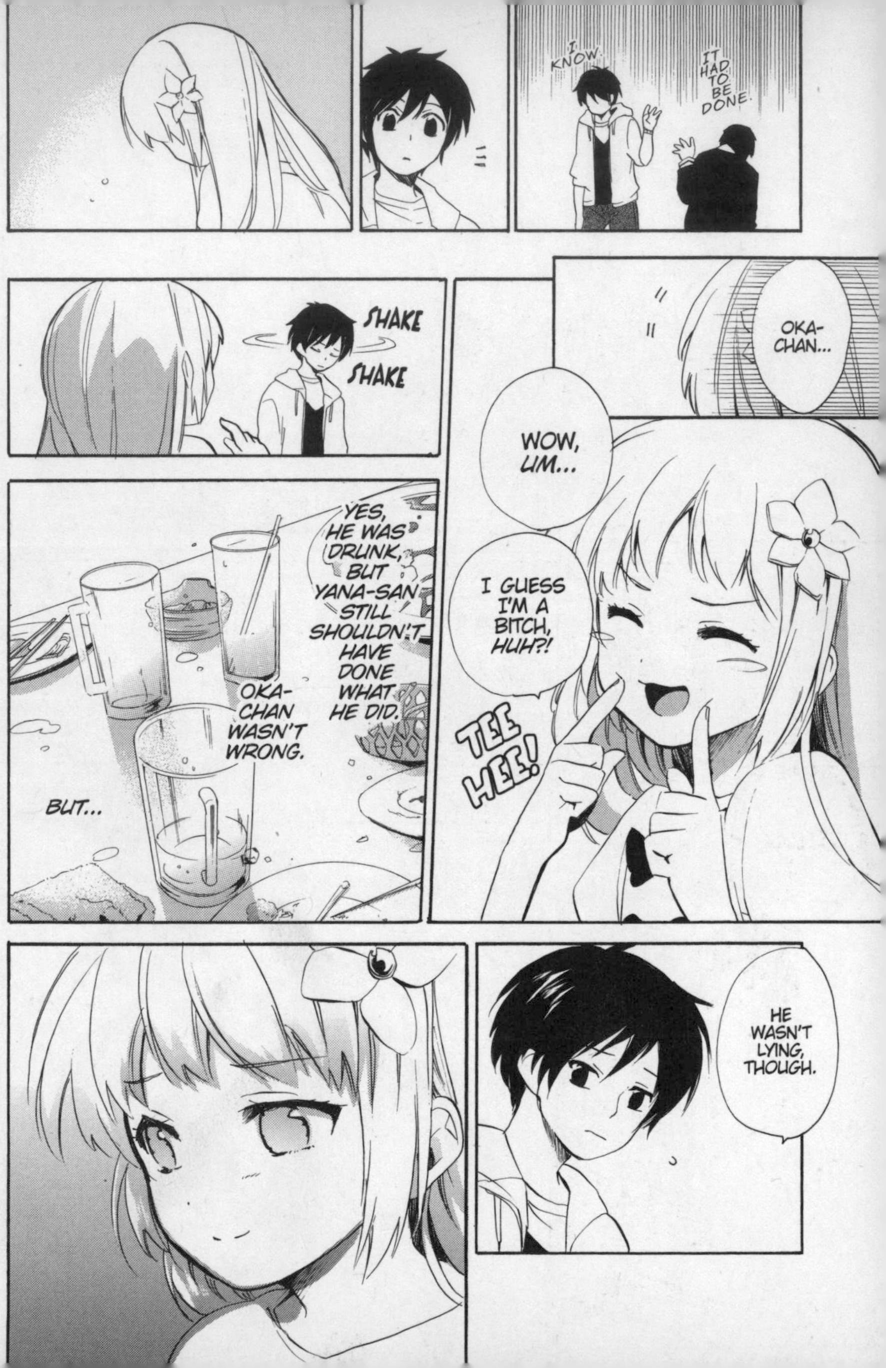
I KNOW.
IT HAD TO BE DONE.
OKA-CHAN...
WOW, UM...
I GUESS I'M A BITCH, HUH?!
TEE HEE!
SHAKE
SHAKE
YES, HE WAS DRUNK, BUT YANA-SAN STILL SHOULDN'T HAVE DONE WHAT HE DID.
OKA-CHAN WASN'T WRONG.
BUT...
HE WASN'T LYING, THOUGH.

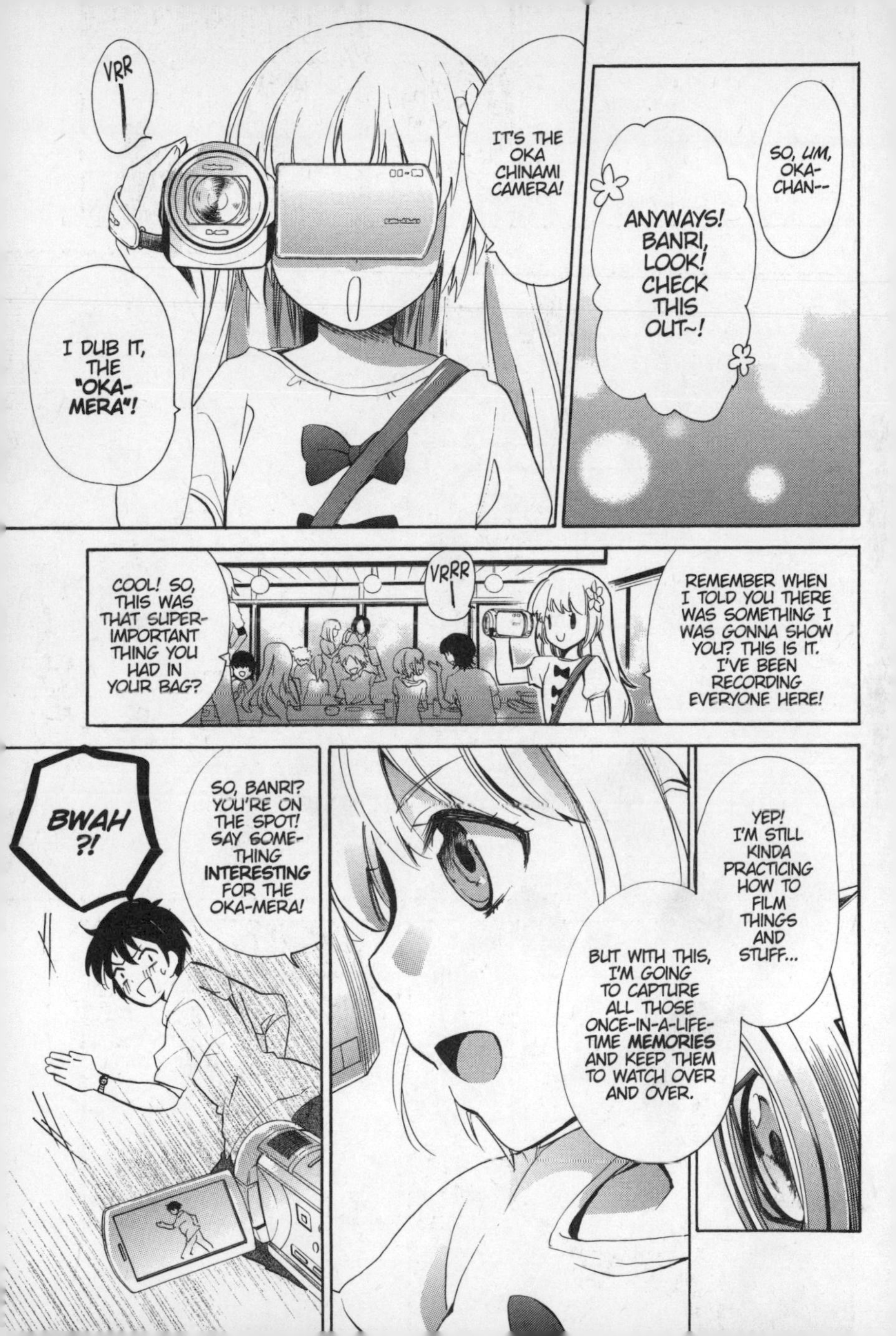
SO, UM, OKA-CHAN--
ANYWAYS! BANRI, LOOK! CHECK THIS OUT~!
IT'S THE OKA CHINAMI CAMERA!
VRR
I DUB IT, THE "OKA-MERA"!
REMEMBER WHEN I TOLD YOU THERE WAS SOMETHING I WAS GONNA SHOW YOU? THIS IS IT. I'VE BEEN RECORDING EVERYONE HERE!
VRRR
COOL! SO, THIS WAS THAT SUPER-IMPORTANT THING YOU HAD IN YOUR BAG?
YEP! I'M STILL KINDA PRACTICING HOW TO FILM THINGS AND STUFF...
BUT WITH THIS, I'M GOING TO CAPTURE ALL THOSE ONCE-IN-A-LIFE-TIME MEMORIES AND KEEP THEM TO WATCH OVER AND OVER.
SO, BANRI? YOU'RE ON THE SPOT! SAY SOME-THING INTERESTING FOR THE OKA-MERA!
BWAH ?!

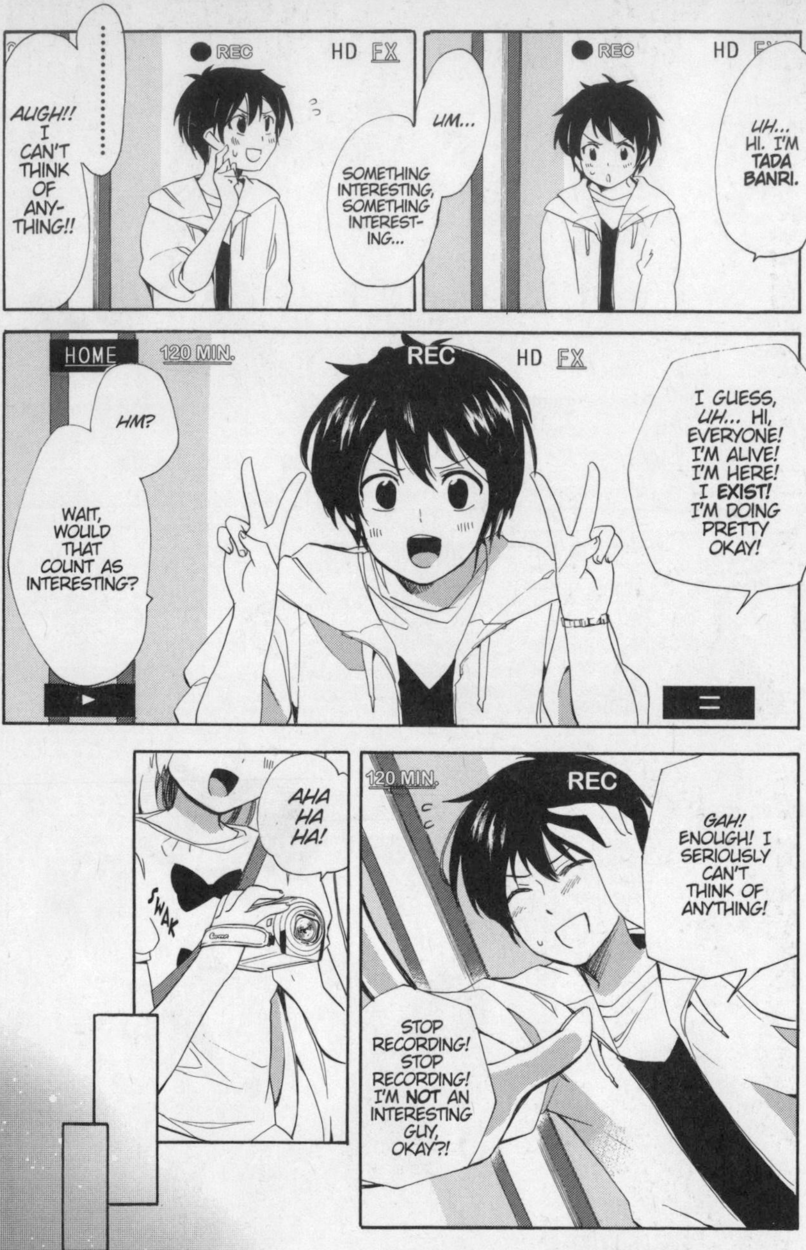
REC
HD FX
UH... HI. I'M TADA BANRI.
REC
HD FX
UM...
SOMETHING INTERESTING, SOMETHING INTEREST-ING...
......
AUGH!! I CAN'T THINK OF ANY-THING!!
HOME
120 MIN.
REC
HD FX
I GUESS, UH... HI, EVERYONE! I'M ALIVE! I'M HERE! I EXIST! I'M DOING PRETTY OKAY!
HM?
WAIT, WOULD THAT COUNT AS INTERESTING?
120 MIN.
REC
GAH! ENOUGH! I SERIOUSLY CAN'T THINK OF ANYTHING!
STOP RECORDING! STOP RECORDING! I'M NOT AN INTERESTING GUY, OKAY?!
AHA HA HA!
SWAK

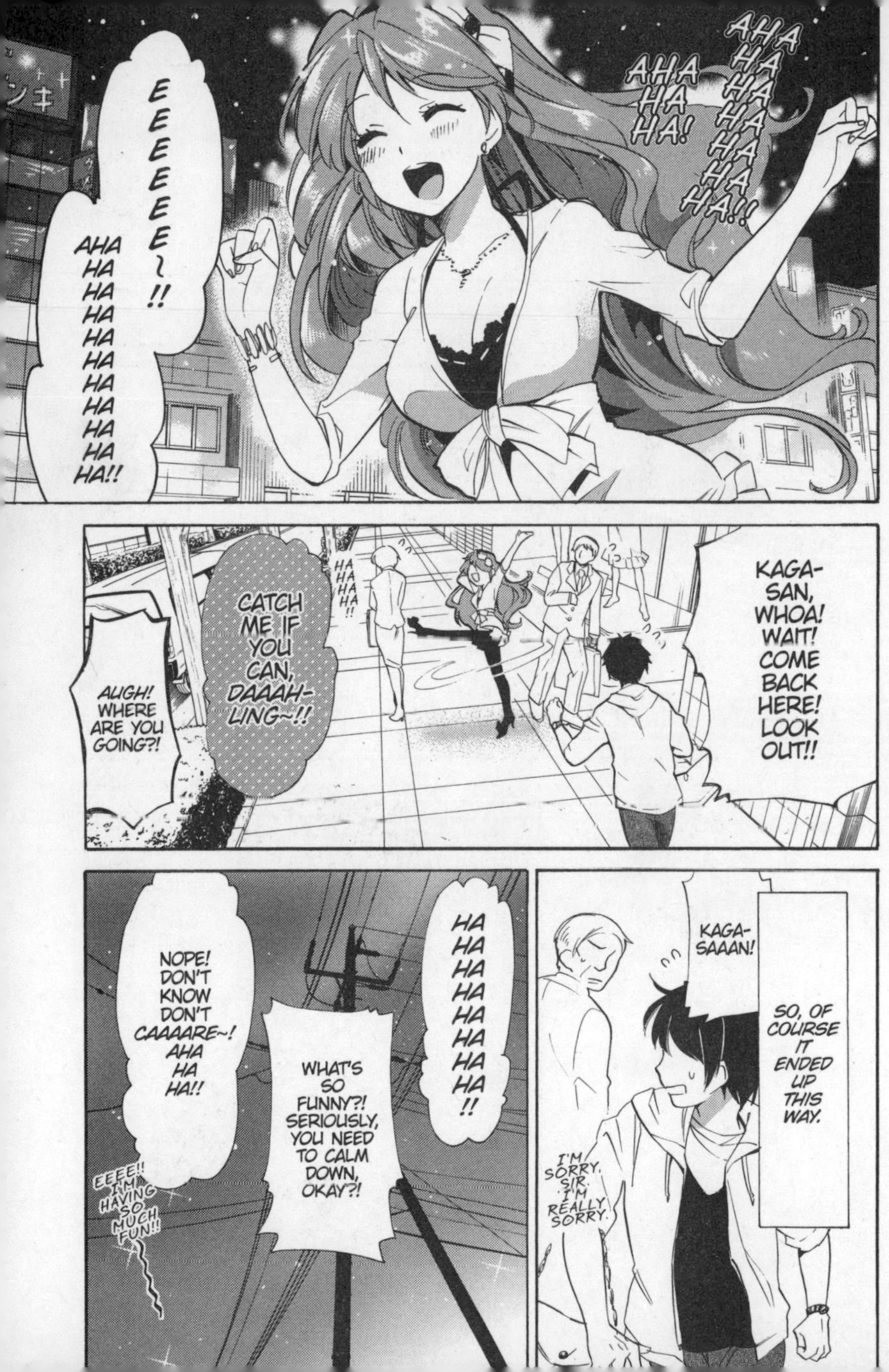
AHA HA HA HA HA HA HA HA!!
AHA HA HA HA!
EEEEEEE~!!
AHA HA HA HA HA HA HA HA HA HA HA!!
KAGA-SAN, WHOA! WAIT! COME BACK HERE! LOOK OUT!!
HA HA HA HA!!
CATCH ME IF YOU CAN, DAAAH-LING~!!
AUGH! WHERE ARE YOU GOING?!
KAGA-SAAAN!
SO, OF COURSE IT ENDED UP THIS WAY.
I'M SORRY, SIR. I'M REALLY SORRY.
HA HA HA HA HA HA HA HA HA!!
NOPE! DON'T KNOW DON'T CAAAARE~! AHA HA HA!!
WHAT'S SO FUNNY?! SERIOUSLY, YOU NEED TO CALM DOWN, OKAY?!
EEEE!! I'M HAVING SO MUCH FUN!!

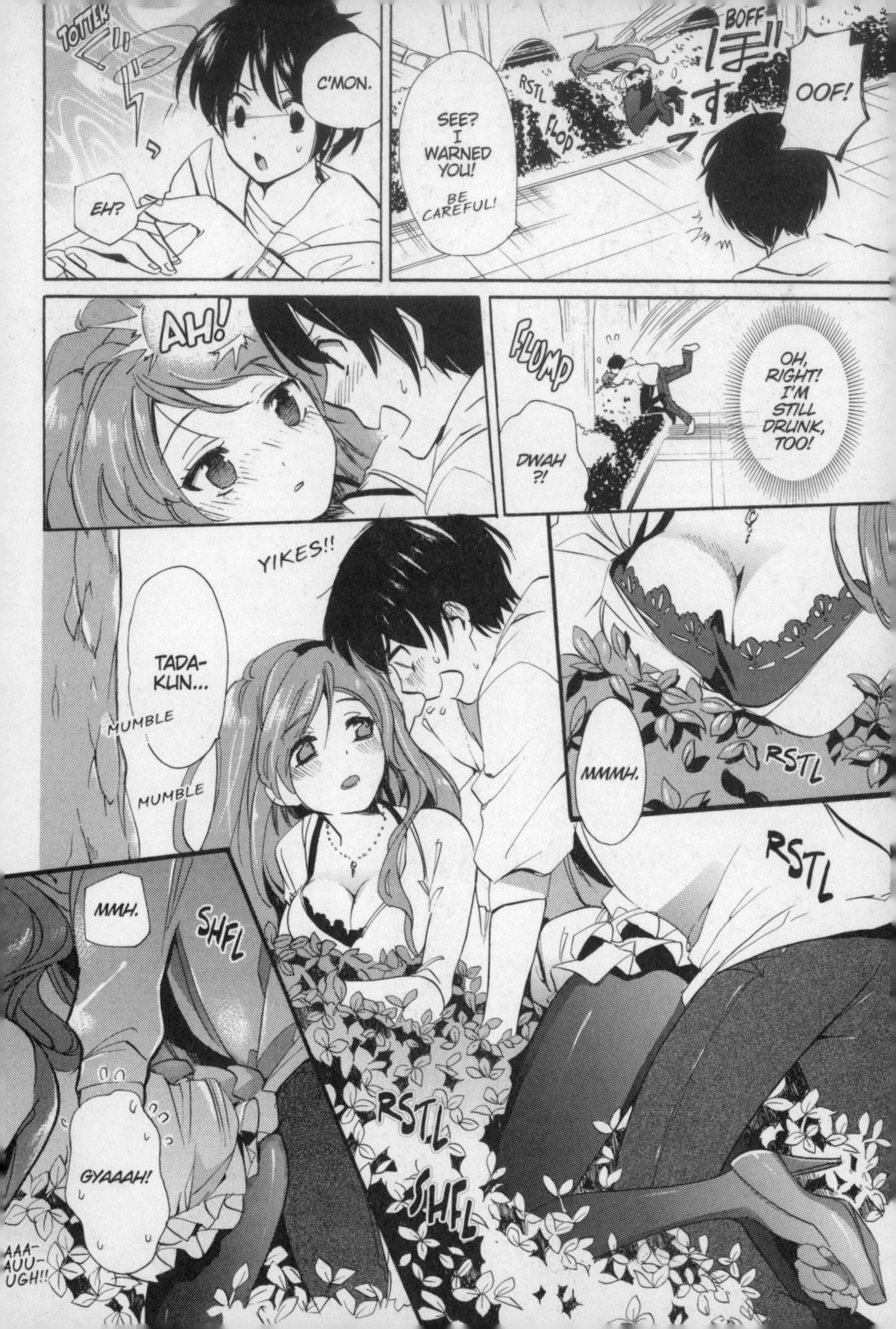
BOFF
OOF!
RSTL
FLOP
SEE? I WARNED YOU!
BE CAREFUL!
TOTTEK
C'MON.
EH?
OH, RIGHT! I'M STILL DRUNK, TOO!
FLUMP
DWAH?!
AH!
MMMH.
RSTL
RSTL
YIKES!!
TADA-KUN...
MUMBLE
MUMBLE
MMH.
SHFL
RSTL
SHFL
GYAAAH!
AAA-AUUU-UGH!!

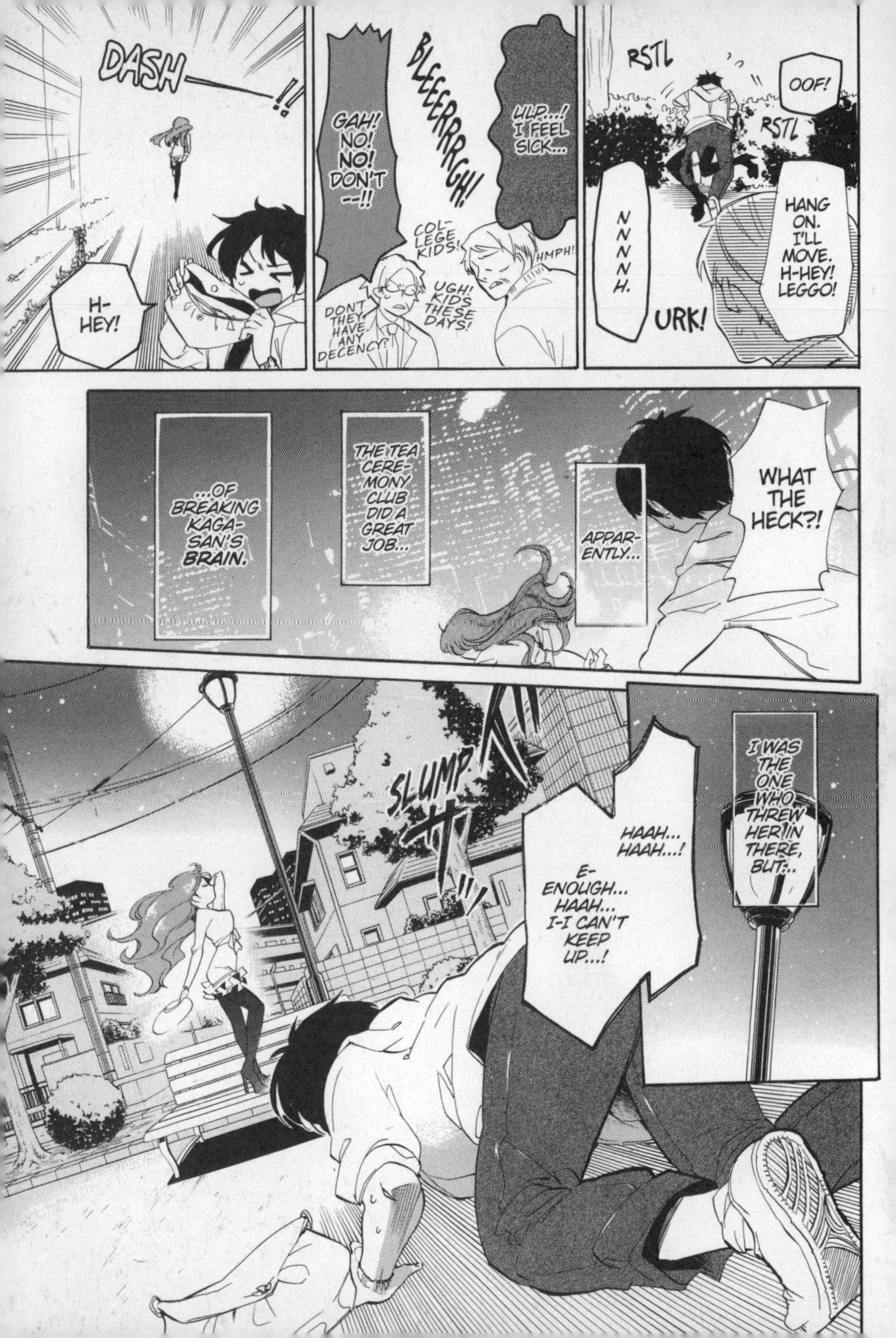
OOF!
RSTL
RSTL
HANG ON. I'LL MOVE. H-HEY! LEGGO!
NNNNNH.
URK!
BLEEERRGH!
ULP...! I FEEL SICK...
GAH! NO! NO! DON'T --!!
COLLEGE KIDS!
HMPH!
UGH! KIDS THESE DAYS!
DON'T THEY HAVE ANY DECENCY?
DASH—!!
H-HEY!
WHAT THE HECK?!
APPARENTLY...
THE TEA CEREMONY CLUB DID A GREAT JOB...
...OF BREAKING KAGA-SAN'S BRAIN.
I WAS THE ONE WHO THREW HER IN THERE, BUT...
HAAH... HAAH...!
E-ENOUGH... HAAH... I-I CAN'T KEEP UP...!
SLUMP

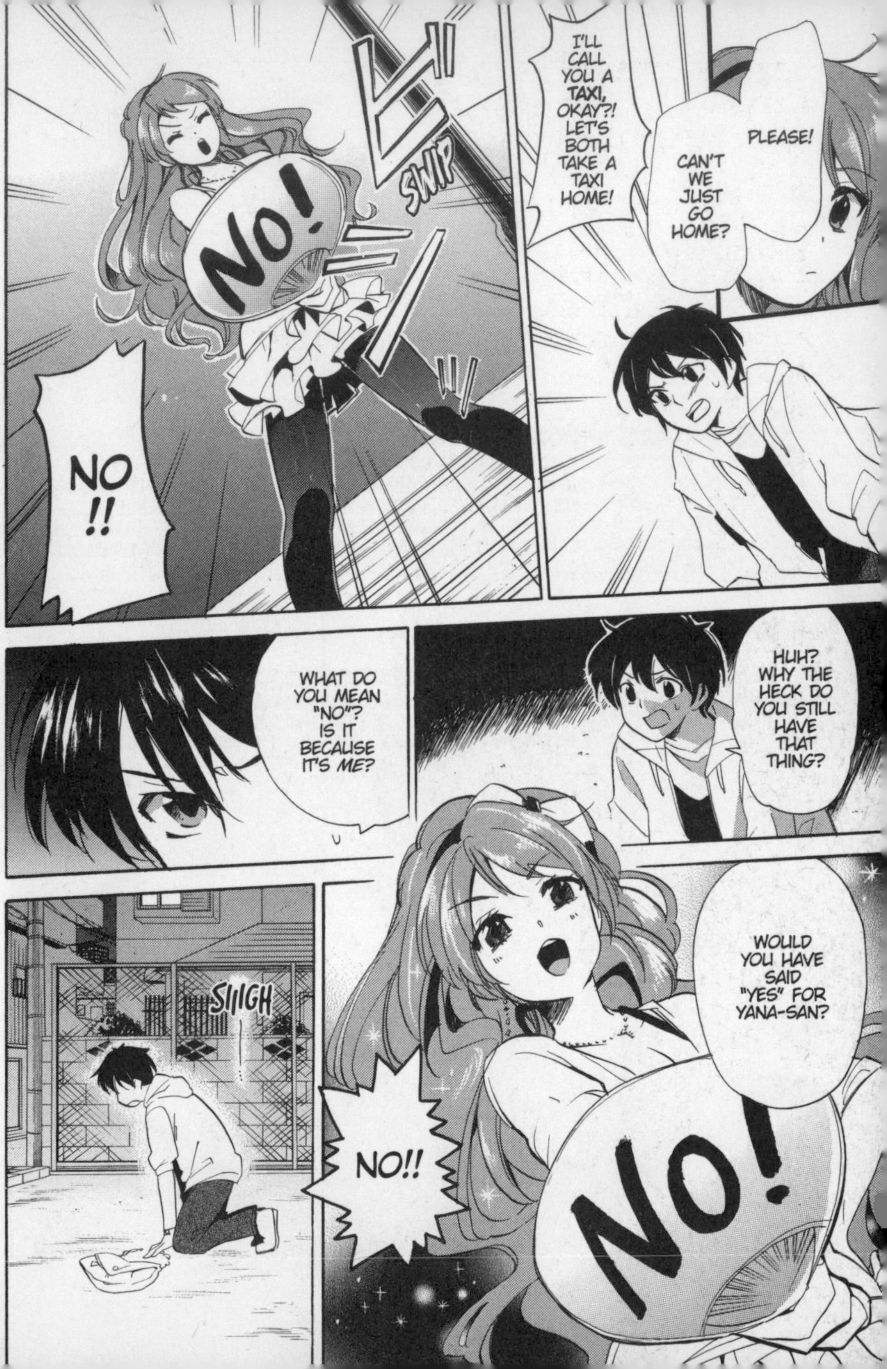
PLEASE!
CAN'T WE JUST GO HOME?
I'LL CALL YOU A TAXI, OKAY?! LET'S BOTH TAKE A TAXI HOME!
NO!
SWIP
NO !!
HUH? WHY THE HECK DO YOU STILL HAVE THAT THING?
WHAT DO YOU MEAN "NO"? IS IT BECAUSE IT'S *ME*?
WOULD YOU HAVE SAID "YES" FOR YANA-SAN?
NO!!
NO!
SIIIGH

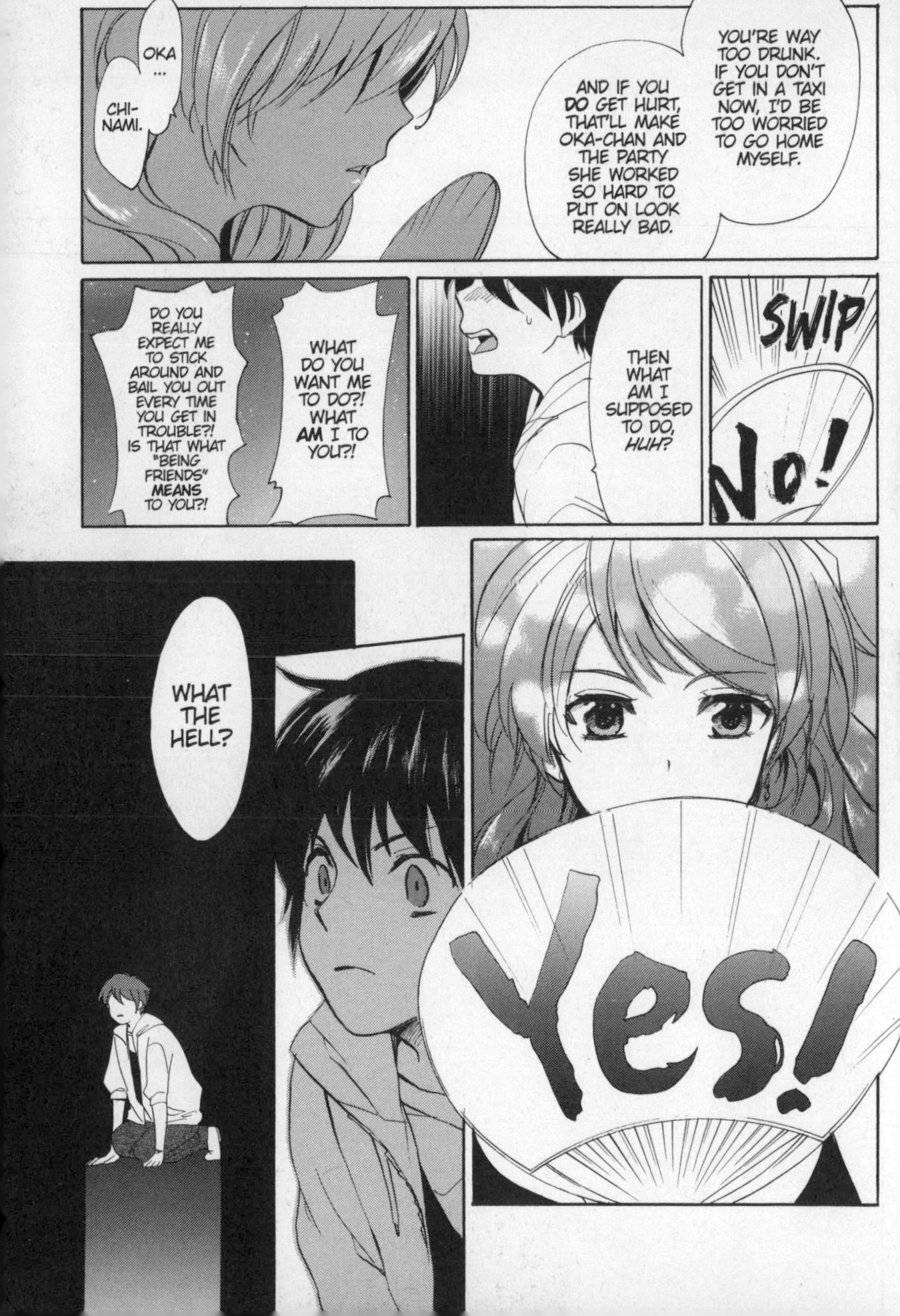

YOU'RE WAY TOO DRUNK. IF YOU DON'T GET IN A TAXI NOW, I'D BE TOO WORRIED TO GO HOME MYSELF.
AND IF YOU DO GET HURT, THAT'LL MAKE OKA-CHAN AND THE PARTY SHE WORKED SO HARD TO PUT ON LOOK REALLY BAD.
OKA...
CHI-NAMI.
SWIP
NO!
THEN WHAT AM I SUPPOSED TO DO, HUH?
WHAT DO YOU WANT ME TO DO?! WHAT AM I TO YOU?!
DO YOU REALLY EXPECT ME TO STICK AROUND AND BAIL YOU OUT EVERY TIME YOU GET IN TROUBLE?! IS THAT WHAT "BEING FRIENDS" MEANS TO YOU?!
YES!
WHAT THE HELL?

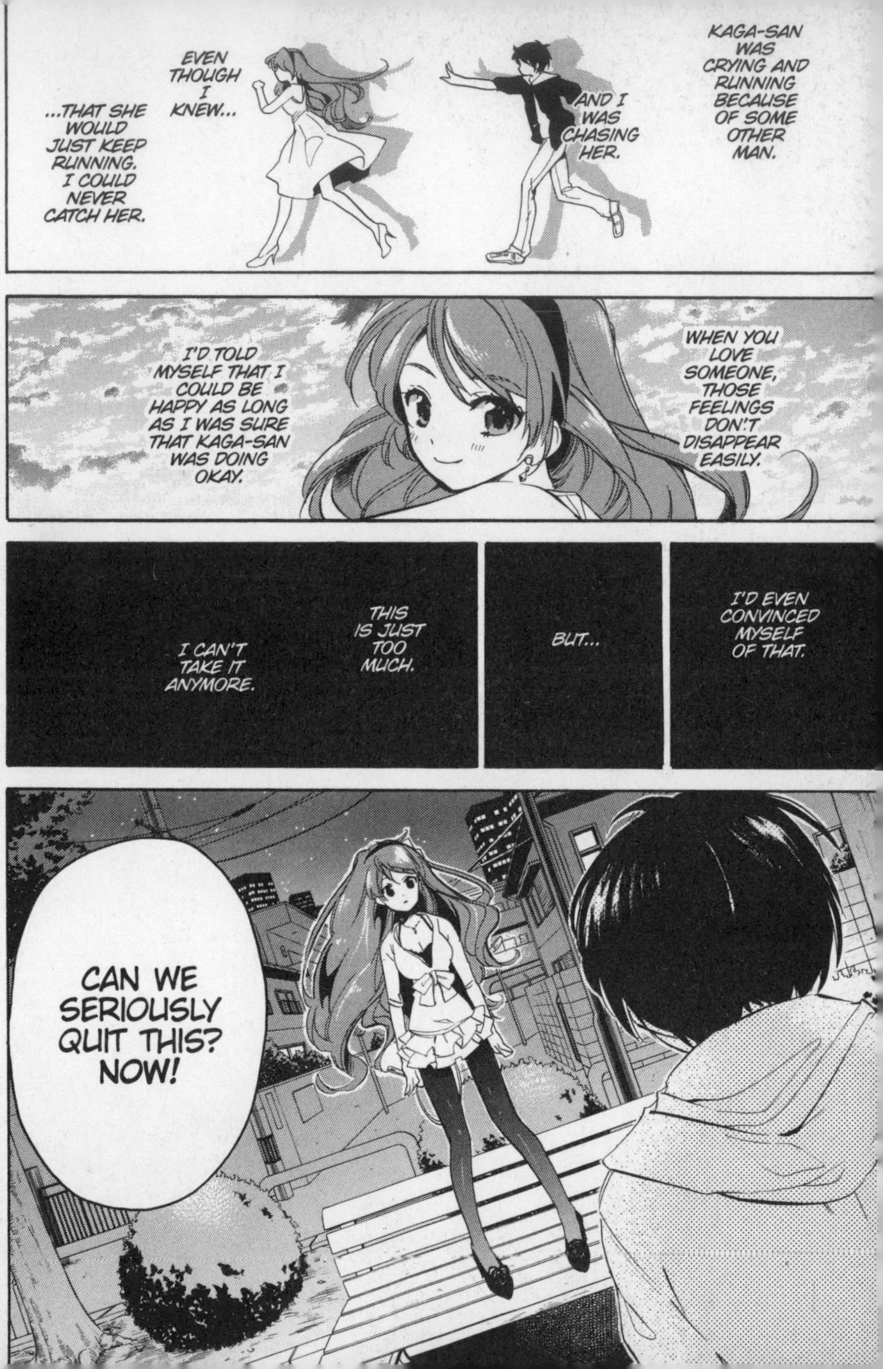
KAGA-SAN WAS CRYING AND RUNNING BECAUSE OF SOME OTHER MAN.
AND I WAS CHASING HER.
EVEN THOUGH I KNEW...
...THAT SHE WOULD JUST KEEP RUNNING. I COULD NEVER CATCH HER.
WHEN YOU LOVE SOMEONE, THOSE FEELINGS DON'T DISAPPEAR EASILY.
I'D TOLD MYSELF THAT I COULD BE HAPPY AS LONG AS I WAS SURE THAT KAGA-SAN WAS DOING OKAY.
I'D EVEN CONVINCED MYSELF OF THAT.
BUT...
THIS IS JUST TOO MUCH.
I CAN'T TAKE IT ANYMORE.
CAN WE SERIOUSLY QUIT THIS? NOW!

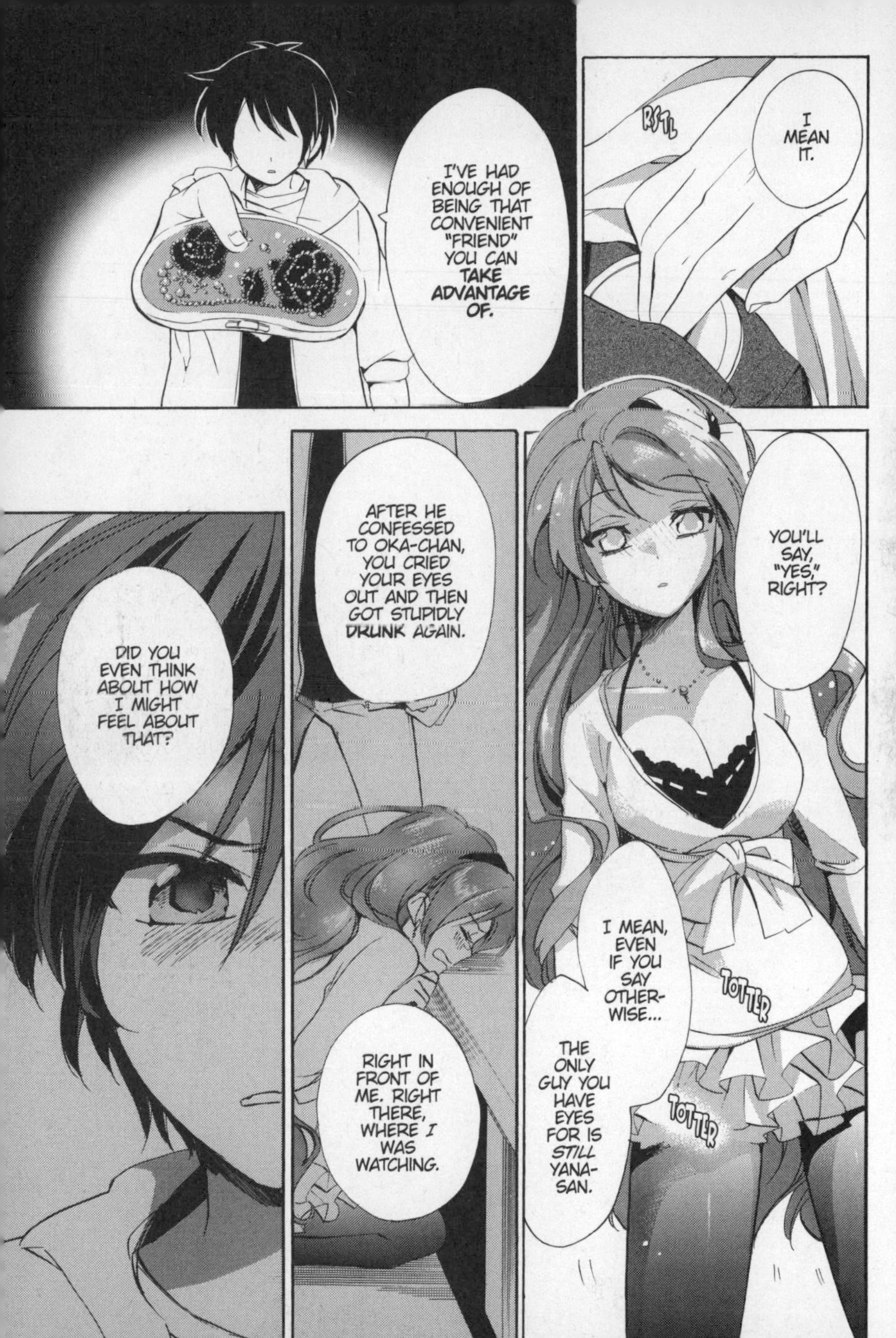
RSTL
I MEAN IT.
I'VE HAD ENOUGH OF BEING THAT CONVENIENT "FRIEND" YOU CAN TAKE ADVANTAGE OF.
YOU'LL SAY, "YES," RIGHT?
I MEAN, EVEN IF YOU SAY OTHERWISE...
TOTTER
THE ONLY GUY YOU HAVE EYES FOR IS STILL YANA-SAN.
TOTTER
AFTER HE CONFESSED TO OKA-CHAN, YOU CRIED YOUR EYES OUT AND THEN GOT STUPIDLY DRUNK AGAIN.
RIGHT IN FRONT OF ME. RIGHT THERE, WHERE I WAS WATCHING.
DID YOU EVEN THINK ABOUT HOW I MIGHT FEEL ABOUT THAT?

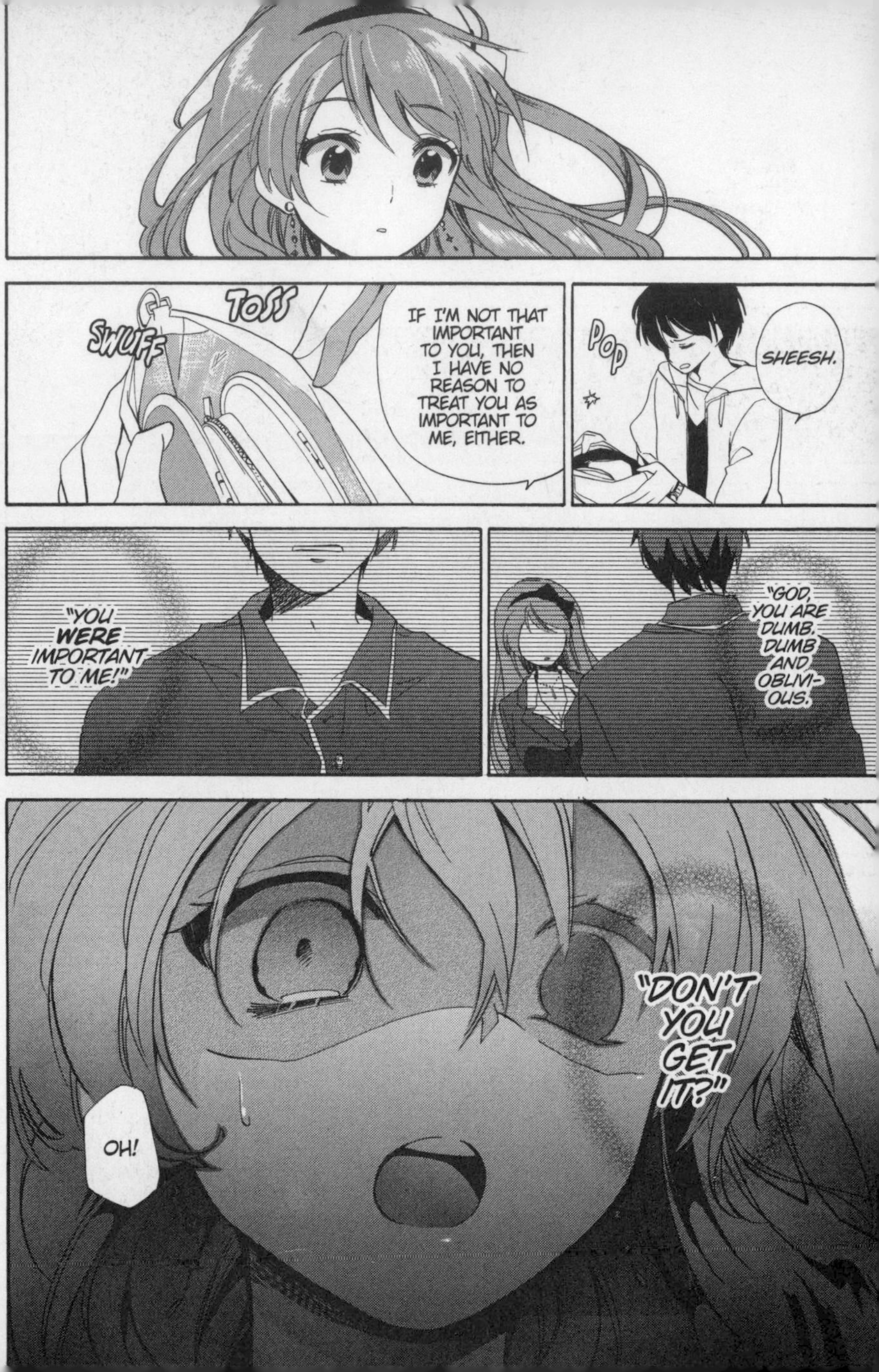
POP
SHEESH.
TOSS
SWUFF
IF I'M NOT THAT IMPORTANT TO YOU, THEN I HAVE NO REASON TO TREAT YOU AS IMPORTANT TO ME, EITHER.
"GOD, YOU ARE DUMB. DUMB AND OBLIVI-OUS.
"YOU WERE IMPORTANT TO ME!"
"DON'T YOU GET IT?"
OH!

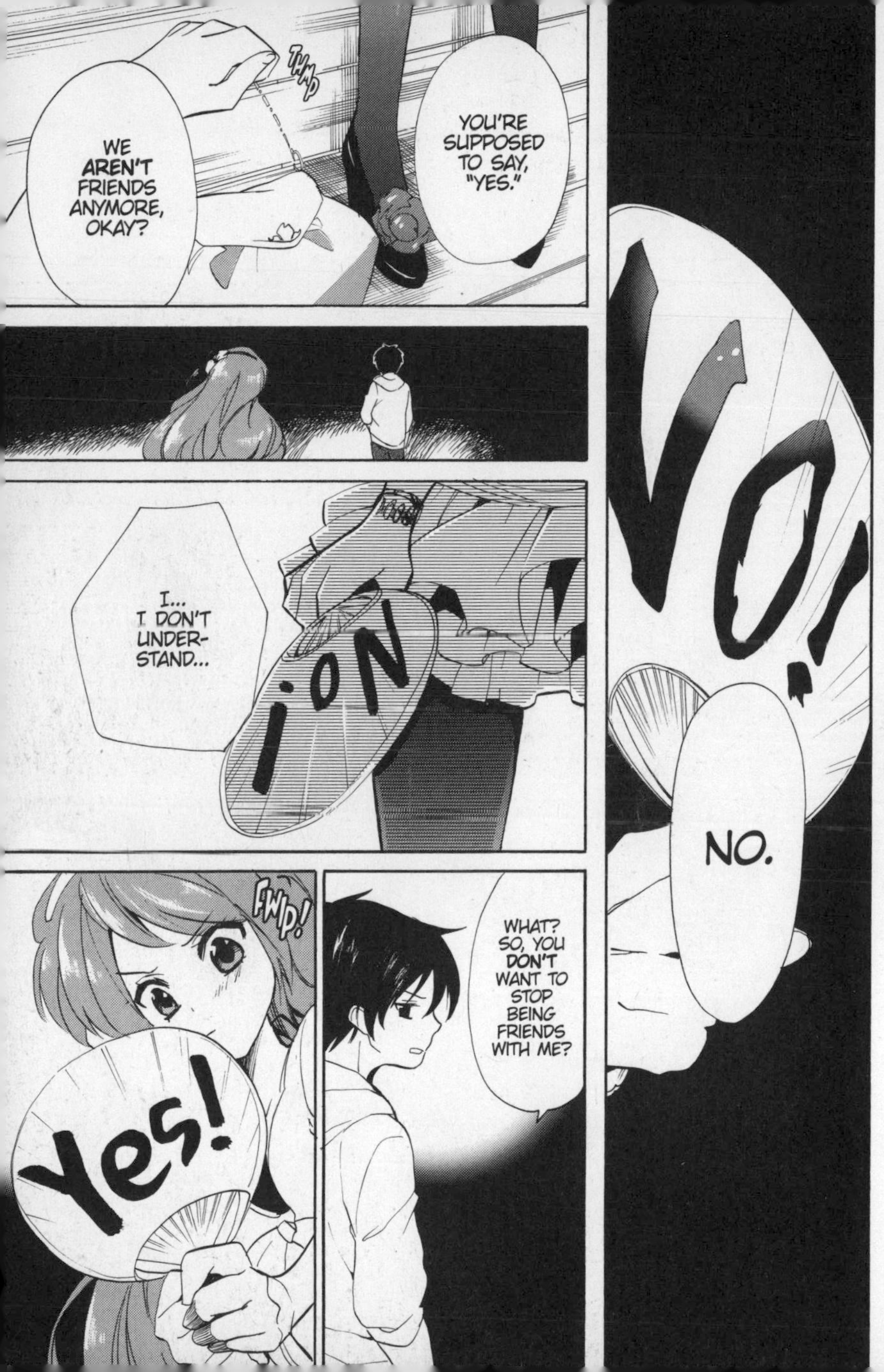
NO!
NO.
YOU'RE SUPPOSED TO SAY, "YES."
THMP
WE AREN'T FRIENDS ANYMORE, OKAY?
I... I DON'T UNDERSTAND...
WHAT? SO, YOU DON'T WANT TO STOP BEING FRIENDS WITH ME?
FWIP!
Yes!

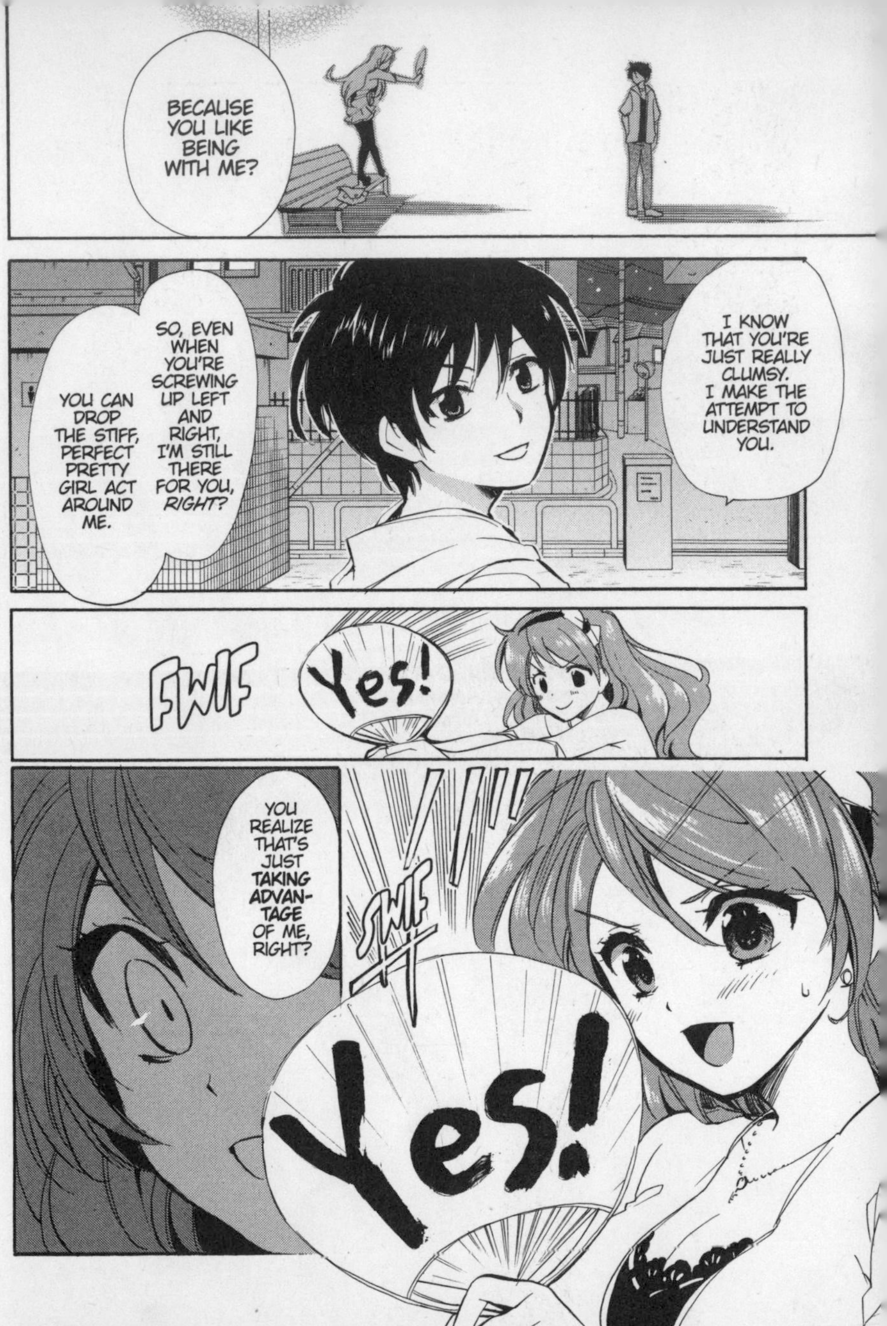
BECAUSE YOU LIKE BEING WITH ME?
I KNOW THAT YOU'RE JUST REALLY CLUMSY. I MAKE THE ATTEMPT TO UNDERSTAND YOU.
SO, EVEN WHEN YOU'RE SCREWING UP LEFT AND RIGHT, I'M STILL THERE FOR YOU, *RIGHT?*
YOU CAN DROP THE STIFF, PERFECT PRETTY GIRL ACT AROUND ME.
Yes!
FWIF
Yes!
SWIF
YOU REALIZE THAT'S JUST **TAKING ADVANTAGE** OF ME, RIGHT?

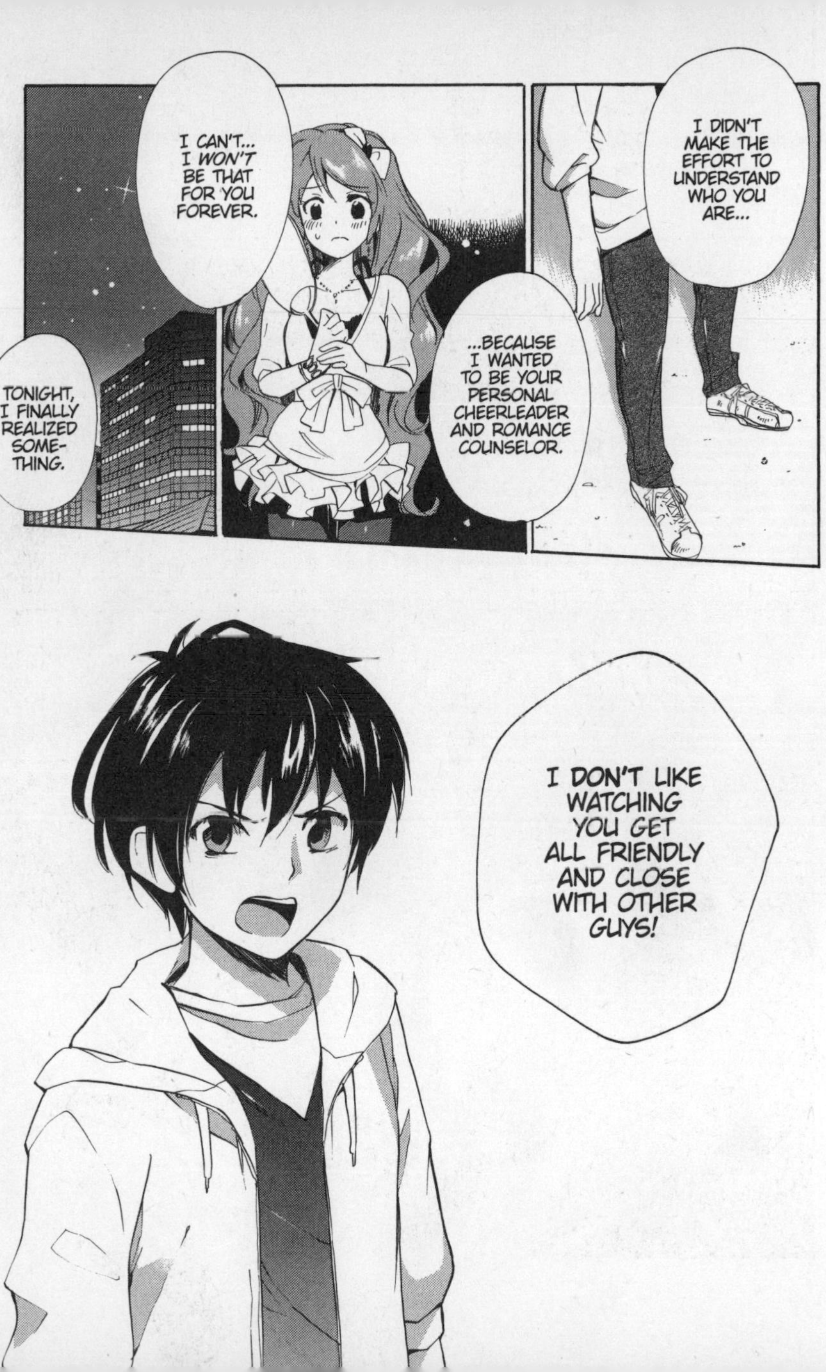
I DIDN'T MAKE THE EFFORT TO UNDERSTAND WHO YOU ARE...
...BECAUSE I WANTED TO BE YOUR PERSONAL CHEERLEADER AND ROMANCE COUNSELOR.
I CAN'T... I *WON'T* BE THAT FOR YOU FOREVER.
TONIGHT, I FINALLY REALIZED SOME-THING.
I DON'T LIKE WATCHING YOU GET ALL FRIENDLY AND CLOSE WITH OTHER GUYS!

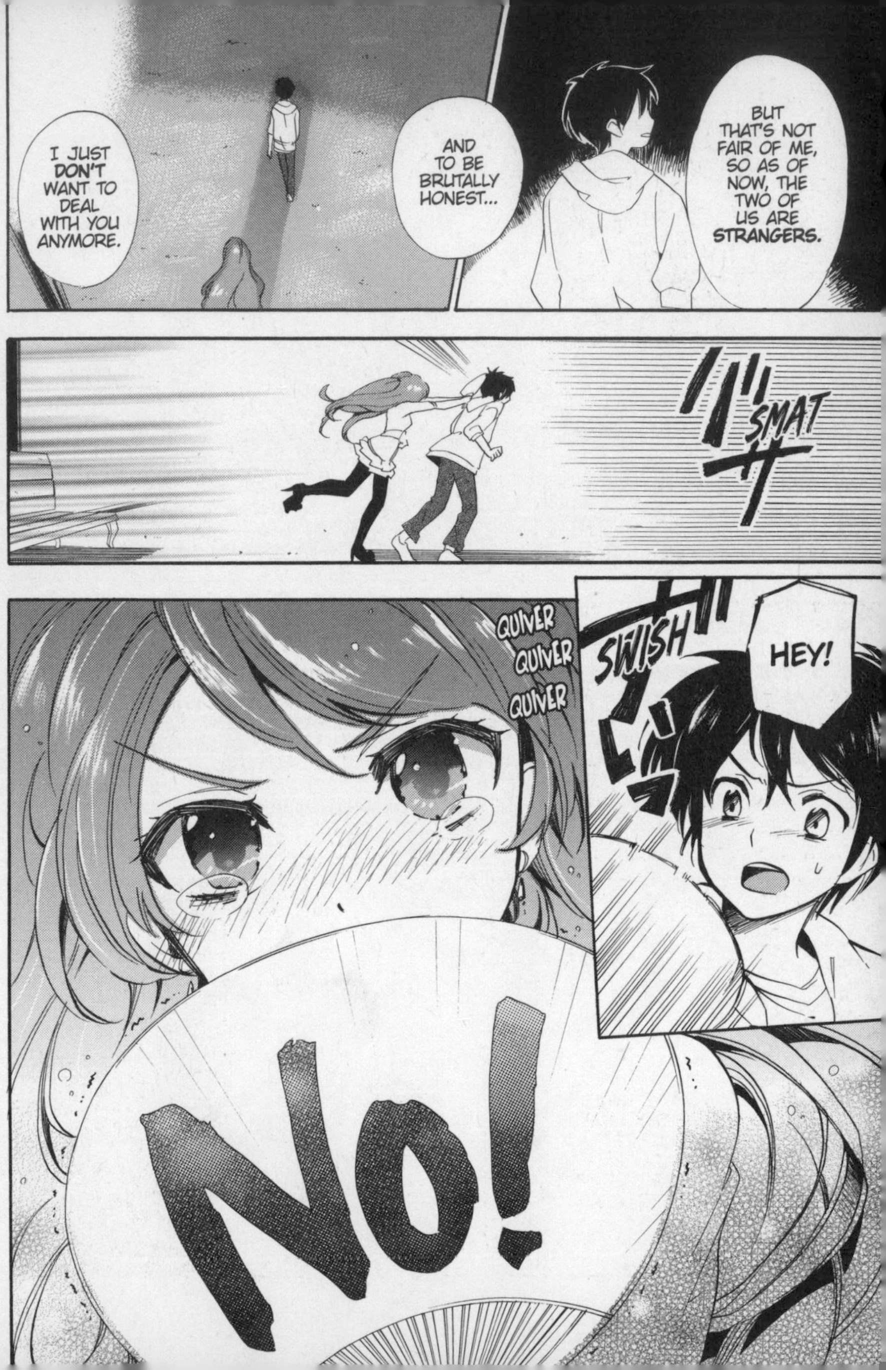
BUT THAT'S NOT FAIR OF ME, SO AS OF NOW, THE TWO OF US ARE STRANGERS.
AND TO BE BRUTALLY HONEST...
I JUST DON'T WANT TO DEAL WITH YOU ANYMORE.
SMAT
HEY!
SWISH
QUIVER QUIVER QUIVER
NO!

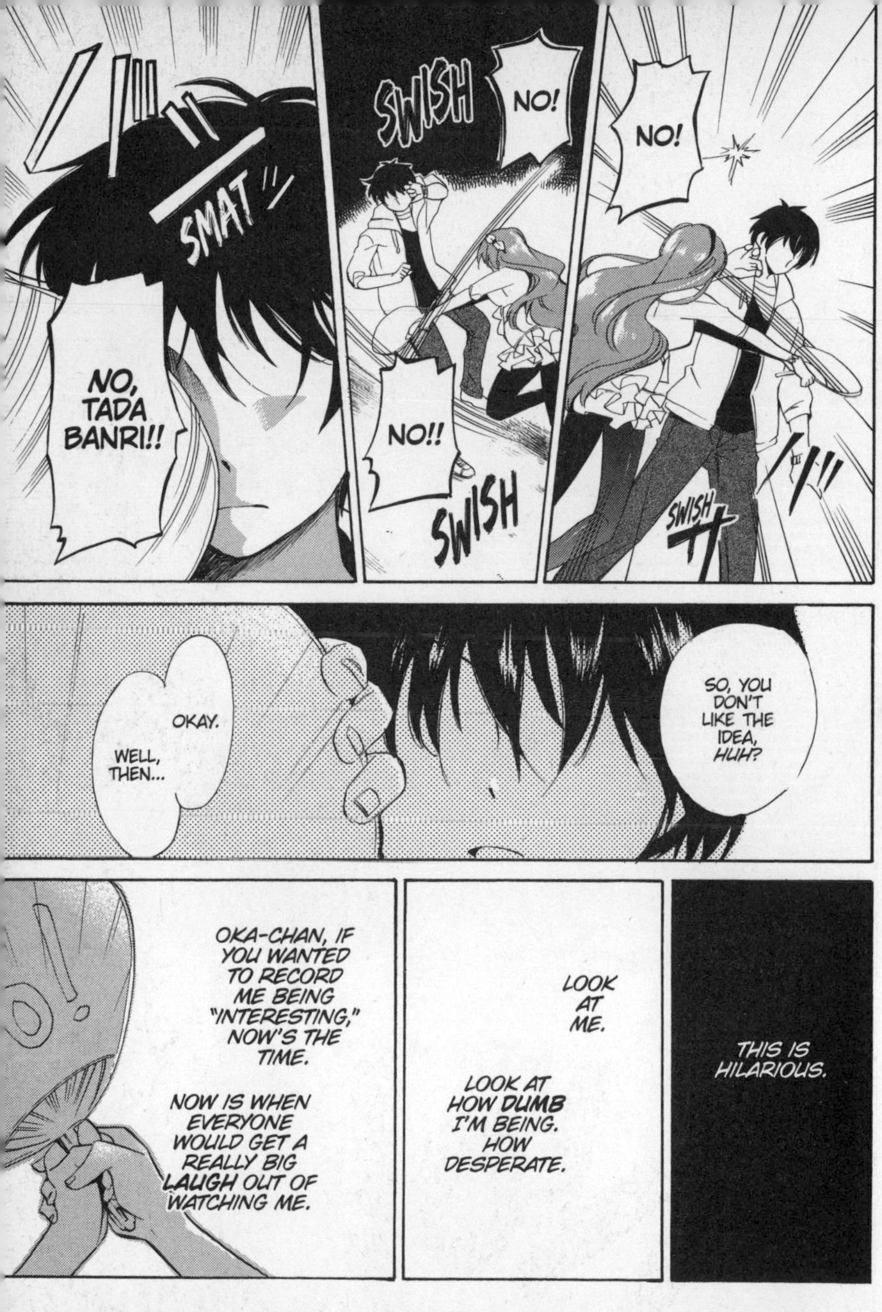
NO!
SWISH
NO!
SWISH
NO!!
SWISH
SMAT
NO, TADA BANRI!!
SO, YOU DON'T LIKE THE IDEA, HUH?
OKAY.
WELL, THEN...
THIS IS HILARIOUS.
LOOK AT ME.
LOOK AT HOW DUMB I'M BEING. HOW DESPERATE.
OKA-CHAN, IF YOU WANTED TO RECORD ME BEING "INTERESTING," NOW'S THE TIME.
NOW IS WHEN EVERYONE WOULD GET A REALLY BIG LAUGH OUT OF WATCHING ME.

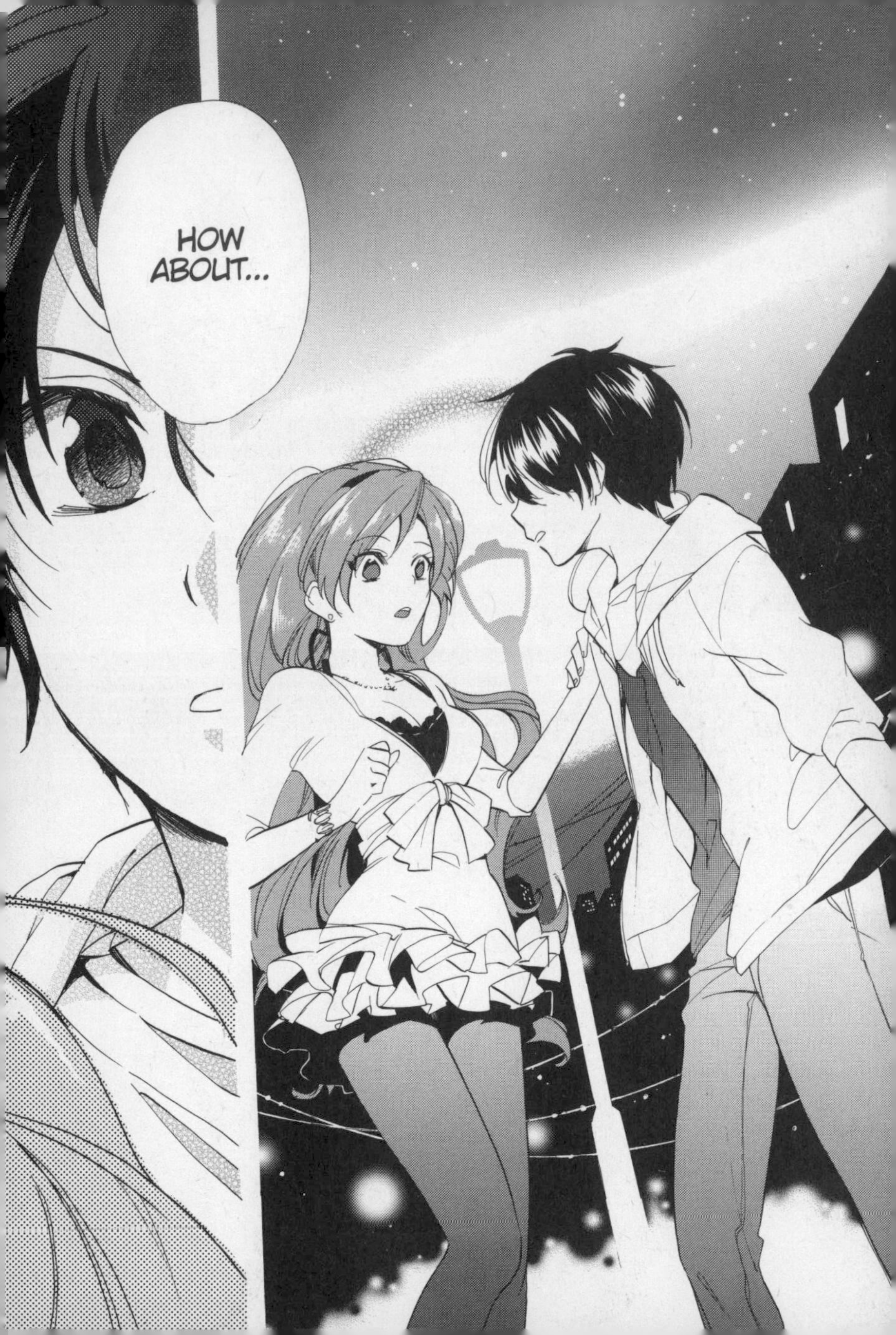
HOW ABOUT...

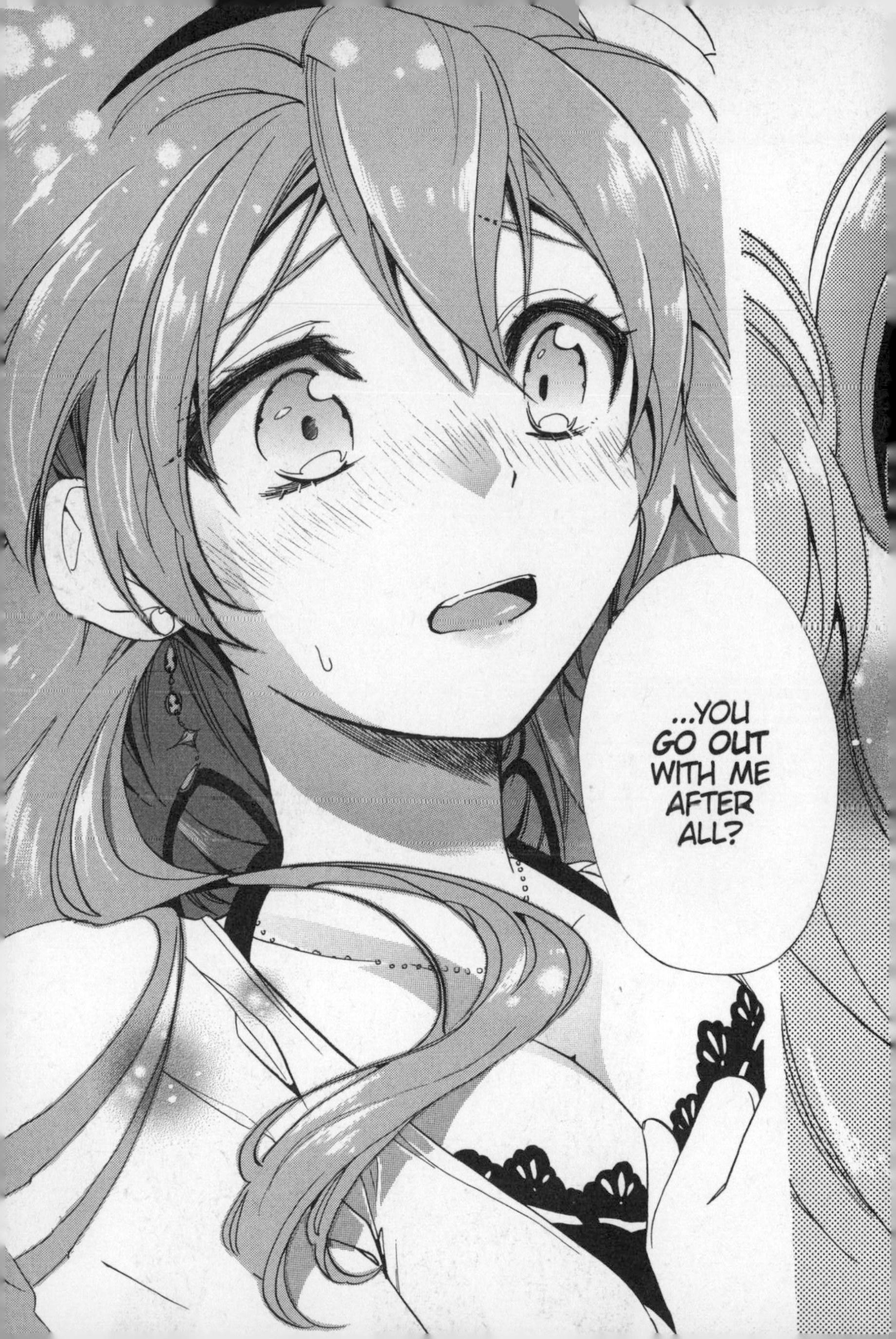
...YOU GO OUT WITH ME AFTER ALL?

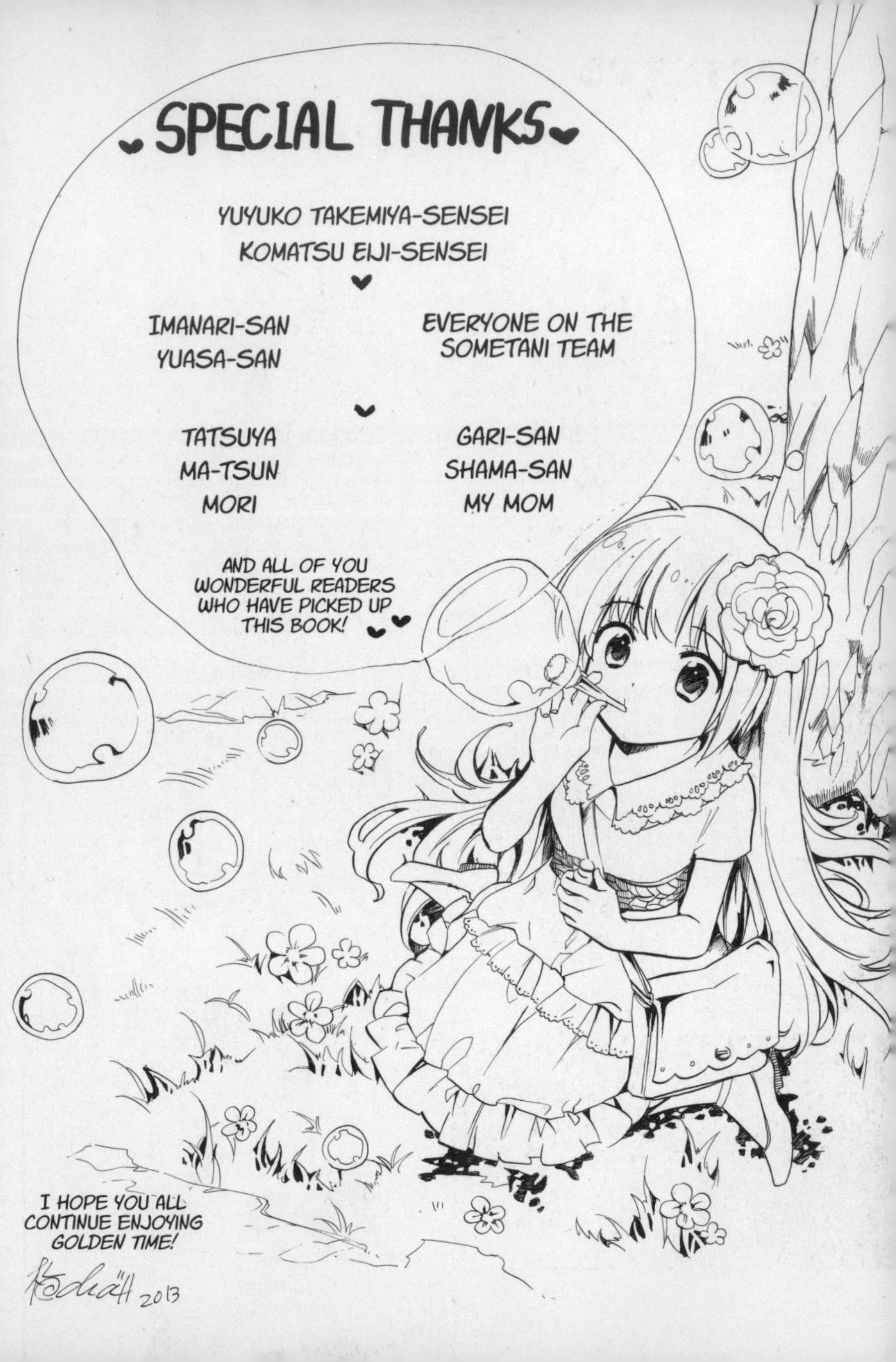
SPECIAL THANKS
YUYUKO TAKEMIYA-SENSEI
KOMATSU EIJI-SENSEI
IMANARI-SAN
YUASA-SAN
EVERYONE ON THE SOMETANI TEAM
TATSUYA
MA-TSUN
MORI
GARI-SAN
SHAMA-SAN
MY MOM
AND ALL OF YOU WONDERFUL READERS WHO HAVE PICKED UP THIS BOOK!
I HOPE YOU ALL CONTINUE ENJOYING GOLDEN TIME!
2013

CHAPTER 20

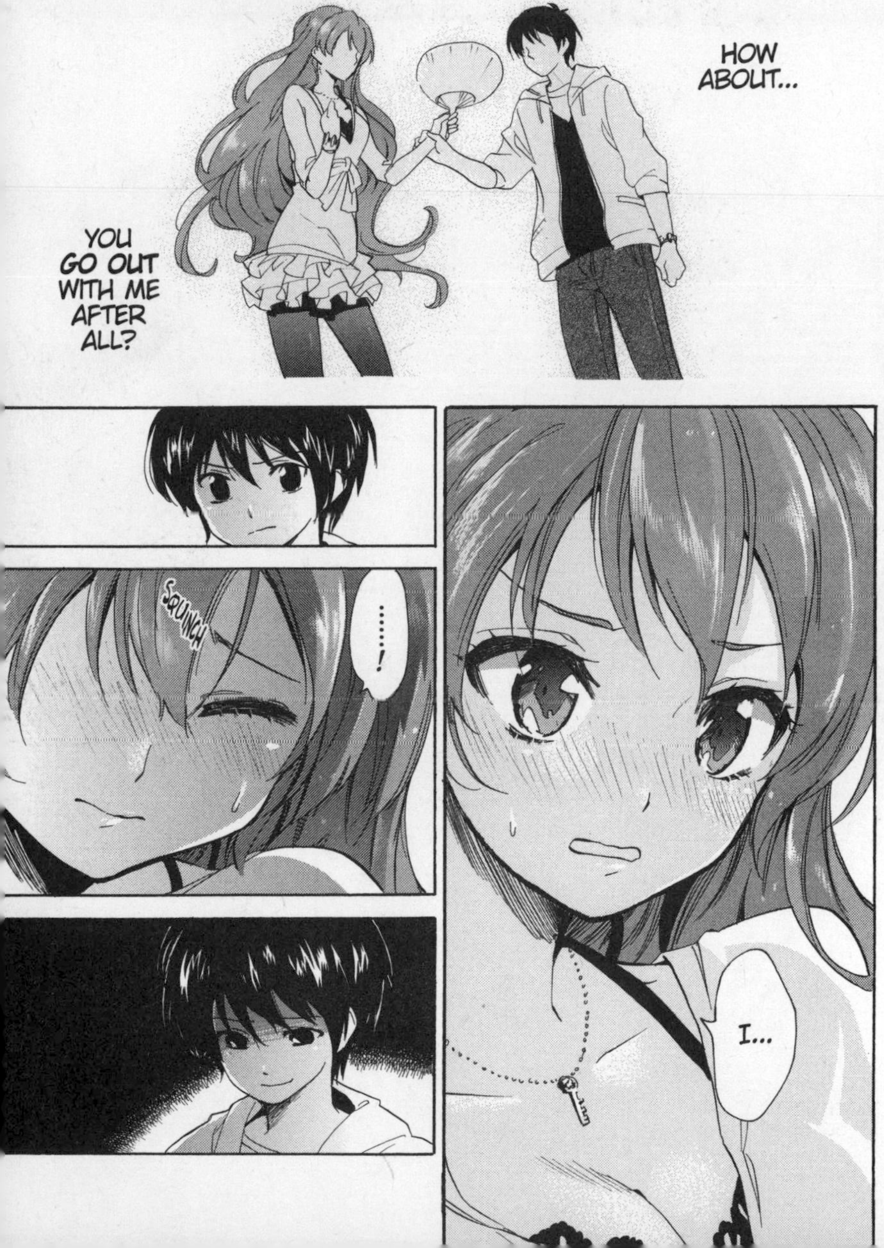
HOW ABOUT...
YOU GO OUT WITH ME AFTER ALL?
I...
......!
SQUINCH

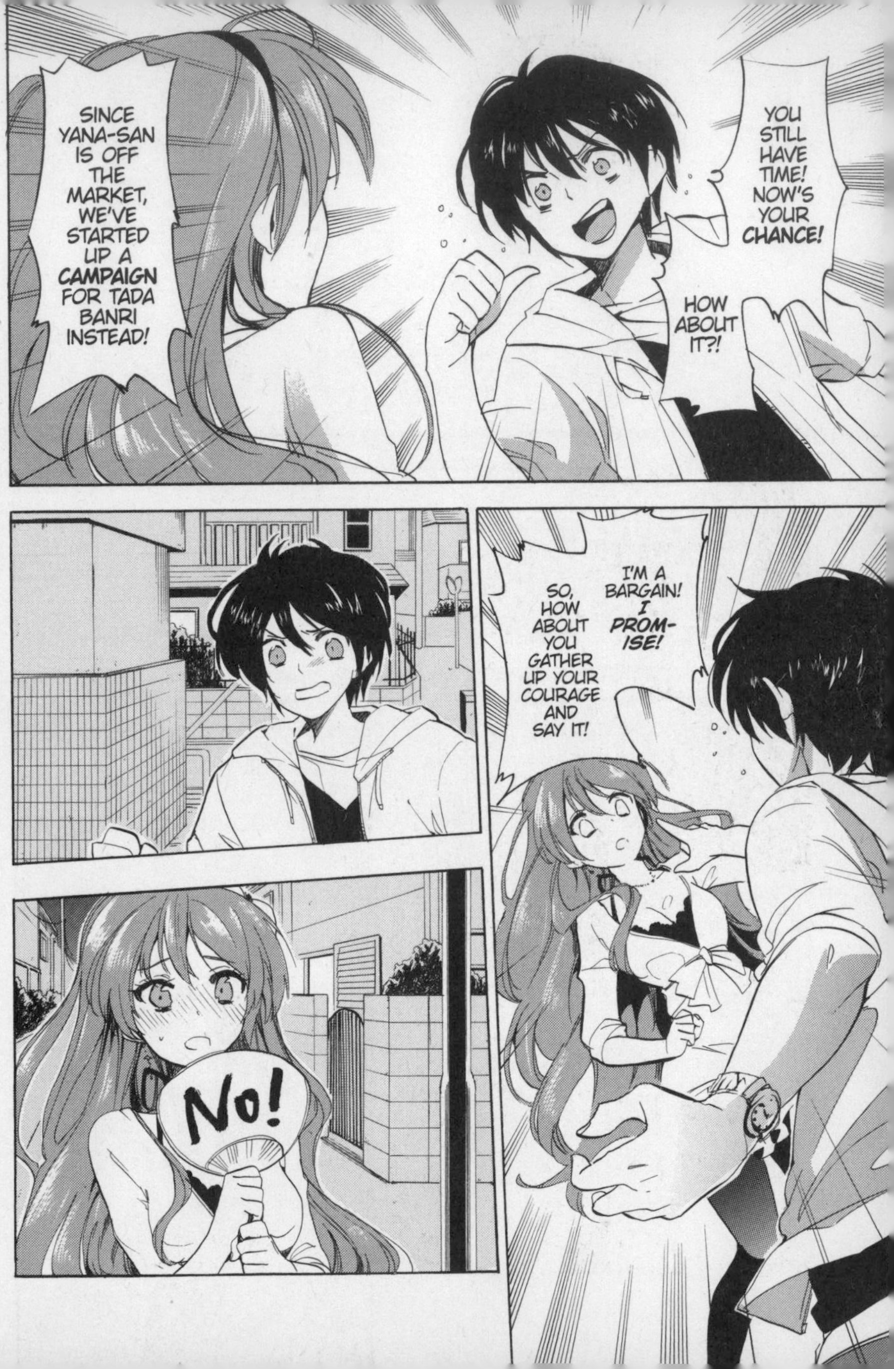
YOU STILL HAVE TIME! NOW'S YOUR CHANCE!
SINCE YANA-SAN IS OFF THE MARKET, WE'VE STARTED UP A CAMPAIGN FOR TADA BANRI INSTEAD!
HOW ABOUT IT?!
I'M A BARGAIN! I PROMISE!
SO, HOW ABOUT YOU GATHER UP YOUR COURAGE AND SAY IT!
No!

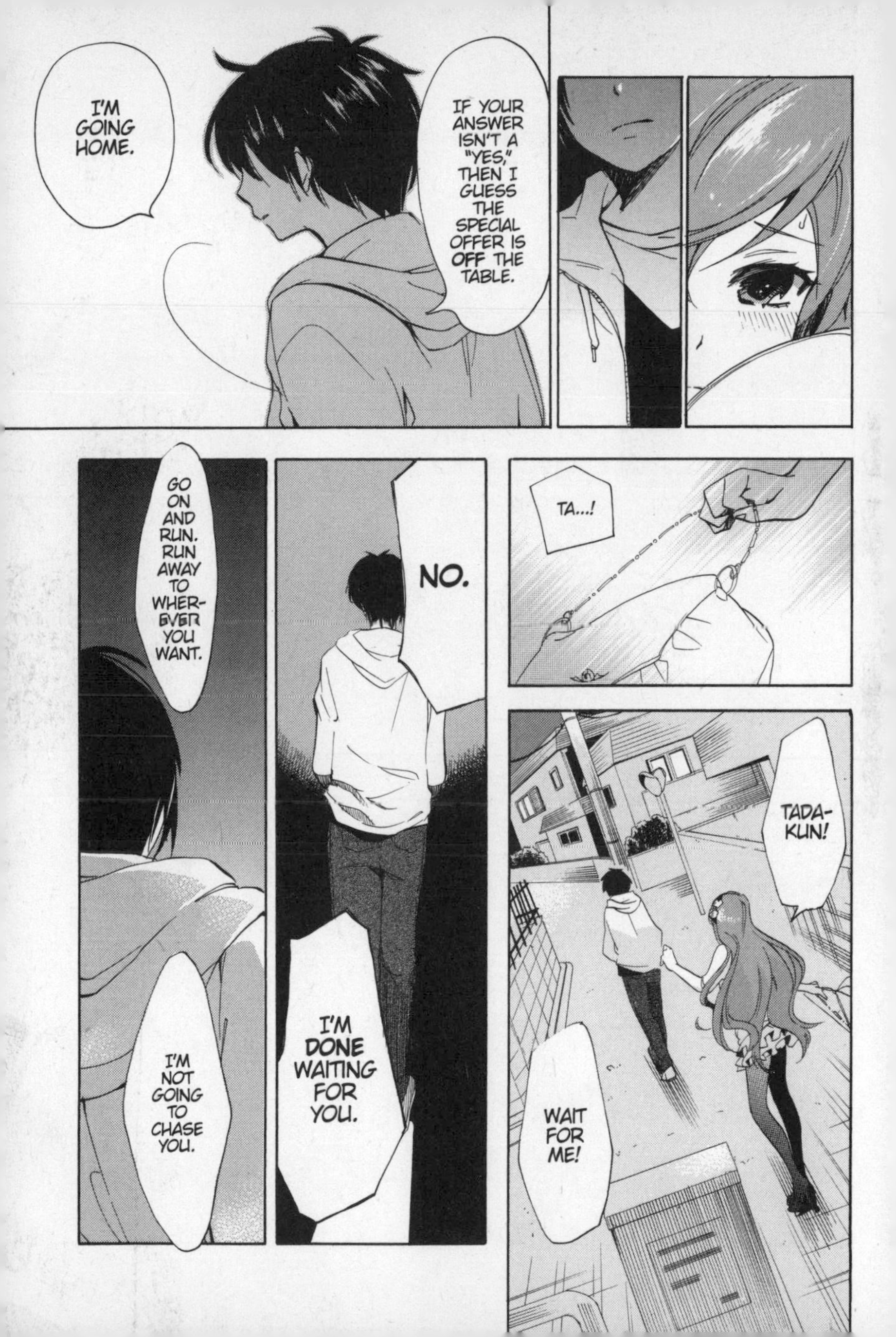
IF YOUR ANSWER ISN'T A "YES," THEN I GUESS THE SPECIAL OFFER IS OFF THE TABLE.
I'M GOING HOME.
TA...!
TADA-KUN!
WAIT FOR ME!
NO.
I'M DONE WAITING FOR YOU.
GO ON AND RUN. RUN AWAY TO WHER-EVER YOU WANT.
I'M NOT GOING TO CHASE YOU.

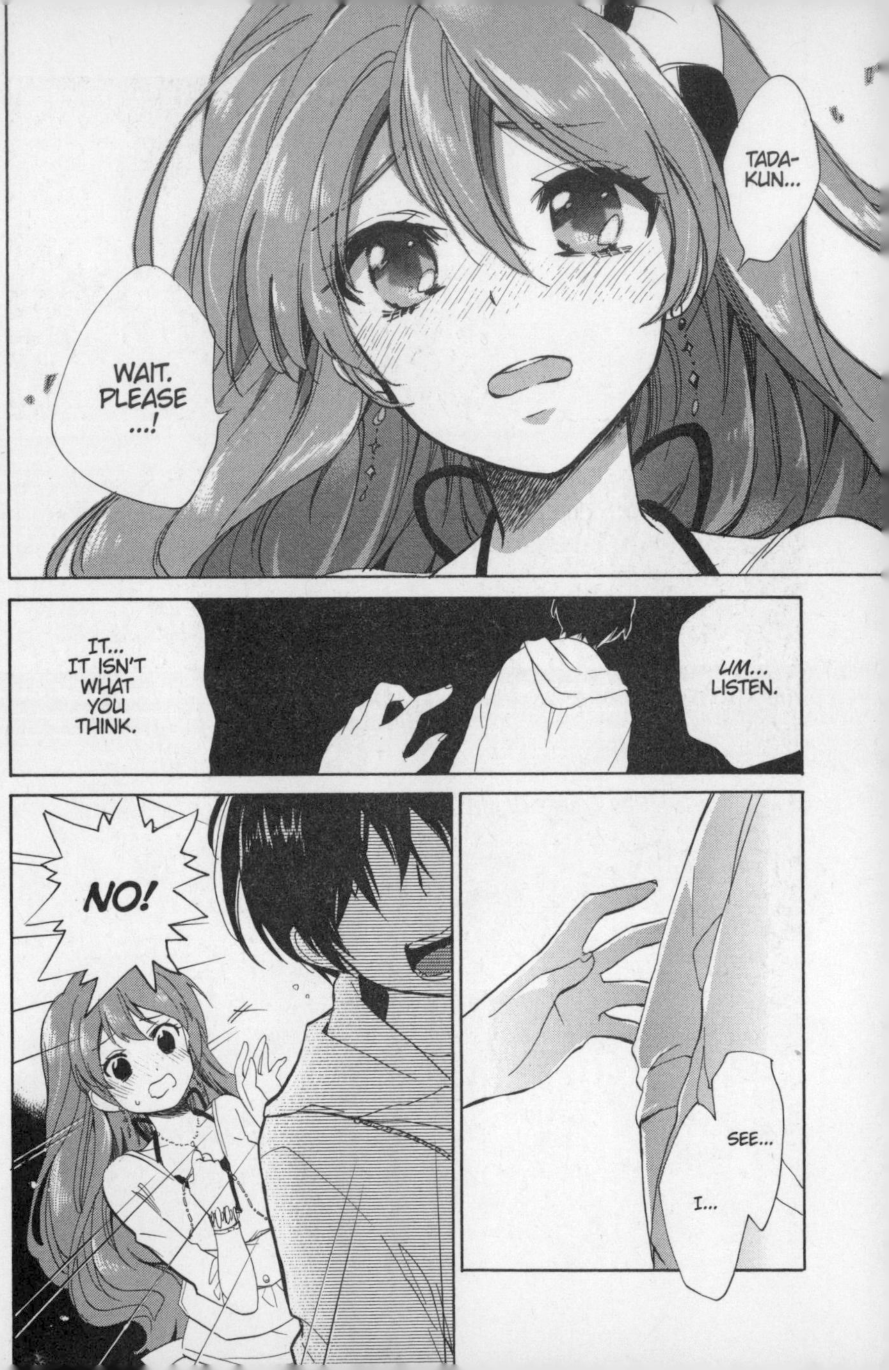
TADA-KUN...
WAIT. PLEASE ...!
UM... LISTEN.
IT... IT ISN'T WHAT YOU THINK.
SEE...
I...
NO!

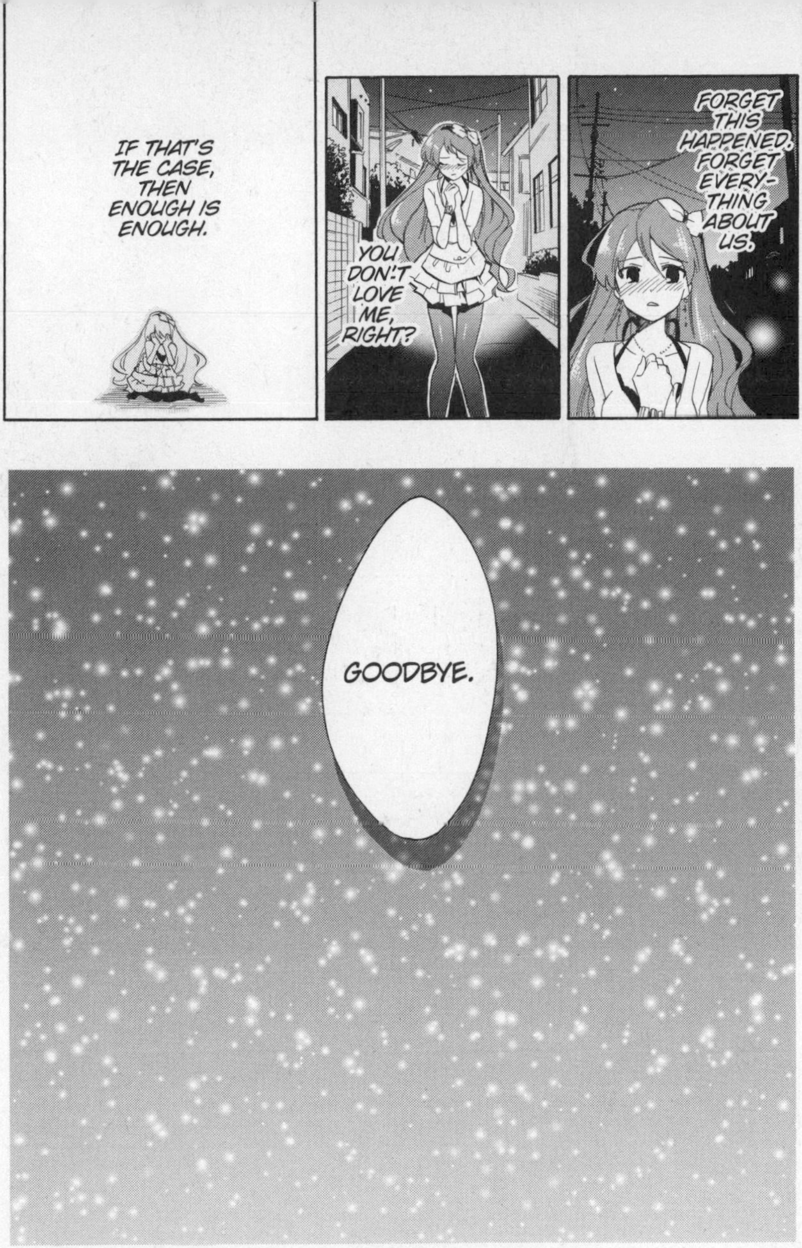
FORGET THIS HAPPENED. FORGET EVERYTHING ABOUT US.
YOU DON'T LOVE ME, RIGHT?
IF THAT'S THE CASE, THEN ENOUGH IS ENOUGH.
GOODBYE.

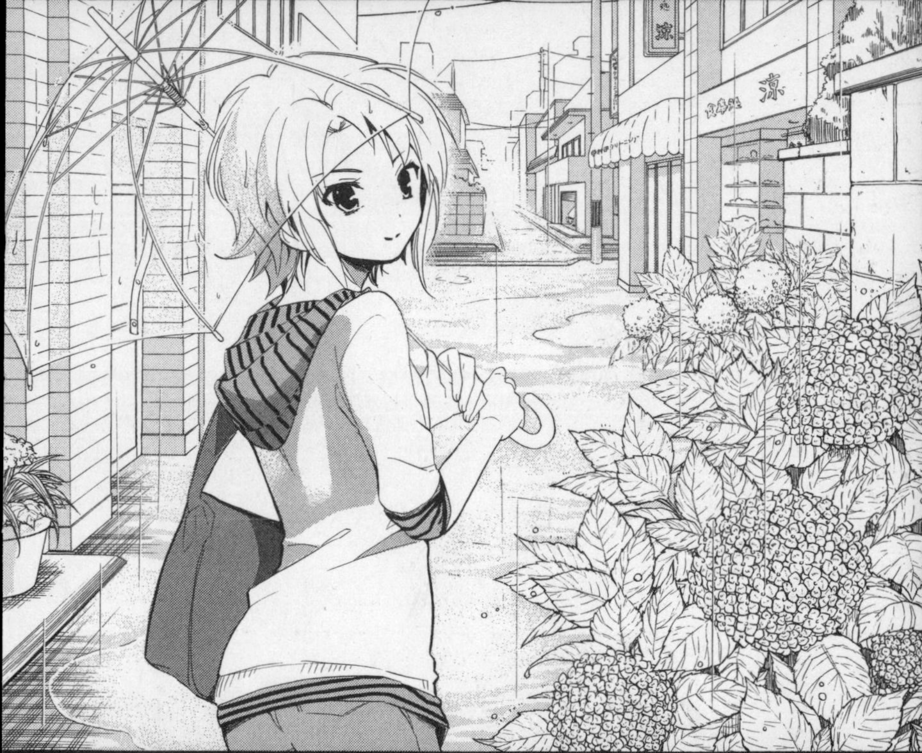
涼

CHAPTER 20: The Answer is "No"

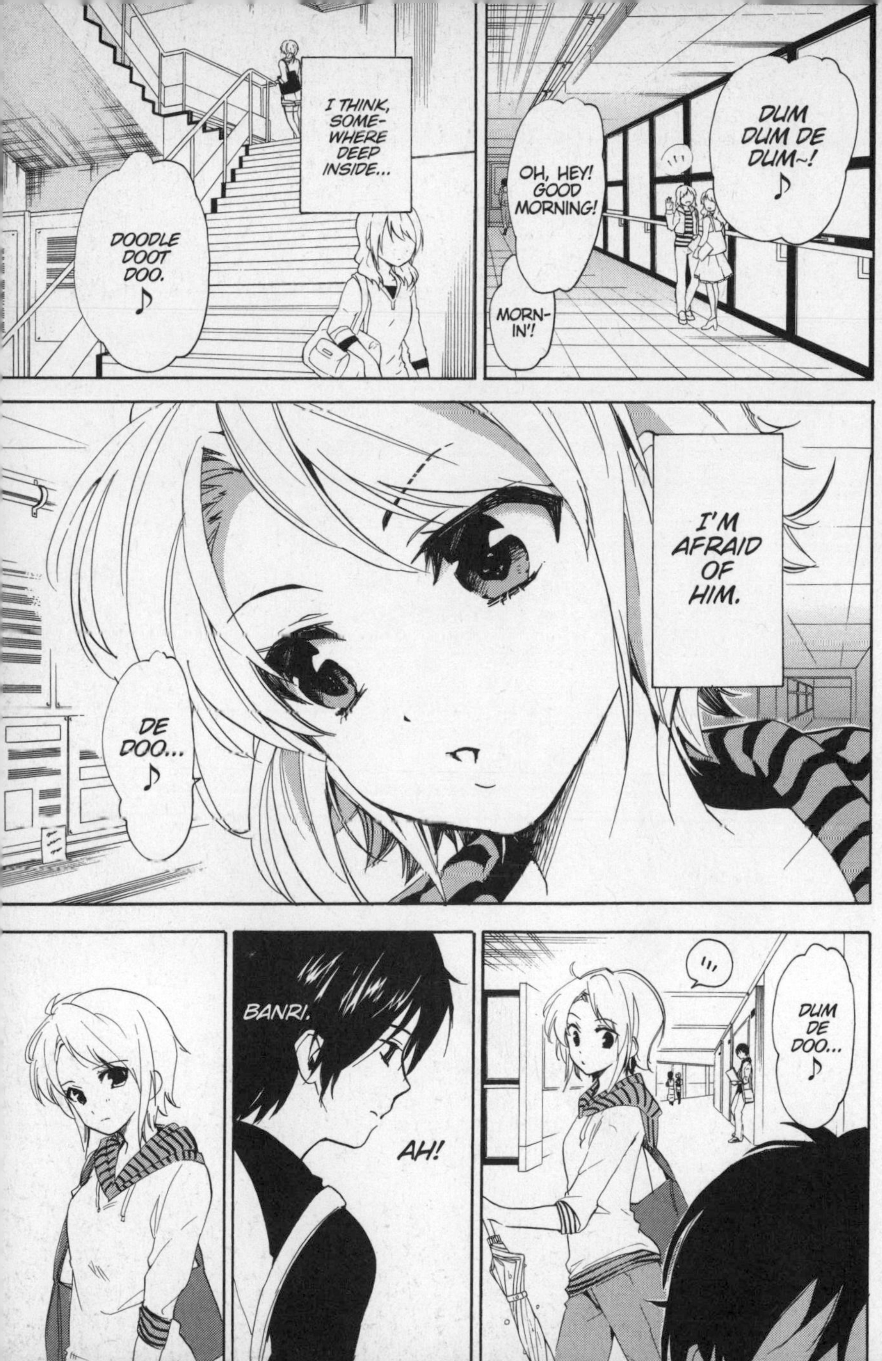

DUM DUM DE DUM~! ♪
OH, HEY! GOOD MORNING!
MORN-IN'!
I THINK, SOMEWHERE DEEP INSIDE...
DOODLE DOOT DOO. ♪
I'M AFRAID OF HIM.
DE DOO... ♪
DUM DE DOO... ♪
BANRI.
AH!

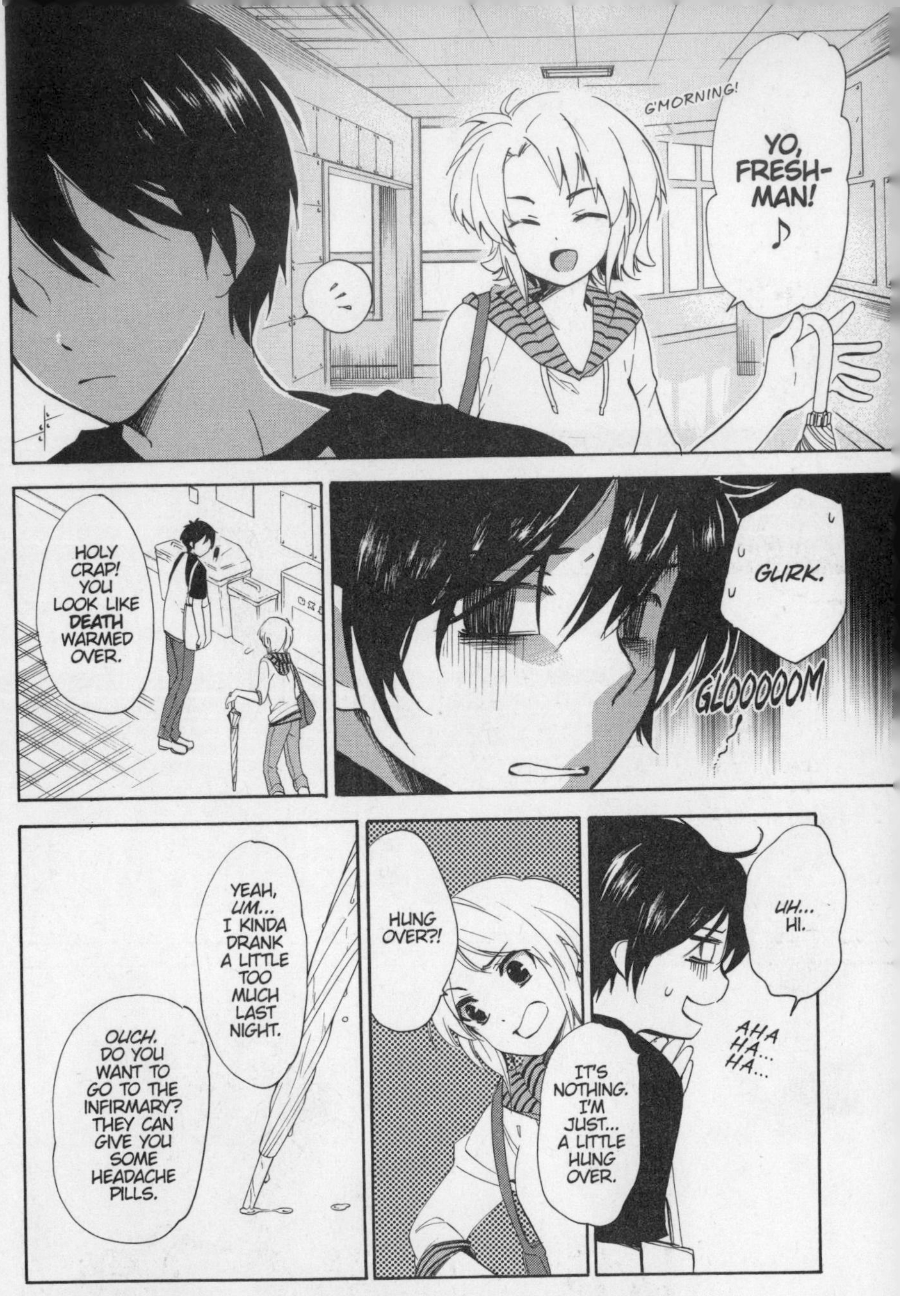
YO, FRESH-MAN! ♪
G'MORNING!
GURK.
GLOOOOOM
HOLY CRAP! YOU LOOK LIKE DEATH WARMED OVER.
UH... HI.
AHA HA... HA...
IT'S NOTHING. I'M JUST... A LITTLE HUNG OVER.
HUNG OVER?!
YEAH, UM... I KINDA DRANK A LITTLE TOO MUCH LAST NIGHT.
OUCH. DO YOU WANT TO GO TO THE INFIRMARY? THEY CAN GIVE YOU SOME HEADACHE PILLS.

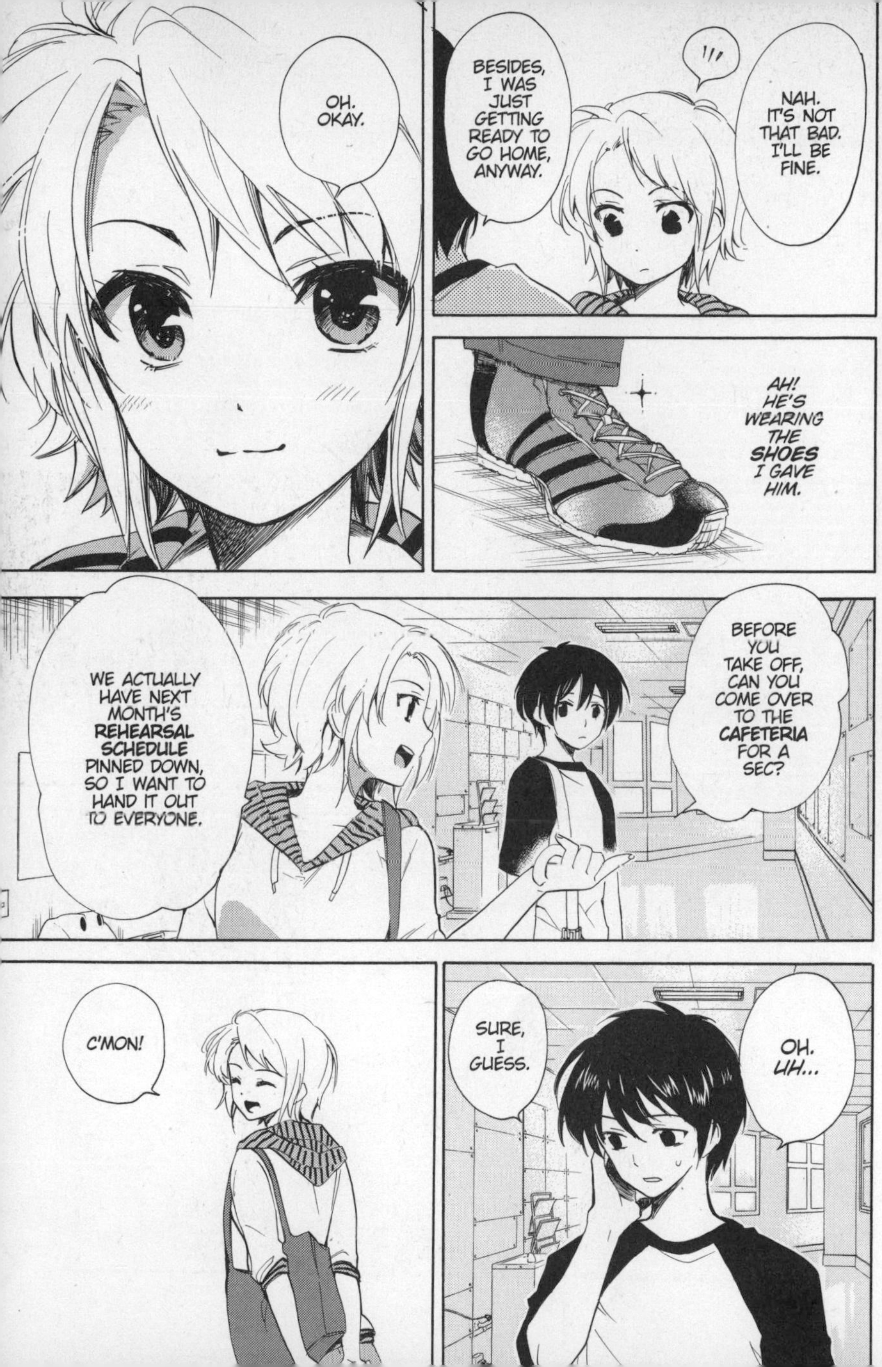
NAH. IT'S NOT THAT BAD. I'LL BE FINE.
BESIDES, I WAS JUST GETTING READY TO GO HOME, ANYWAY.
AH! HE'S WEARING THE SHOES I GAVE HIM.
OH. OKAY.
BEFORE YOU TAKE OFF, CAN YOU COME OVER TO THE CAFETERIA FOR A SEC?
WE ACTUALLY HAVE NEXT MONTH'S REHEARSAL SCHEDULE PINNED DOWN, SO I WANT TO HAND IT OUT TO EVERYONE.
OH. UH...
SURE, I GUESS.
C'MON!

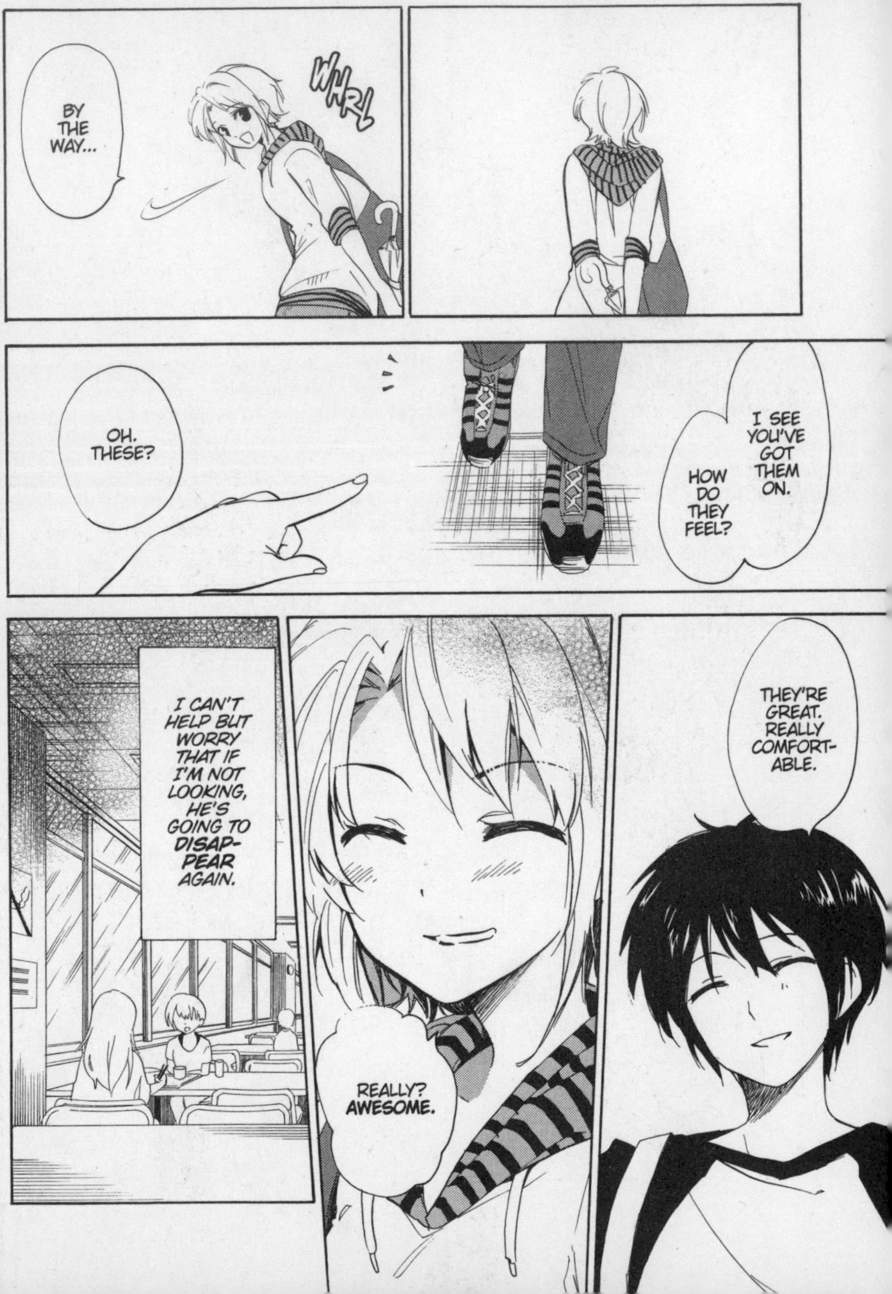
WHIRL
BY THE WAY...
I SEE YOU'VE GOT THEM ON. HOW DO THEY FEEL?
OH. THESE?
THEY'RE GREAT. REALLY COMFORT-ABLE.
REALLY? **AWESOME.**
I CAN'T HELP BUT WORRY THAT IF I'M NOT LOOKING, HE'S GOING TO ***DISAP-PEAR*** *AGAIN.*

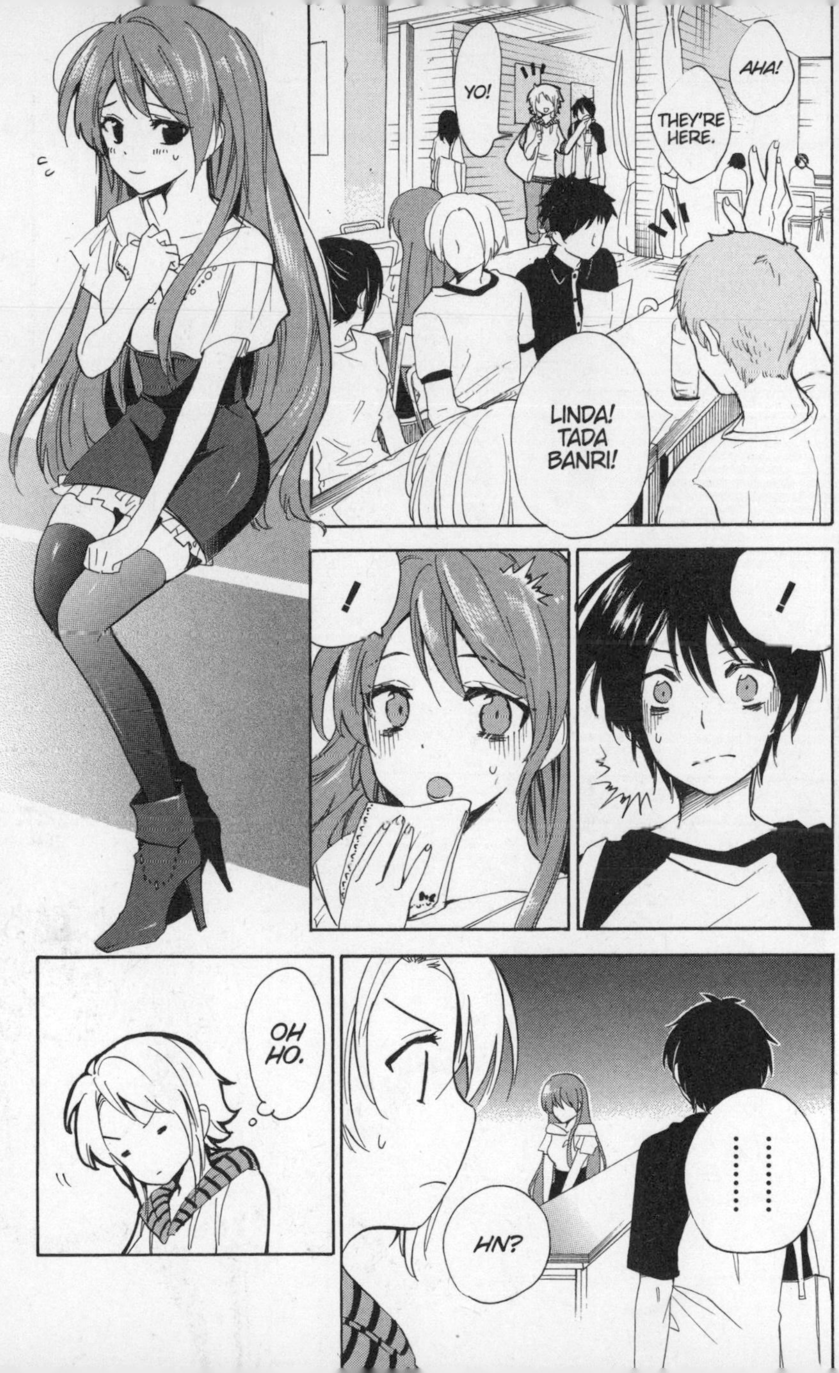
AHA!
THEY'RE HERE.
YO!
LINDA! TADA BANRI!
!
!
......
HN?
OH HO.

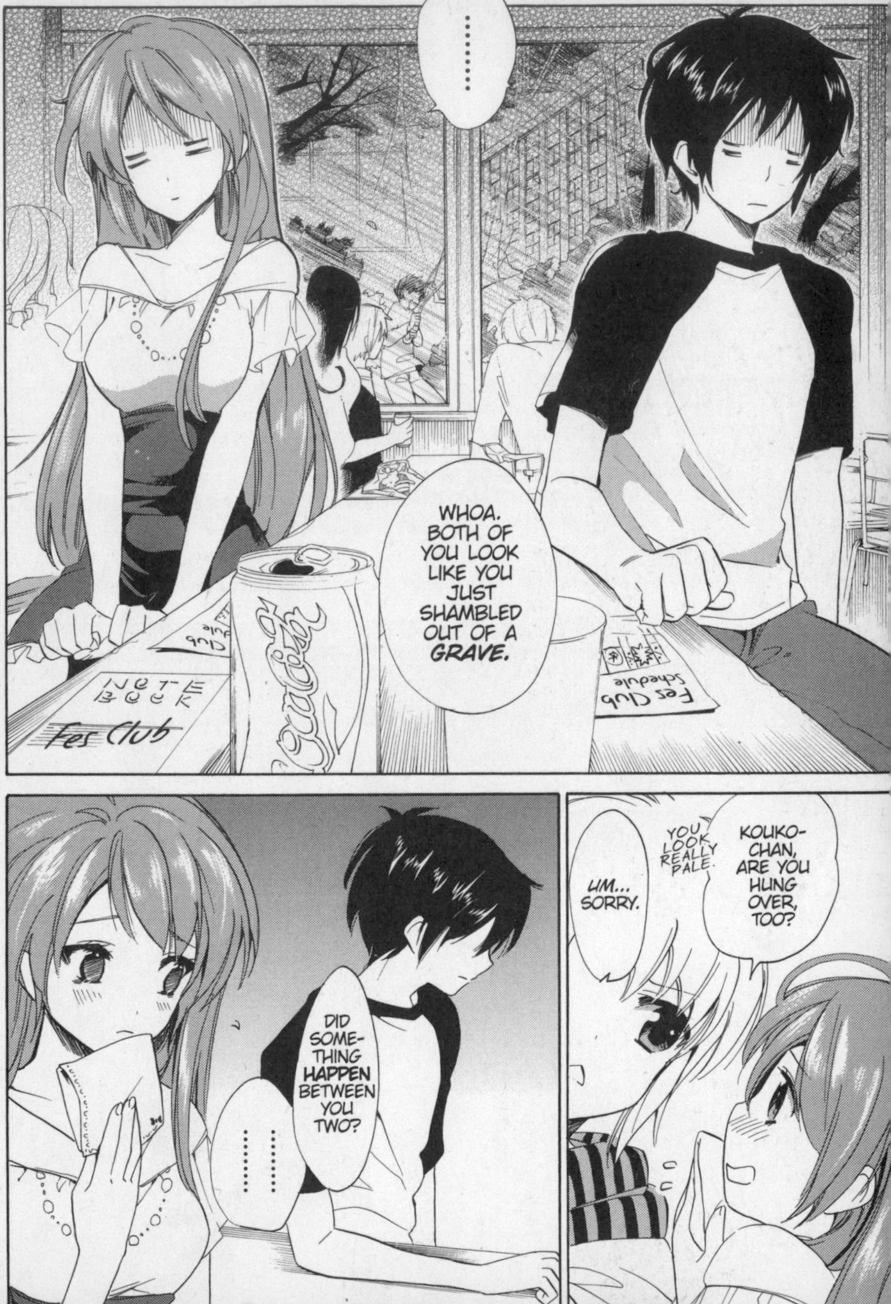
......
Fes Club Schedule
WHOA. BOTH OF YOU LOOK LIKE YOU JUST SHAMBLED OUT OF A GRAVE.
Fes Club
KOUKO-CHAN, ARE YOU HUNG OVER, TOO?
YOU LOOK REALLY PALE.
UM... SORRY.
DID SOMETHING HAPPEN BETWEEN YOU TWO?
......

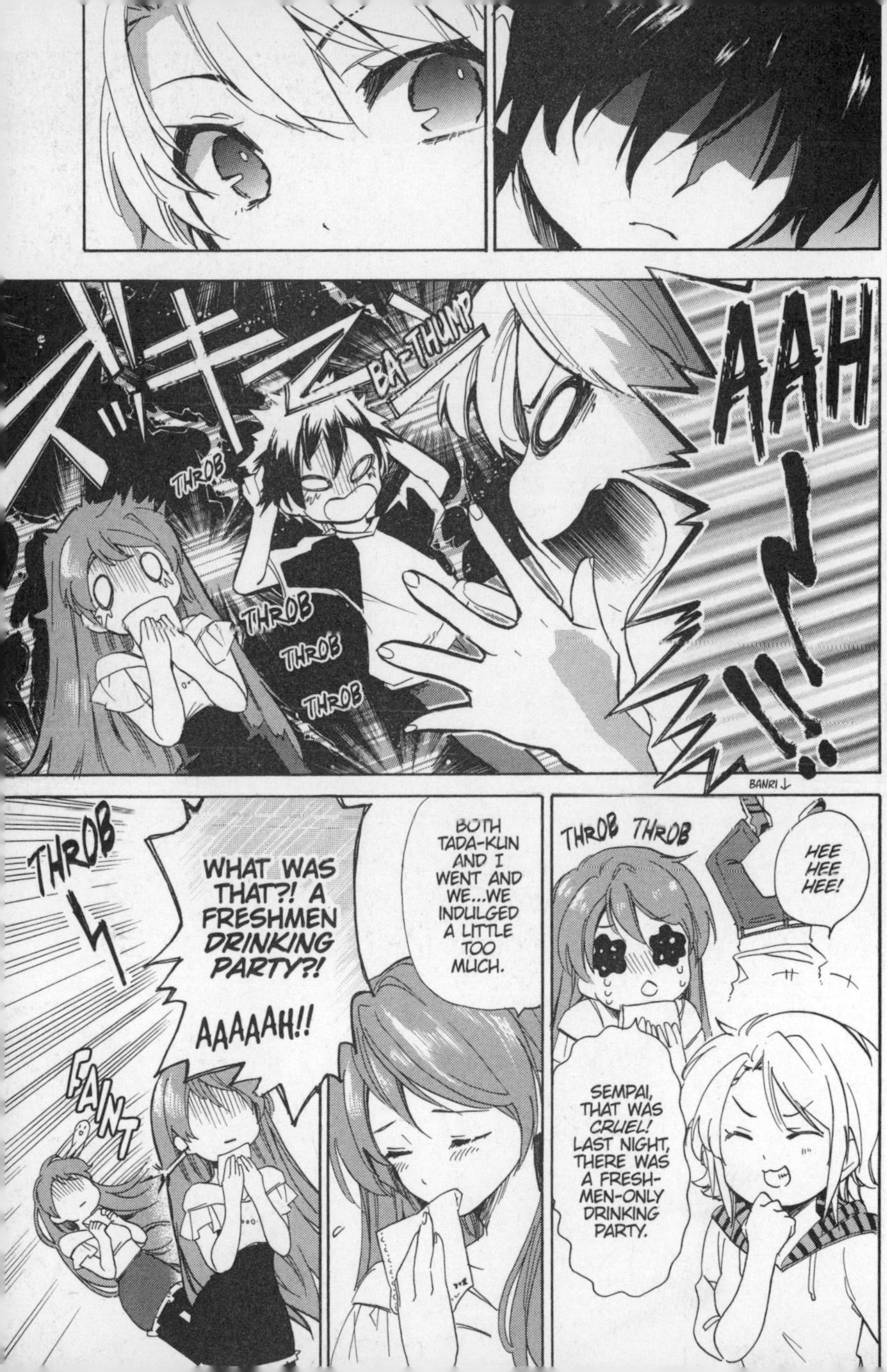
AAH!!!
BA-THUMP
THROB
THROB
THROB
THROB
BANRI ↓
HEE HEE HEE!
THROB THROB
SEMPAI, THAT WAS CRUEL! LAST NIGHT, THERE WAS A FRESH-MEN-ONLY DRINKING PARTY.
BOTH TADA-KUN AND I WENT AND WE...WE INDULGED A LITTLE TOO MUCH.
WHAT WAS THAT?! A FRESHMEN DRINKING PARTY?!
AAAAAH!!
THROB
FAINT

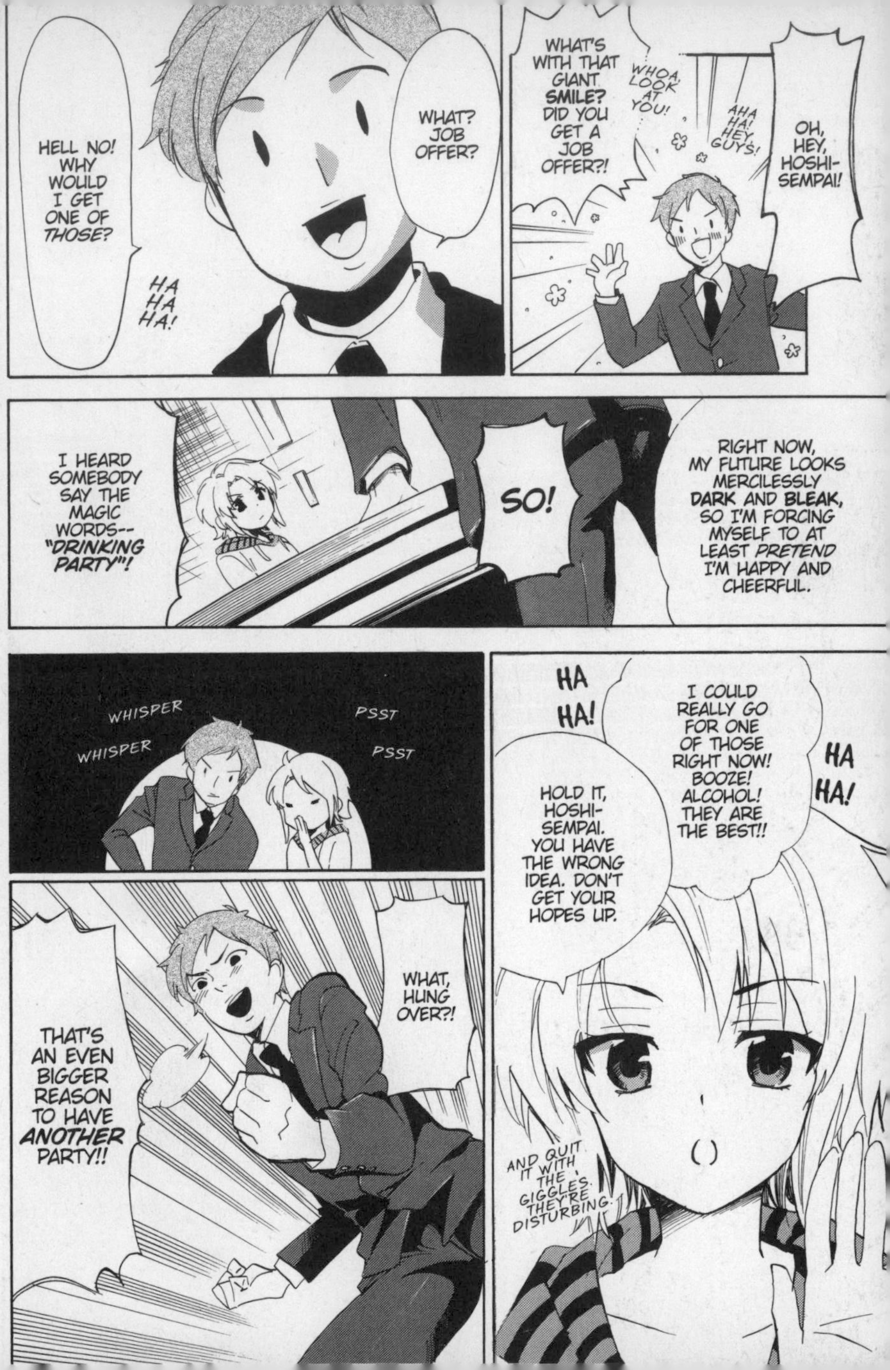
OH, HEY, HOSHI-SEMPAI!
AHA HA! HEY, GUYS!
WHOA, LOOK AT YOU!
WHAT'S WITH THAT GIANT SMILE? DID YOU GET A JOB OFFER?!
WHAT? JOB OFFER?
HELL NO! WHY WOULD I GET ONE OF THOSE?
HA HA HA!
RIGHT NOW, MY FUTURE LOOKS MERCILESSLY DARK AND BLEAK, SO I'M FORCING MYSELF TO AT LEAST PRETEND I'M HAPPY AND CHEERFUL.
SO!
I HEARD SOMEBODY SAY THE MAGIC WORDS-- "DRINKING PARTY"!
HA HA!
I COULD REALLY GO FOR ONE OF THOSE RIGHT NOW! BOOZE! ALCOHOL! THEY ARE THE BEST!!
HA HA!
HOLD IT, HOSHI-SEMPAI. YOU HAVE THE WRONG IDEA. DON'T GET YOUR HOPES UP.
AND QUIT IT WITH THE GIGGLES. THEY'RE DISTURBING.
WHISPER
WHISPER
PSST
PSST
WHAT, HUNG OVER?!
THAT'S AN EVEN BIGGER REASON TO HAVE ANOTHER PARTY!!

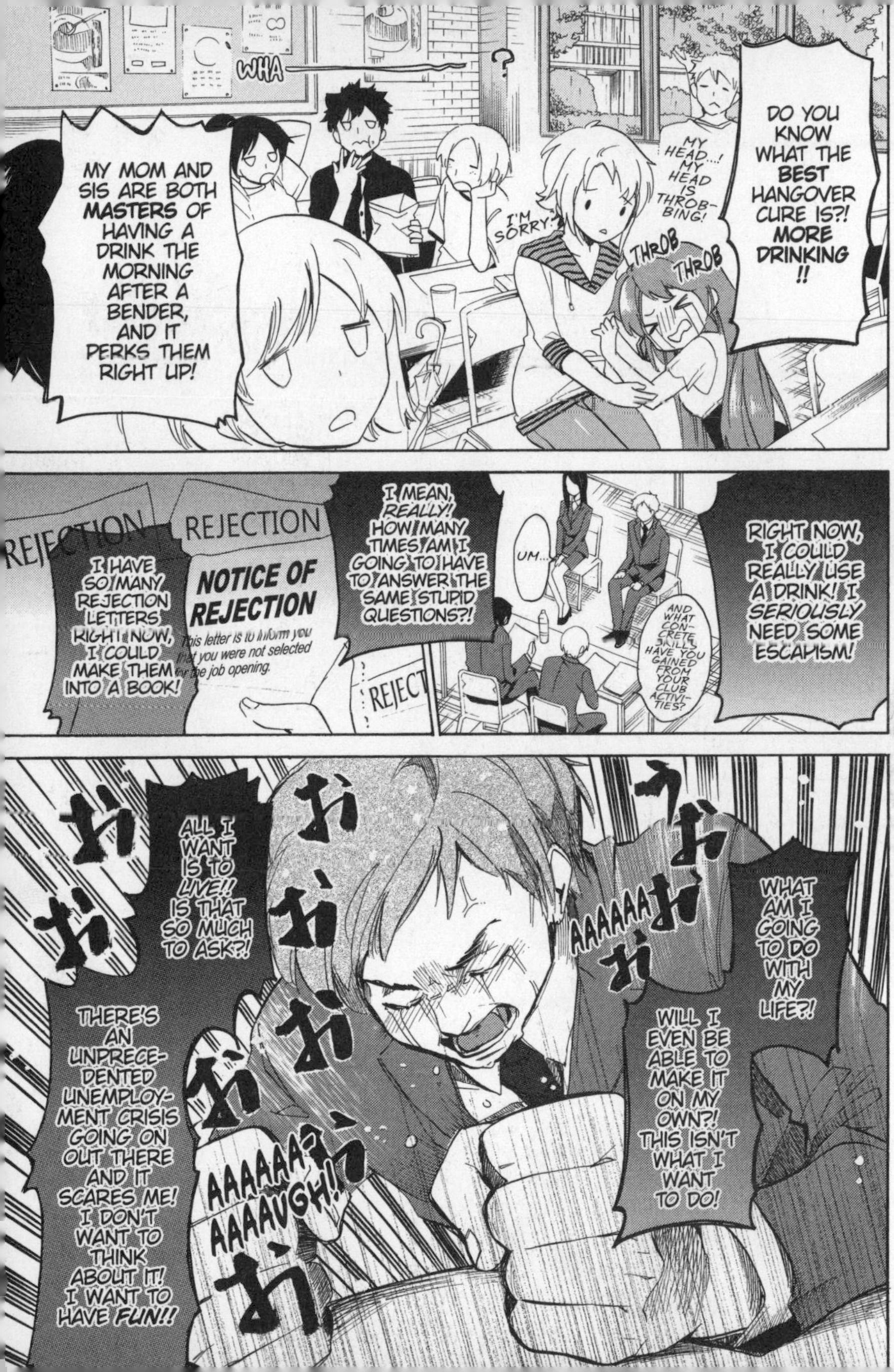
DO YOU KNOW WHAT THE BEST HANGOVER CURE IS?! MORE DRINKING!!
MY HEAD...! MY HEAD IS THROBBING!
I'M SORRY!
THROB THROB
WHA
?
MY MOM AND SIS ARE BOTH MASTERS OF HAVING A DRINK THE MORNING AFTER A BENDER, AND IT PERKS THEM RIGHT UP!
RIGHT NOW, I COULD REALLY USE A DRINK! I SERIOUSLY NEED SOME ESCAPISM!
AND WHAT CONCRETE SKILLS HAVE YOU GAINED FROM YOUR CLUB ACTIVITIES?
UM...
I MEAN, REALLY! HOW MANY TIMES AM I GOING TO HAVE TO ANSWER THE SAME STUPID QUESTIONS?!
REJECTION
REJECTION
NOTICE OF REJECTION
This letter is to inform you that you were not selected for the job opening.
REJECT
I HAVE SO MANY REJECTION LETTERS RIGHT NOW, I COULD MAKE THEM INTO A BOOK!
WHAT AM I GOING TO DO WITH MY LIFE?!
WILL I EVEN BE ABLE TO MAKE IT ON MY OWN?! THIS ISN'T WHAT I WANT TO DO!
AAAAAA
AAAAAA AAAAUGH!
ALL I WANT IS TO LIVE!! IS THAT SO MUCH TO ASK?!
THERE'S AN UNPRECEDENTED UNEMPLOYMENT CRISIS GOING ON OUT THERE AND IT SCARES ME! I DON'T WANT TO THINK ABOUT IT! I WANT TO HAVE FUN!!

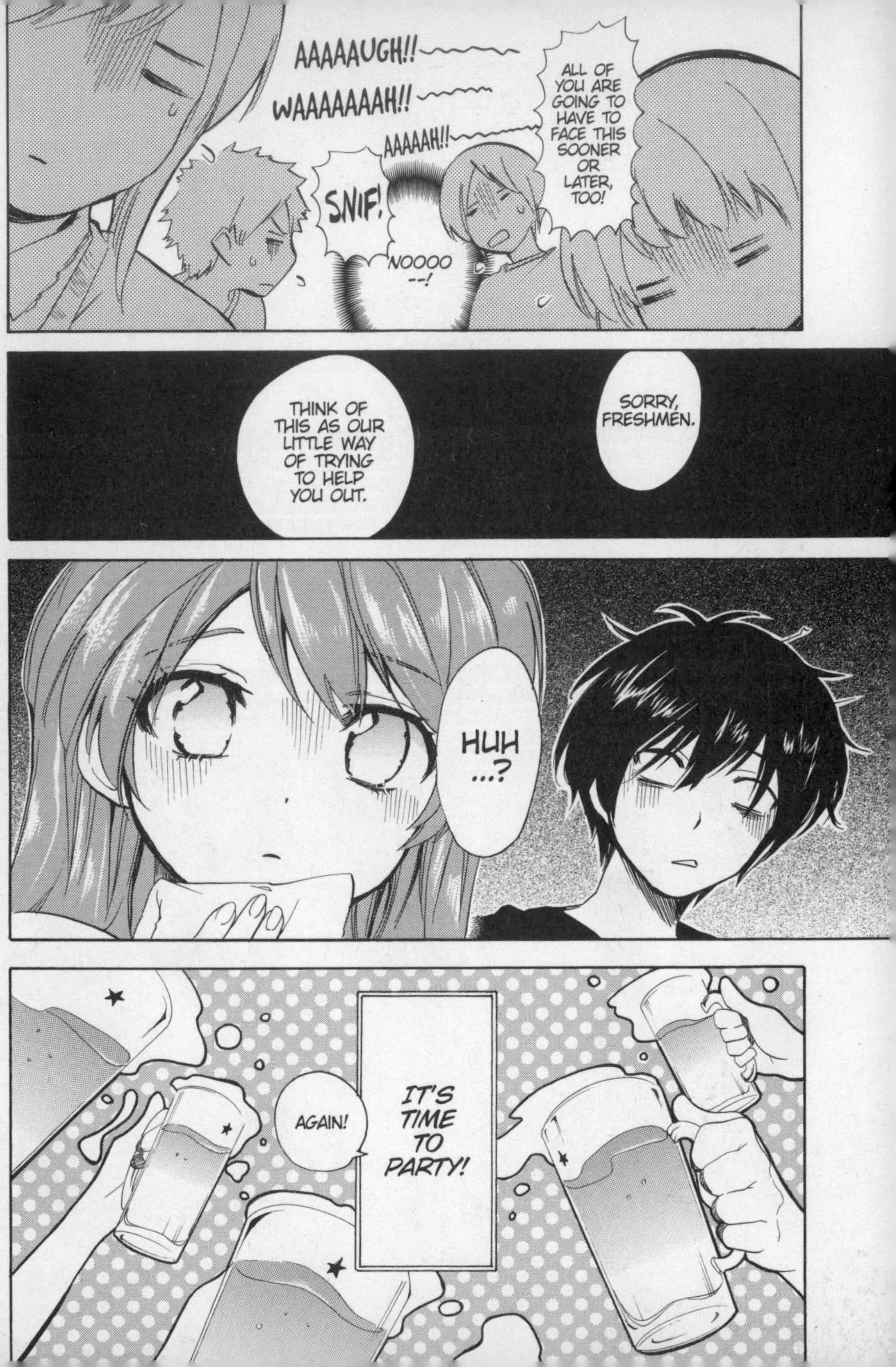
ALL OF YOU ARE GOING TO HAVE TO FACE THIS SOONER OR LATER, TOO!
AAAAAUGH!!
WAAAAAAAAH!!
AAAAAH!!
SNIF!
NOOOO--!
SORRY, FRESHMEN.
THINK OF THIS AS OUR LITTLE WAY OF TRYING TO HELP YOU OUT.
HUH ...?
IT'S TIME TO PARTY!
AGAIN!

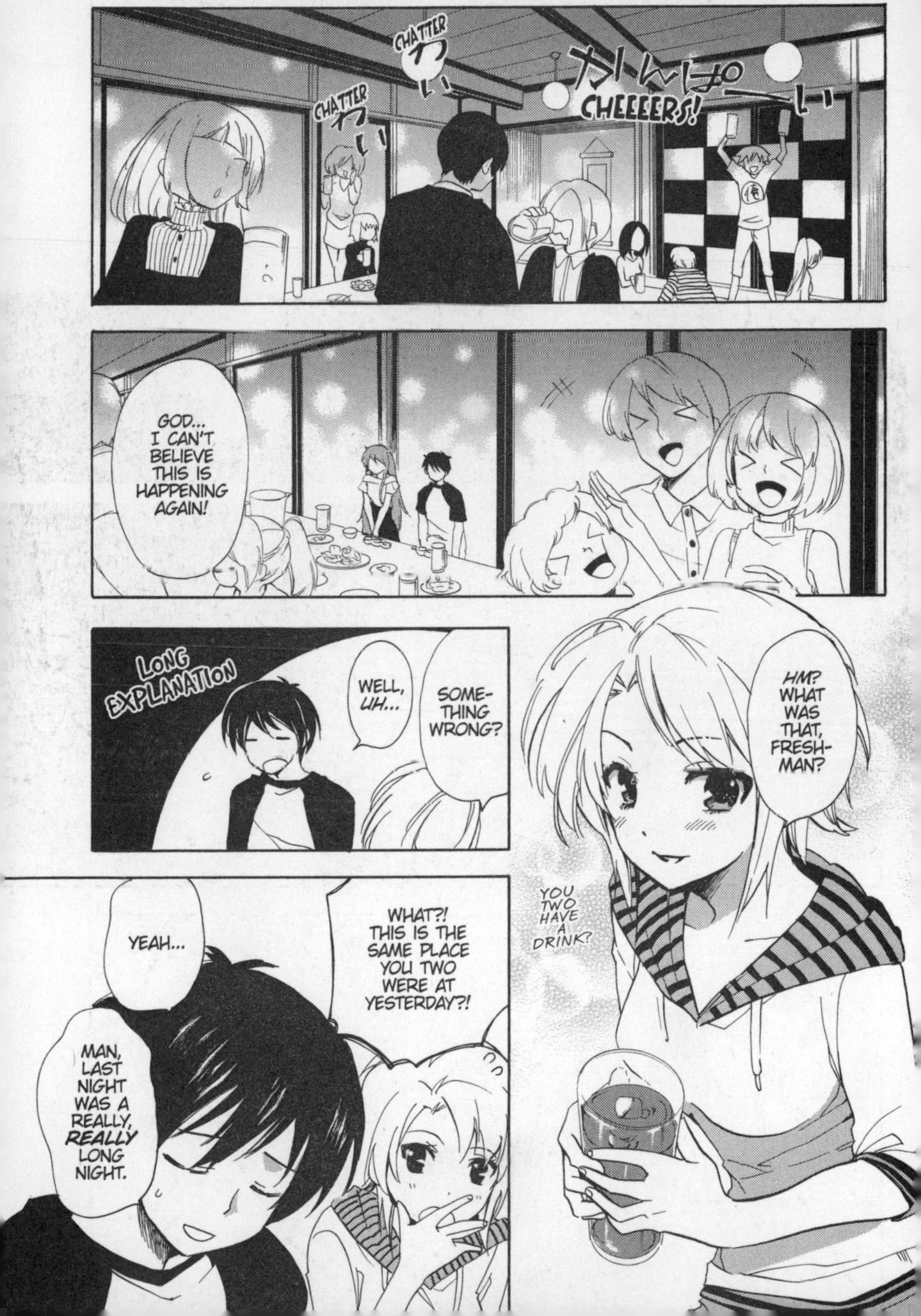
かんぱーい
CHEEEERS!
CHATTER
わい
CHATTER
わい
GOD... I CAN'T BELIEVE THIS IS HAPPENING AGAIN!
HM? WHAT WAS THAT, FRESH-MAN?
YOU TWO HAVE A DRINK?
SOME-THING WRONG?
WELL, UH...
LONG EXPLANATION
WHAT?! THIS IS THE SAME PLACE YOU TWO WERE AT YESTERDAY?!
YEAH...
MAN, LAST NIGHT WAS A REALLY, ***REALLY*** LONG NIGHT.

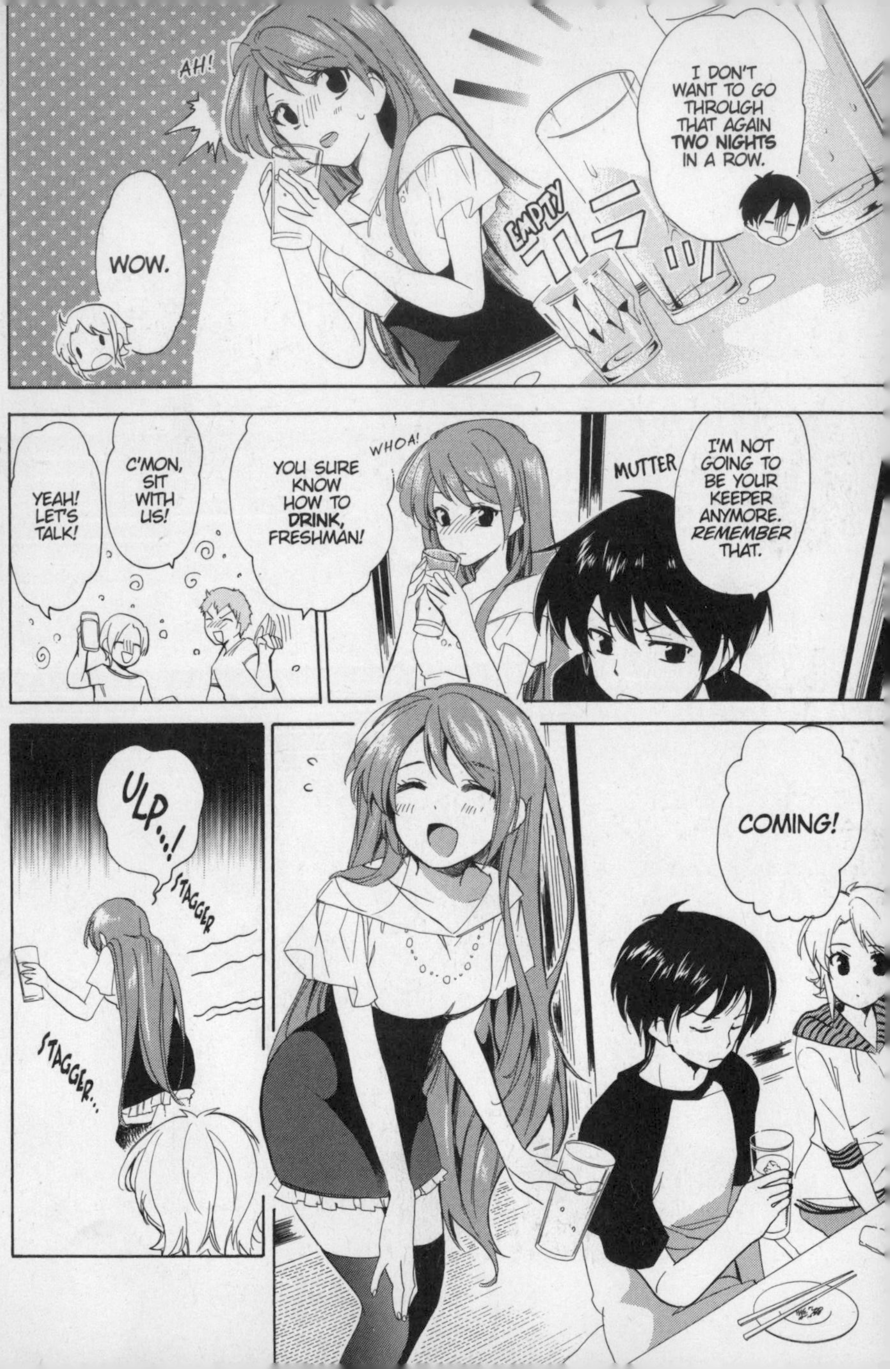
I DON'T WANT TO GO THROUGH THAT AGAIN TWO NIGHTS IN A ROW.
EMPTY
AH!
WOW.
I'M NOT GOING TO BE YOUR KEEPER ANYMORE. REMEMBER THAT.
MUTTER
WHOA!
YOU SURE KNOW HOW TO DRINK, FRESHMAN!
C'MON, SIT WITH US!
YEAH! LET'S TALK!
COMING!
ULP...!
STAGGER
STAGGER...

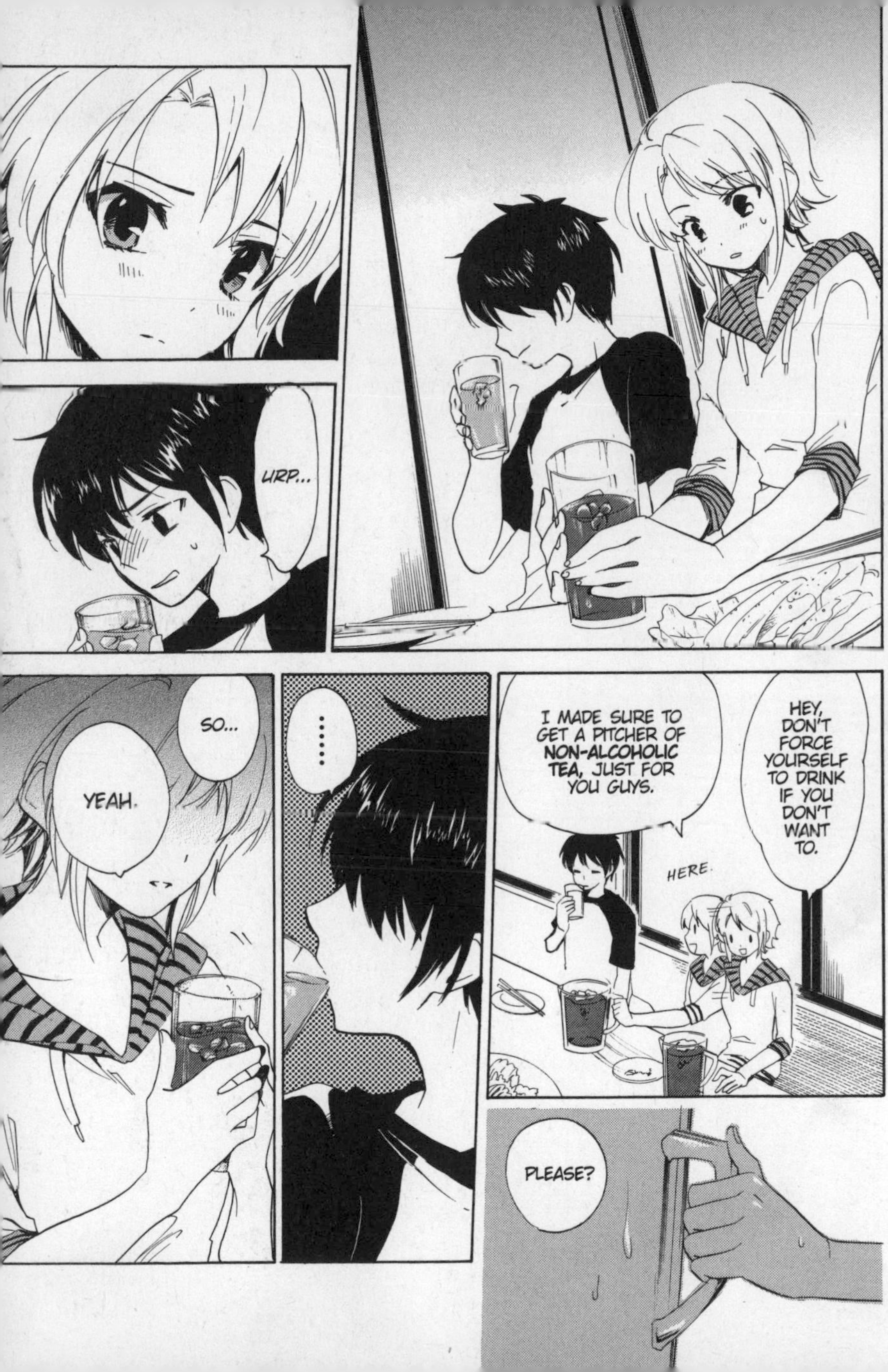
URP...
HEY, DON'T FORCE YOURSELF TO DRINK IF YOU DON'T WANT TO.
I MADE SURE TO GET A PITCHER OF **NON-ALCOHOLIC** TEA, JUST FOR YOU GUYS.
HERE.
PLEASE?
......
SO...
YEAH.

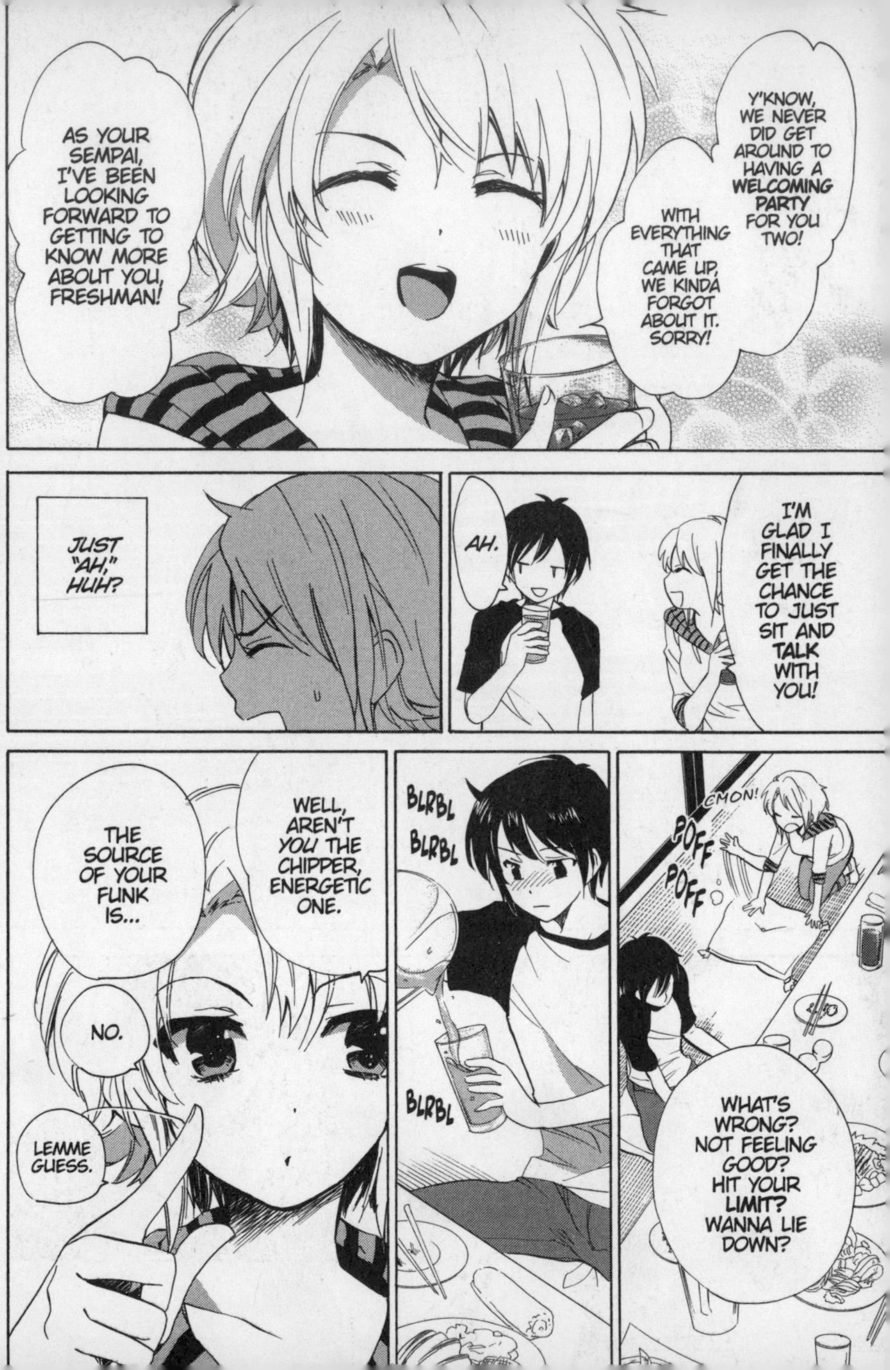
Y'KNOW, WE NEVER DID GET AROUND TO HAVING A WELCOMING PARTY FOR YOU TWO!
WITH EVERYTHING THAT CAME UP, WE KINDA FORGOT ABOUT IT. SORRY!
AS YOUR SEMPAI, I'VE BEEN LOOKING FORWARD TO GETTING TO KNOW MORE ABOUT YOU, FRESHMAN!
I'M GLAD I FINALLY GET THE CHANCE TO JUST SIT AND TALK WITH YOU!
AH.
JUST "AH," HUH?
C'MON!
POFF
POFF
WHAT'S WRONG? NOT FEELING GOOD? HIT YOUR LIMIT? WANNA LIE DOWN?
BLRBL
BLRBL
BLRBL
WELL, AREN'T YOU THE CHIPPER, ENERGETIC ONE.
THE SOURCE OF YOUR FUNK IS...
NO.
LEMME GUESS.

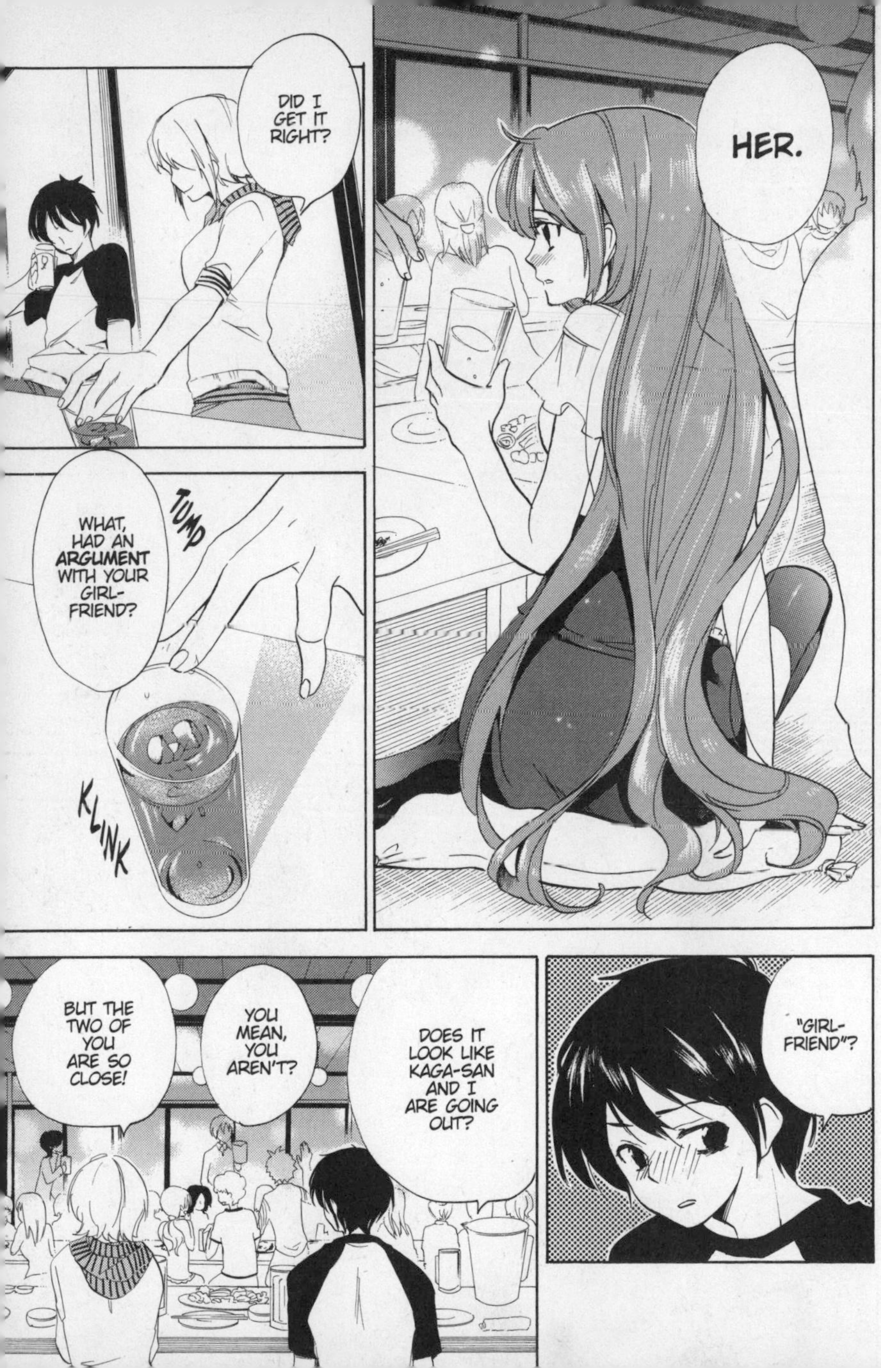
HER.
DID I GET IT RIGHT?
WHAT, HAD AN ARGUMENT WITH YOUR GIRL-FRIEND?
TUMP
KLINK
"GIRL-FRIEND"?
DOES IT LOOK LIKE KAGA-SAN AND I ARE GOING OUT?
YOU MEAN, YOU AREN'T?
BUT THE TWO OF YOU ARE SO CLOSE!

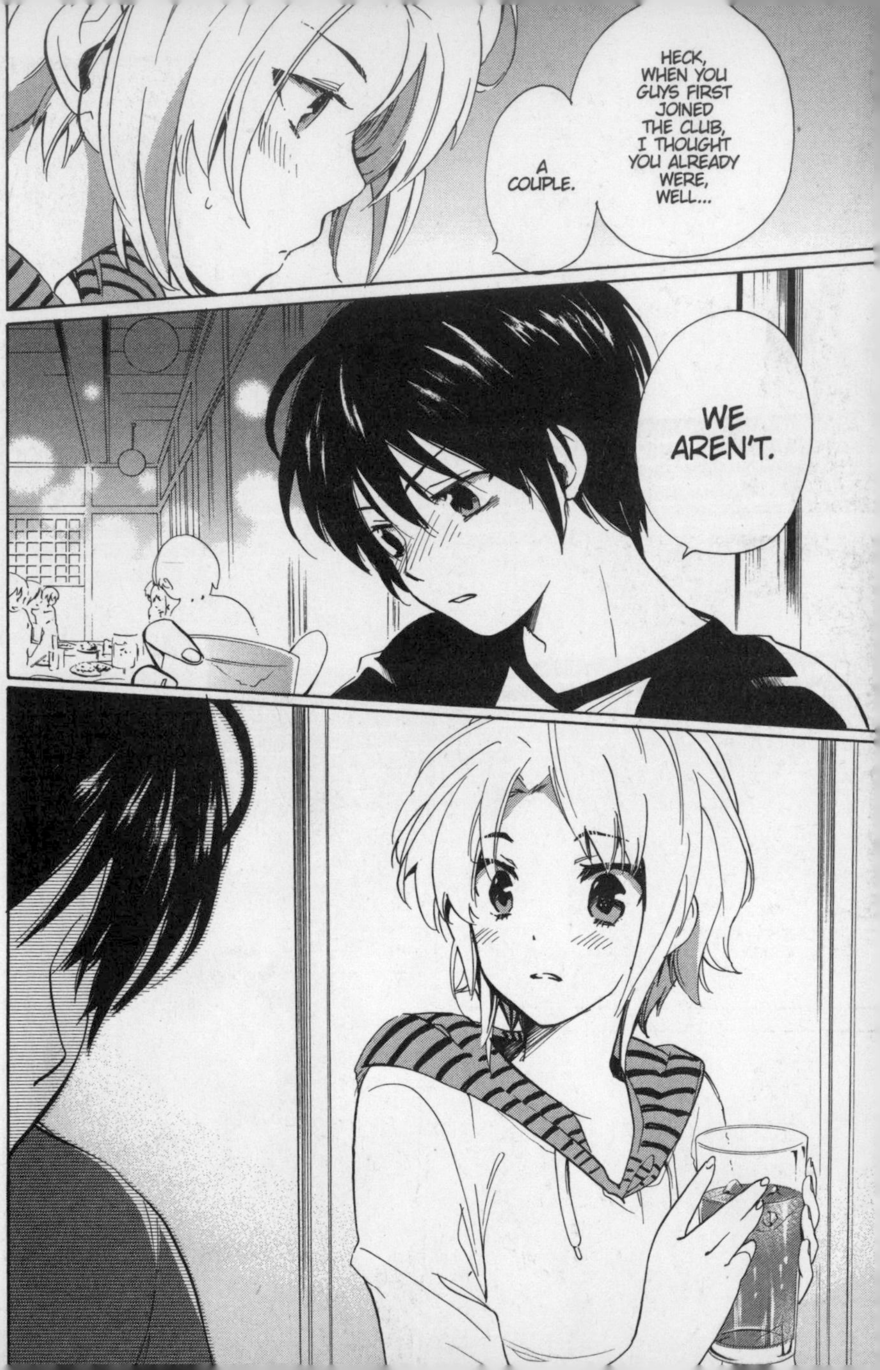
HECK, WHEN YOU GUYS FIRST JOINED THE CLUB, I THOUGHT YOU ALREADY WERE, WELL...
A COUPLE.
WE AREN'T.

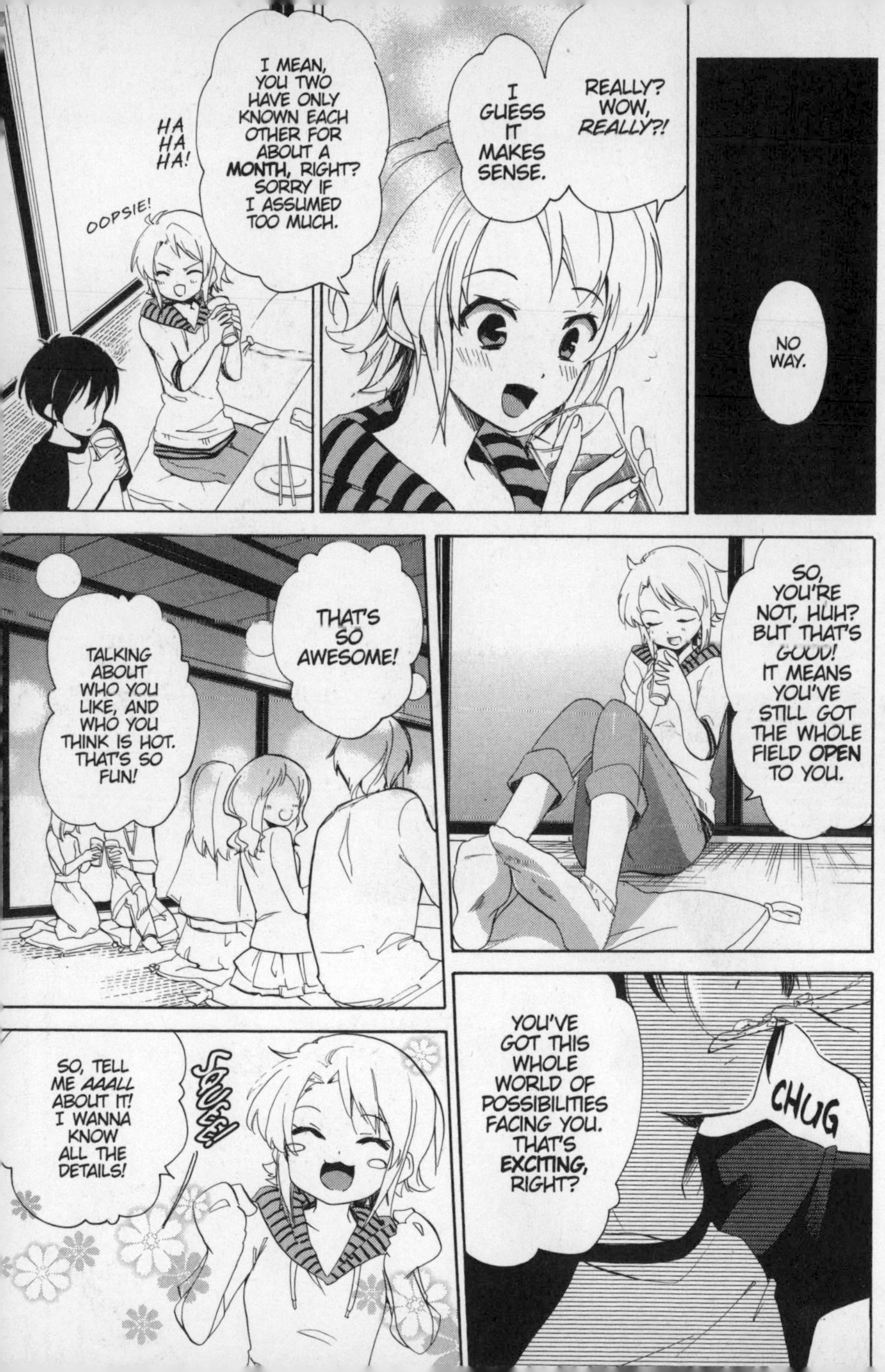
NO WAY.
REALLY? WOW, REALLY?!
I GUESS IT MAKES SENSE.
I MEAN, YOU TWO HAVE ONLY KNOWN EACH OTHER FOR ABOUT A MONTH, RIGHT? SORRY IF I ASSUMED TOO MUCH.
HA HA HA!
OOPSIE!
SO, YOU'RE NOT, HUH? BUT THAT'S GOOD! IT MEANS YOU'VE STILL GOT THE WHOLE FIELD OPEN TO YOU.
THAT'S SO AWESOME!
TALKING ABOUT WHO YOU LIKE, AND WHO YOU THINK IS HOT. THAT'S SO FUN!
YOU'VE GOT THIS WHOLE WORLD OF POSSIBILITIES FACING YOU. THAT'S EXCITING, RIGHT?
CHUG
SO, TELL ME AAALL ABOUT IT! I WANNA KNOW ALL THE DETAILS!

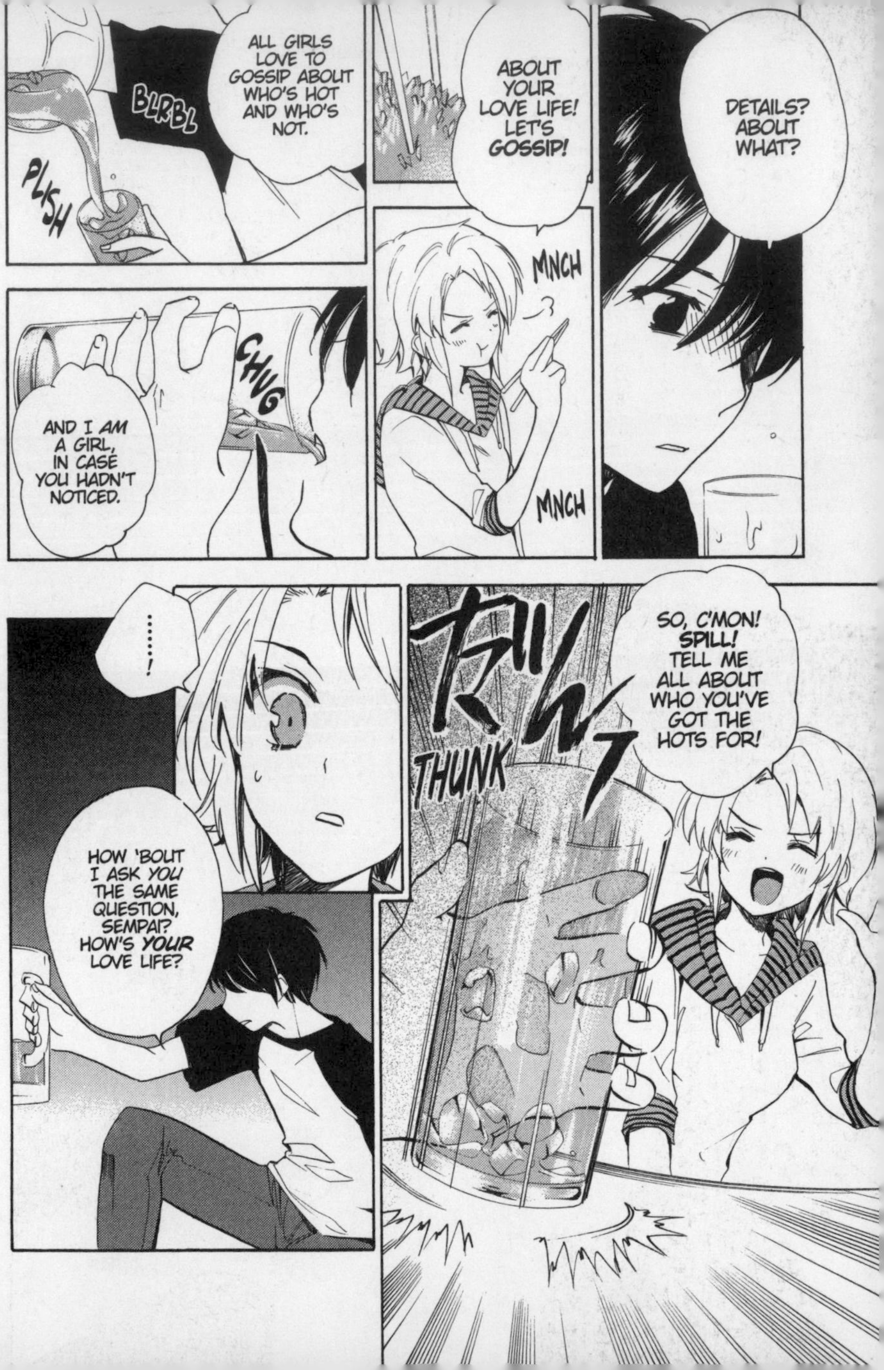
DETAILS? ABOUT WHAT?
ABOUT YOUR LOVE LIFE! LET'S GOSSIP!
MNCH
MNCH
ALL GIRLS LOVE TO GOSSIP ABOUT WHO'S HOT AND WHO'S NOT.
BLRBL
PLISH
AND I *AM* A GIRL, IN CASE YOU HADN'T NOTICED.
CHUG
SO, C'MON! **SPILL!** TELL ME ALL ABOUT WHO YOU'VE GOT THE HOTS FOR!
THUNK
......!
HOW 'BOUT I ASK *YOU* THE SAME QUESTION, SEMPAI? HOW'S ***YOUR*** LOVE LIFE?

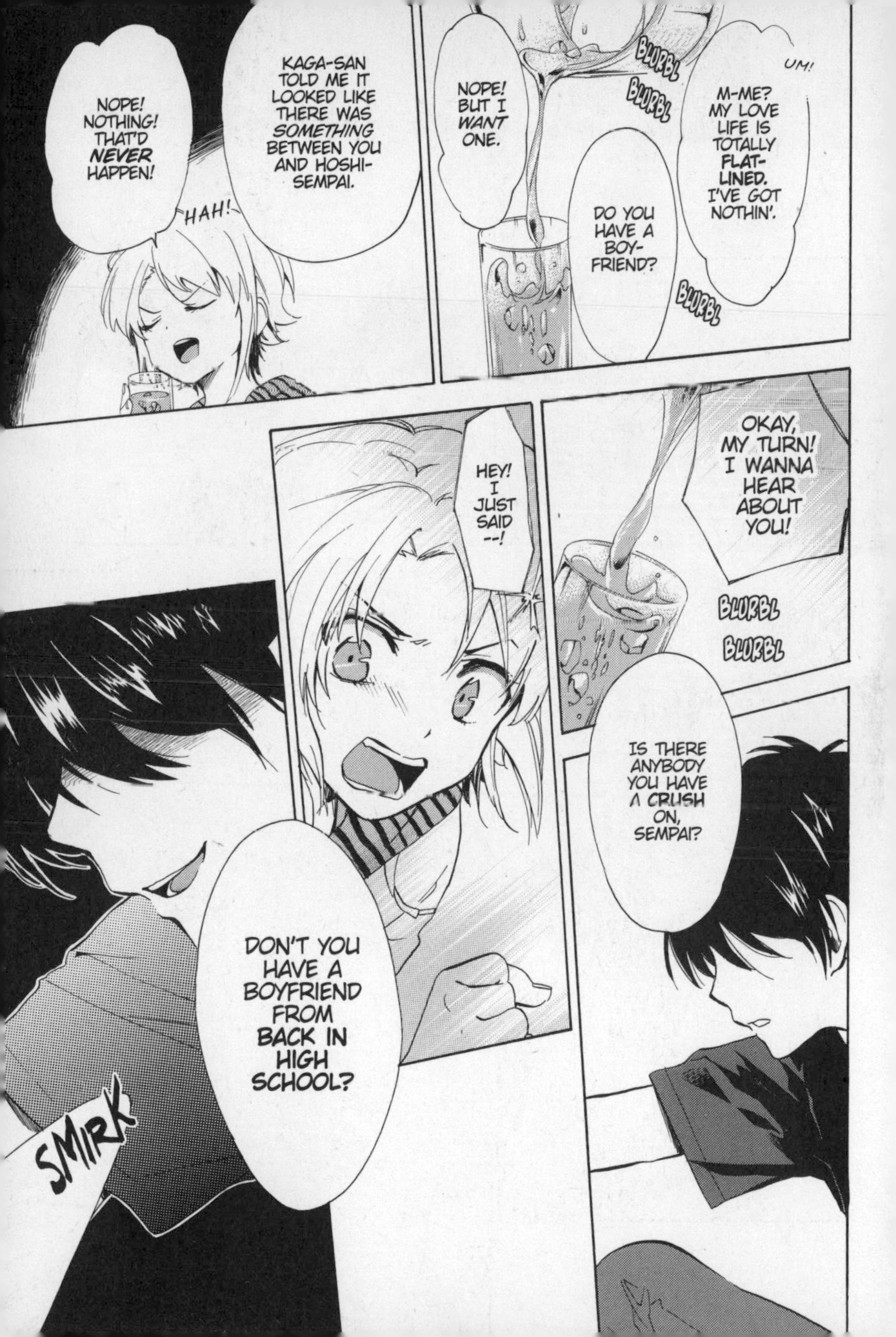
BLURBL
BLURBL
UM!
M-ME? MY LOVE LIFE IS TOTALLY FLAT-LINED. I'VE GOT NOTHIN'.
DO YOU HAVE A BOY-FRIEND?
BLURBL
NOPE! BUT I *WANT* ONE.
KAGA-SAN TOLD ME IT LOOKED LIKE THERE WAS *SOMETHING* BETWEEN YOU AND HOSHI-SEMPAI.
HAH!
NOPE! NOTHING! THAT'D ***NEVER*** HAPPEN!
OKAY, MY TURN! I WANNA HEAR ABOUT YOU!
BLURBL
BLURBL
IS THERE ANYBODY YOU HAVE A CRUSH ON, SEMPAI?
HEY! I JUST SAID --!
DON'T YOU HAVE A BOYFRIEND FROM BACK IN HIGH SCHOOL?
SMIRK

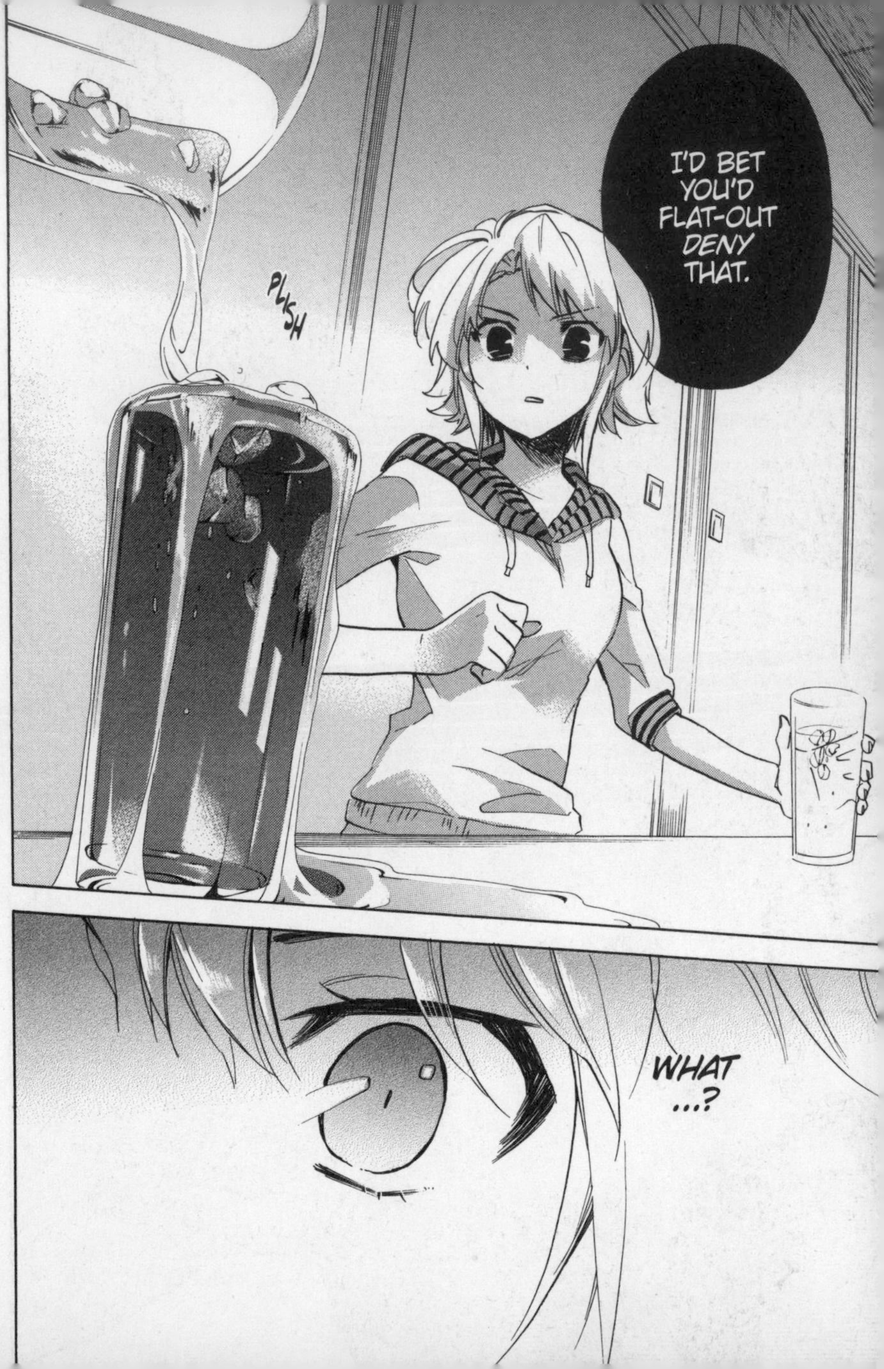
I'D BET YOU'D FLAT-OUT DENY THAT.
PLISH
WHAT ...?

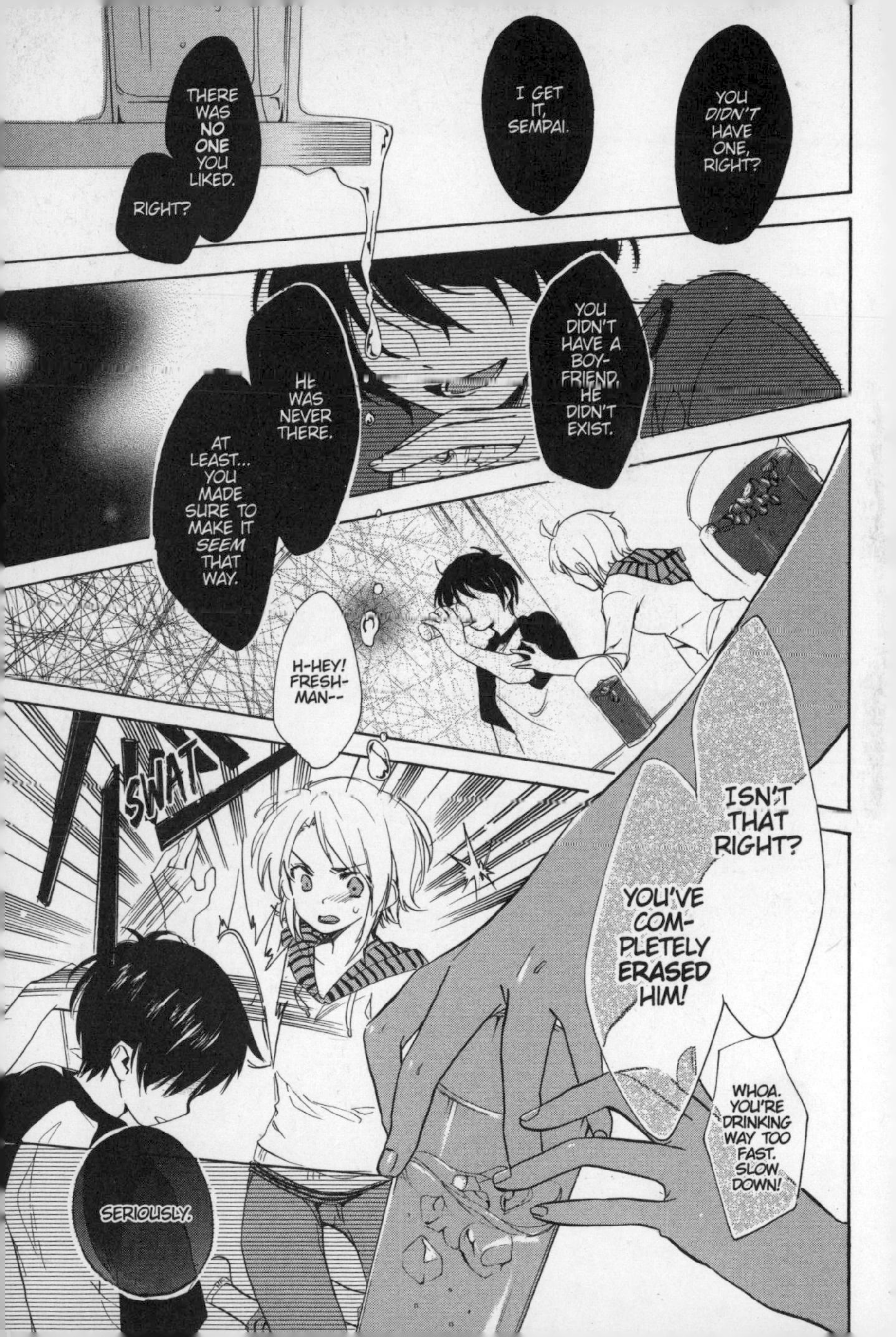

YOU DIDN'T HAVE ONE, RIGHT?
I GET IT, SEMPAI.
THERE WAS NO ONE YOU LIKED.
RIGHT?
YOU DIDN'T HAVE A BOY-FRIEND, HE DIDN'T EXIST.
HE WAS NEVER THERE.
AT LEAST... YOU MADE SURE TO MAKE IT SEEM THAT WAY.
ISN'T THAT RIGHT?
YOU'VE COM-PLETELY ERASED HIM!
H-HEY! FRESH-MAN--
SWAT
WHOA. YOU'RE DRINKING WAY TOO FAST. SLOW DOWN!
SERIOUSLY.

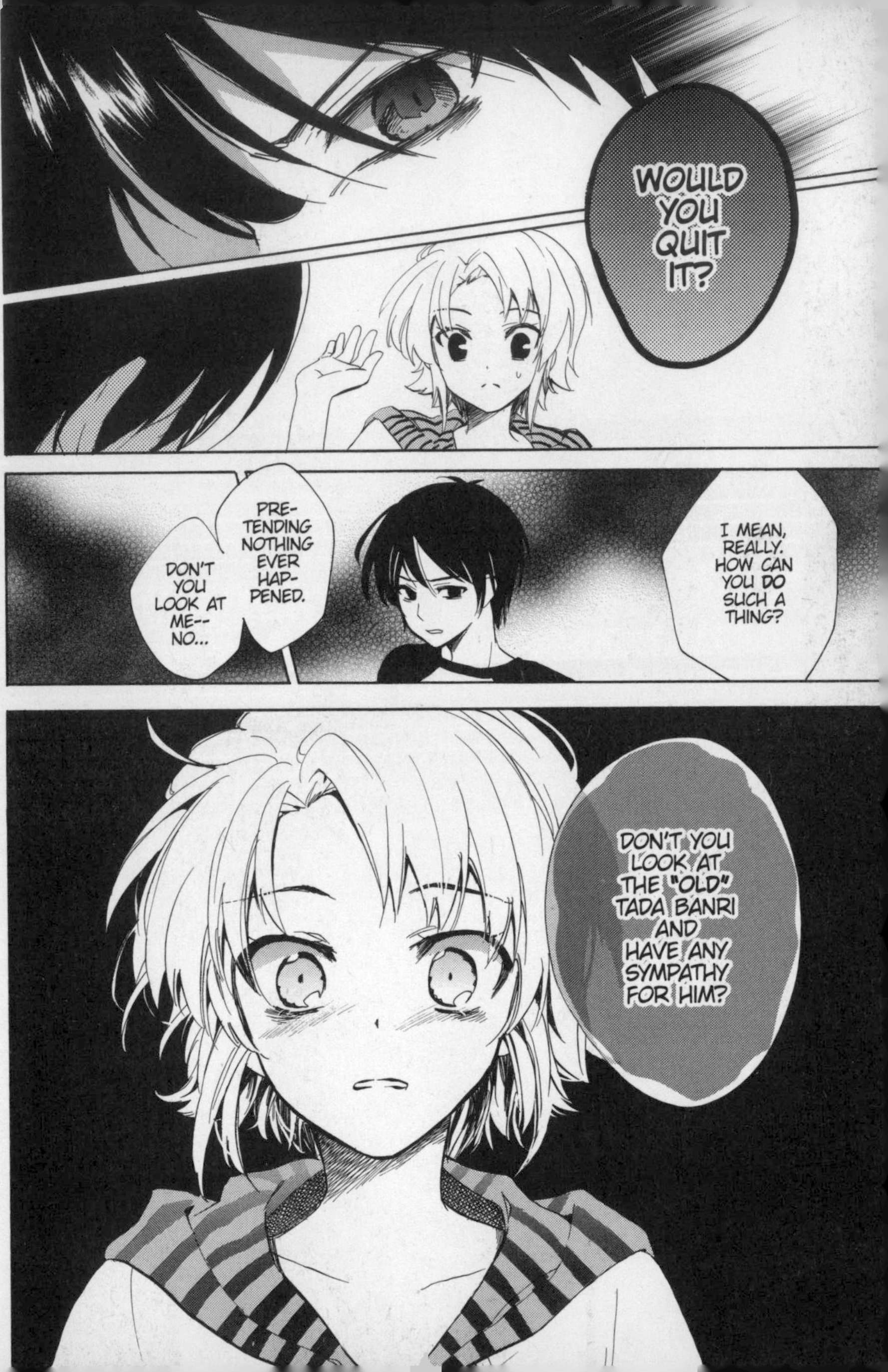
WOULD YOU QUIT IT?
I MEAN, REALLY. HOW CAN YOU DO SUCH A THING?
PRE-TENDING NOTHING EVER HAP-PENED.
DON'T YOU LOOK AT ME-- NO...
DON'T YOU LOOK AT THE "OLD" TADA BANRI AND HAVE ANY SYMPATHY FOR HIM?

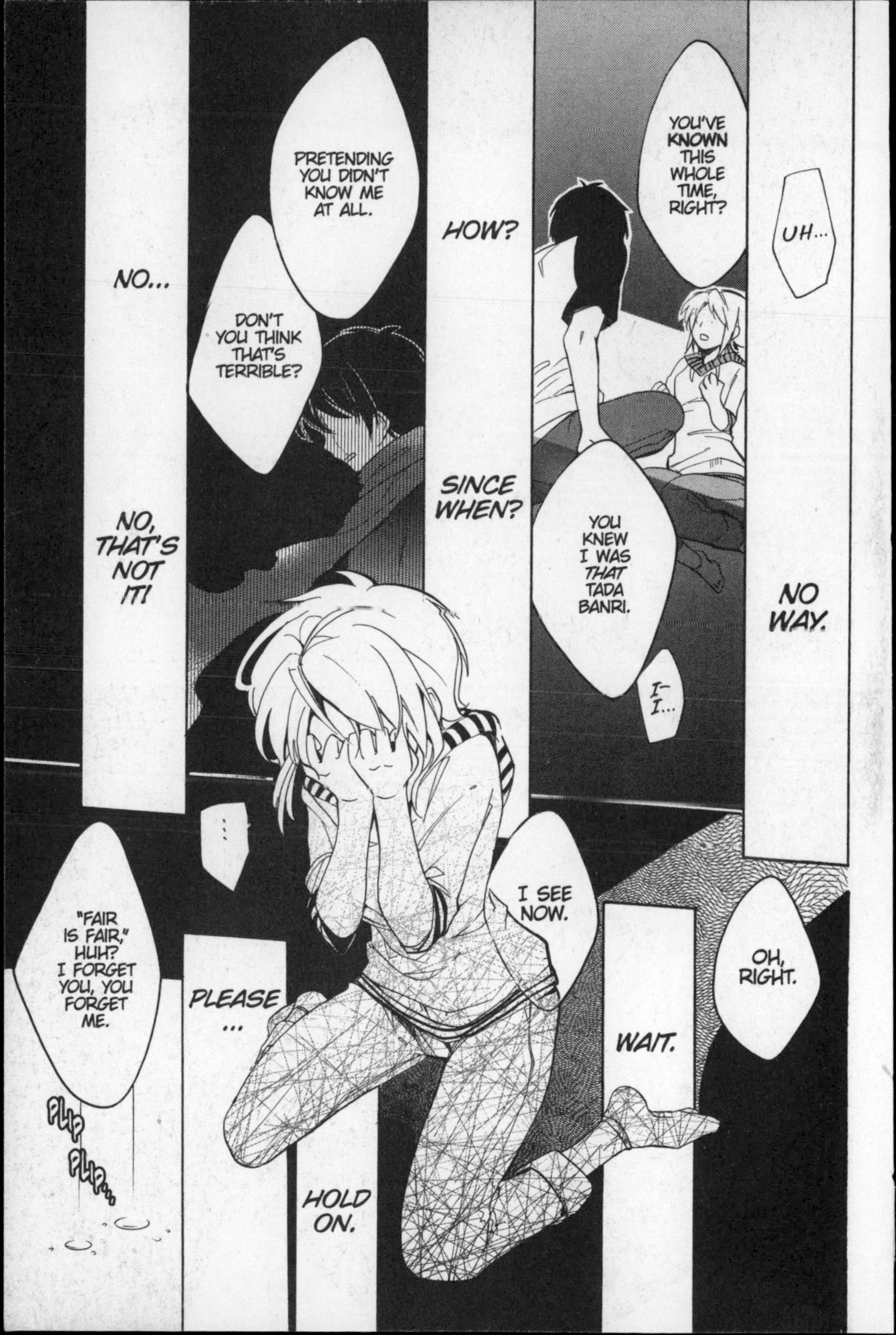
UH...
NO WAY.
YOU'VE KNOWN THIS WHOLE TIME, RIGHT?
YOU KNEW I WAS *THAT* TADA BANRI.
I- I...
HOW?
SINCE WHEN?
PRETENDING YOU DIDN'T KNOW ME AT ALL.
DON'T YOU THINK THAT'S TERRIBLE?
NO...
NO, THAT'S NOT IT!
OH, RIGHT.
WAIT.
I SEE NOW.
HOLD ON.
PLEASE...
...
"FAIR IS FAIR," HUH? I FORGET YOU, YOU FORGET ME.
PLIP PLIP...

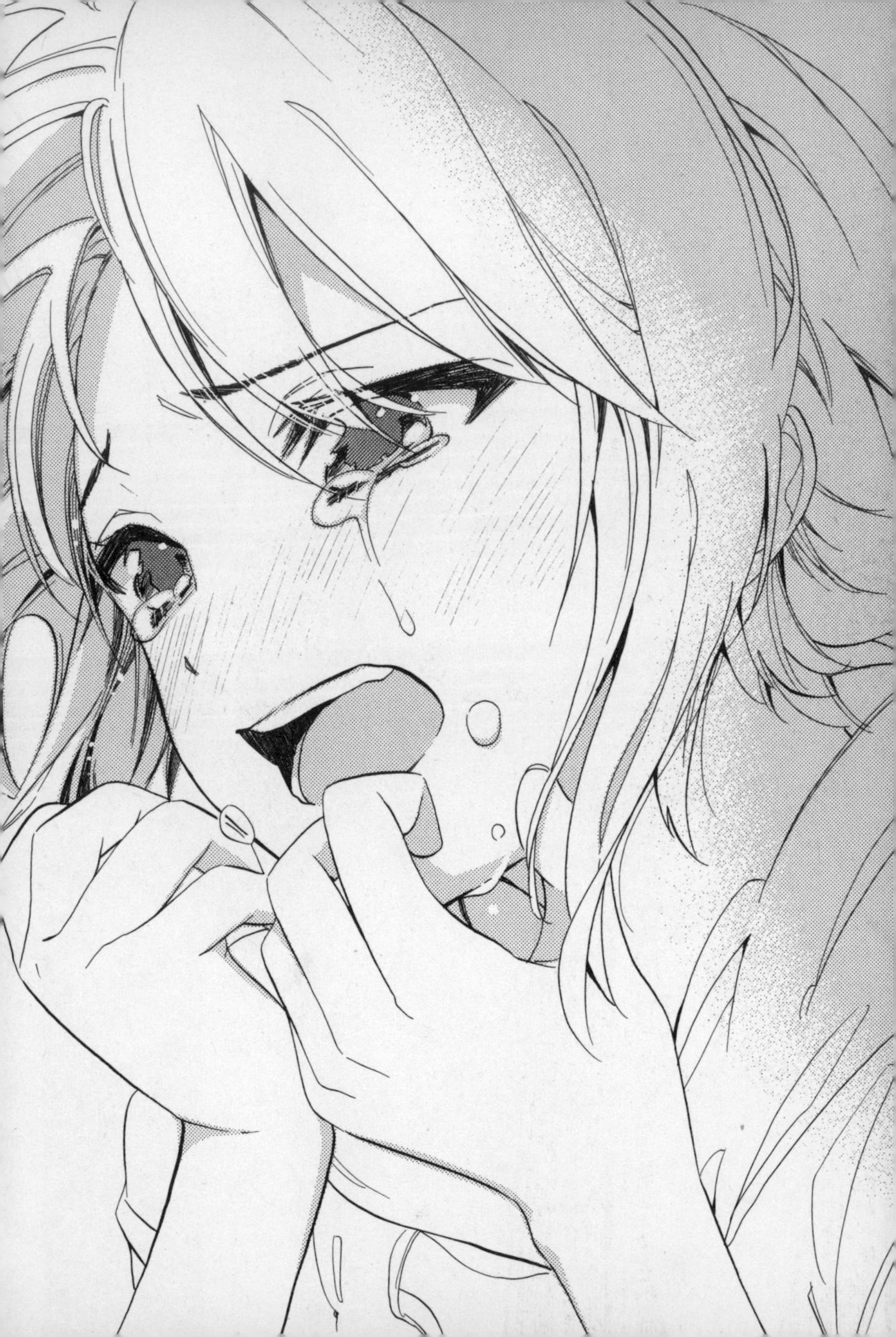

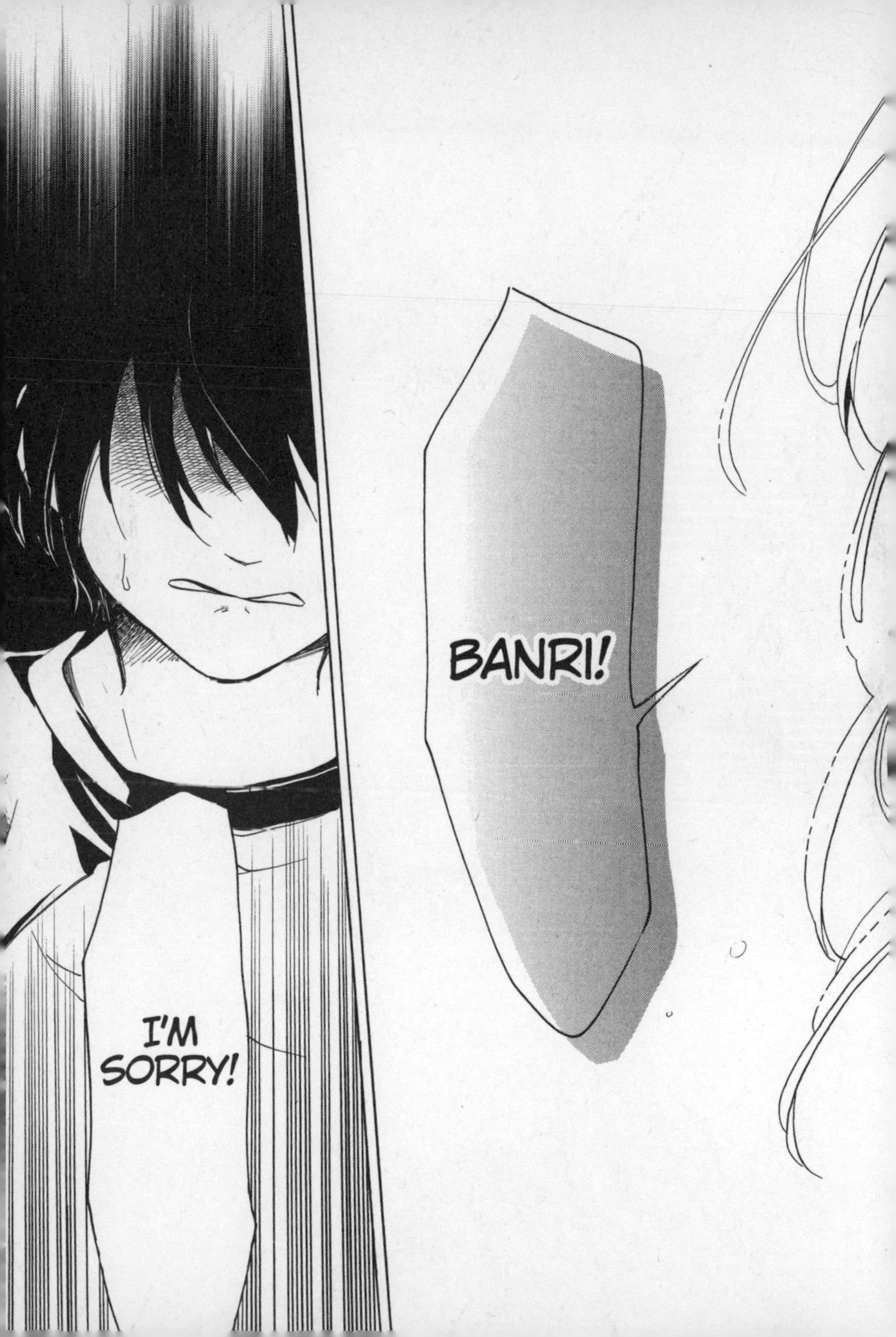
BANRI!
I'M SORRY!

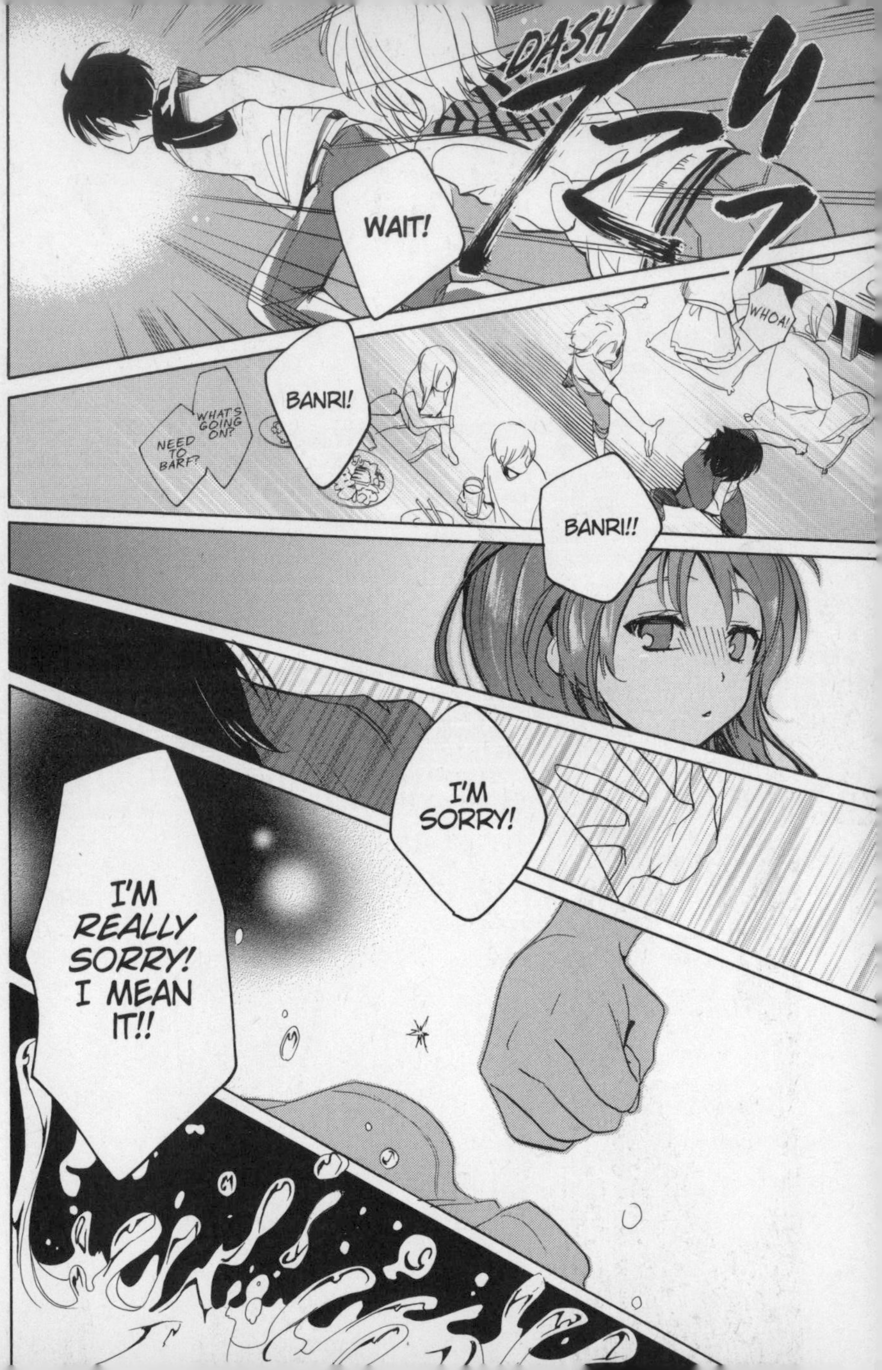

DASH
WAIT!
WHOA!
BANRI!
WHAT'S GOING ON?
NEED TO BARF?
BANRI!!
I'M SORRY!
I'M REALLY SORRY! I MEAN IT!!

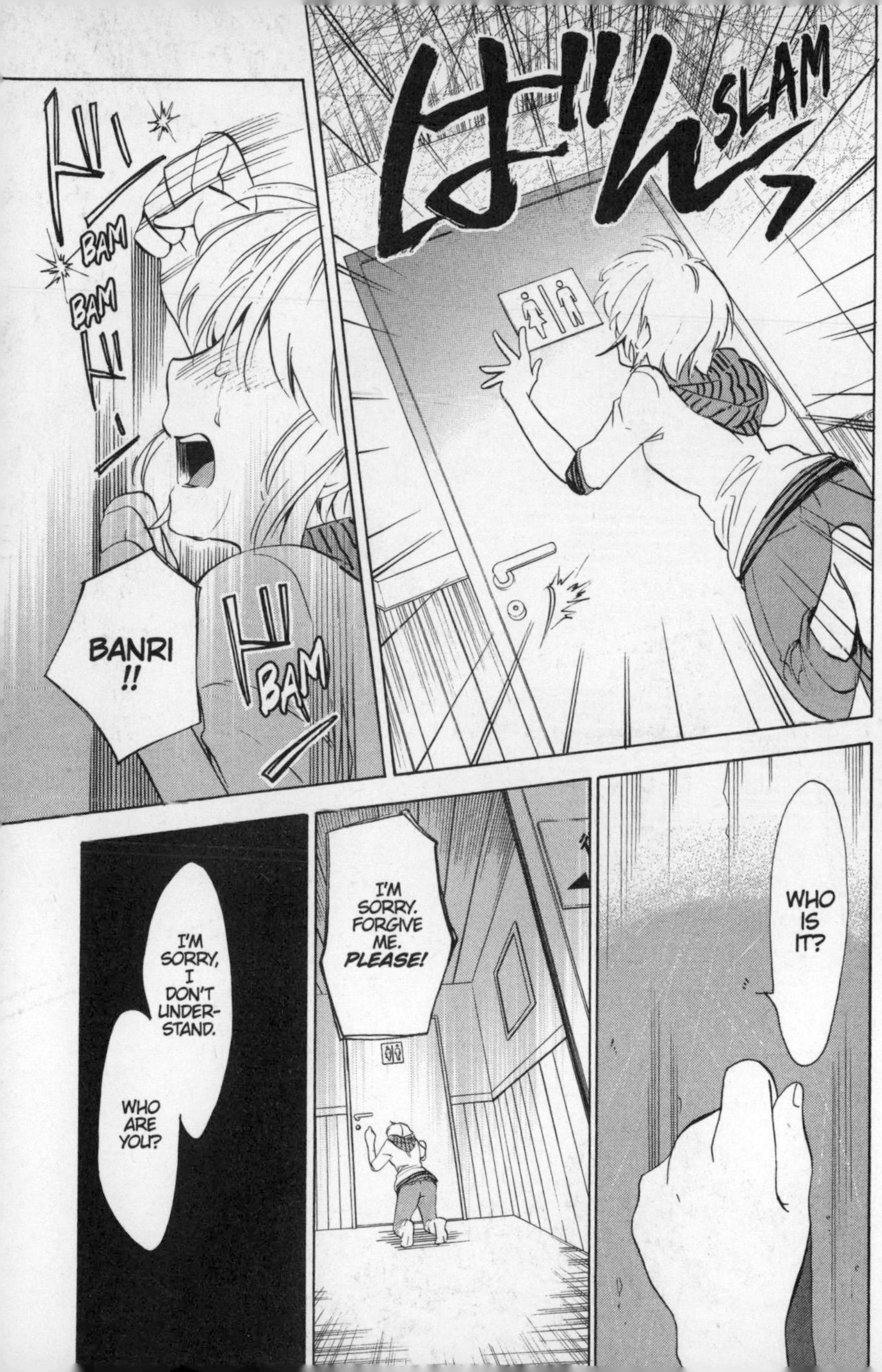
ばん
SLAM
BAM
BAM
BANRI!!
BAM
WHO IS IT?
I'M SORRY. FORGIVE ME. PLEASE!
I'M SORRY, I DON'T UNDERSTAND.
WHO ARE YOU?

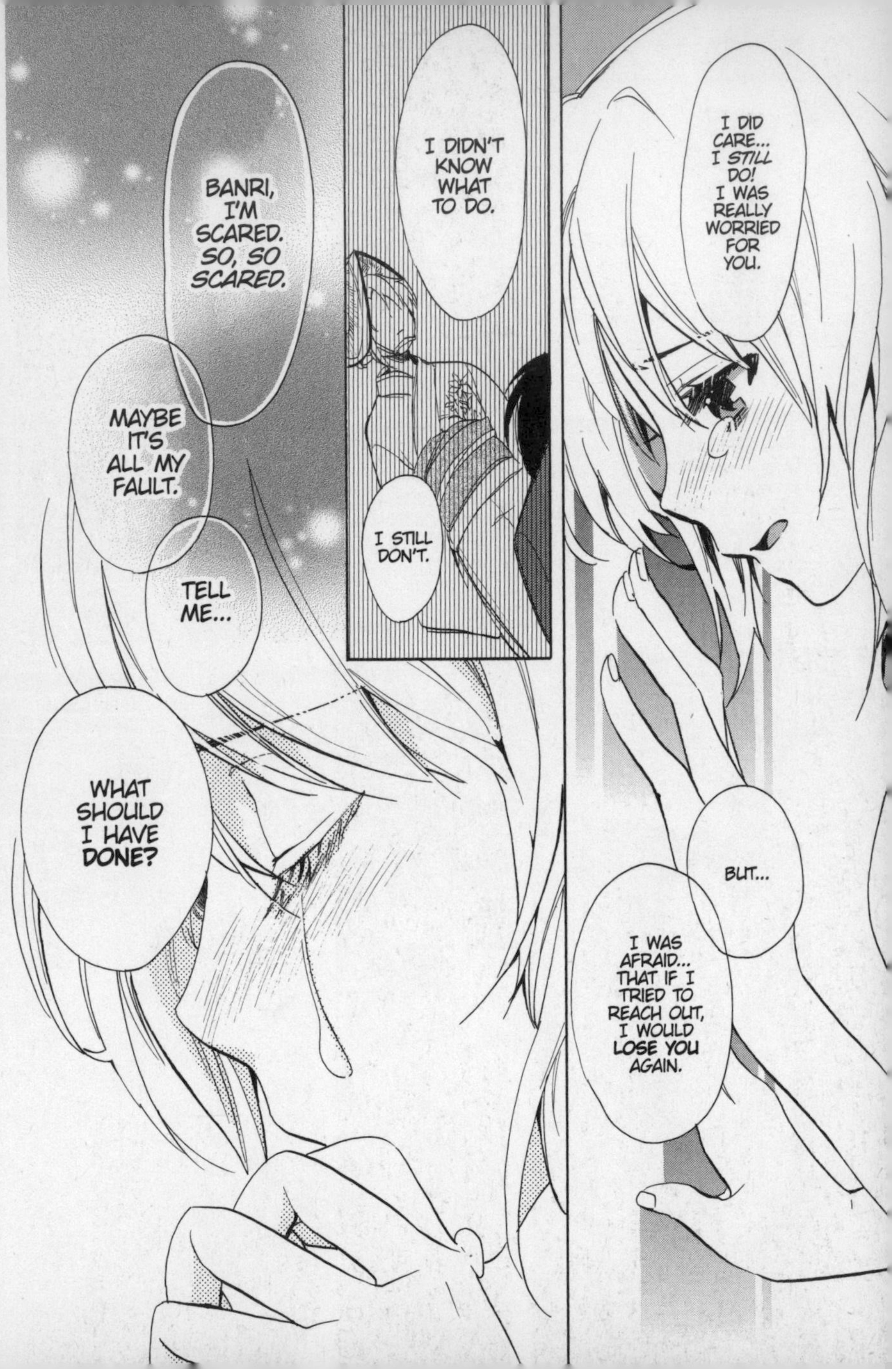
I DID CARE... I STILL DO! I WAS REALLY WORRIED FOR YOU.
BUT...
I WAS AFRAID... THAT IF I TRIED TO REACH OUT, I WOULD LOSE YOU AGAIN.
I DIDN'T KNOW WHAT TO DO.
I STILL DON'T.
BANRI, I'M SCARED. SO, SO SCARED.
MAYBE IT'S ALL MY FAULT.
TELL ME...
WHAT SHOULD I HAVE DONE?

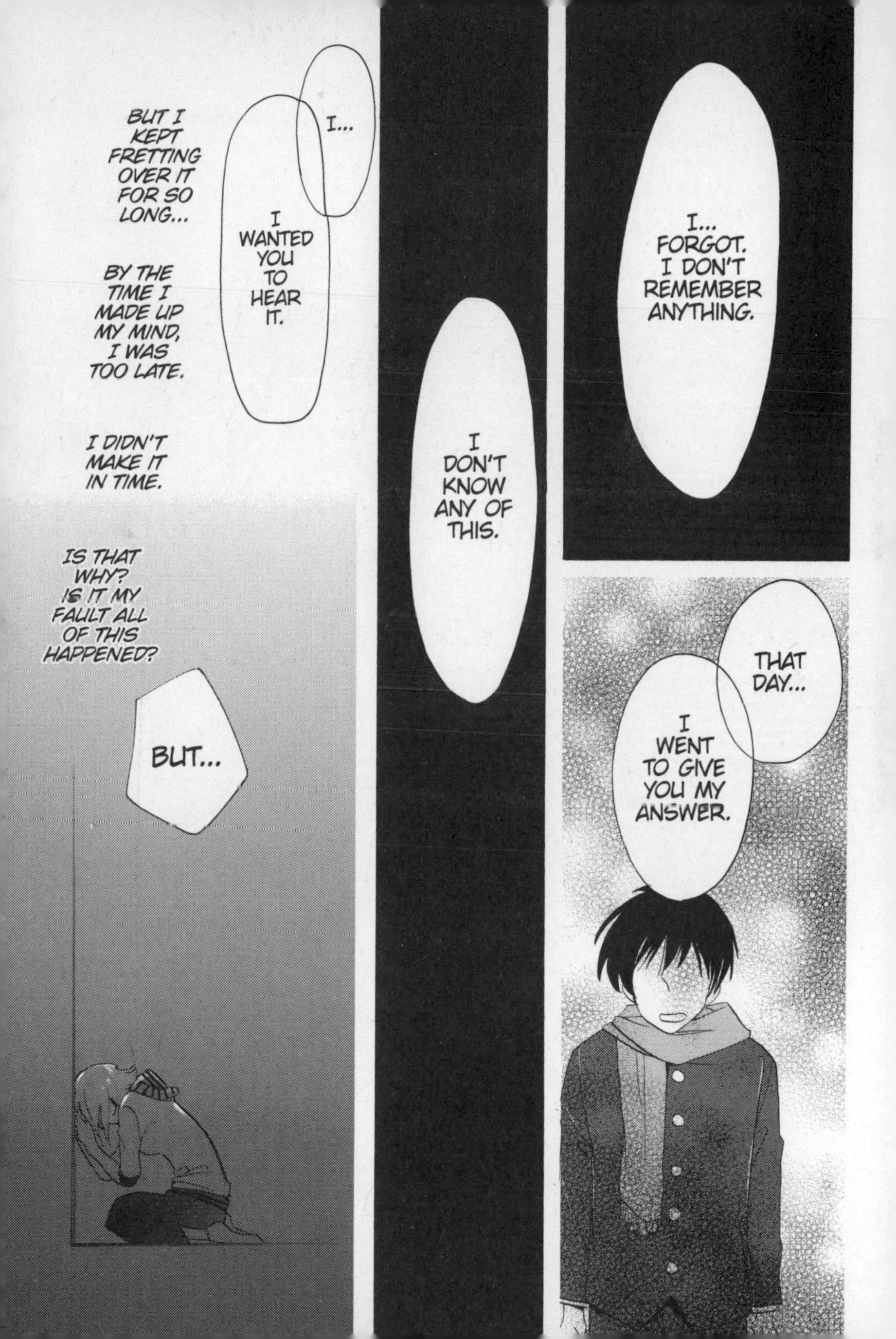
I... FORGOT. I DON'T REMEMBER ANYTHING.
THAT DAY...
I WENT TO GIVE YOU MY ANSWER.
I DON'T KNOW ANY OF THIS.
I...
I WANTED YOU TO HEAR IT.
BUT I KEPT FRETTING OVER IT FOR SO LONG...
BY THE TIME I MADE UP MY MIND, I WAS TOO LATE.
I DIDN'T MAKE IT IN TIME.
IS THAT WHY? IS IT MY FAULT ALL OF THIS HAPPENED?
BUT...

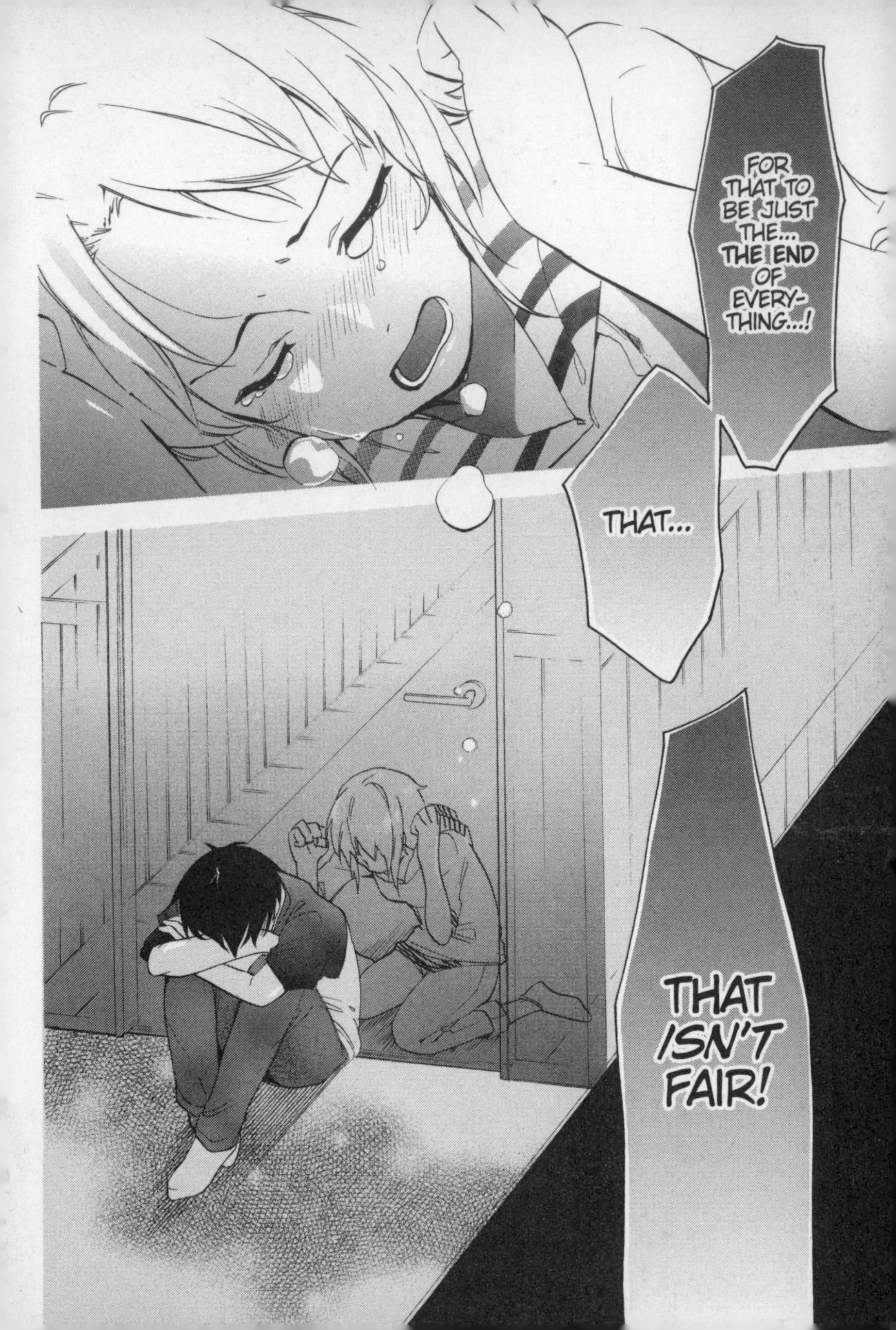
FOR THAT TO BE JUST THE... THE END OF EVERY-THING...!
THAT...
THAT ISN'T FAIR!

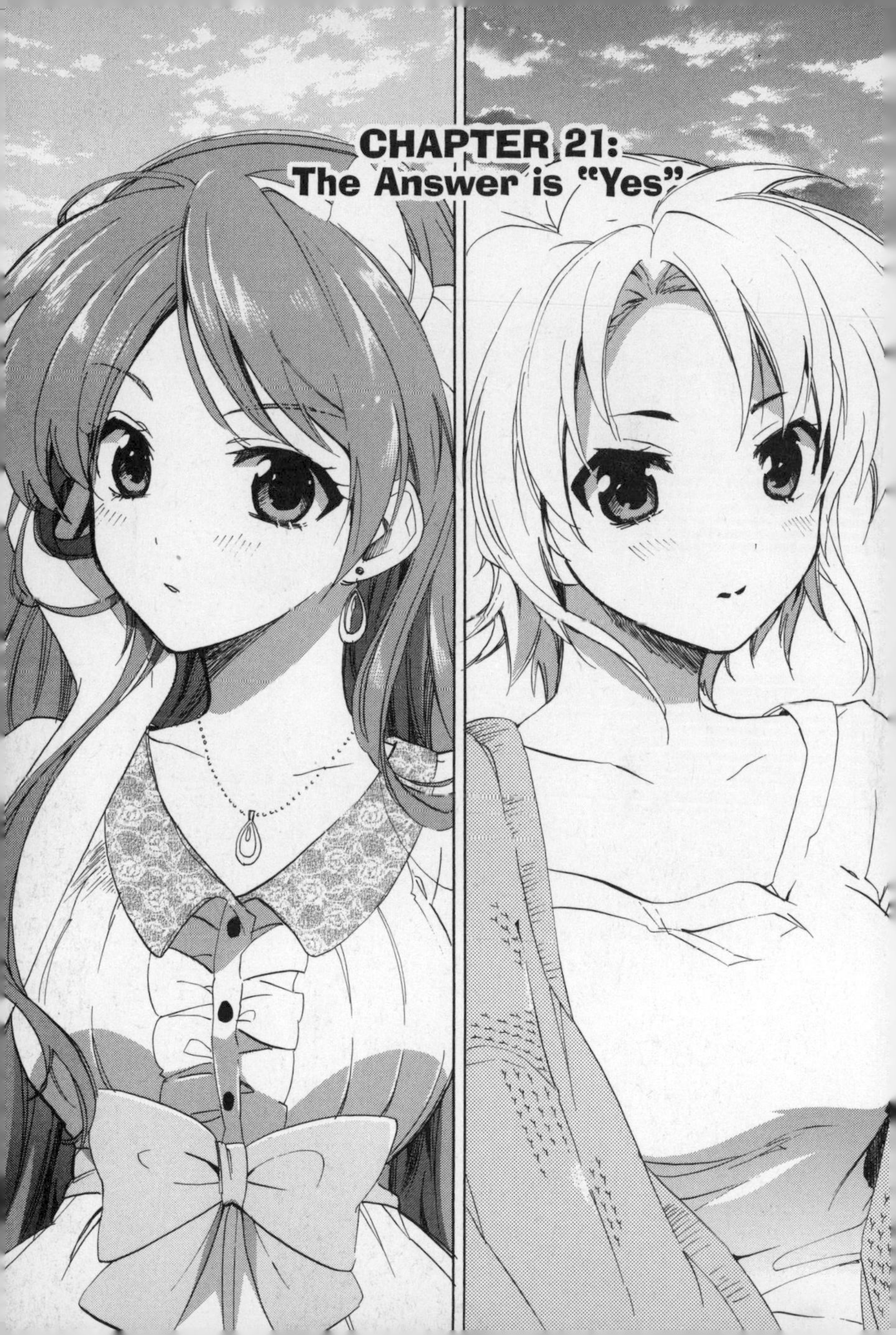
CHAPTER 21:
The Answer is "Yes"

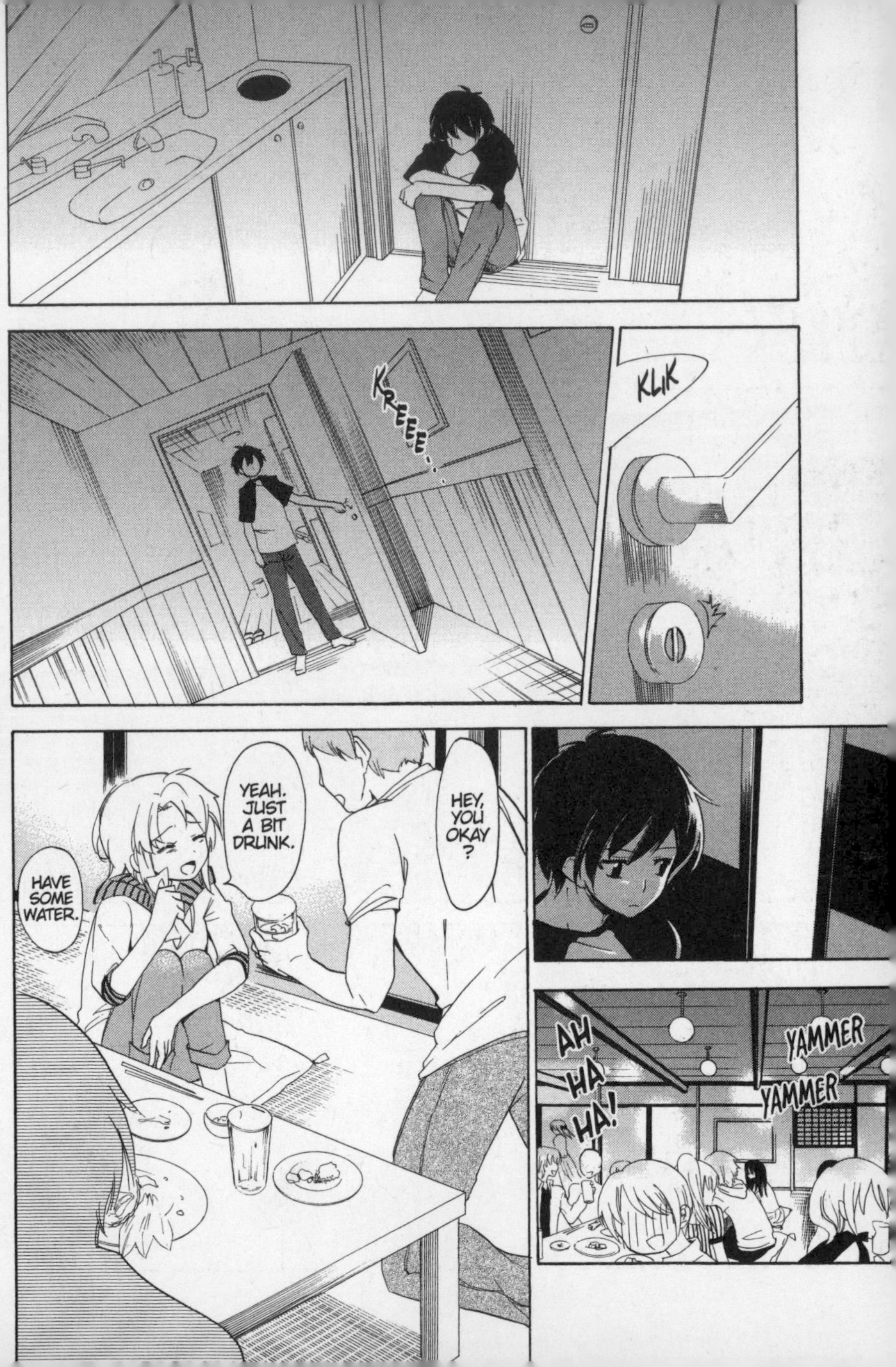
KLIK
KREEEE...
AH HA HA!
YAMMER
YAMMER
HEY, YOU OKAY?
YEAH. JUST A BIT DRUNK.
HAVE SOME WATER.

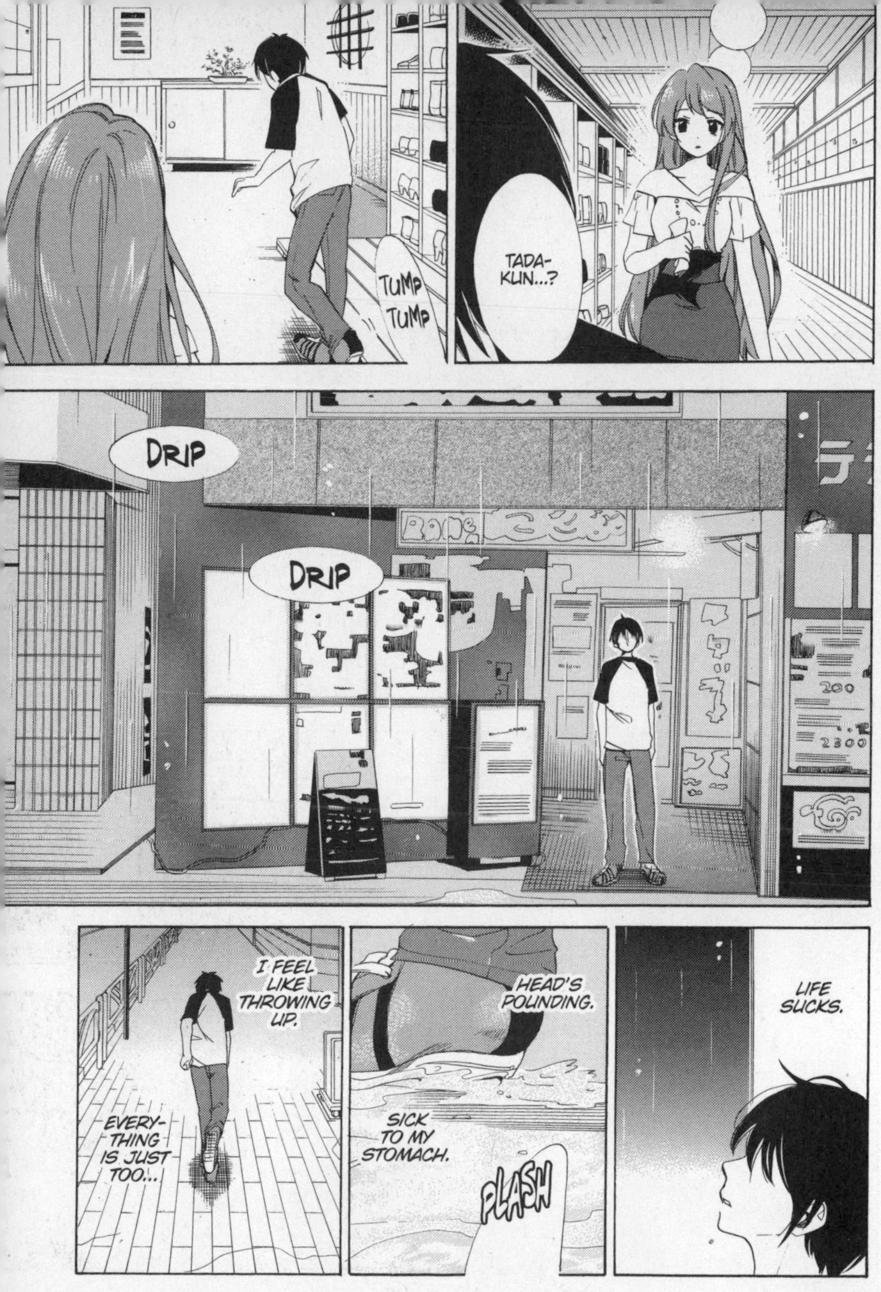
TADA-KUN...?
TUMP TUMP
DRIP
DRIP
200
2300
LIFE SUCKS.
HEAD'S POUNDING.
SICK TO MY STOMACH.
PLASH
I FEEL LIKE THROWING UP.
EVERY-THING IS JUST TOO...

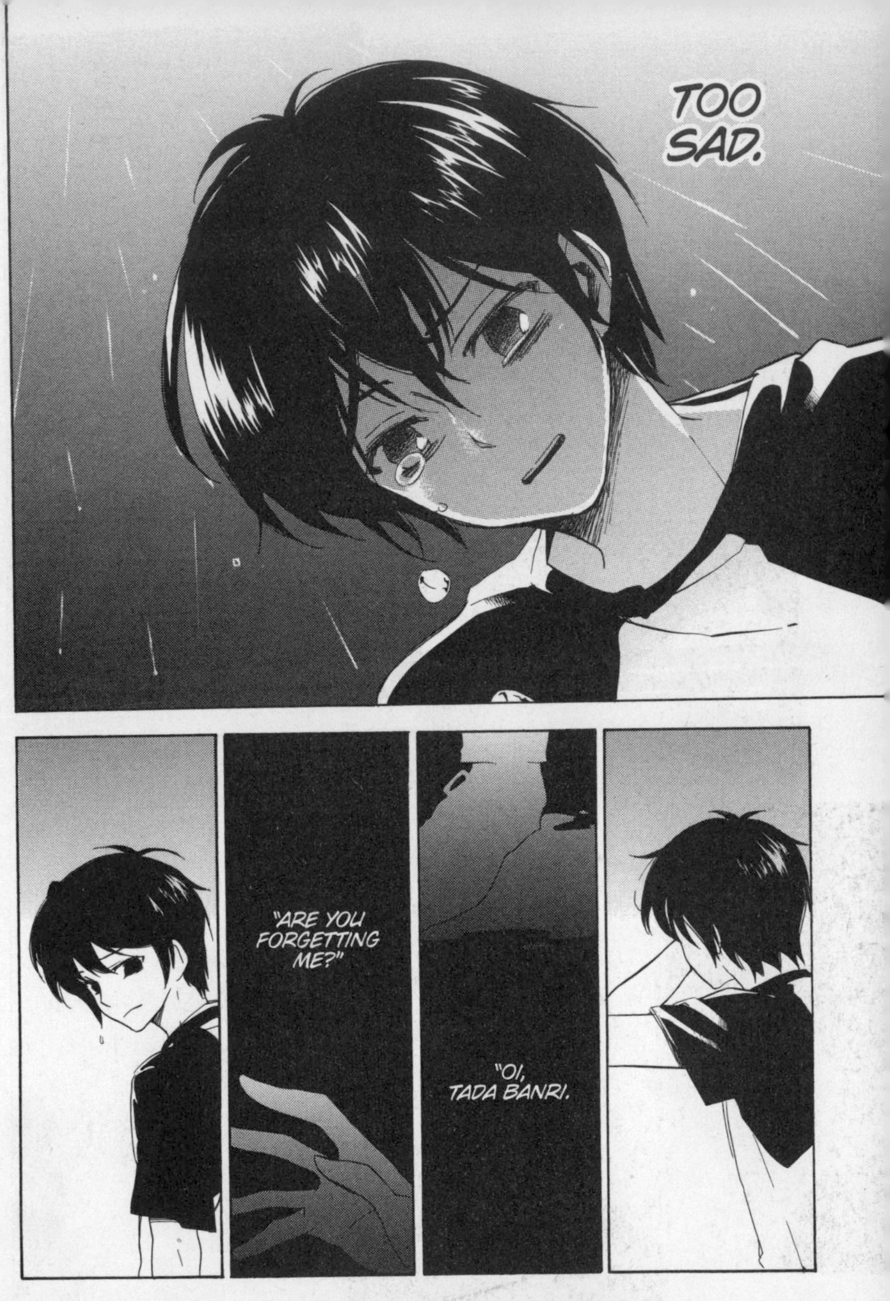
TOO SAD.
"OI, TADA BANRI.
"ARE YOU FORGETTING ME?"

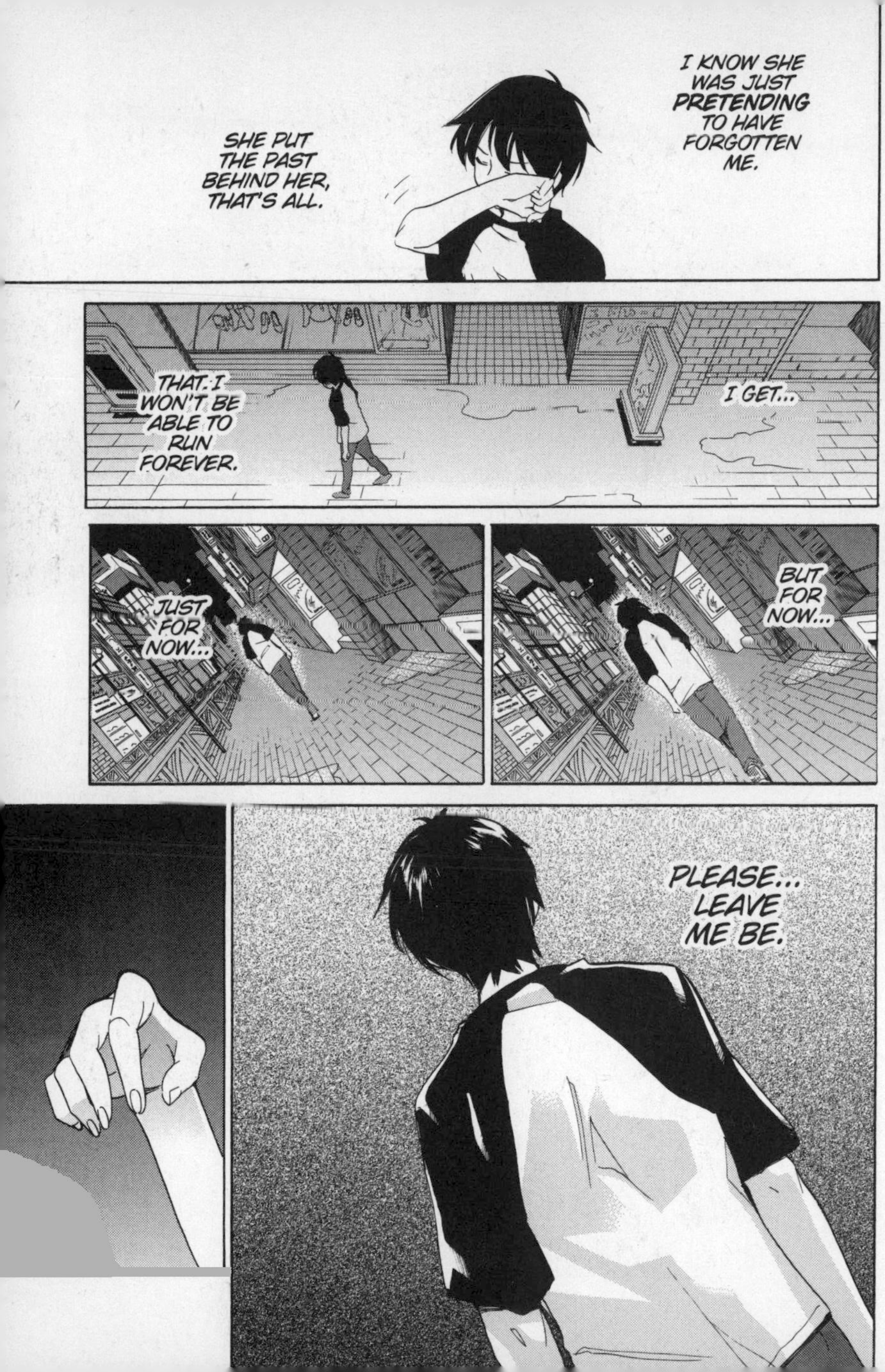
I KNOW SHE WAS JUST PRETENDING TO HAVE FORGOTTEN ME.
SHE PUT THE PAST BEHIND HER, THAT'S ALL.
I GET...
THAT I WON'T BE ABLE TO RUN FOREVER.
BUT FOR NOW...
JUST FOR NOW...
PLEASE... LEAVE ME BE.

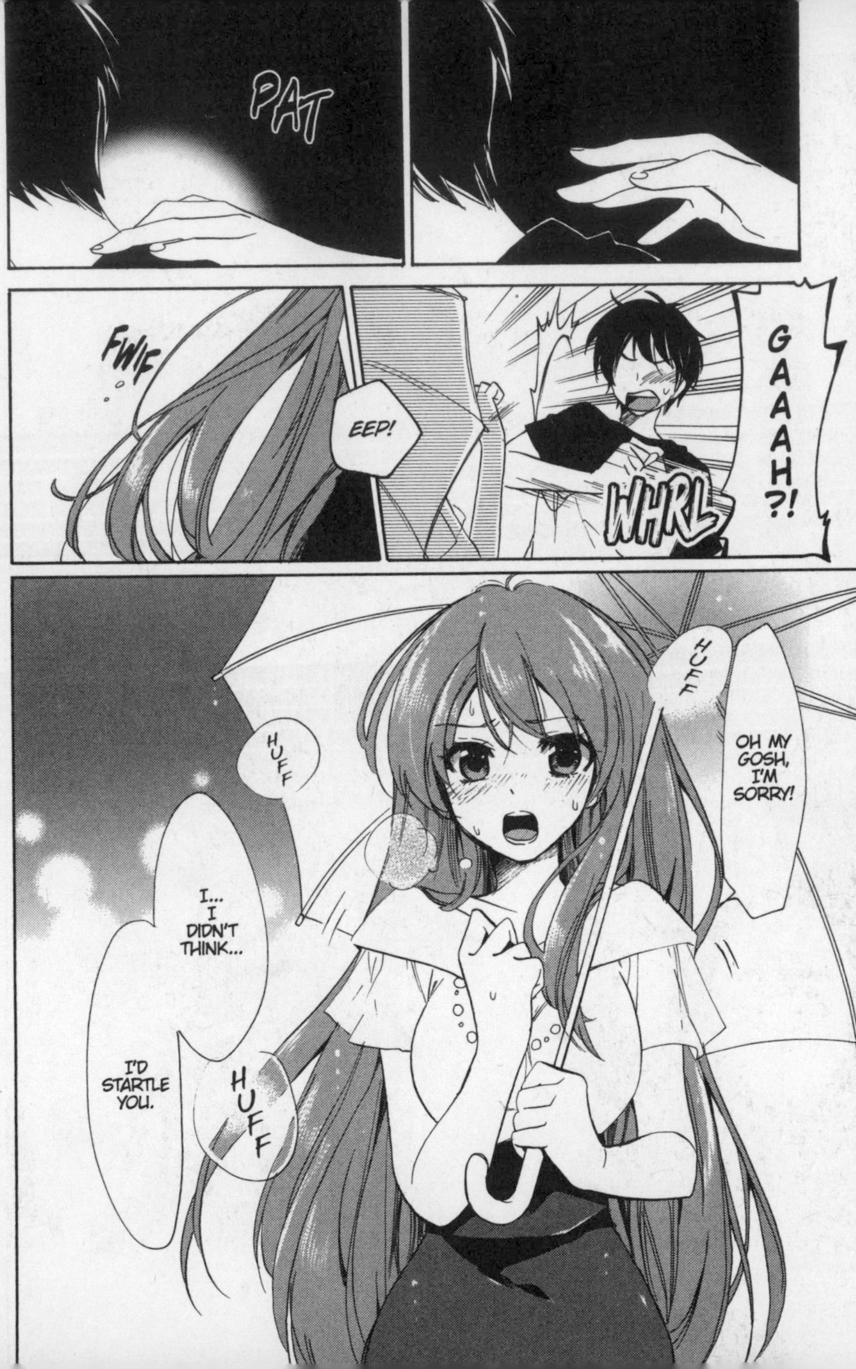
PAT
GAAAH?!
WHRL
EEP!
FWIP
HUFF
OH MY GOSH, I'M SORRY!
HUFF
I... I DIDN'T THINK...
I'D STARTLE YOU.
HUFF

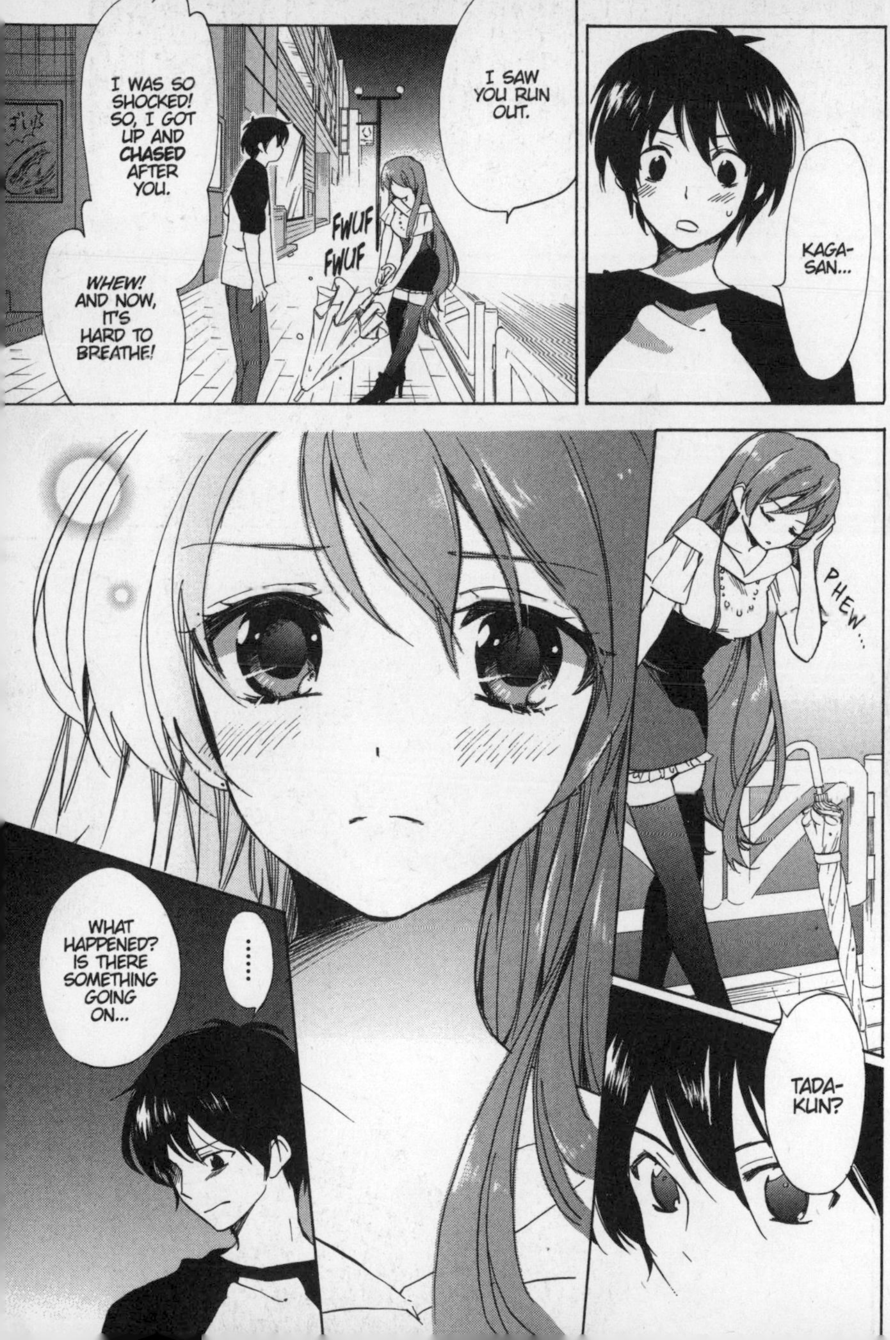
KAGA-SAN...
I SAW YOU RUN OUT.
I WAS SO SHOCKED! SO, I GOT UP AND CHASED AFTER YOU.
FWUF FWUF
WHEW! AND NOW, IT'S HARD TO BREATHE!
PHEW...
TADA-KUN?
......
WHAT HAPPENED? IS THERE SOMETHING GOING ON...

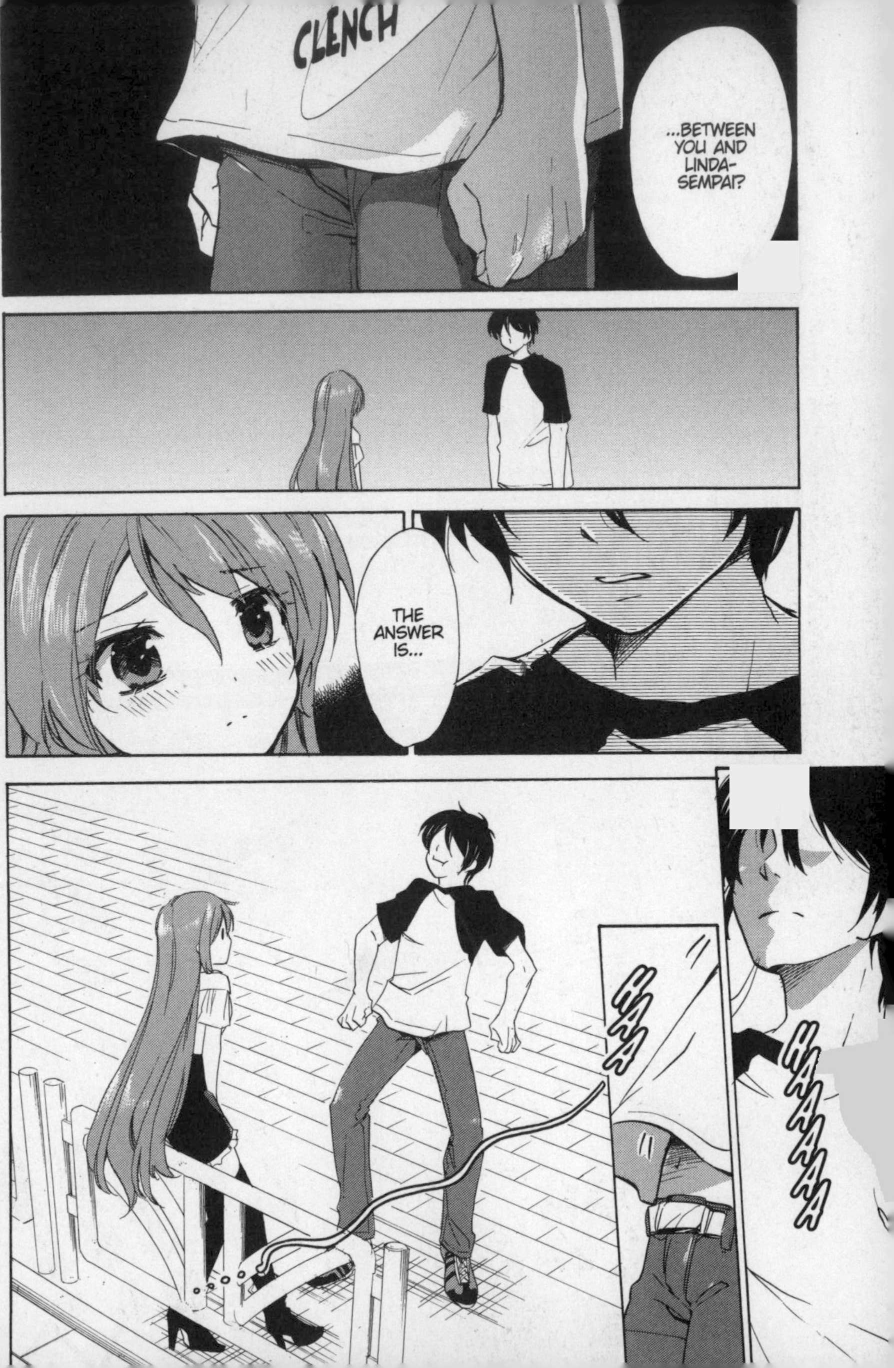
...BETWEEN YOU AND LINDA-SEMPAI?
CLENCH
THE ANSWER IS...
HAAAAAAA
HAA

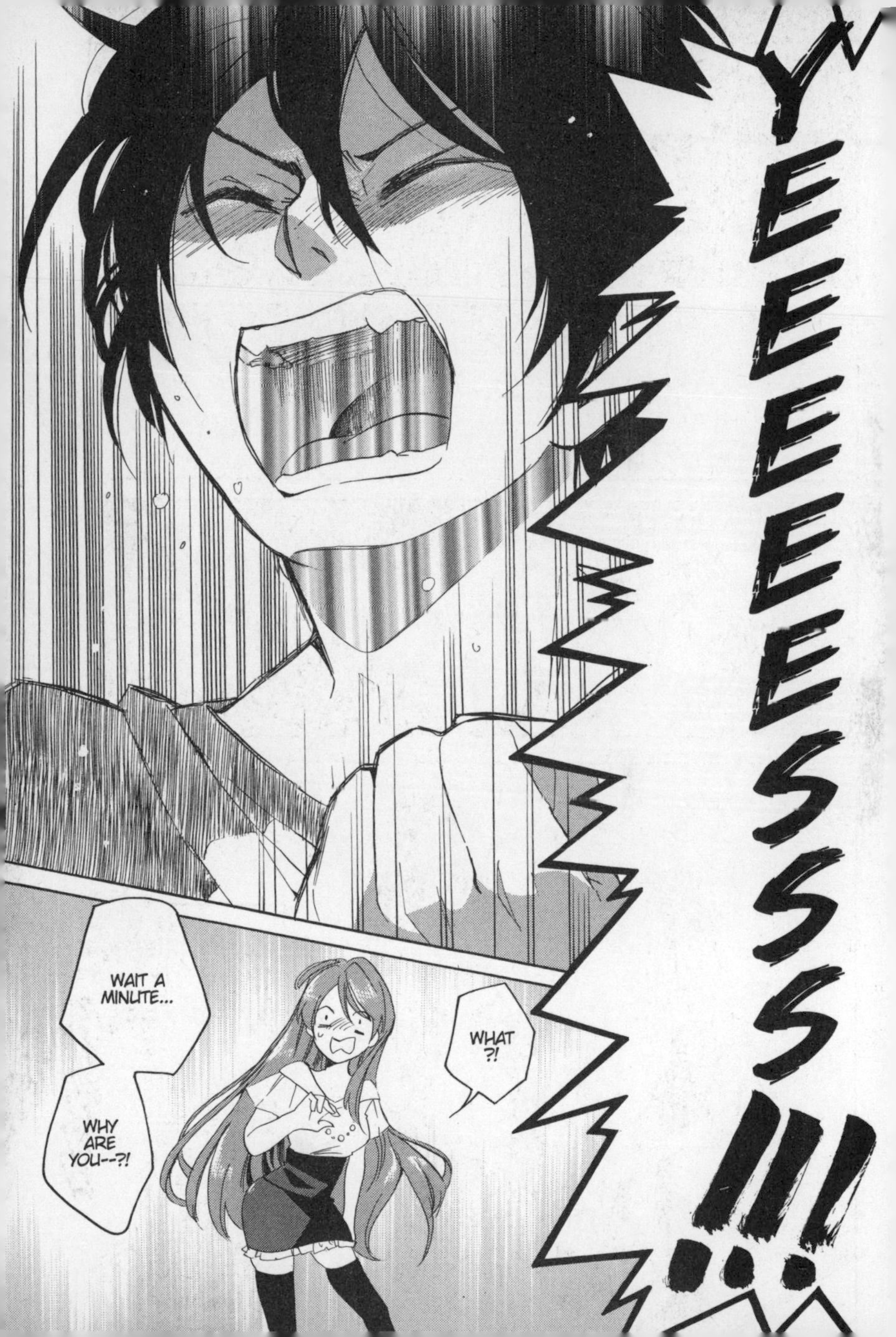
YEEEEEEESSSS!!!!
WHAT ?!
WAIT A MINUTE...
WHY ARE YOU--?!

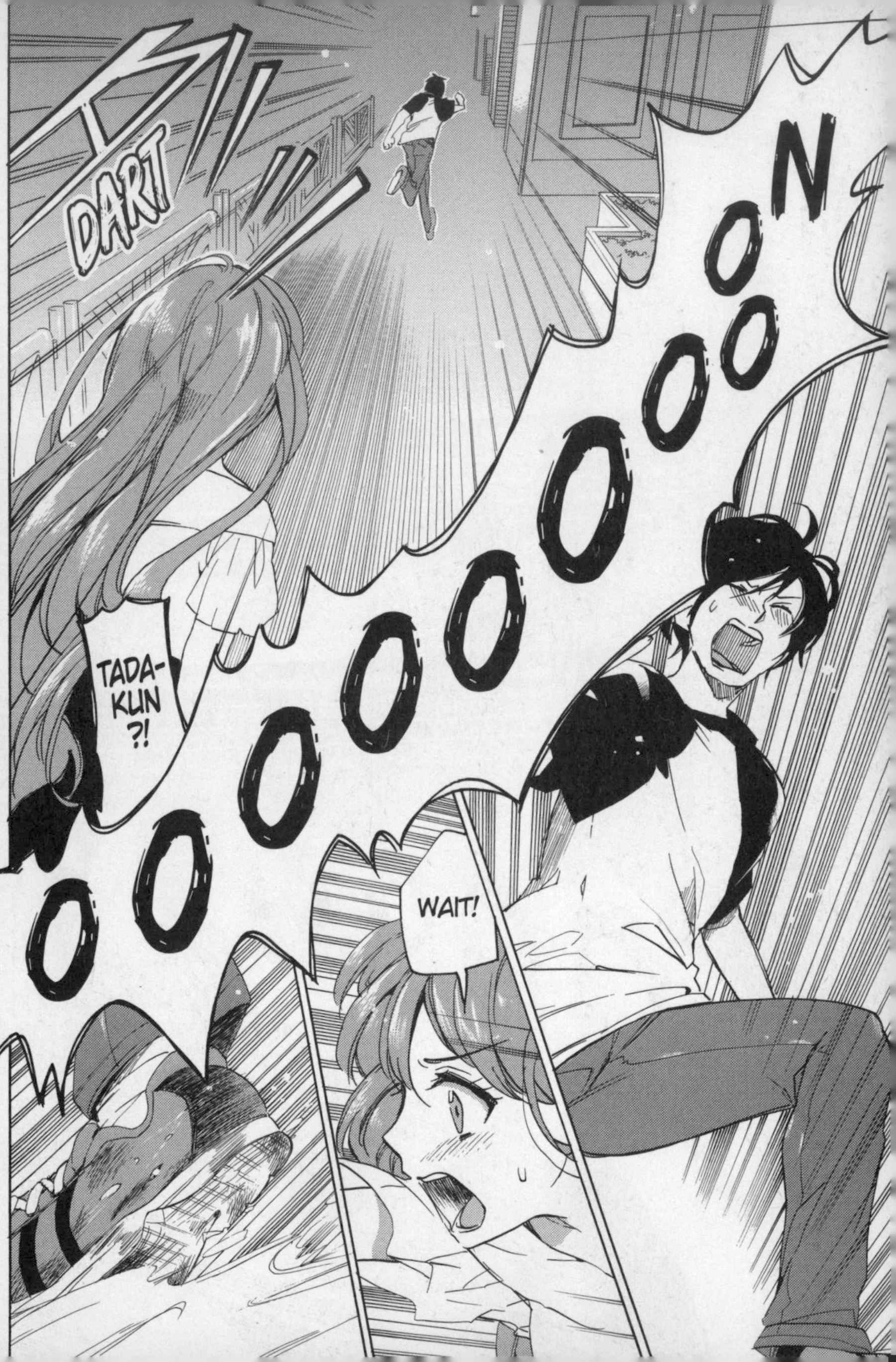
NOOOOOOOOOOOOOO
DART
TADA-KUN?!
WAIT!

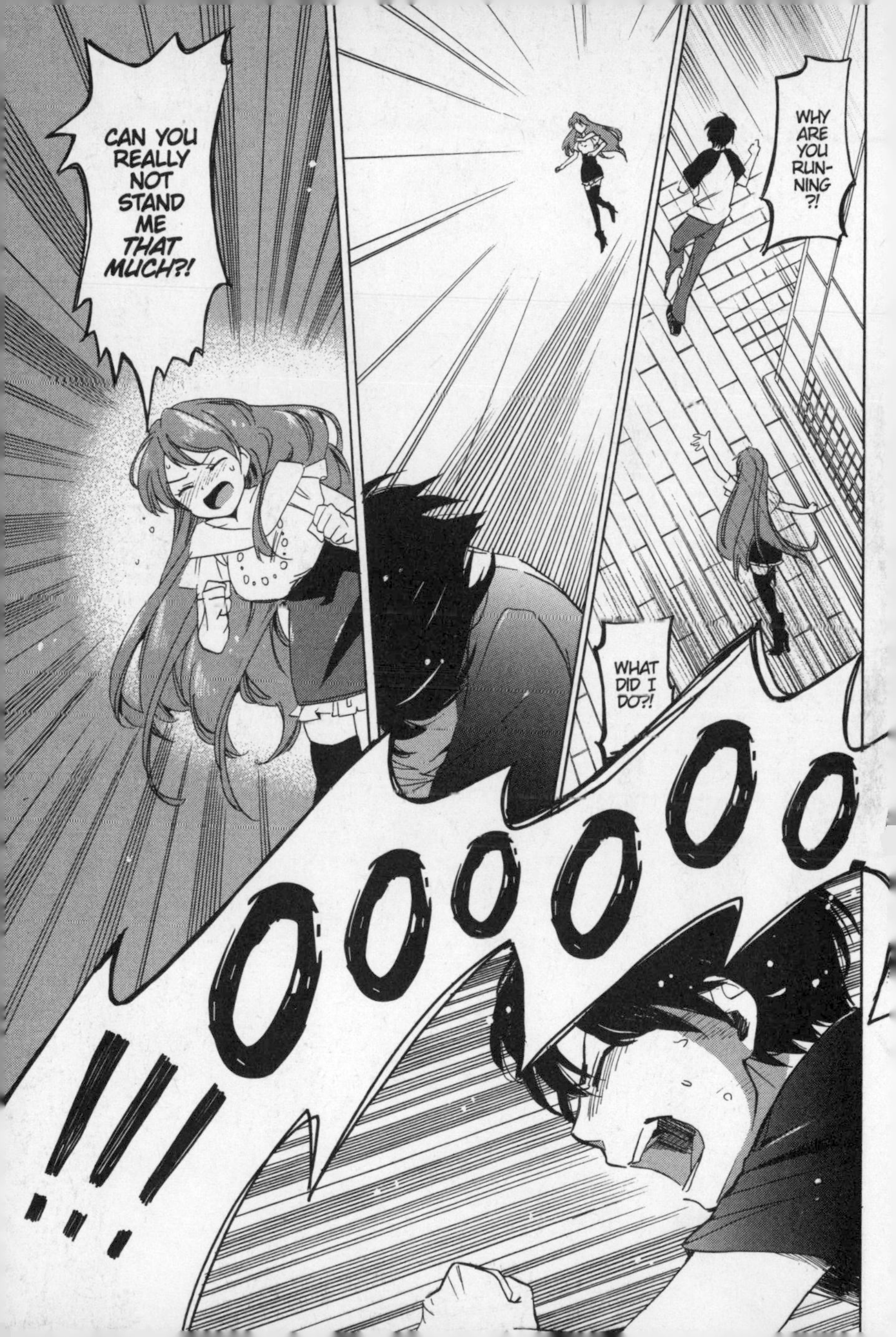
WHY ARE YOU RUN-NING?!
WHAT DID I DO?!
CAN YOU REALLY NOT STAND ME THAT MUCH?!
OOOOOOO!!!

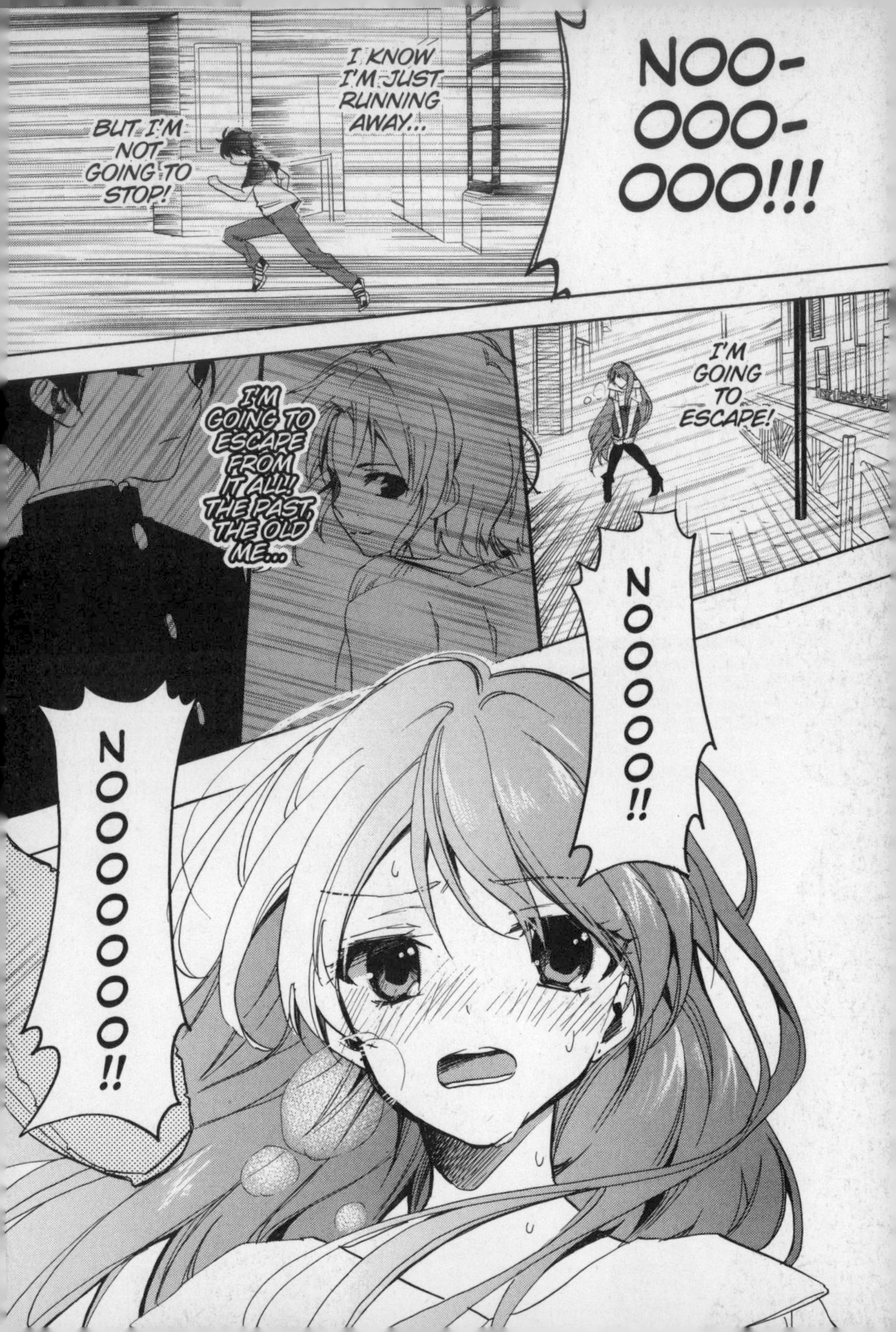
NOO-OOO-OOO!!!
I KNOW I'M JUST RUNNING AWAY...
BUT I'M NOT GOING TO STOP!
I'M GOING TO ESCAPE!
I'M GOING TO ESCAPE FROM IT ALL! THE PAST, THE OLD ME...
NOOOOOO!!
NOOOOOOOOO!!

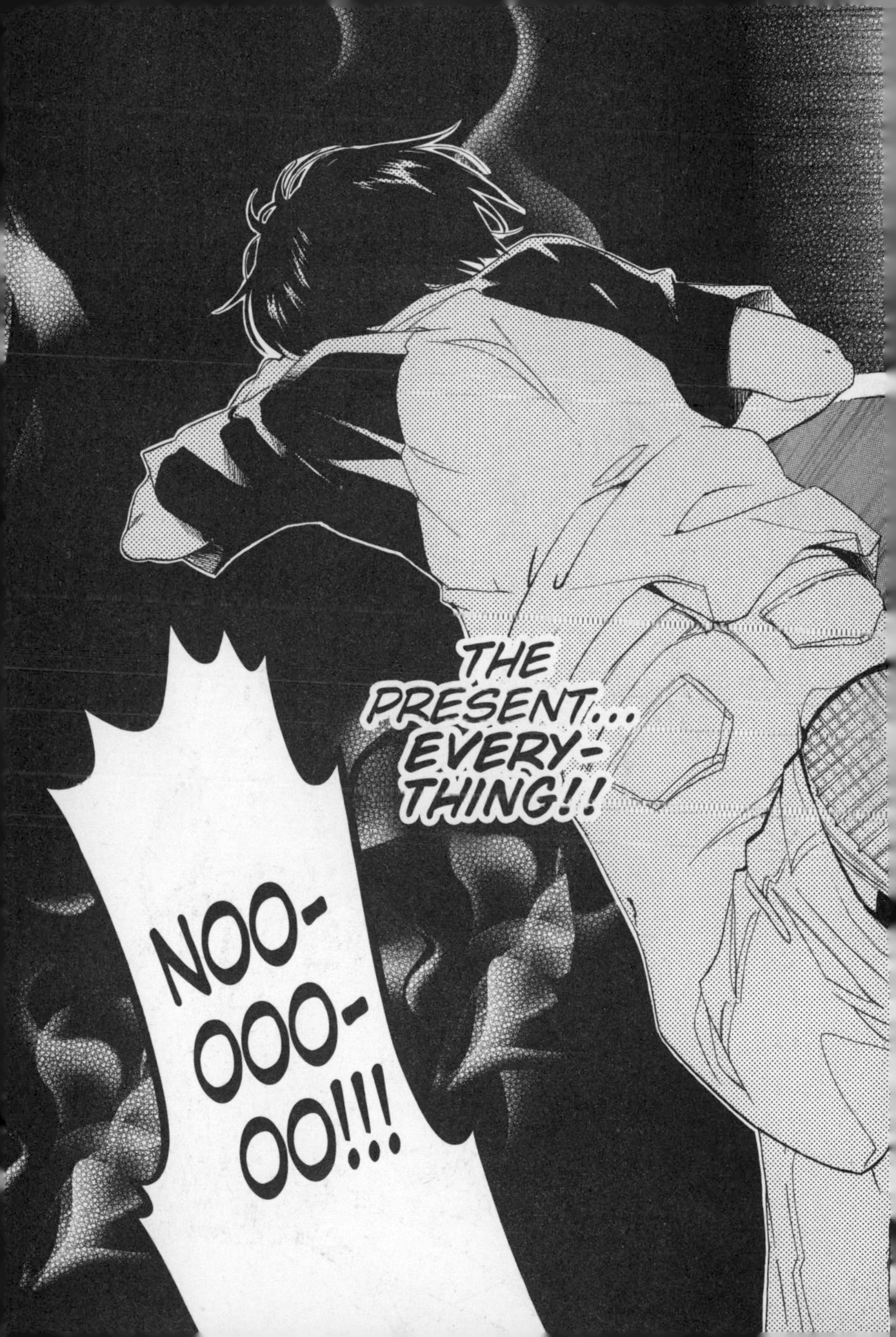
THE PRESENT... EVERY-THING!!
NOO-OOO-OO!!!

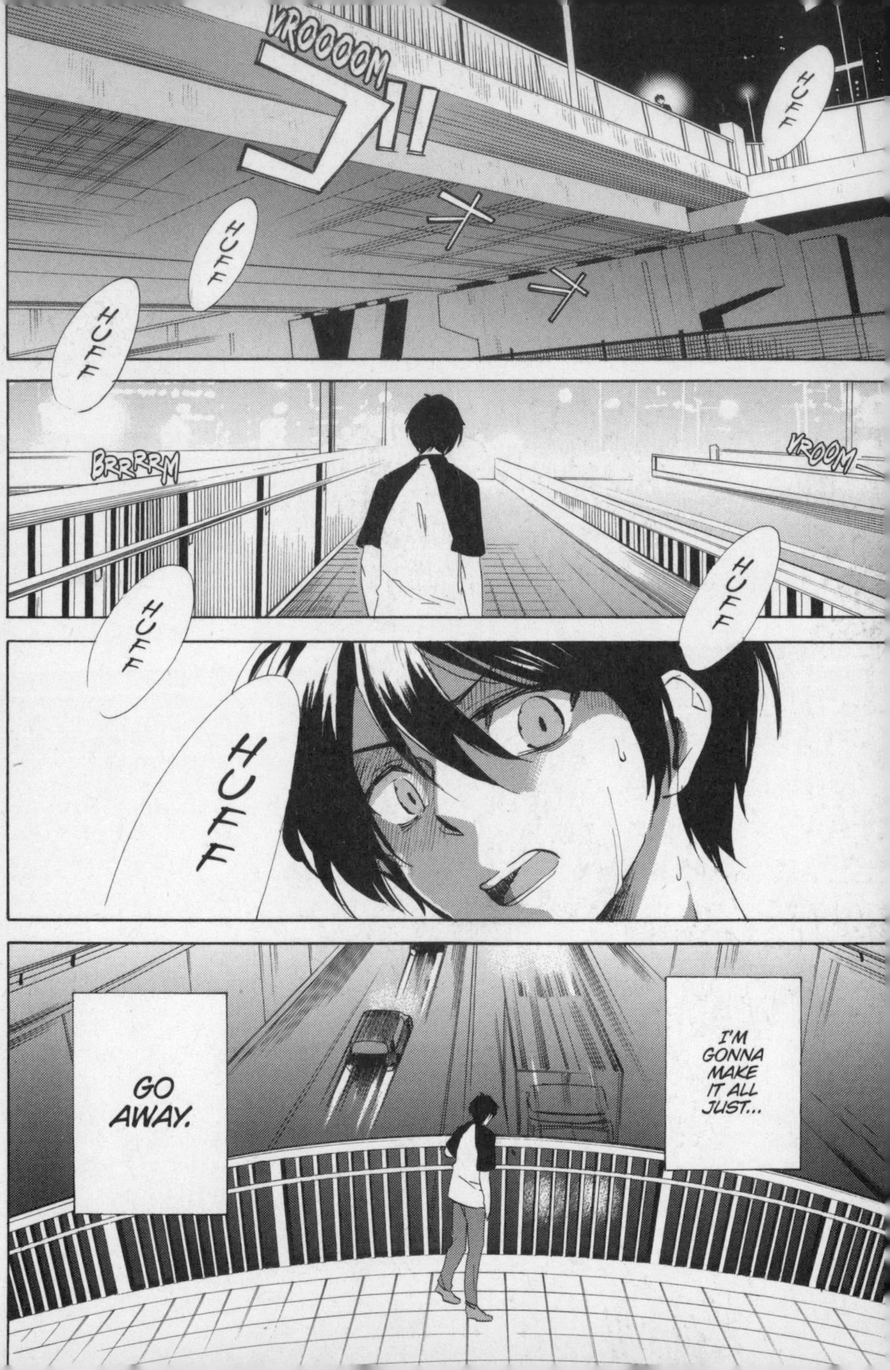
HUFF
VROOOOM
HUFF
HUFF
VROOM
HUFF
BRRRRM
HUFF
HUFF
I'M GONNA MAKE IT ALL JUST...
GO AWAY.

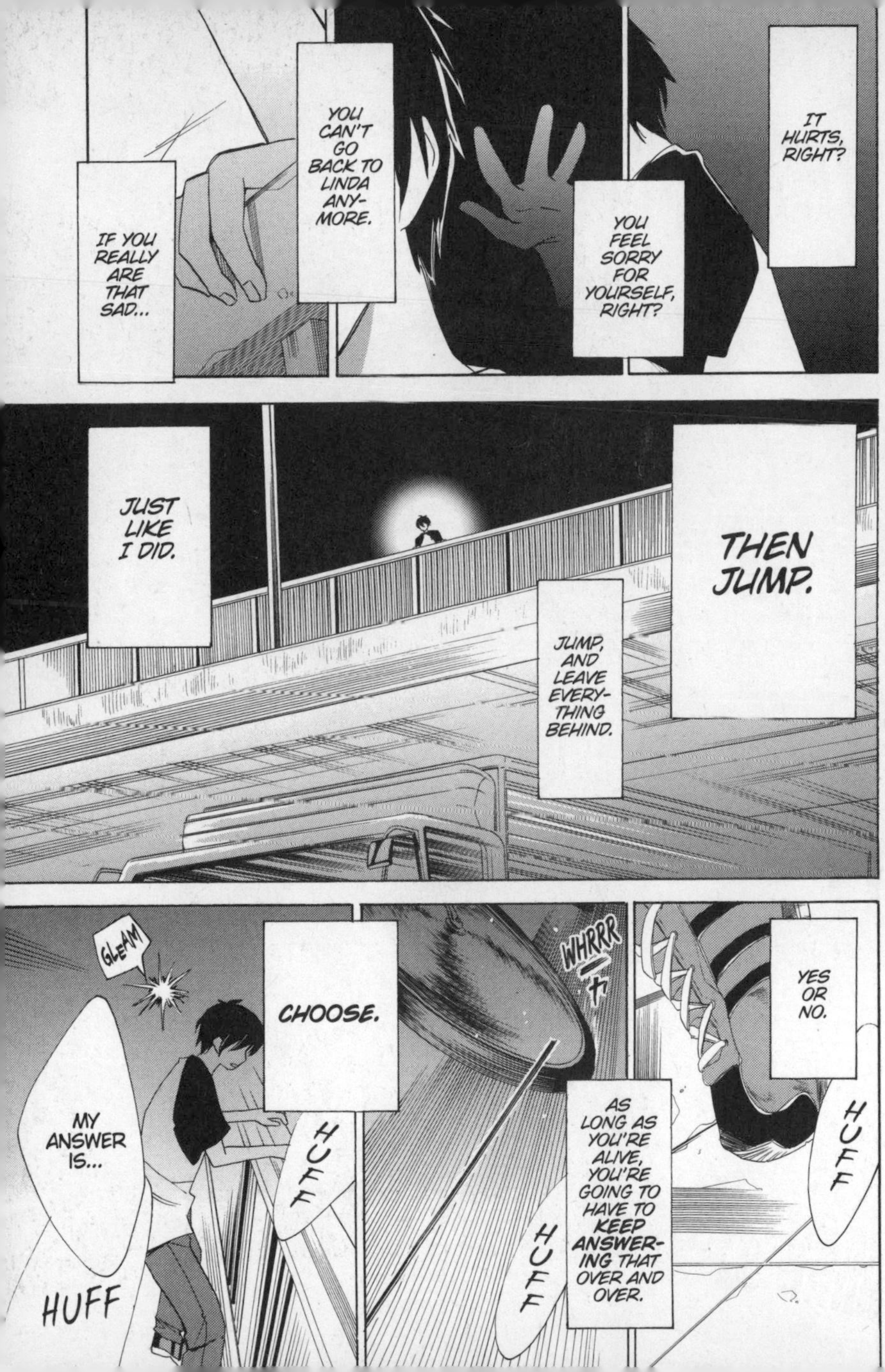

IT HURTS, RIGHT?
YOU FEEL SORRY FOR YOURSELF, RIGHT?
YOU CAN'T GO BACK TO LINDA ANYMORE.
IF YOU REALLY ARE THAT SAD...
THEN JUMP.
JUMP, AND LEAVE EVERYTHING BEHIND.
JUST LIKE I DID.
YES OR NO.
HUFF
AS LONG AS YOU'RE ALIVE, YOU'RE GOING TO HAVE TO KEEP ANSWERING THAT OVER AND OVER.
HUFF
WHRRR
CHOOSE.
HUFF
GLEAM
MY ANSWER IS...
HUFF

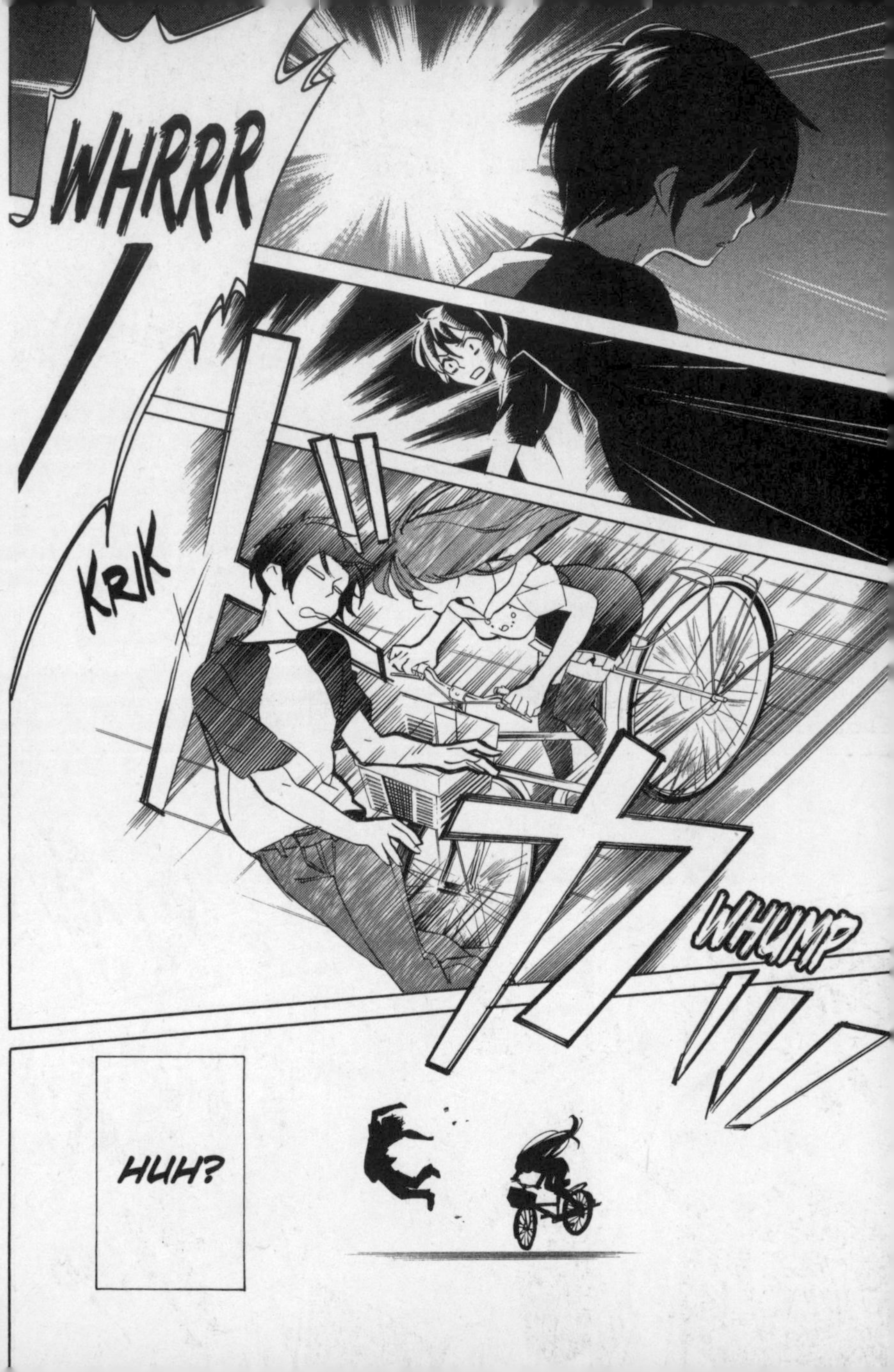
WHRRR
KRIK
WHUMP
HUH?

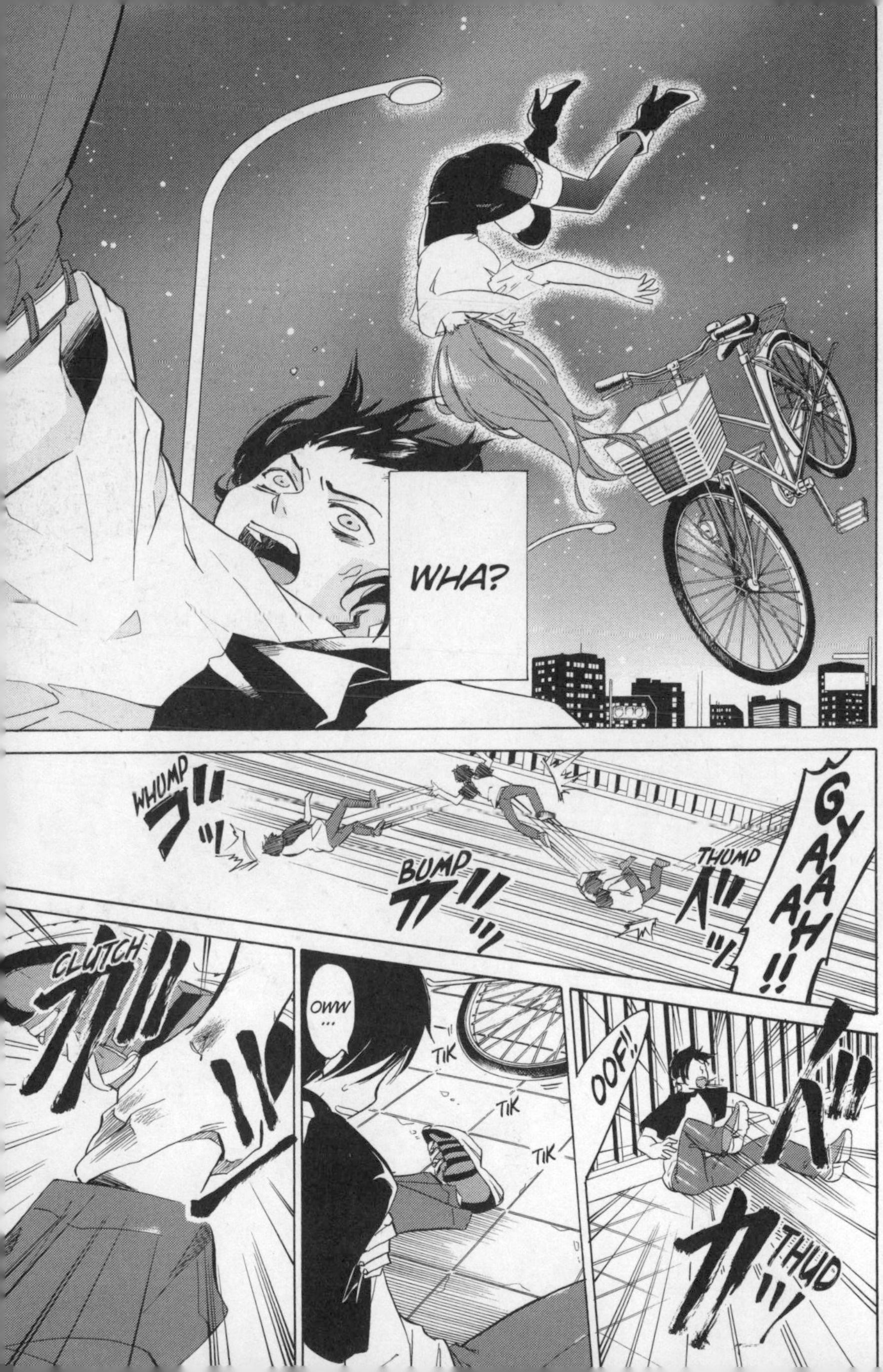
WHA?
GYAAAH!!
THUMP
WHUMP
BUMP
OOF!!
THUD
OWW ...
TIK
TIK
TIK
CLUTCH

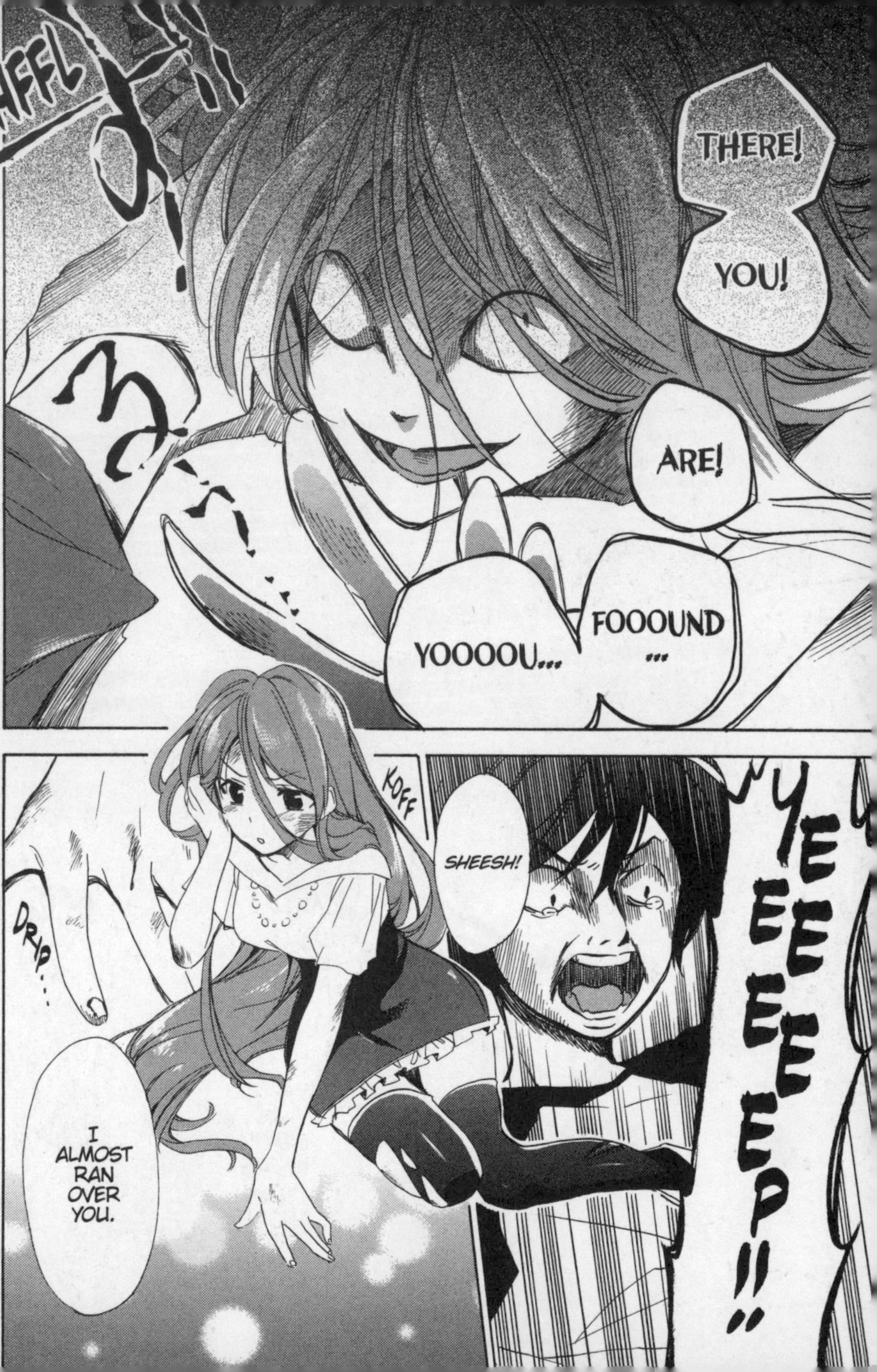

THERE! YOU!
ARE!
FOOOUND...
YOOOOU...
SHFFL
YEEEEEEP!!
SHEESH!
KOFF
DRIP...
I ALMOST RAN OVER YOU.

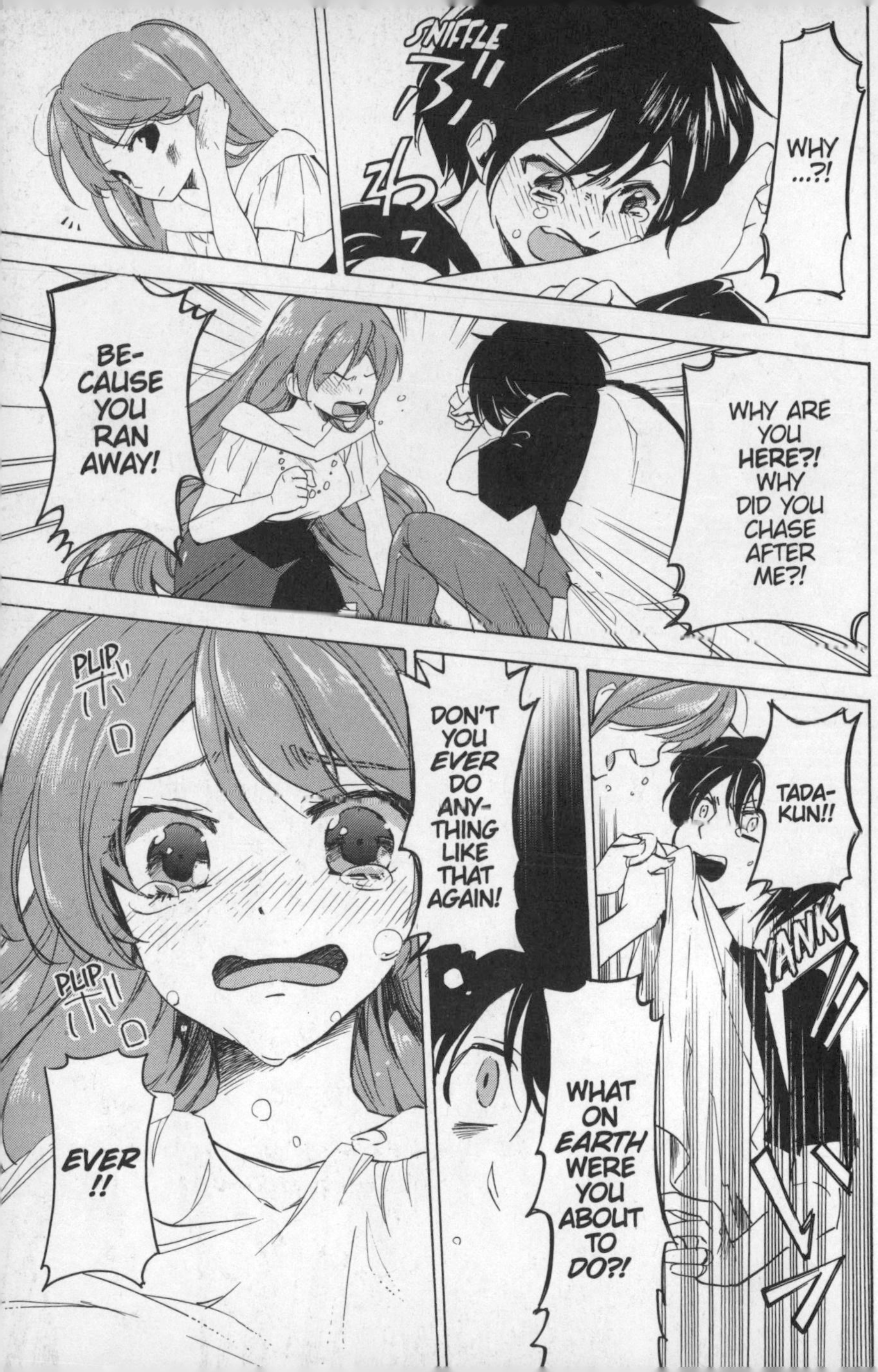
SNIFFLE
WHY ...?!
WHY ARE YOU HERE?! WHY DID YOU CHASE AFTER ME?!
BE-CAUSE YOU RAN AWAY!
TADA-KUN!!
YANK
WHAT ON EARTH WERE YOU ABOUT TO DO?!
PLIP
PLIP
DON'T YOU EVER DO ANY-THING LIKE THAT AGAIN!
EVER!!

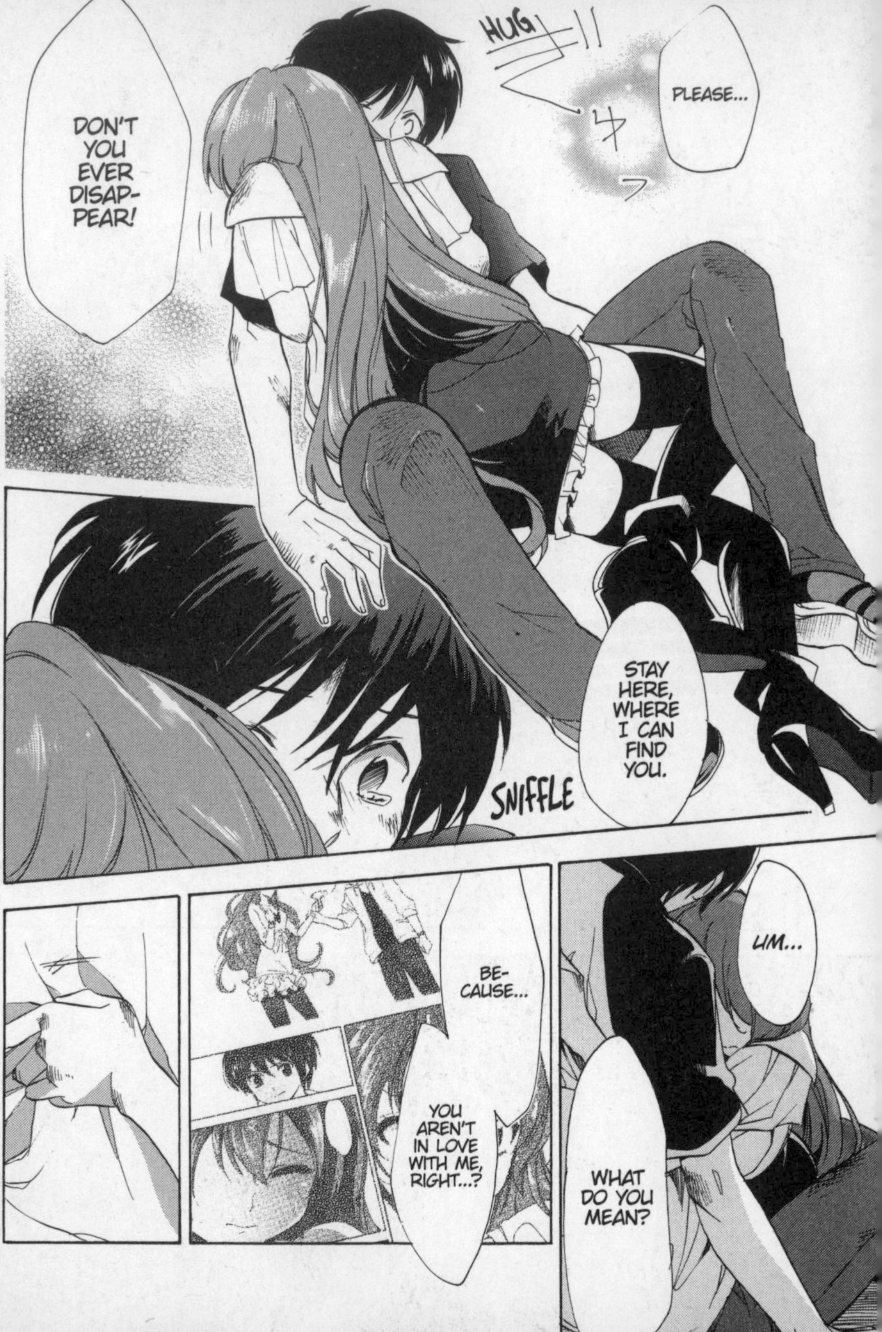
HUG
PLEASE...
DON'T YOU EVER DISAP-PEAR!
STAY HERE, WHERE I CAN FIND YOU.
SNIFFLE
UM...
WHAT DO YOU MEAN?
BE-CAUSE...
YOU AREN'T IN LOVE WITH ME, RIGHT...?

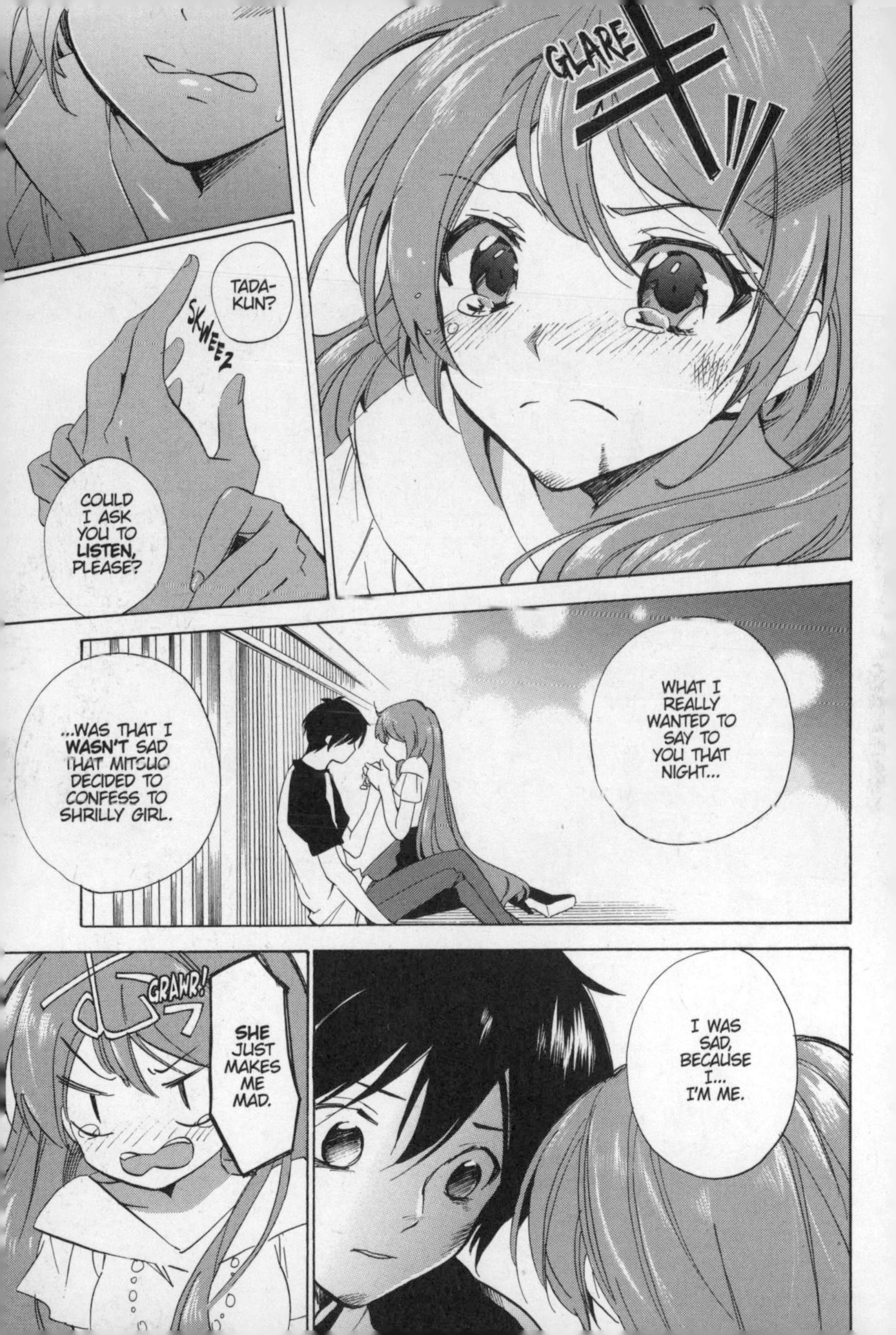
GLARE
TADA-KUN?
SKWEEZ
COULD I ASK YOU TO **LISTEN,** PLEASE?
WHAT I REALLY WANTED TO SAY TO YOU THAT NIGHT...
...WAS THAT I **WASN'T** SAD THAT MITSUO DECIDED TO CONFESS TO SHRILLY GIRL.
I WAS SAD, BECAUSE I... I'M ME.
GRAWR!
SHE JUST MAKES ME MAD.

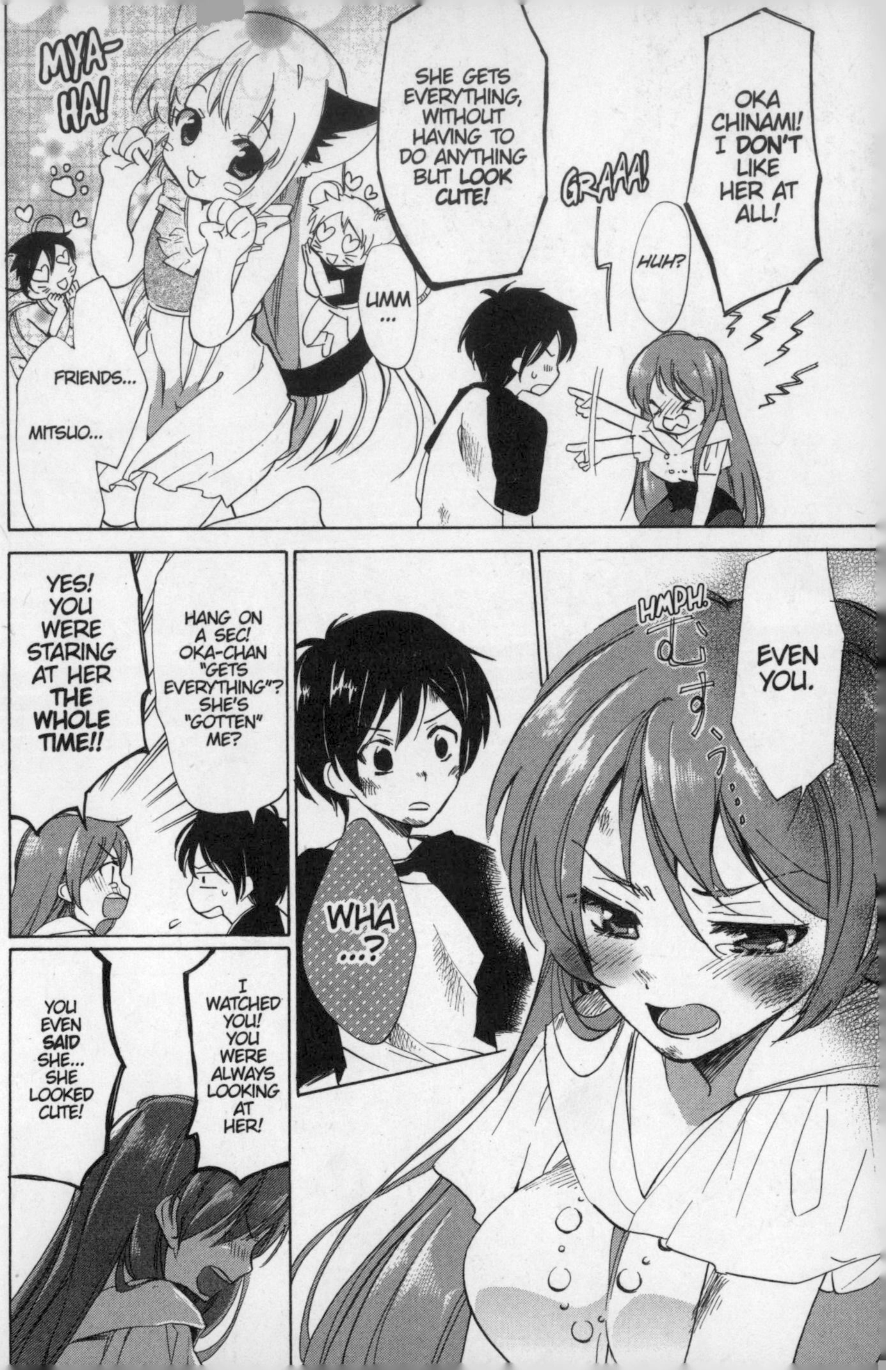
OKA CHINAMI! I DON'T LIKE HER AT ALL!
GRAAA!
HUH?
SHE GETS EVERYTHING, WITHOUT HAVING TO DO ANYTHING BUT LOOK CUTE!
UMM ...
MYA-HA!
FRIENDS...
MITSUO...
HMPH.
むすぅ...
EVEN YOU.
HANG ON A SEC! OKA-CHAN "GETS EVERYTHING"? SHE'S "GOTTEN" ME?
WHA ...?
YES! YOU WERE STARING AT HER THE WHOLE TIME!!
I WATCHED YOU! YOU WERE ALWAYS LOOKING AT HER!
YOU EVEN SAID SHE... SHE LOOKED CUTE!

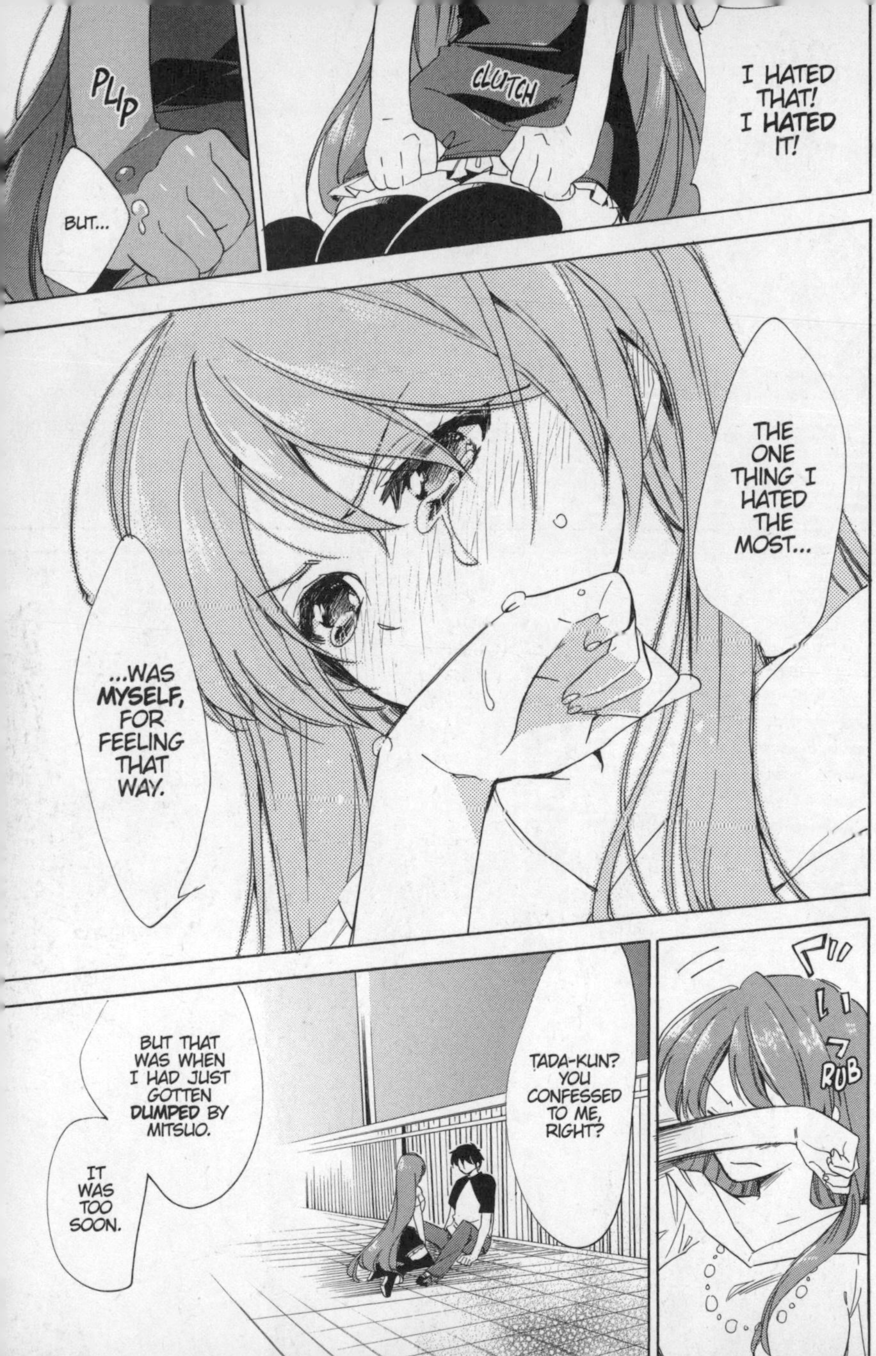
I HATED THAT! I HATED IT!
CLUTCH
PLIP
BUT...
THE ONE THING I HATED THE MOST...
...WAS MYSELF, FOR FEELING THAT WAY.
RUB
TADA-KUN? YOU CONFESSED TO ME, RIGHT?
BUT THAT WAS WHEN I HAD JUST GOTTEN DUMPED BY MITSUO.
IT WAS TOO SOON.

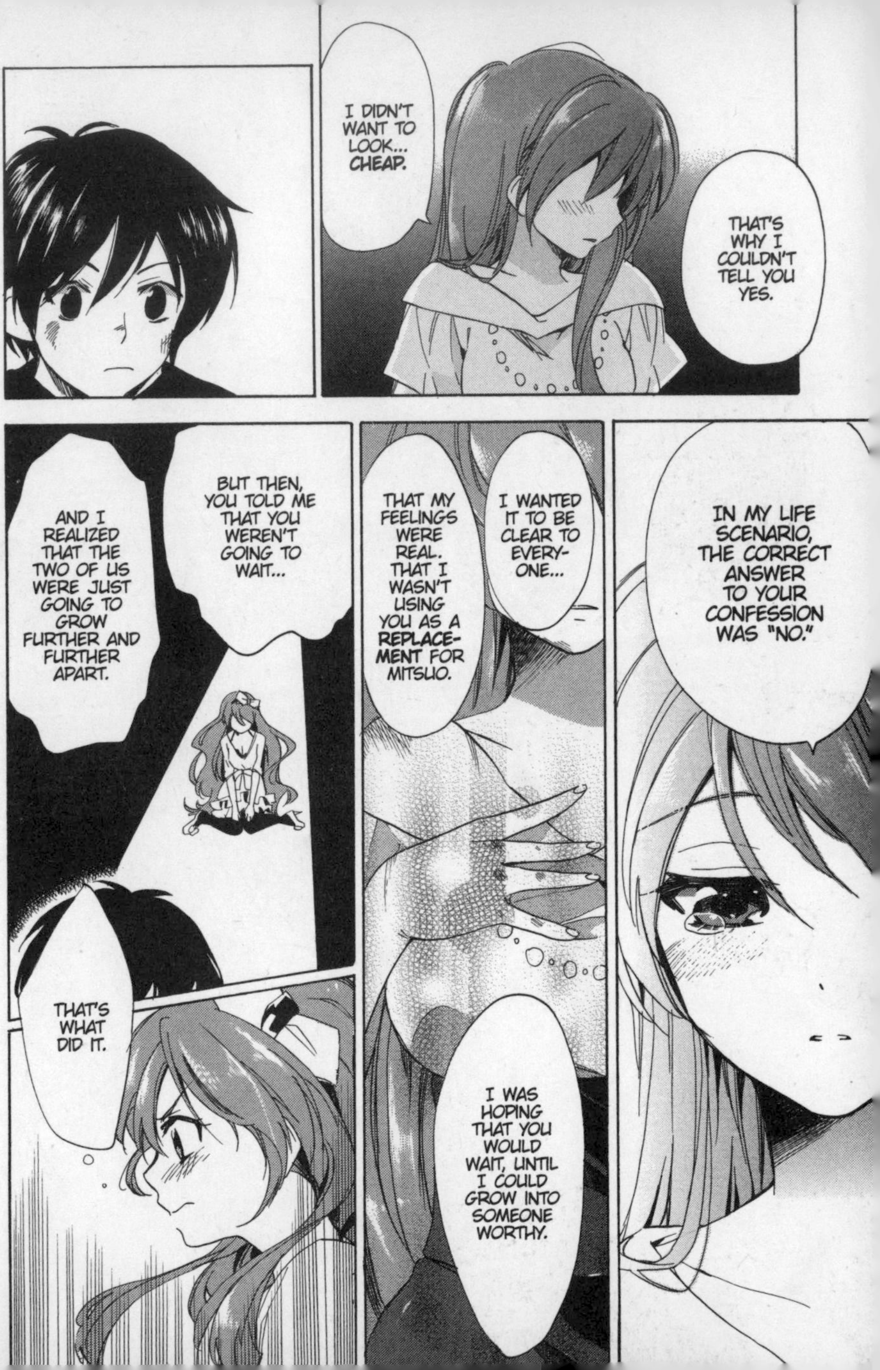
I DIDN'T WANT TO LOOK... CHEAP.
THAT'S WHY I COULDN'T TELL YOU YES.
IN MY LIFE SCENARIO, THE CORRECT ANSWER TO YOUR CONFESSION WAS "NO."
I WANTED IT TO BE CLEAR TO EVERY-ONE...
THAT MY FEELINGS WERE REAL. THAT I WASN'T USING YOU AS A REPLACE-MENT FOR MITSUO.
I WAS HOPING THAT YOU WOULD WAIT, UNTIL I COULD GROW INTO SOMEONE WORTHY.
BUT THEN, YOU TOLD ME THAT YOU WEREN'T GOING TO WAIT...
AND I REALIZED THAT THE TWO OF US WERE JUST GOING TO GROW FURTHER AND FURTHER APART.
THAT'S WHAT DID IT.

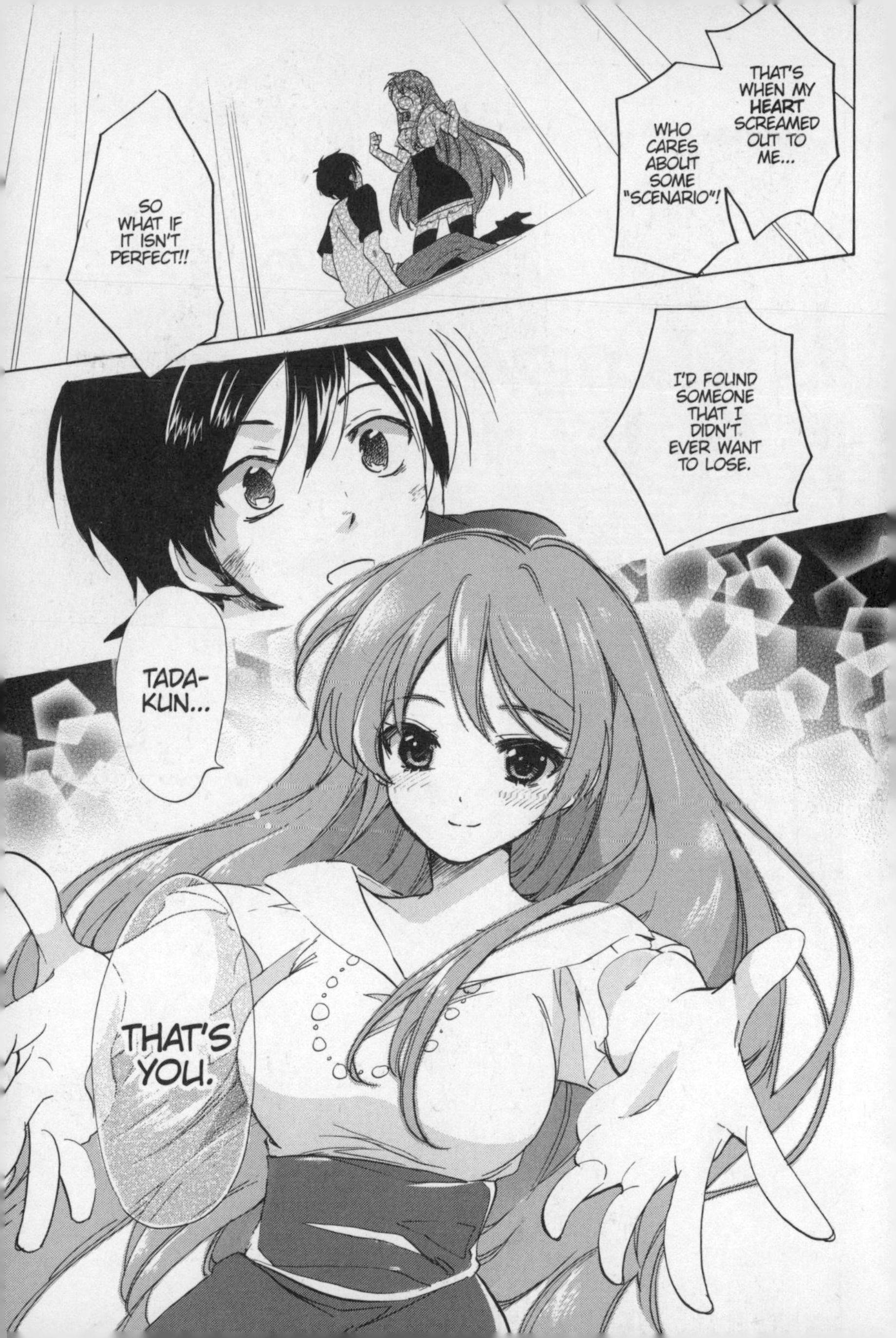
THAT'S WHEN MY HEART SCREAMED OUT TO ME...
WHO CARES ABOUT SOME "SCENARIO"!
SO WHAT IF IT ISN'T PERFECT!!
I'D FOUND SOMEONE THAT I DIDN'T EVER WANT TO LOSE.
TADA-KUN...
THAT'S YOU.

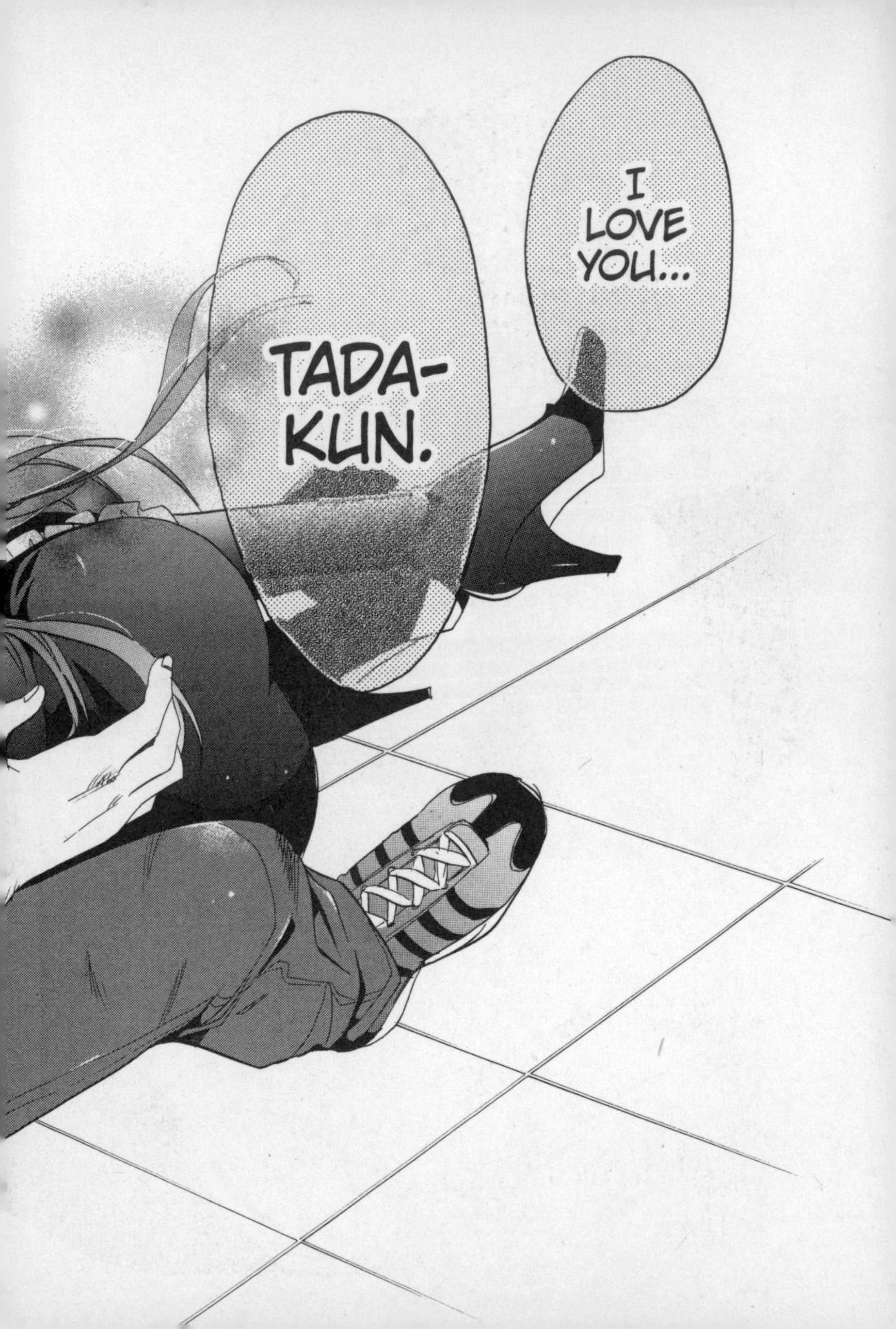
I LOVE YOU...
TADA-KUN.

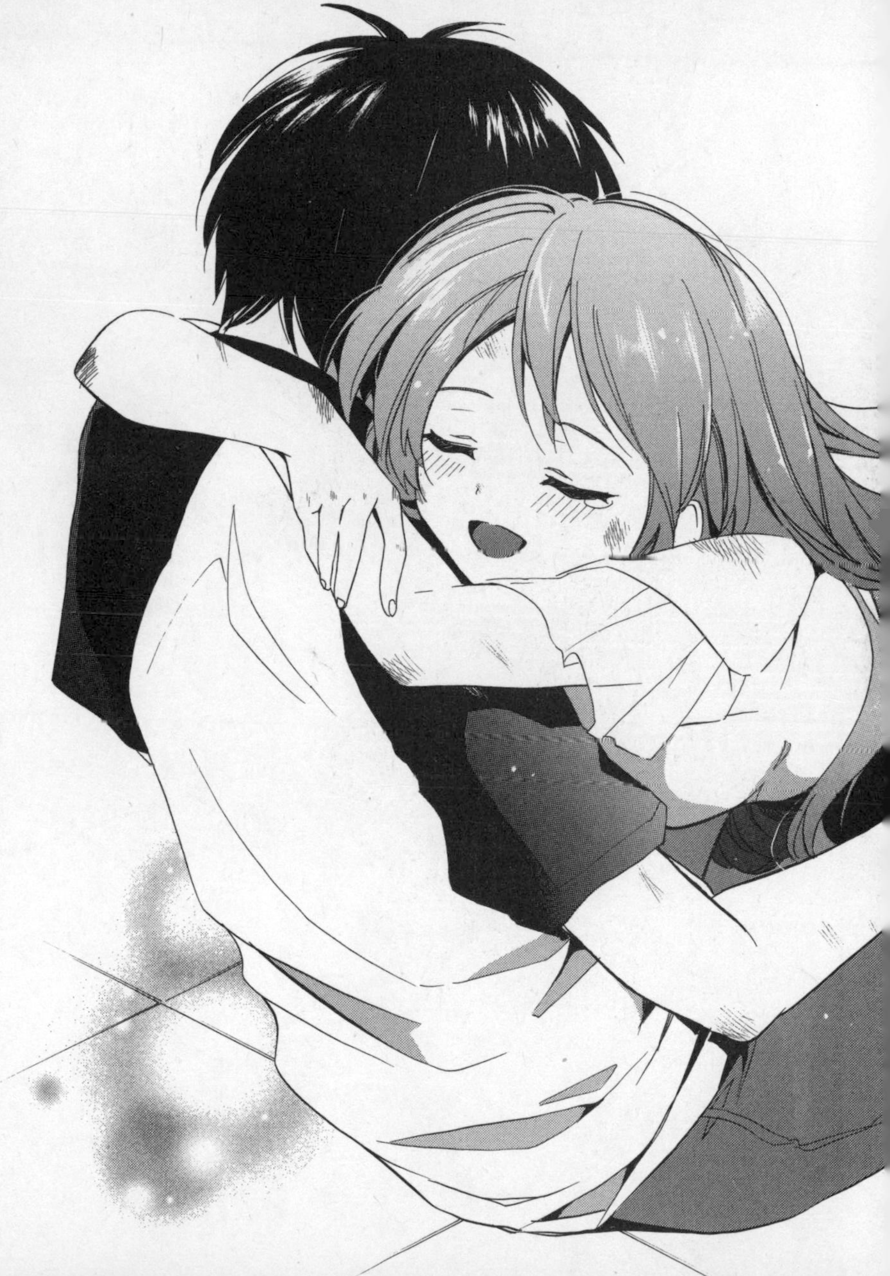

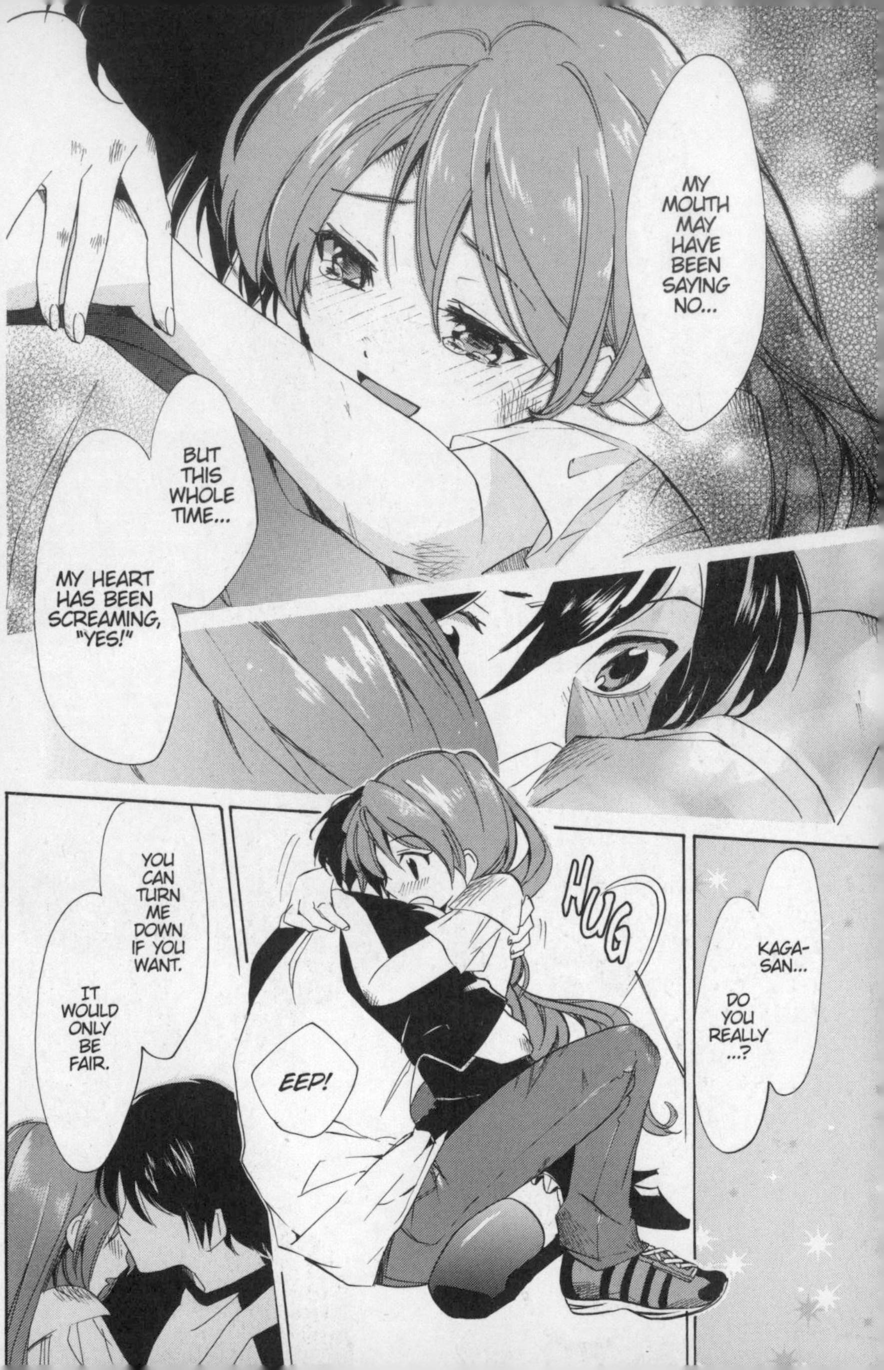
MY MOUTH MAY HAVE BEEN SAYING NO...
BUT THIS WHOLE TIME...
MY HEART HAS BEEN SCREAMING, "YES!"
KAGA-SAN...
DO YOU REALLY ...?
HUG
EEP!
YOU CAN TURN ME DOWN IF YOU WANT.
IT WOULD ONLY BE FAIR.

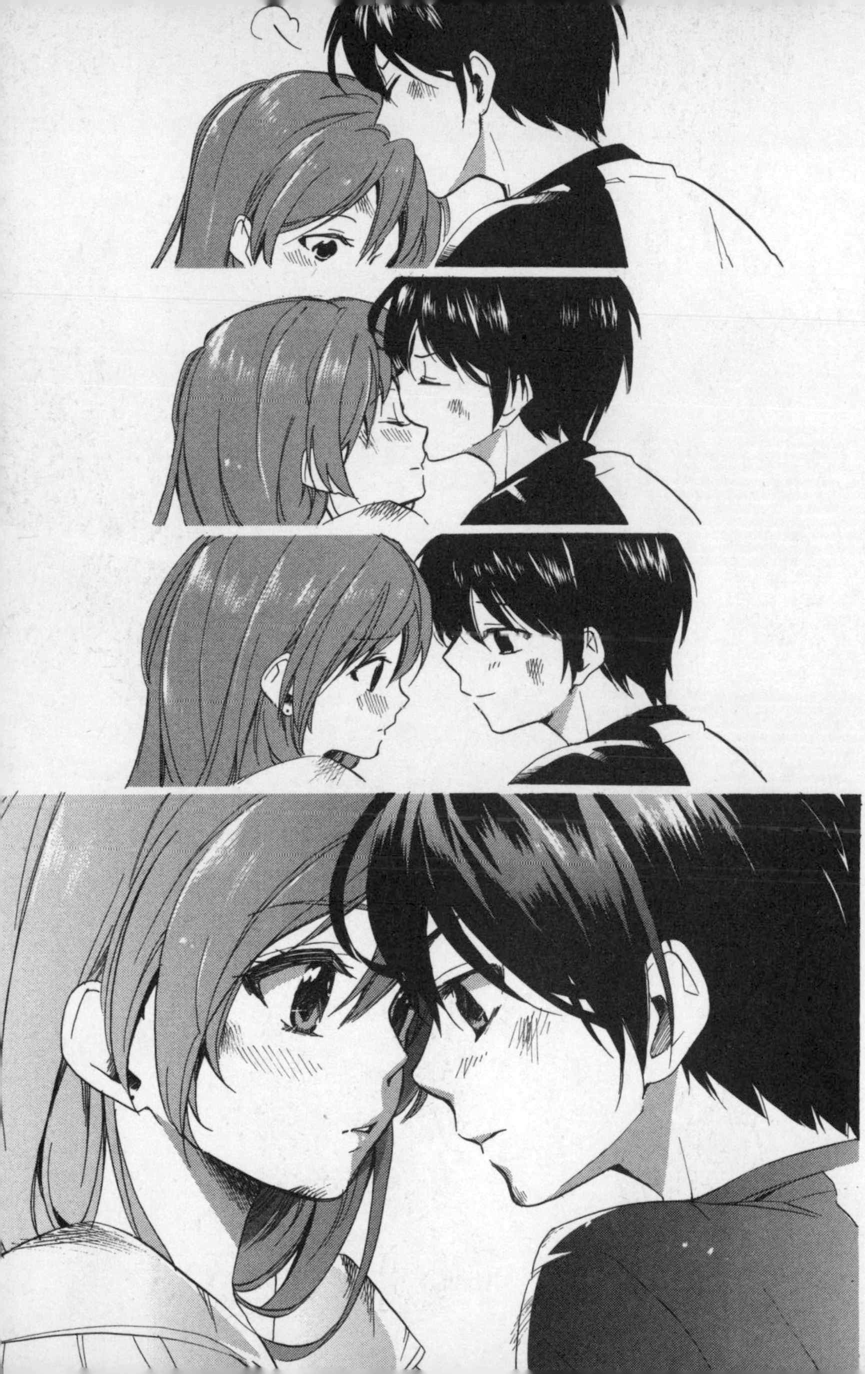

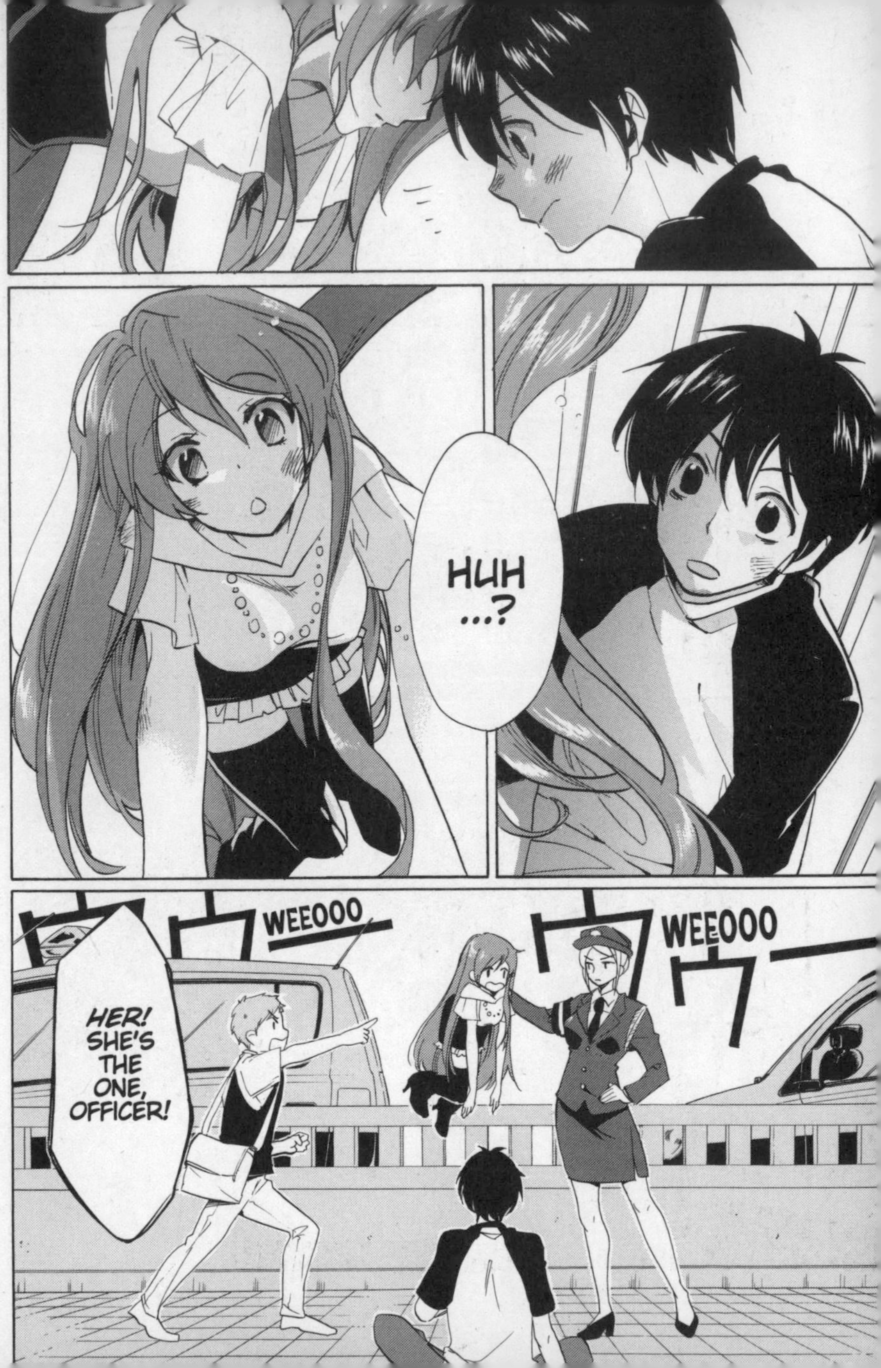
HUH ...?
WEEOOO
WEEOOO
HER! SHE'S THE ONE, OFFICER!

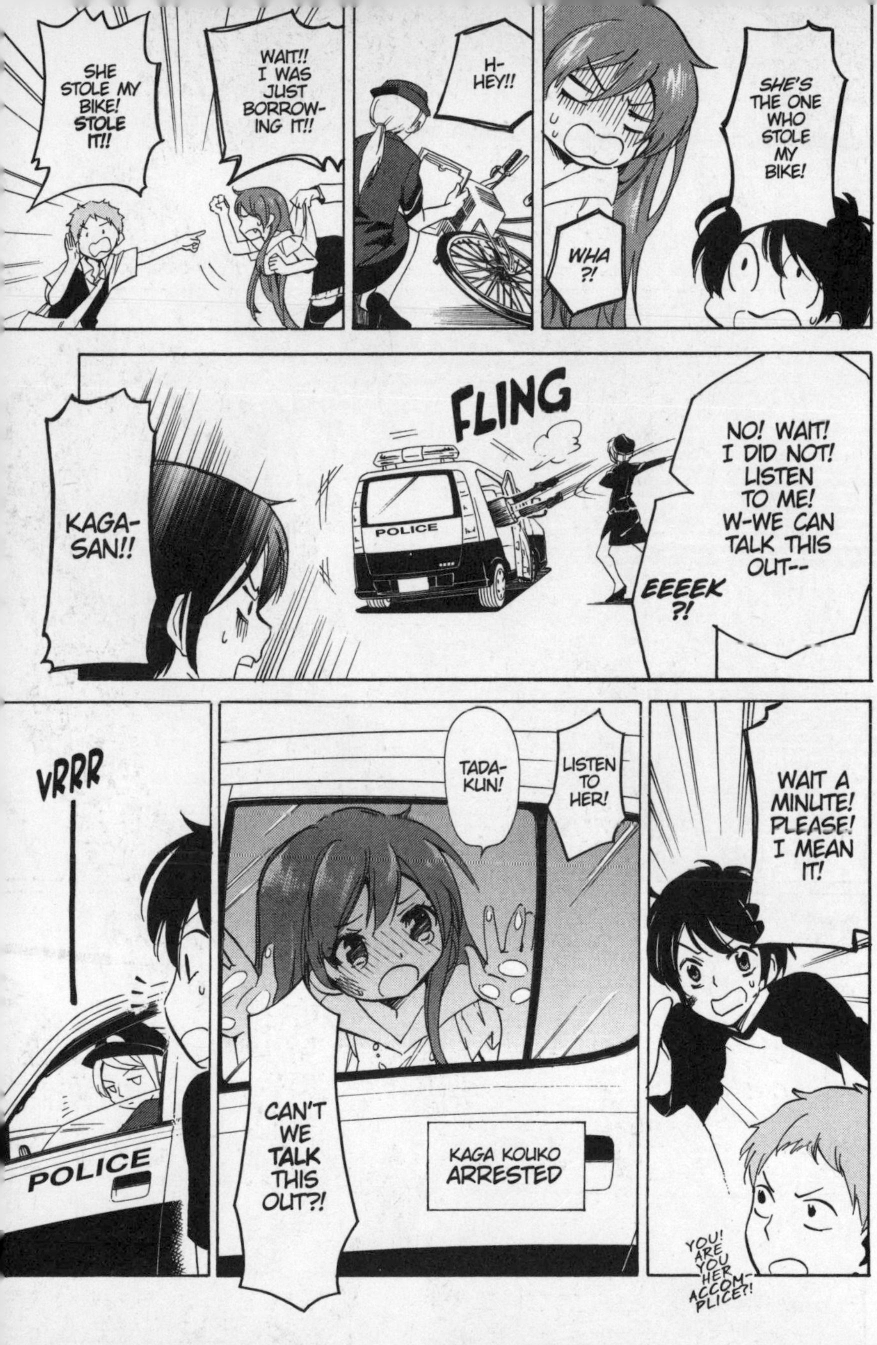

SHE'S THE ONE WHO STOLE MY BIKE!
WHA?!
H-HEY!!
WAIT!! I WAS JUST BORROWING IT!!
SHE STOLE MY BIKE! STOLE IT!!
NO! WAIT! I DID NOT! LISTEN TO ME! W-WE CAN TALK THIS OUT--
FLING
EEEEK?!
KAGA-SAN!!
WAIT A MINUTE! PLEASE! I MEAN IT!
YOU! ARE YOU HER ACCOMPLICE?!
LISTEN TO HER!
TADA-KUN!
CAN'T WE TALK THIS OUT?!
KAGA KOUKO ARRESTED
VRRR
POLICE

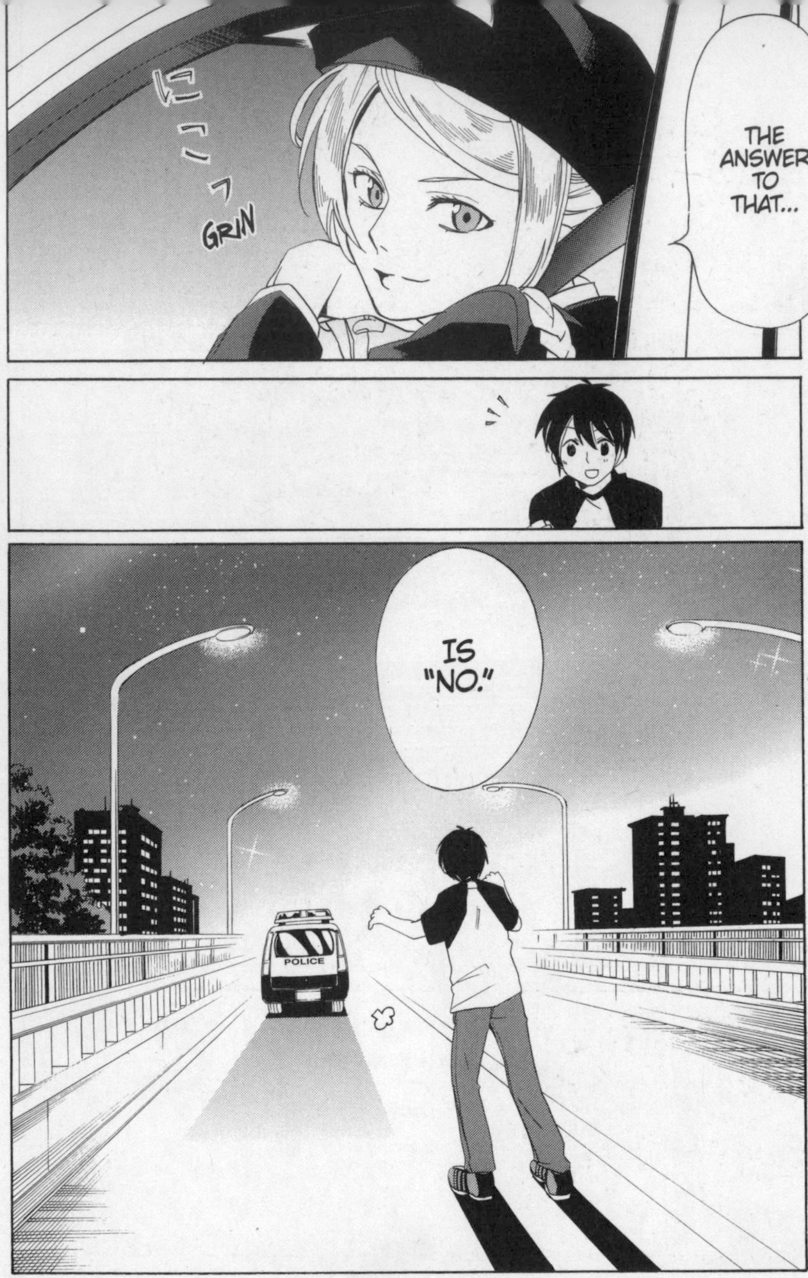
THE ANSWER TO THAT...
にこっ
GRIN
IS "NO."
POLICE

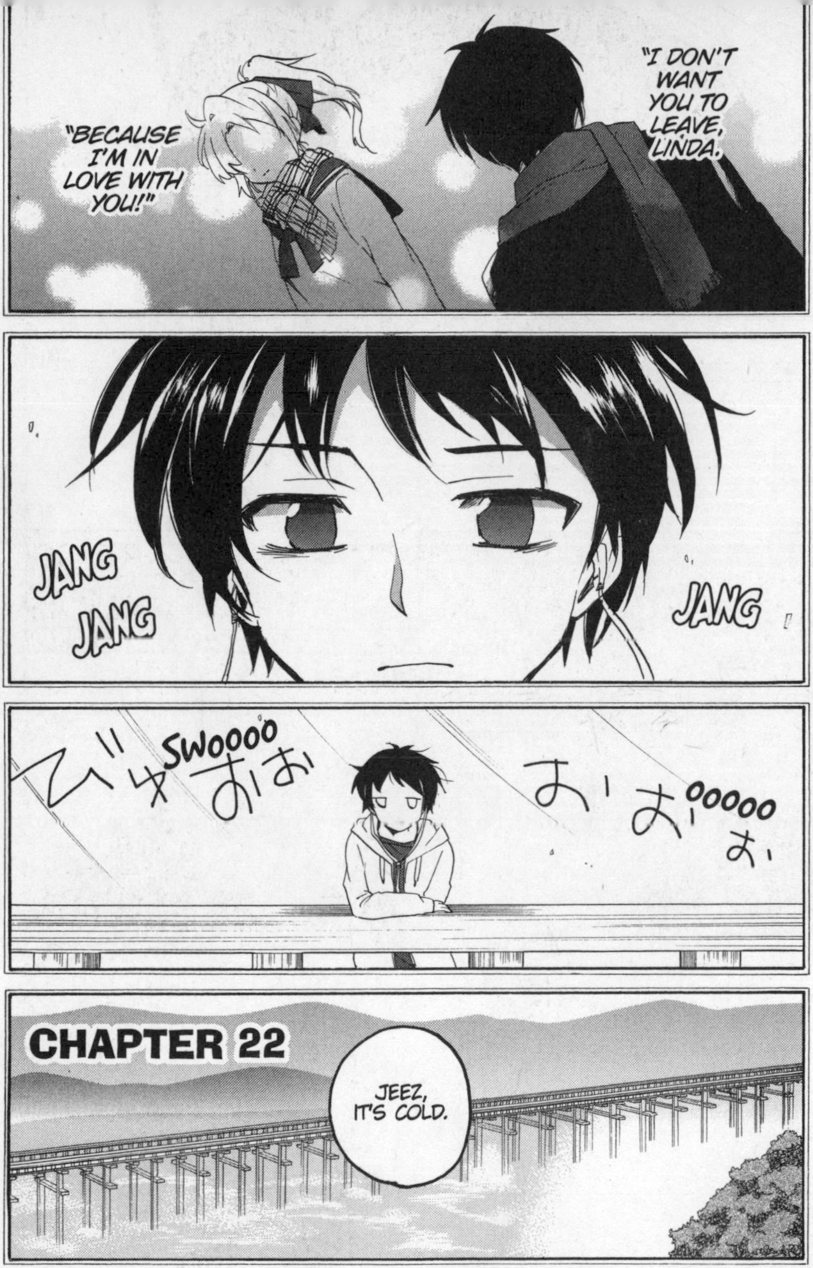
"I DON'T WANT YOU TO LEAVE, LINDA.
"BECAUSE I'M IN LOVE WITH YOU!"
JANG
JANG JANG
SWOOOO
OOOOO
CHAPTER 22
JEEZ, IT'S COLD.

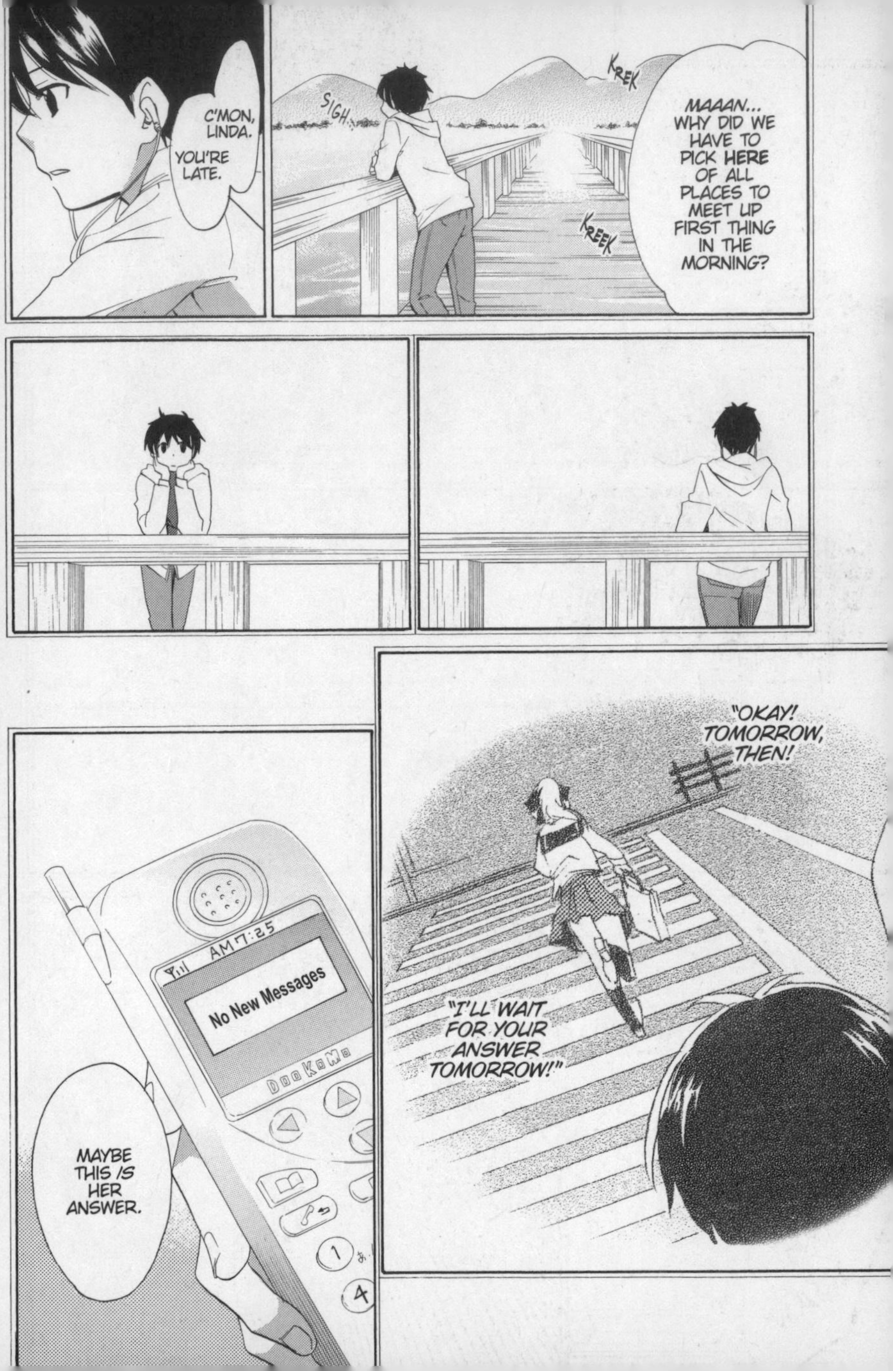
MAAAN... WHY DID WE HAVE TO PICK HERE OF ALL PLACES TO MEET UP FIRST THING IN THE MORNING?
KREK
SIGH
KREEK
C'MON, LINDA.
YOU'RE LATE.
"OKAY! TOMORROW, THEN!
"I'LL WAIT FOR YOUR ANSWER TOMORROW!"
AM7:25
No New Messages
DooKoMo
MAYBE THIS IS HER ANSWER.

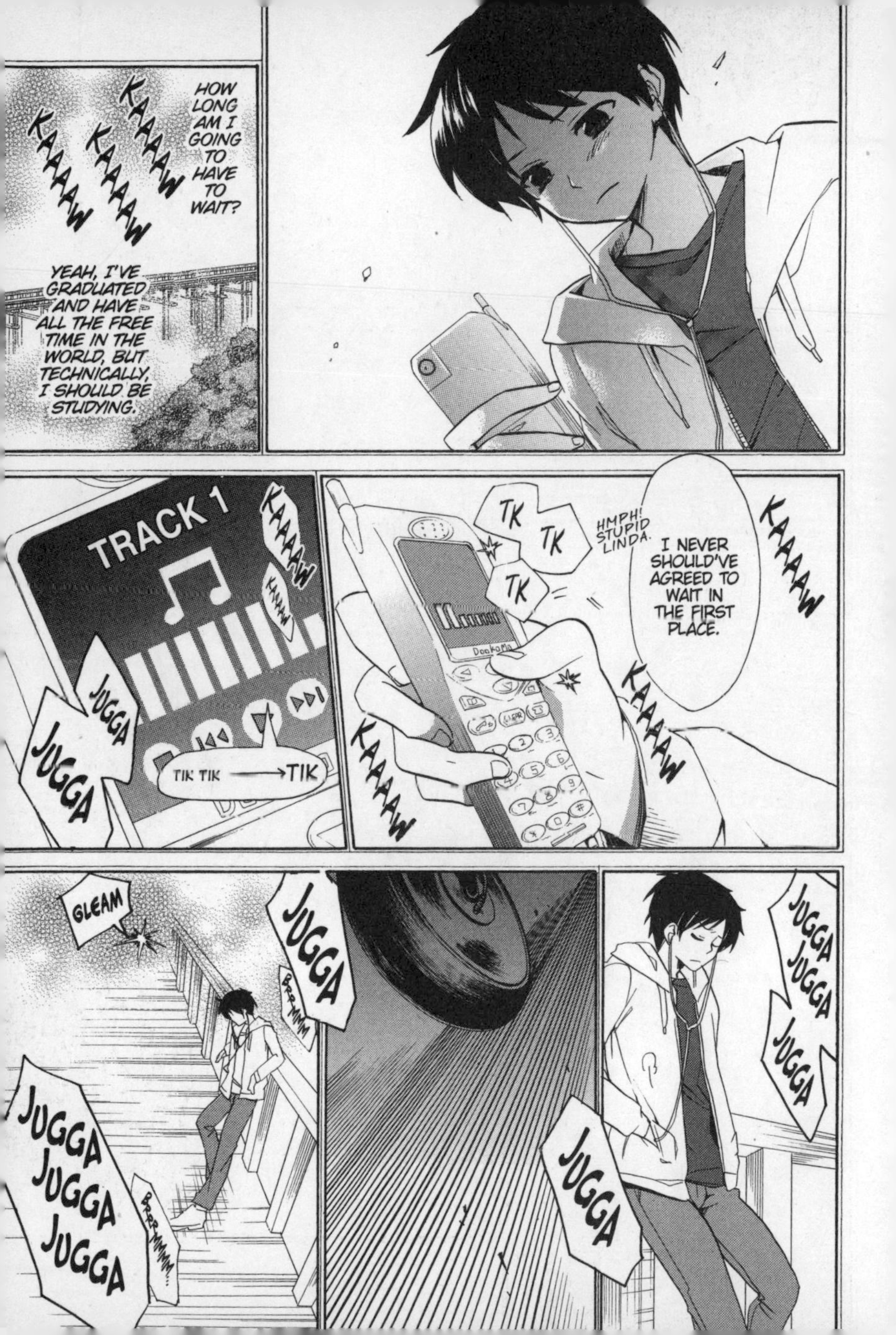
HOW LONG AM I GOING TO HAVE TO WAIT?
KAAAAAW
KAAAAAW
KAAAAAW
YEAH, I'VE GRADUATED AND HAVE ALL THE FREE TIME IN THE WORLD, BUT TECHNICALLY, I SHOULD BE STUDYING.
KAAAAAW
I NEVER SHOULD'VE AGREED TO WAIT IN THE FIRST PLACE.
HMPH! STUPID LINDA.
TK
TK
TK
KAAAAAW
KAAAAAW
TRACK 1
KAAAAAW
KAAAAW
JUGGA
JUGGA
JUGGA
TIK TIK ⟶ TIK
JUGGA JUGGA JUGGA
JUGGA
JUGGA
JUGGA
BRR-MMM
GLEAM
JUGGA JUGGA JUGGA
BRRR-MMM...

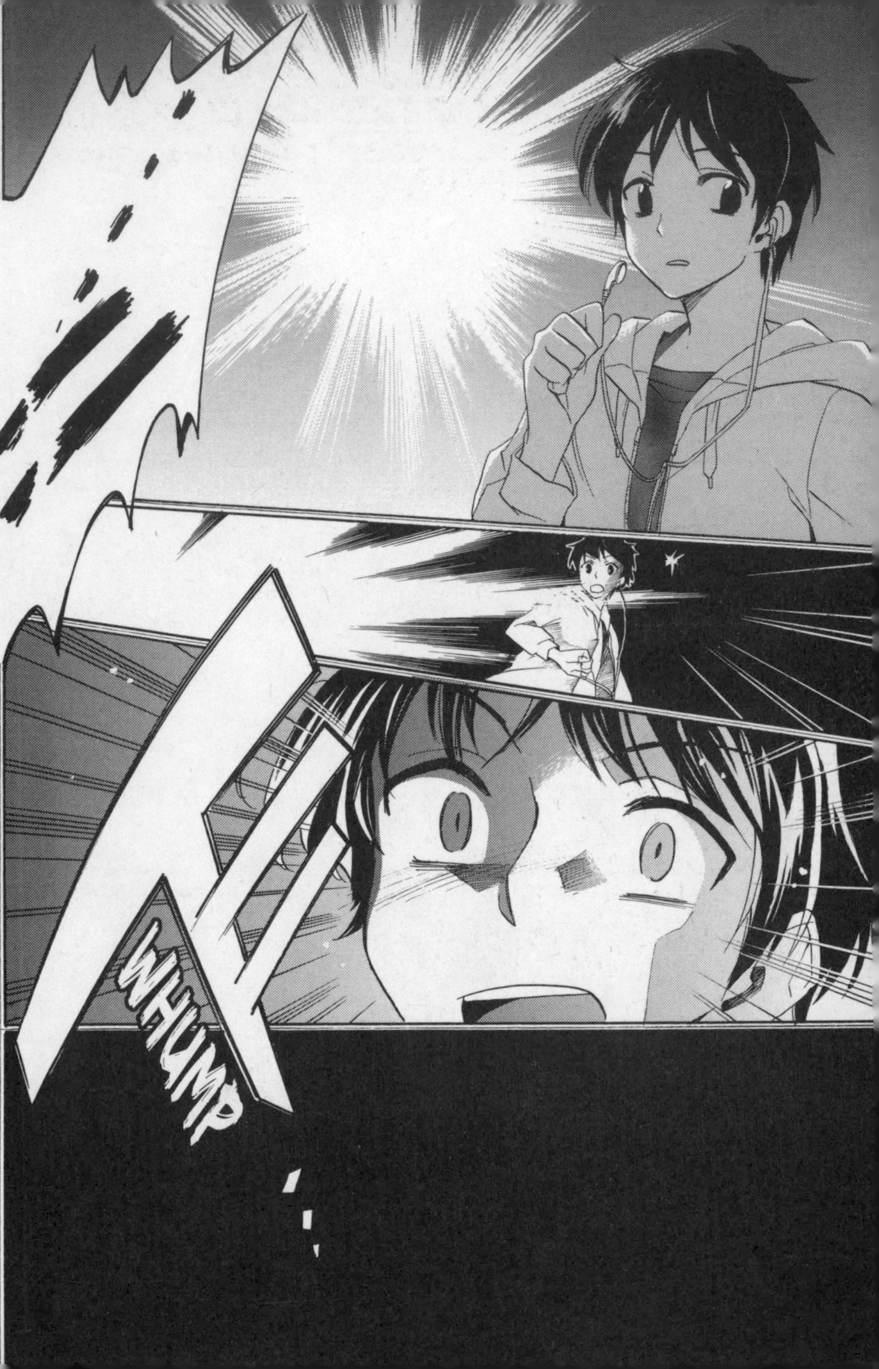
WHUMP

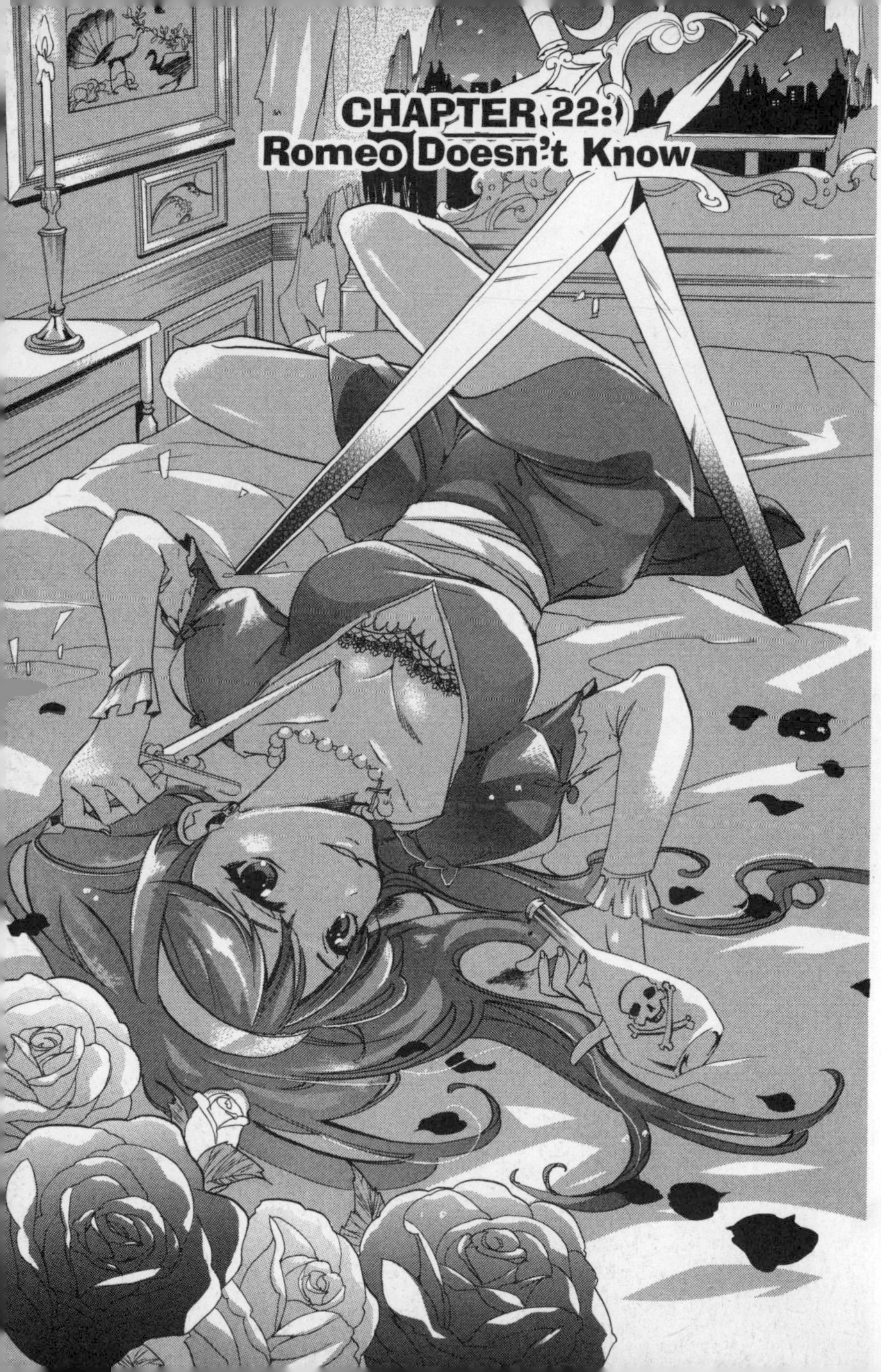
CHAPTER 22:
Romeo Doesn't Know

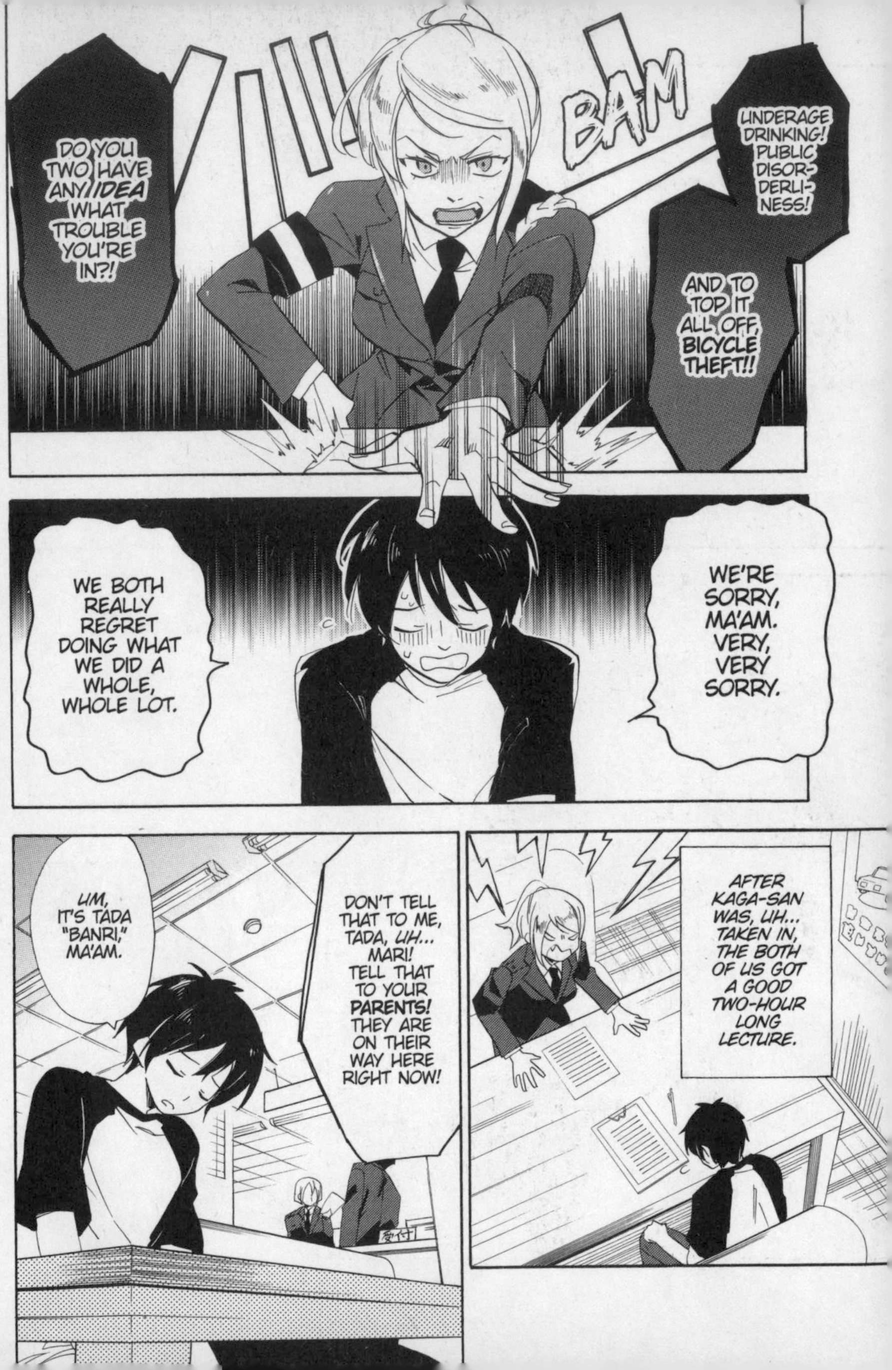
BAM
UNDERAGE DRINKING! PUBLIC DISORDERLINESS!
DO YOU TWO HAVE ANY IDEA WHAT TROUBLE YOU'RE IN?!
AND TO TOP IT ALL OFF, BICYCLE THEFT!!
WE'RE SORRY, MA'AM. VERY, VERY SORRY.
WE BOTH REALLY REGRET DOING WHAT WE DID A WHOLE, WHOLE LOT.
AFTER KAGA-SAN WAS, UH... TAKEN IN, THE BOTH OF US GOT A GOOD TWO-HOUR LONG LECTURE.
UM, IT'S TADA "BANRI," MA'AM.
DON'T TELL THAT TO ME, TADA, UH... MARI! TELL THAT TO YOUR PARENTS! THEY ARE ON THEIR WAY HERE RIGHT NOW!

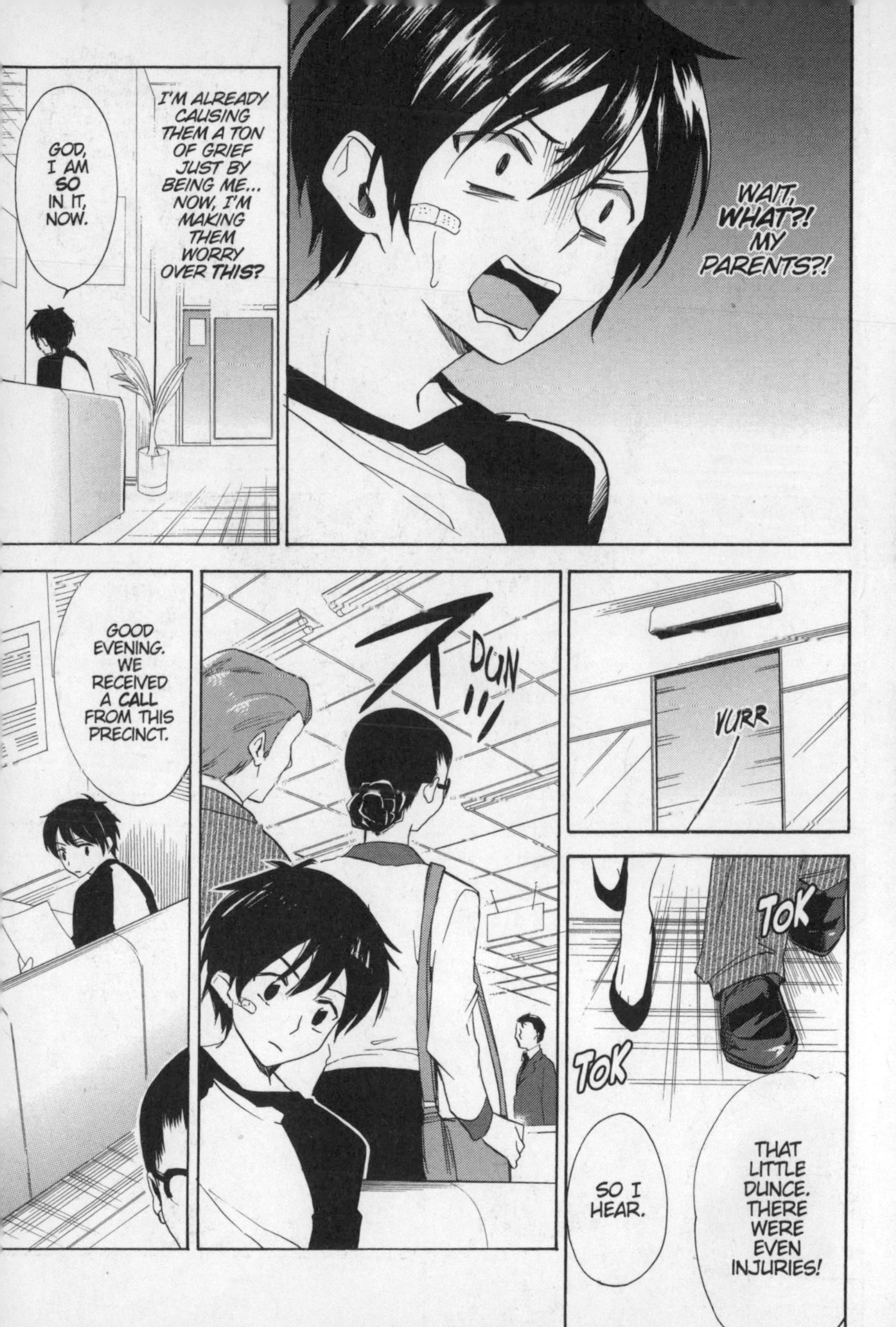
WAIT, WHAT?! MY PARENTS?!
I'M ALREADY CAUSING THEM A TON OF GRIEF JUST BY BEING ME... NOW, I'M MAKING THEM WORRY OVER THIS?
GOD, I AM SO IN IT, NOW.
VURR
TOK
TOK
THAT LITTLE DUNCE. THERE WERE EVEN INJURIES!
SO I HEAR.
DUN
GOOD EVENING. WE RECEIVED A CALL FROM THIS PRECINCT.

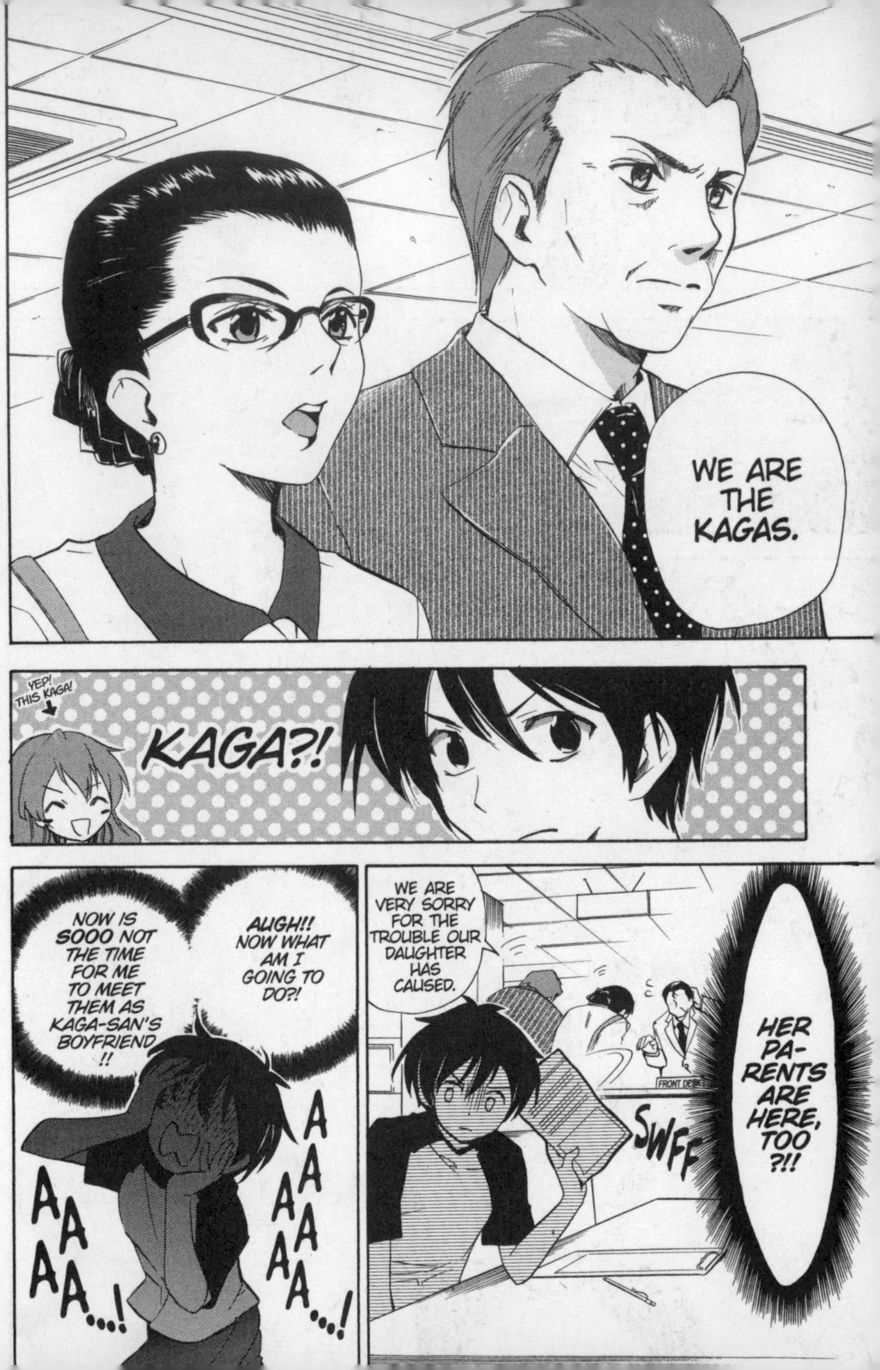
WE ARE THE KAGAS.
KAGA?!
YEP! THIS KAGA!
WE ARE VERY SORRY FOR THE TROUBLE OUR DAUGHTER HAS CAUSED.
FRONT DESK
HER PA-RENTS ARE HERE, TOO?!!
SWFF
AUGH!! NOW WHAT AM I GOING TO DO?!
NOW IS SOOO NOT THE TIME FOR ME TO MEET THEM AS KAGA-SAN'S BOYFRIEND!!
AAAAAAA...!
AAAAAAA...!

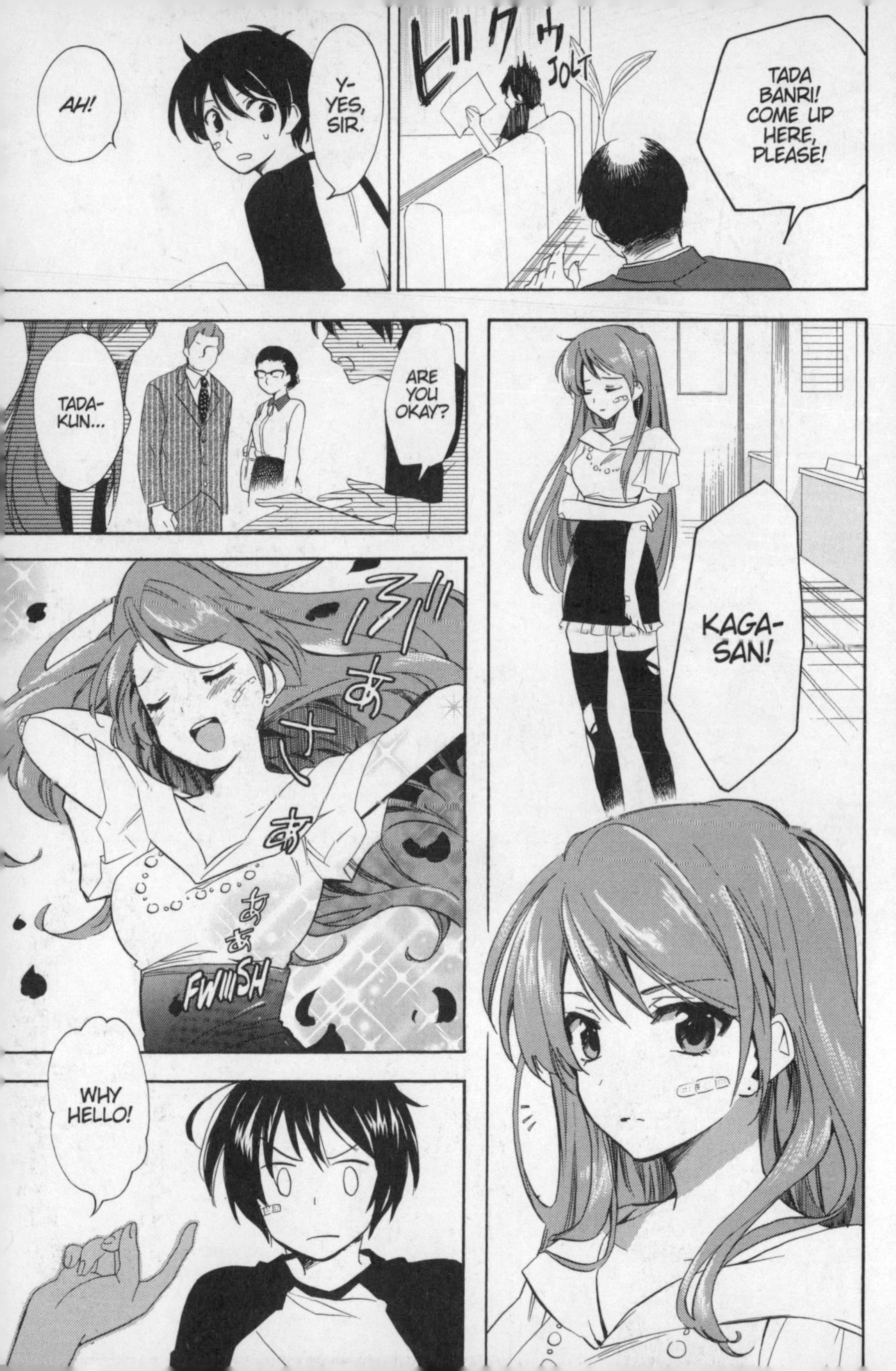
TADA BANRI! COME UP HERE, PLEASE!
JOLT
Y-YES, SIR.
AH!
KAGA-SAN!
ARE YOU OKAY?
TADA-KUN...
FWIIISH
WHY HELLO!

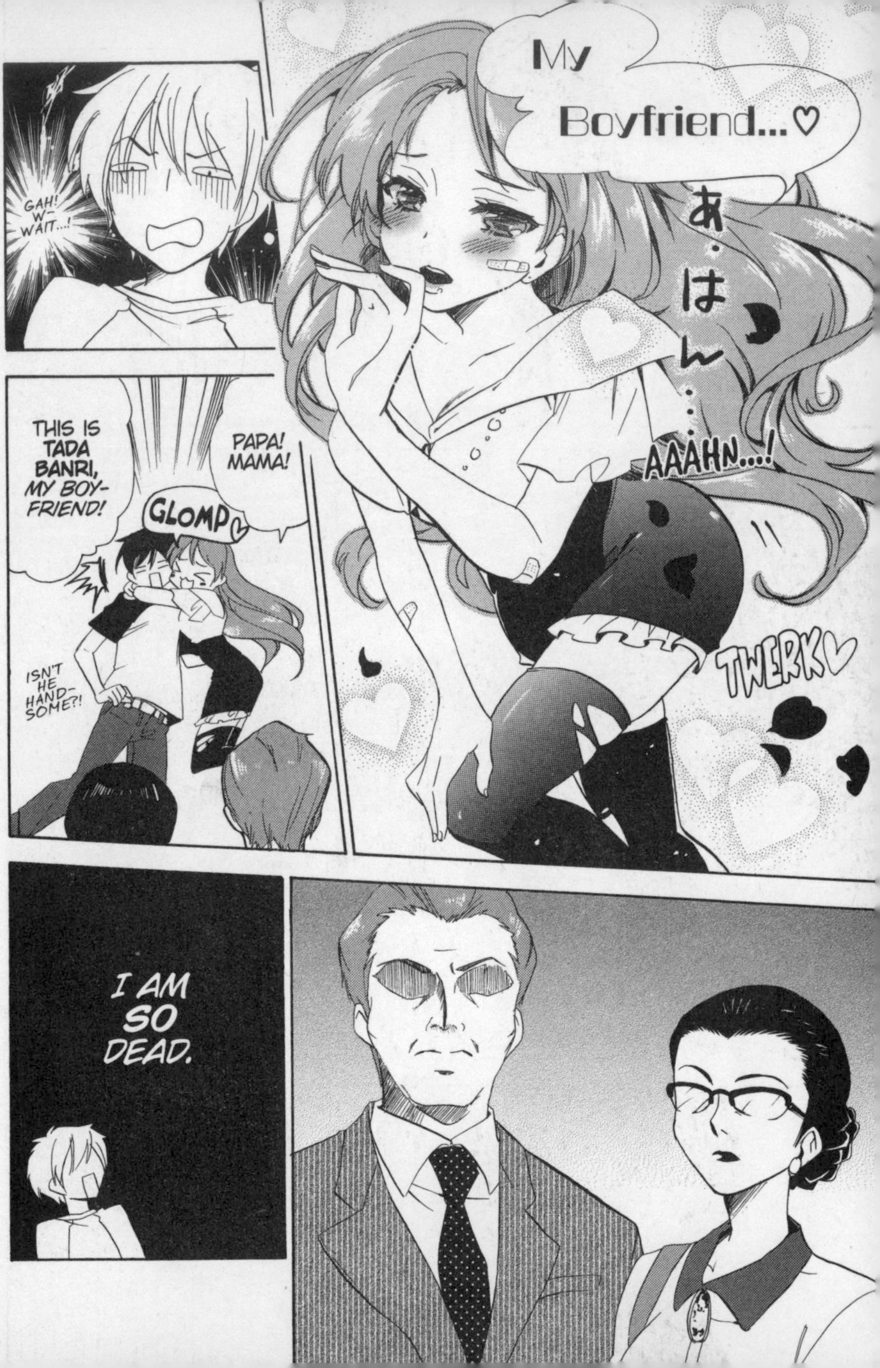
My Boyfriend...♡
あ・は・ん・・・
AAAHN...!
TWERK♡
GAH! W-WAIT...!
PAPA! MAMA!
THIS IS TADA BANRI, MY BOY-FRIEND!
GLOMP♡
ISN'T HE HAND-SOME?!
I AM SO DEAD.

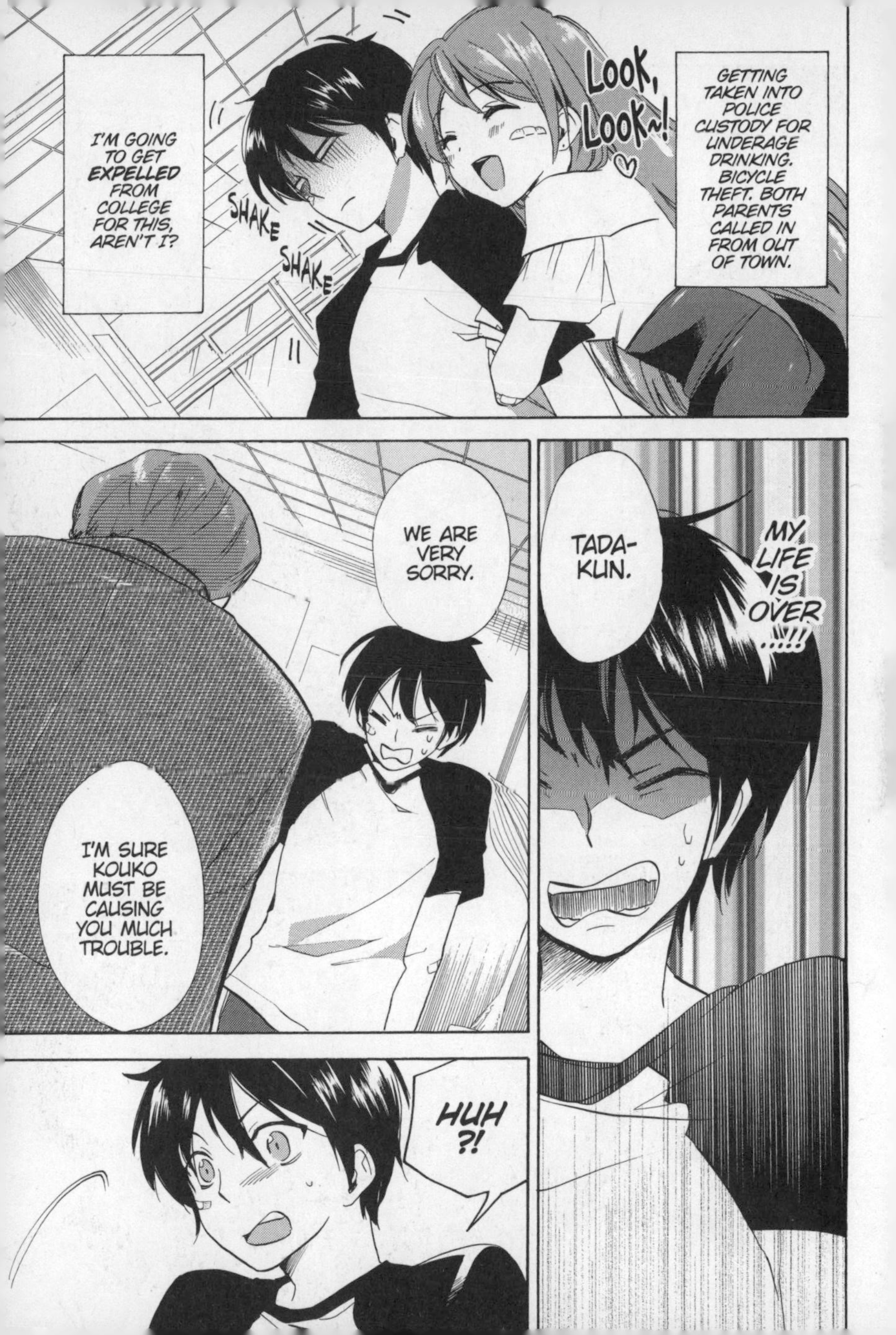
GETTING TAKEN INTO POLICE CUSTODY FOR UNDERAGE DRINKING. BICYCLE THEFT. BOTH PARENTS CALLED IN FROM OUT OF TOWN.
LOOK, LOOK~! ♡
SHAKE
SHAKE
I'M GOING TO GET **EXPELLED** FROM COLLEGE FOR THIS, AREN'T I?
MY LIFE IS OVER ...!!
TADA-KUN.
WE ARE VERY SORRY.
I'M SURE KOUKO MUST BE CAUSING YOU MUCH TROUBLE.
HUH ?!

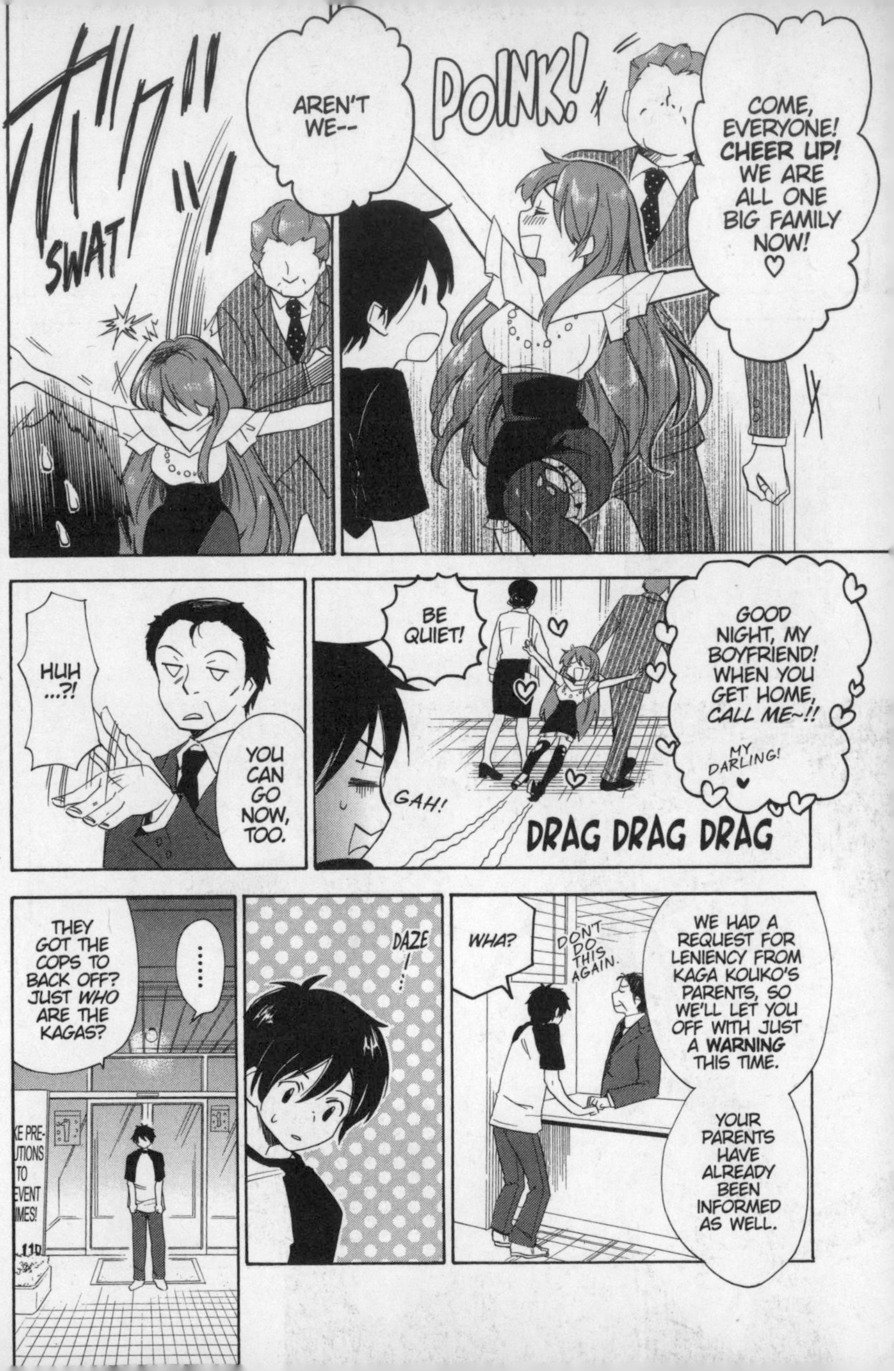
COME, EVERYONE! CHEER UP! WE ARE ALL ONE BIG FAMILY NOW! ♡
POINK!
AREN'T WE--
SWAT
GOOD NIGHT, MY BOYFRIEND! WHEN YOU GET HOME, CALL ME~!!
MY DARLING! ♥
BE QUIET!
DRAG DRAG DRAG
GAH!
YOU CAN GO NOW, TOO.
HUH ...?!
WE HAD A REQUEST FOR LENIENCY FROM KAGA KOUKO'S PARENTS, SO WE'LL LET YOU OFF WITH JUST A WARNING THIS TIME.
WHA?
DON'T DO THIS AGAIN.
YOUR PARENTS HAVE ALREADY BEEN INFORMED AS WELL.
DAZE
......
THEY GOT THE COPS TO BACK OFF? JUST WHO ARE THE KAGAS?

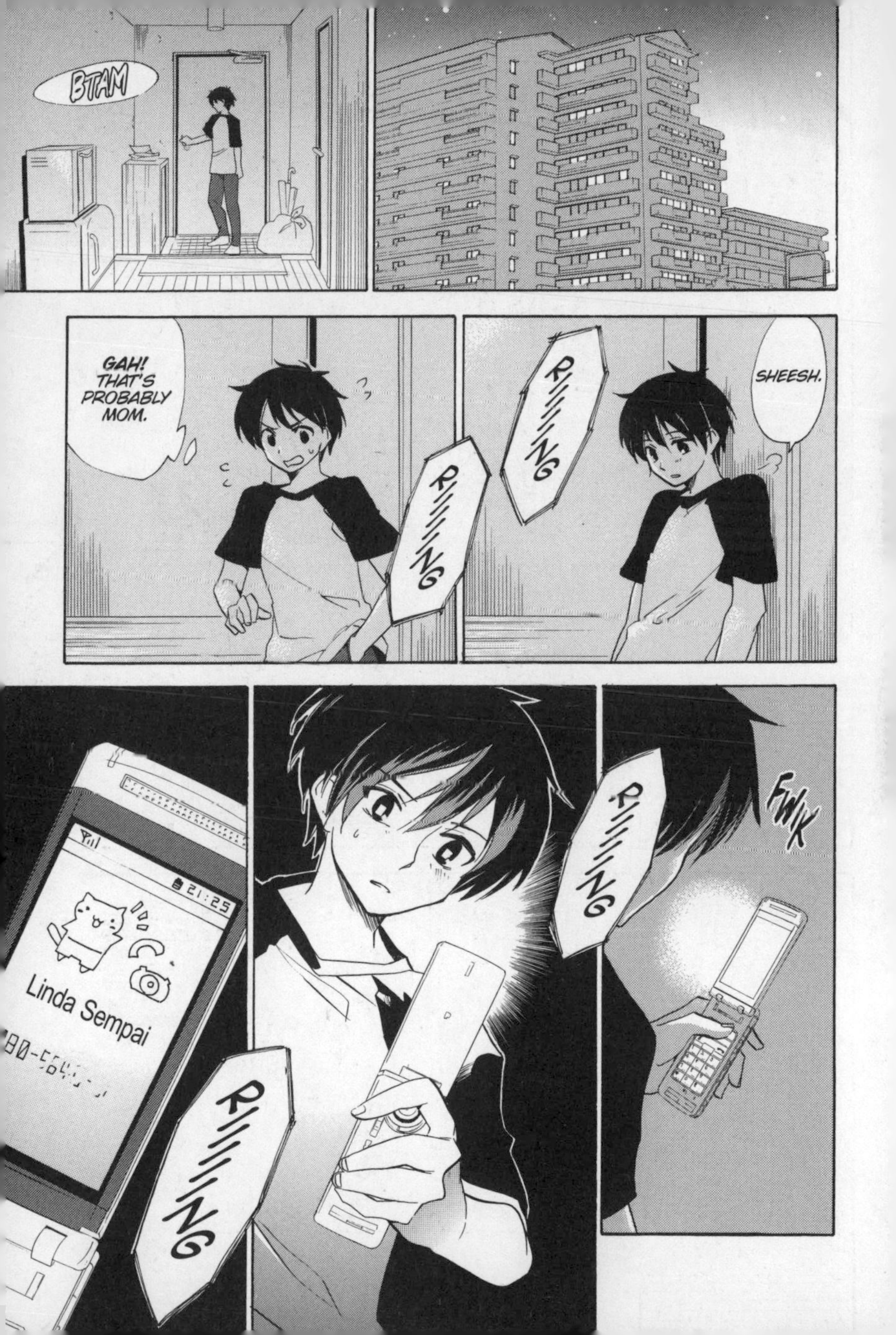

BTAM
SHEESH.
RIIIING
RIIIING
GAH! THAT'S PROBABLY MOM.
FWIK
RIIIING
RIIIING
21:25
Linda Sempai

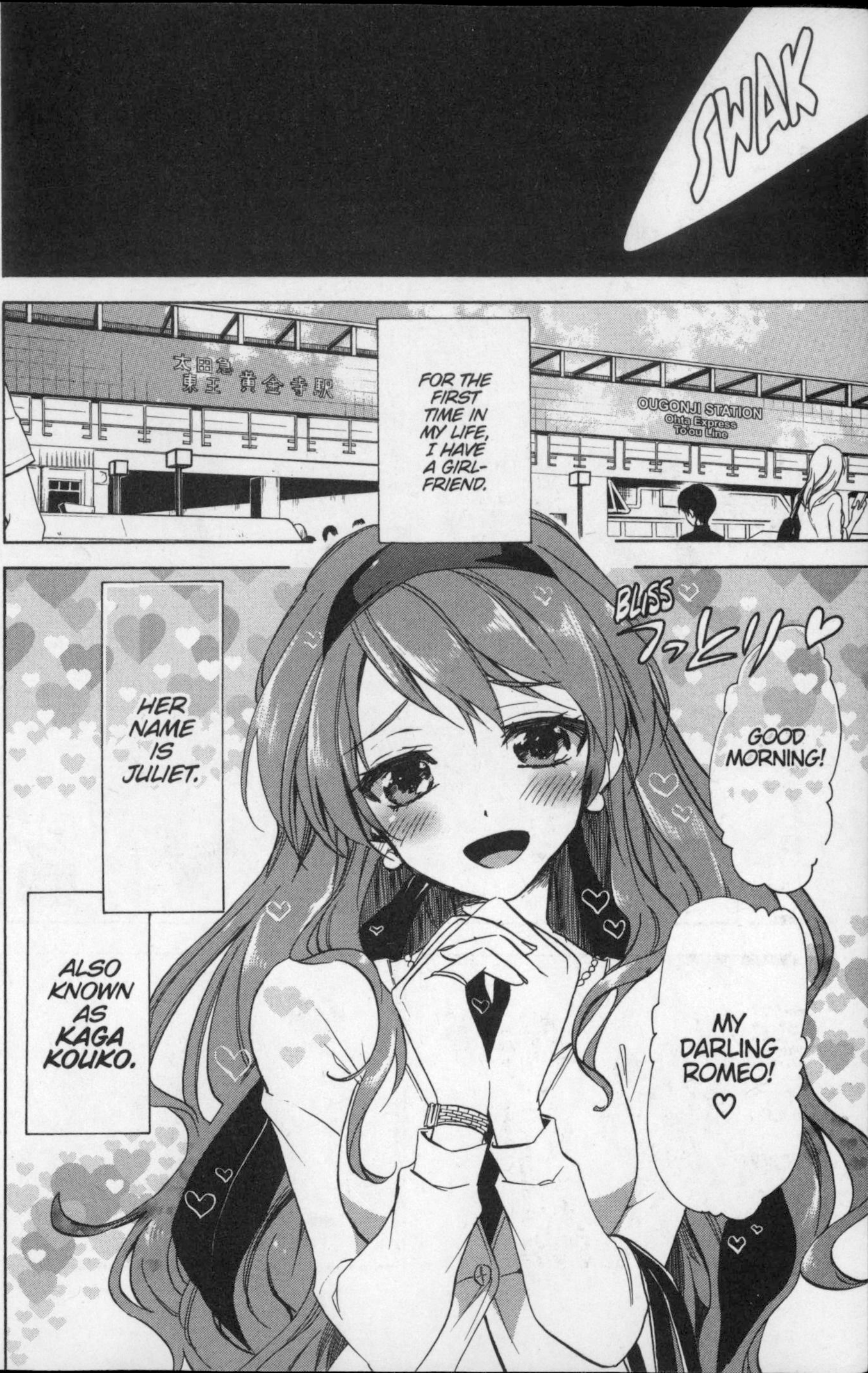
SWAK
FOR THE FIRST TIME IN MY LIFE, I HAVE A GIRLFRIEND.
太田急
東王 黄金寺駅
OUGONJI STATION
Ohta Express
To'ou Line
BLISS
フッとり♡
GOOD MORNING!
MY DARLING ROMEO! ♡
HER NAME IS JULIET.
ALSO KNOWN AS KAGA KOUKO.

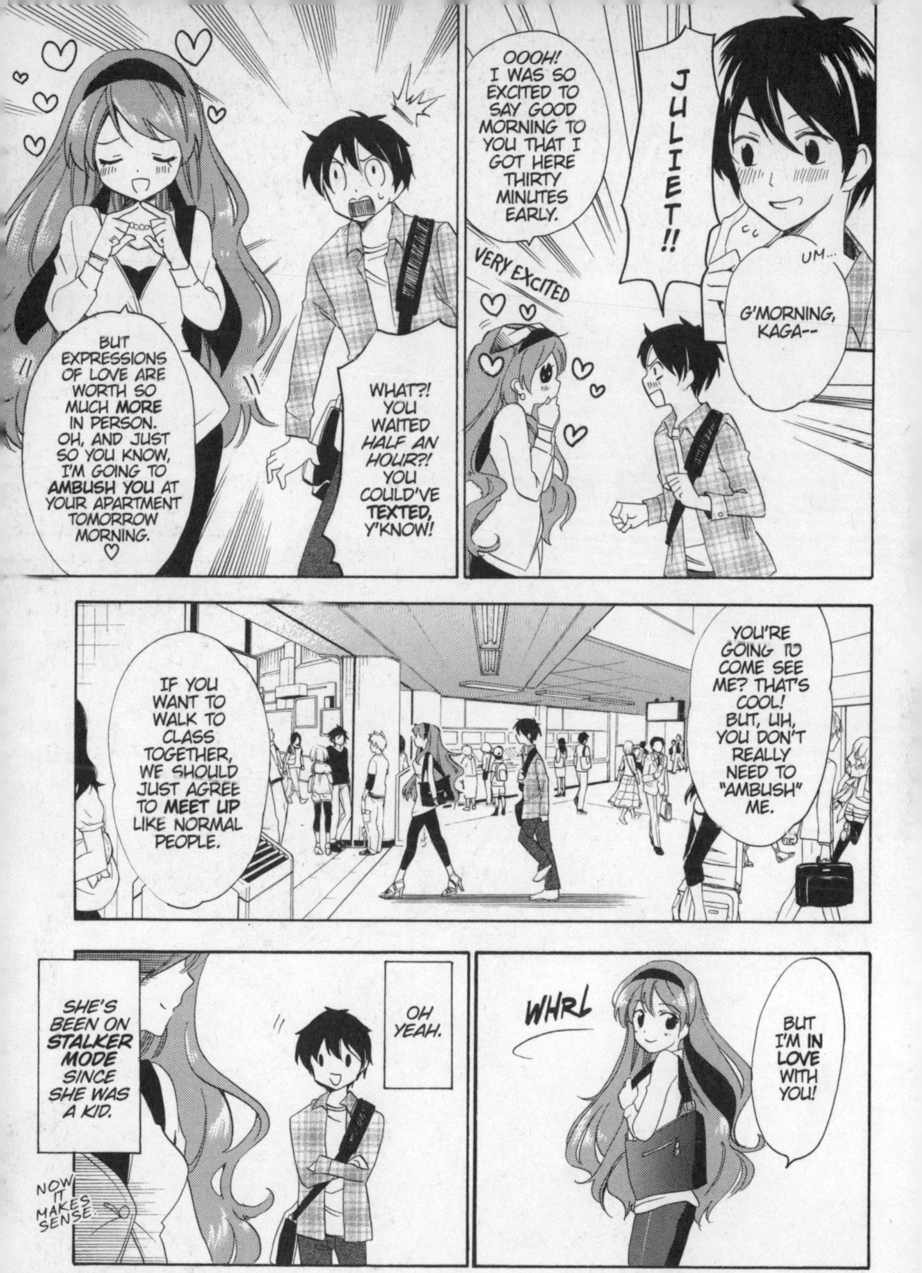
UM... G'MORNING, KAGA--
JULIET!!
OOOH! I WAS SO EXCITED TO SAY GOOD MORNING TO YOU THAT I GOT HERE THIRTY MINUTES EARLY.
VERY EXCITED
WHAT?! YOU WAITED HALF AN HOUR?! YOU COULD'VE TEXTED, Y'KNOW!
BUT EXPRESSIONS OF LOVE ARE WORTH SO MUCH MORE IN PERSON. OH, AND JUST SO YOU KNOW, I'M GOING TO AMBUSH YOU AT YOUR APARTMENT TOMORROW MORNING. ♡
YOU'RE GOING TO COME SEE ME? THAT'S COOL! BUT, UH, YOU DON'T REALLY NEED TO "AMBUSH" ME.
IF YOU WANT TO WALK TO CLASS TOGETHER, WE SHOULD JUST AGREE TO MEET UP LIKE NORMAL PEOPLE.
WHRL
BUT I'M IN LOVE WITH YOU!
OH YEAH.
SHE'S BEEN ON STALKER MODE SINCE SHE WAS A KID.
NOW IT MAKES SENSE.

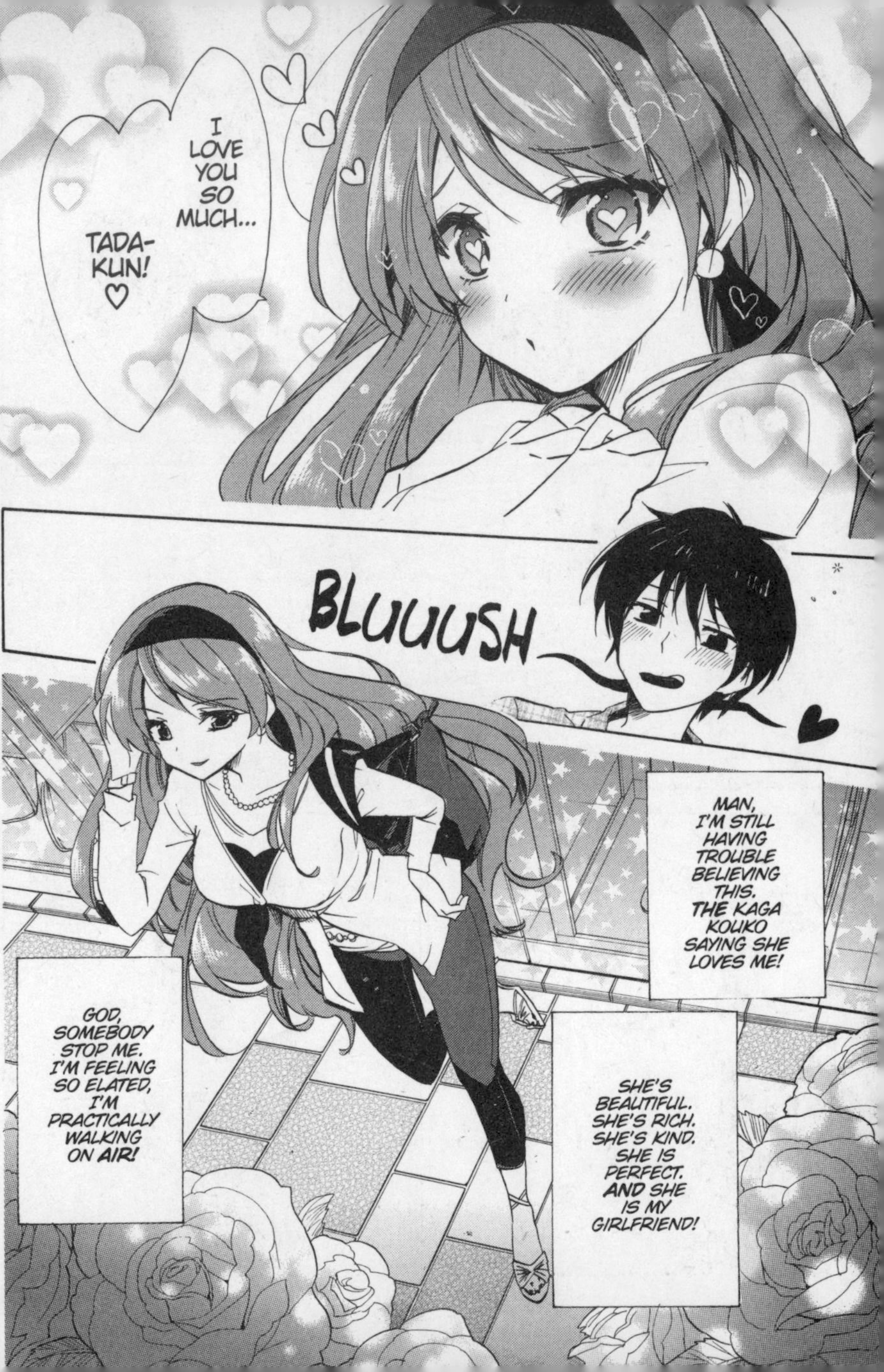
I LOVE YOU SO MUCH... TADA-KUN! ♡
BLUUUSH
MAN, I'M STILL HAVING TROUBLE BELIEVING THIS. THE KAGA KOUKO SAYING SHE LOVES ME!
SHE'S BEAUTIFUL. SHE'S RICH. SHE'S KIND. SHE IS PERFECT. AND SHE IS MY GIRLFRIEND!
GOD, SOMEBODY STOP ME. I'M FEELING SO ELATED, I'M PRACTICALLY WALKING ON AIR!

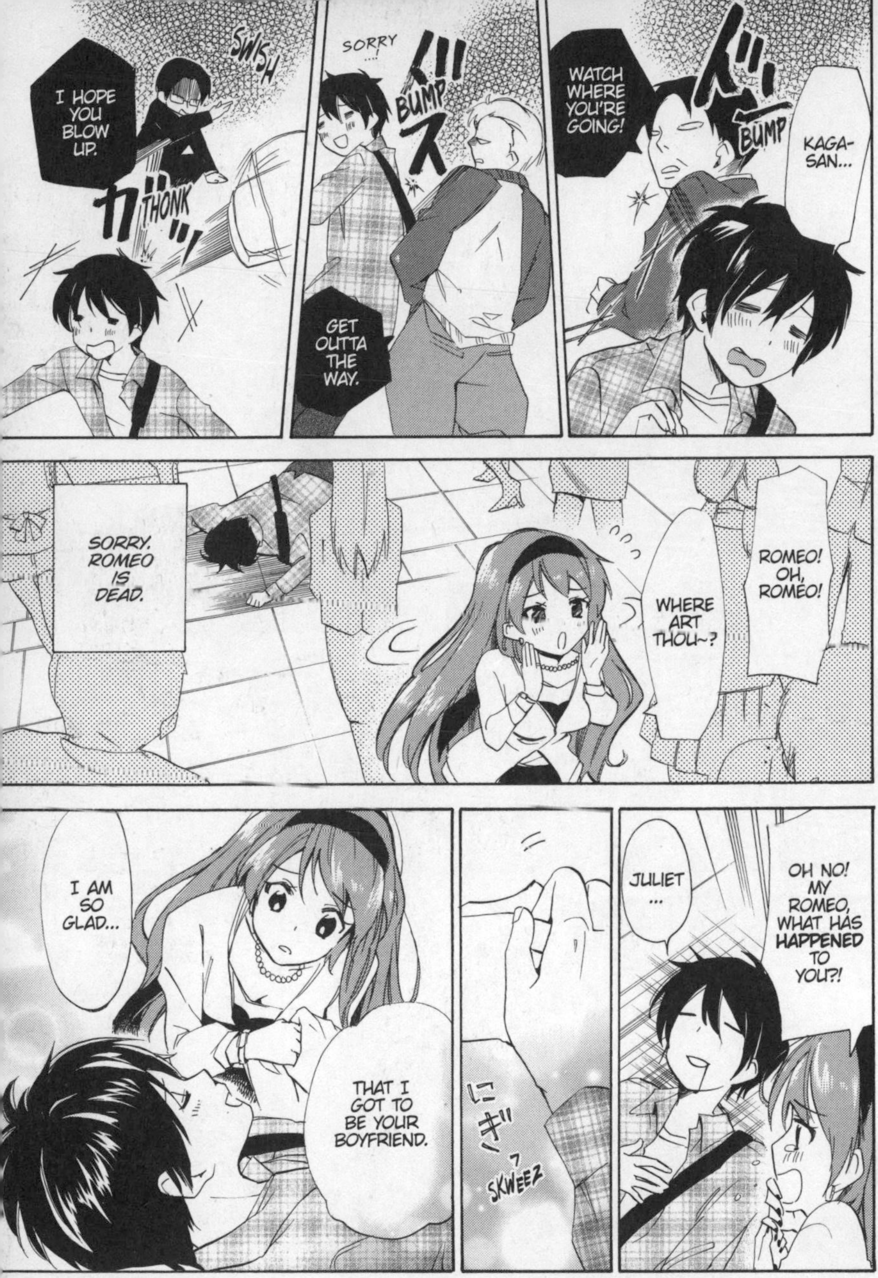
KAGA-SAN...
BUMP
WATCH WHERE YOU'RE GOING!
SORRY ...!
BUMP
GET OUTTA THE WAY.
SWISH
I HOPE YOU BLOW UP.
カッ
THONK
ROMEO! OH, ROMEO!
WHERE ART THOU~?
SORRY. ROMEO IS DEAD.
OH NO! MY ROMEO, WHAT HAS HAPPENED TO YOU?!
JULIET ...
にぎ
SKWEEZ
I AM SO GLAD...
THAT I GOT TO BE YOUR BOYFRIEND.

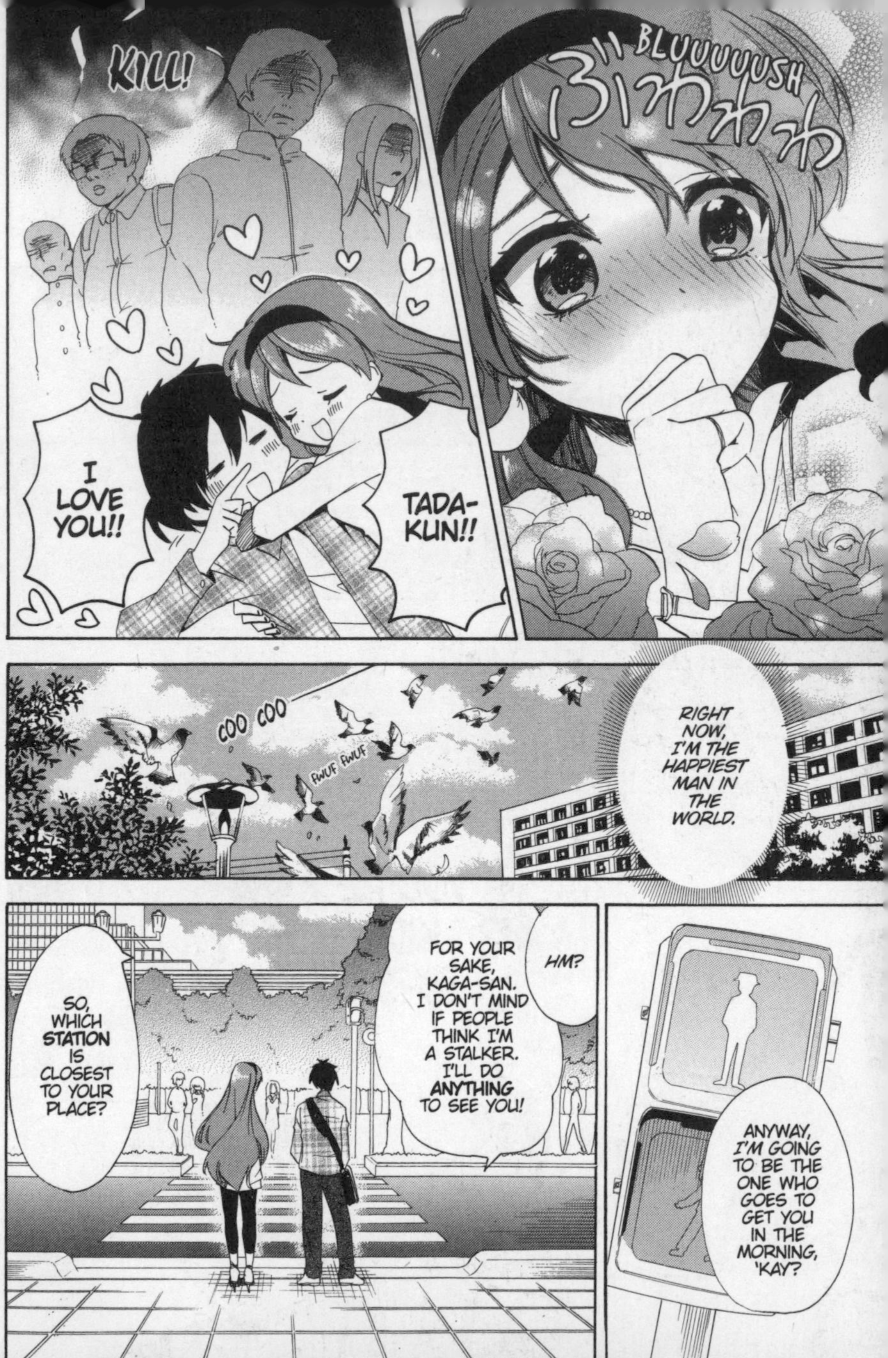
BLUUUUUSH
ぶわわわ
KILL!
TADA-KUN!!
I LOVE YOU!!
RIGHT NOW, I'M THE HAPPIEST MAN IN THE WORLD.
COO COO
FWUF FWUF
ANYWAY, I'M GOING TO BE THE ONE WHO GOES TO GET YOU IN THE MORNING, 'KAY?
HM?
FOR YOUR SAKE, KAGA-SAN. I DON'T MIND IF PEOPLE THINK I'M A STALKER. I'LL DO ANYTHING TO SEE YOU!
SO, WHICH STATION IS CLOSEST TO YOUR PLACE?

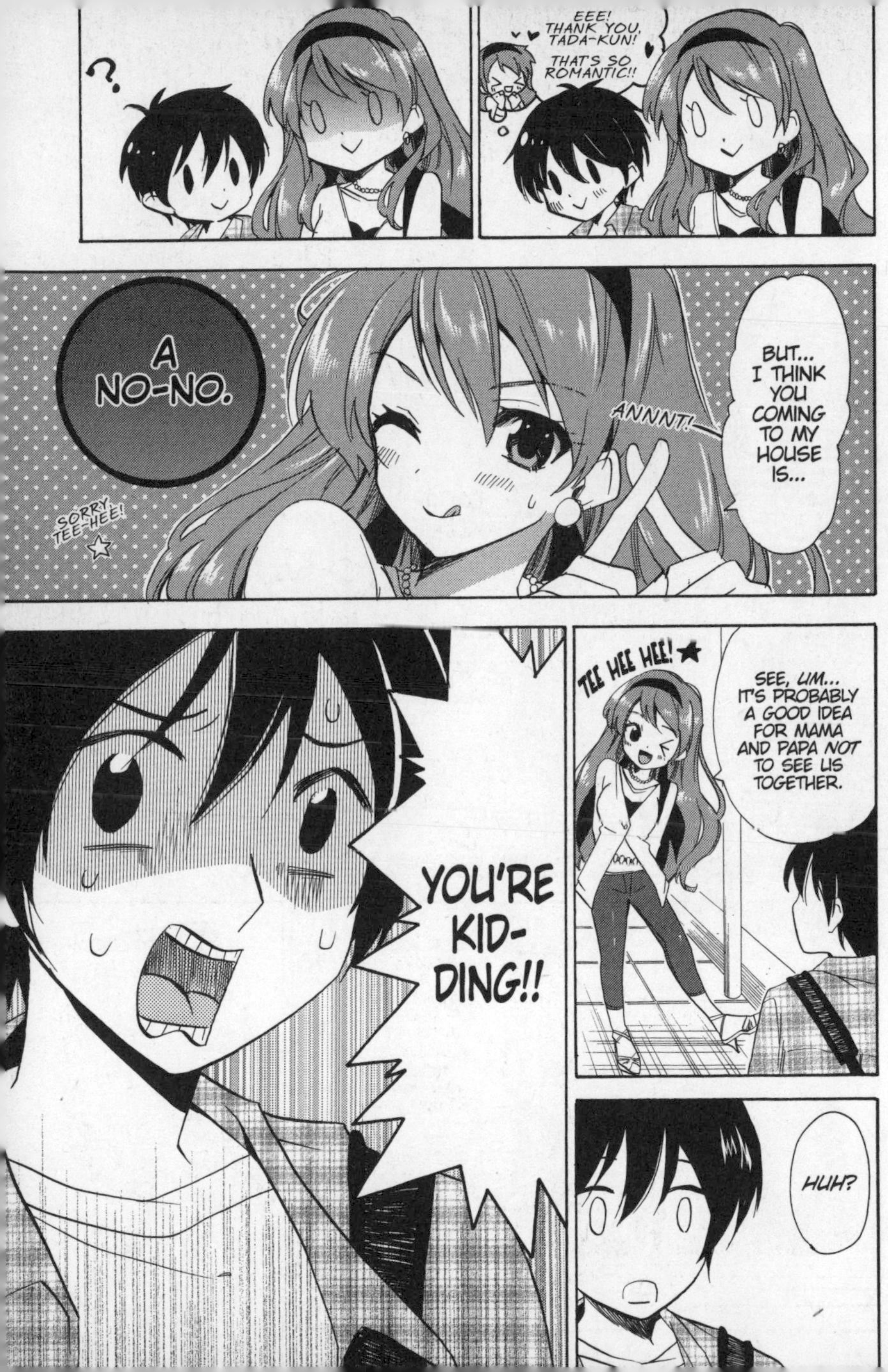
EEE! THANK YOU, TADA-KUN!
THAT'S SO ROMANTIC!!
BUT... I THINK YOU COMING TO MY HOUSE IS...
ANNNT!
A NO-NO.
SORRY, TEE-HEE! ☆
SEE, UM... IT'S PROBABLY A GOOD IDEA FOR MAMA AND PAPA NOT TO SEE US TOGETHER.
TEE HEE HEE! ★
HUH?
YOU'RE KID-DING!!

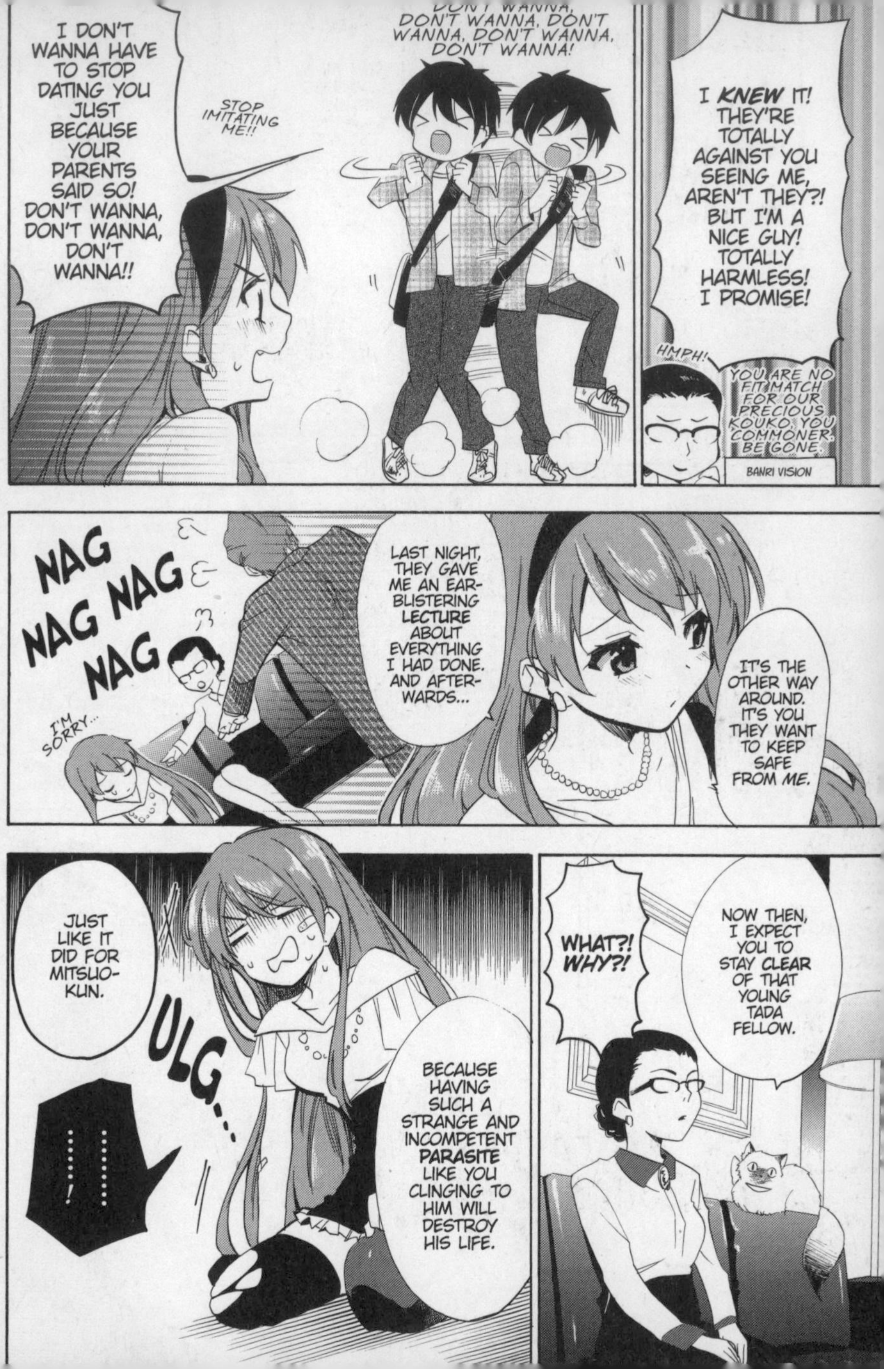
I KNEW IT! THEY'RE TOTALLY AGAINST YOU SEEING ME, AREN'T THEY?! BUT I'M A NICE GUY! TOTALLY HARMLESS! I PROMISE!
HMPH!
YOU ARE NO FIT MATCH FOR OUR PRECIOUS KOUKO, YOU COMMONER. BE GONE.
BANRI VISION
DON'T WANNA, DON'T WANNA, DON'T WANNA, DON'T WANNA, DON'T WANNA!
STOP IMITATING ME!!
I DON'T WANNA HAVE TO STOP DATING YOU JUST BECAUSE YOUR PARENTS SAID SO! DON'T WANNA, DON'T WANNA, DON'T WANNA!!
IT'S THE OTHER WAY AROUND. IT'S YOU THEY WANT TO KEEP SAFE FROM ME.
LAST NIGHT, THEY GAVE ME AN EAR-BLISTERING LECTURE ABOUT EVERYTHING I HAD DONE. AND AFTER-WARDS...
NAG NAG NAG NAG NAG
I'M SORRY...
NOW THEN, I EXPECT YOU TO STAY CLEAR OF THAT YOUNG TADA FELLOW.
WHAT?! WHY?!
BECAUSE HAVING SUCH A STRANGE AND INCOMPETENT PARASITE LIKE YOU CLINGING TO HIM WILL DESTROY HIS LIFE.
JUST LIKE IT DID FOR MITSUO-KUN.
ULG...
......!

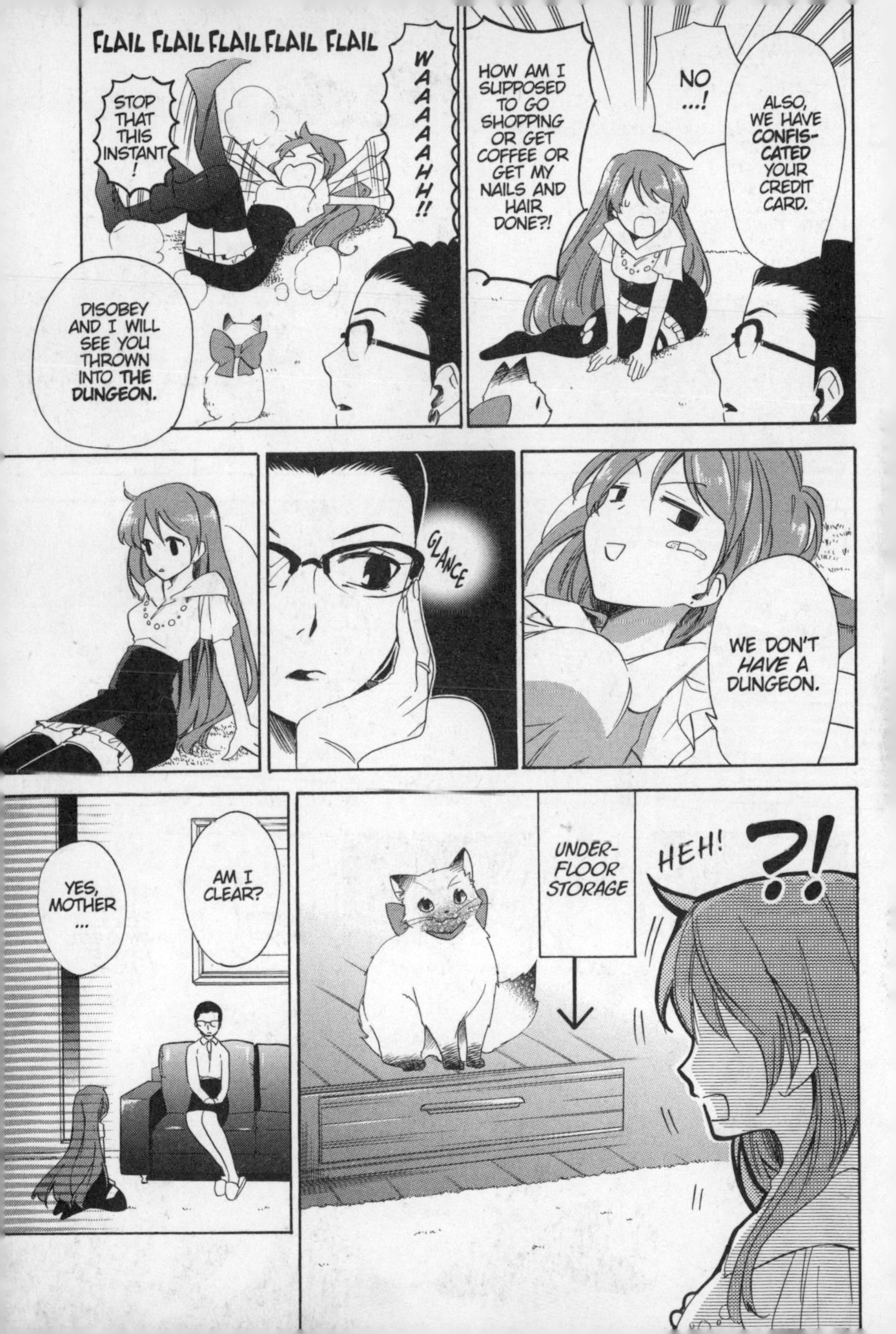
ALSO, WE HAVE CONFIS-CATED YOUR CREDIT CARD.
NO ...!
HOW AM I SUPPOSED TO GO SHOPPING OR GET COFFEE OR GET MY NAILS AND HAIR DONE?!
WAAAAAAHH!!
FLAIL FLAIL FLAIL FLAIL FLAIL
STOP THAT THIS INSTANT!
DISOBEY AND I WILL SEE YOU THROWN INTO THE DUNGEON.
WE DON'T HAVE A DUNGEON.
GLANCE
?!
HEH!
UNDER-FLOOR STORAGE
AM I CLEAR?
YES, MOTHER ...

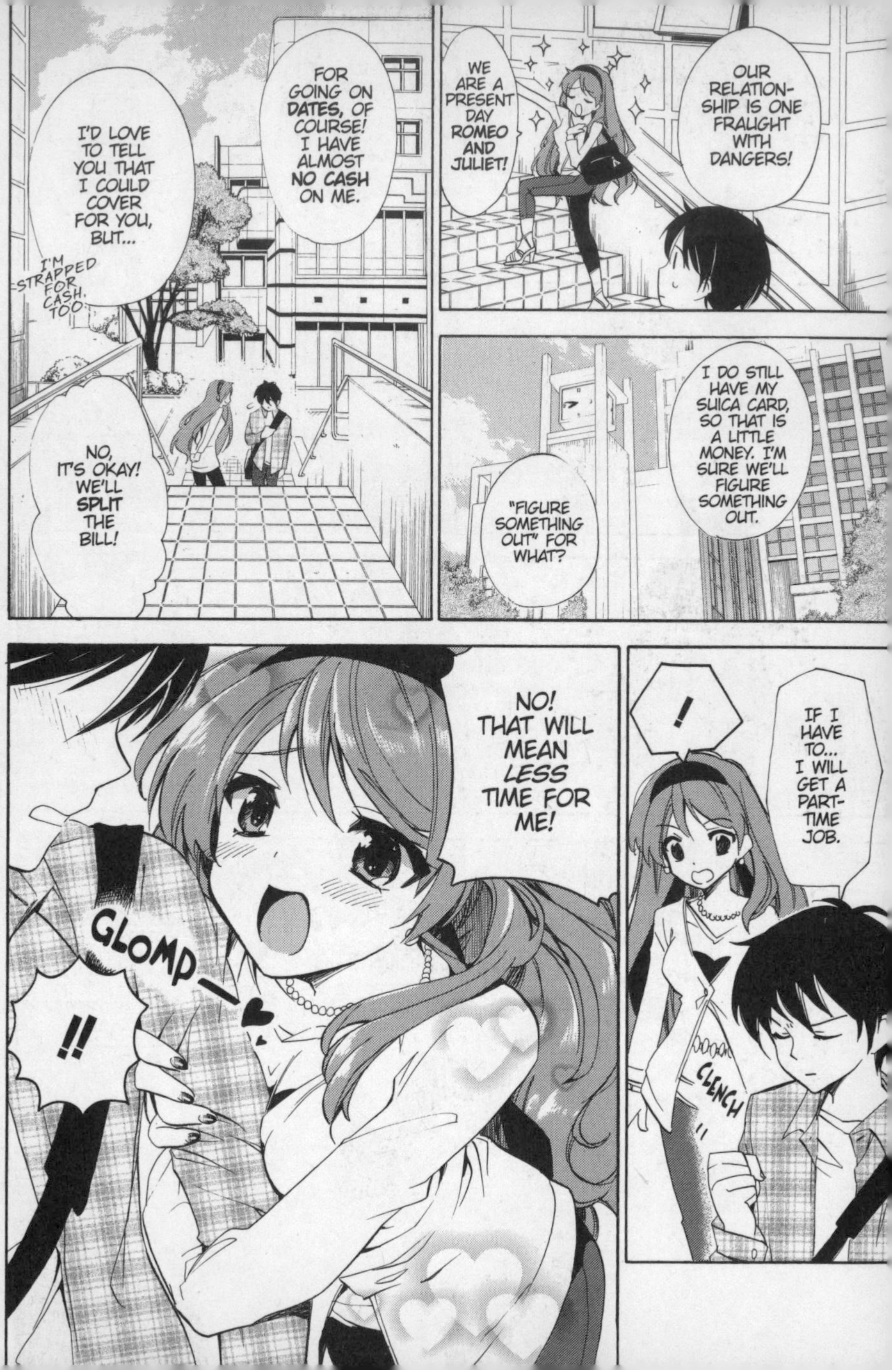
OUR RELATIONSHIP IS ONE FRAUGHT WITH DANGERS!
WE ARE A PRESENT DAY ROMEO AND JULIET!
I DO STILL HAVE MY SUICA CARD, SO THAT IS A LITTLE MONEY. I'M SURE WE'LL FIGURE SOMETHING OUT.
"FIGURE SOMETHING OUT" FOR WHAT?
FOR GOING ON DATES, OF COURSE! I HAVE ALMOST NO CASH ON ME.
I'D LOVE TO TELL YOU THAT I COULD COVER FOR YOU, BUT...
I'M STRAPPED FOR CASH, TOO.
NO, IT'S OKAY! WE'LL SPLIT THE BILL!
!
IF I HAVE TO... I WILL GET A PART-TIME JOB.
CLENCH
NO! THAT WILL MEAN LESS TIME FOR ME!
GLOMP—
!!

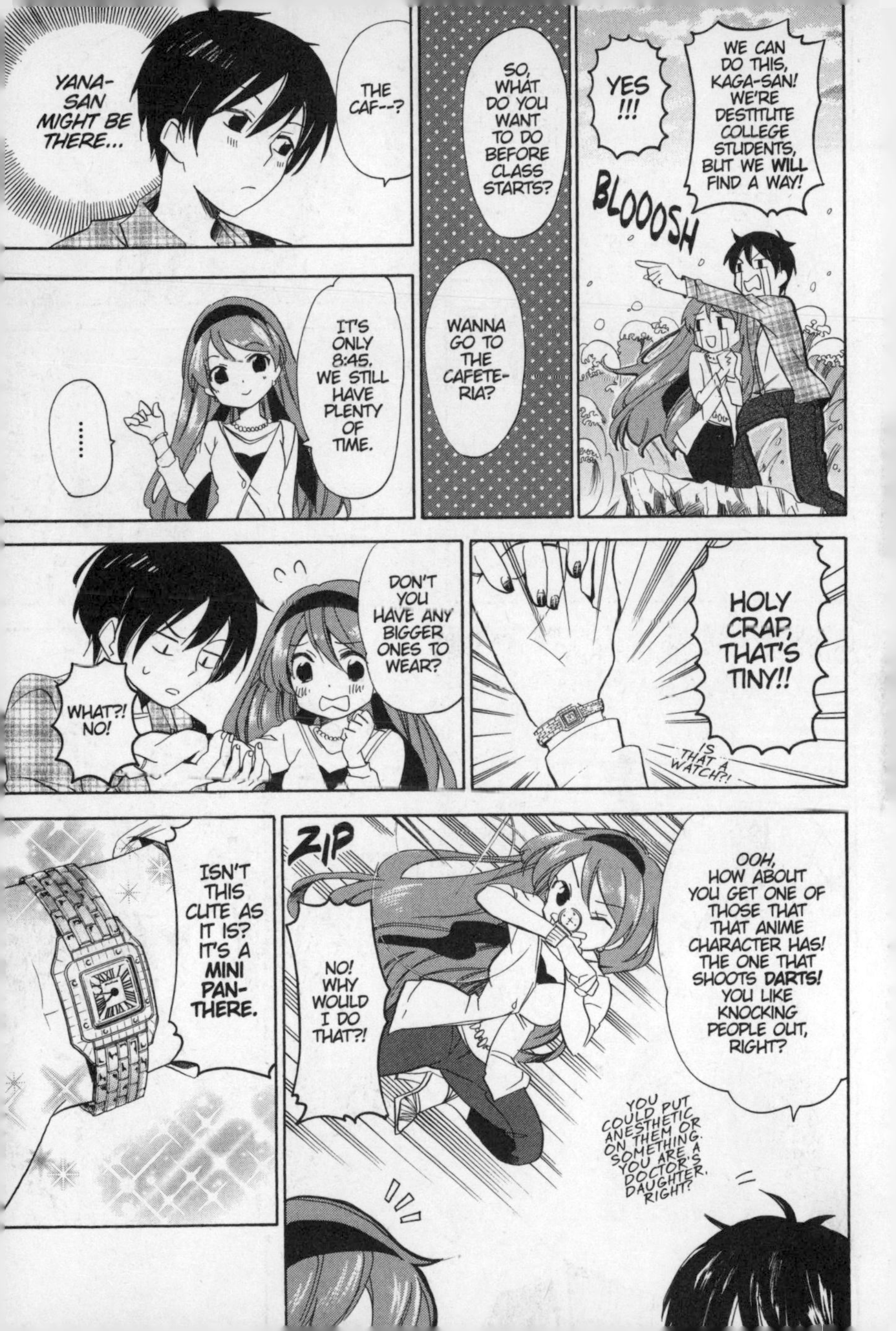
WE CAN DO THIS, KAGA-SAN! WE'RE DESTITUTE COLLEGE STUDENTS, BUT WE WILL FIND A WAY!
YES!!!
BLOOOSH
SO, WHAT DO YOU WANT TO DO BEFORE CLASS STARTS?
WANNA GO TO THE CAFETERIA?
THE CAF--?
YANA-SAN MIGHT BE THERE...
IT'S ONLY 8:45. WE STILL HAVE PLENTY OF TIME.
......
HOLY CRAP, THAT'S TINY!!
IS THAT A WATCH?!
DON'T YOU HAVE ANY BIGGER ONES TO WEAR?
WHAT?! NO!
OOH, HOW ABOUT YOU GET ONE OF THOSE THAT THAT ANIME CHARACTER HAS! THE ONE THAT SHOOTS DARTS! YOU LIKE KNOCKING PEOPLE OUT, RIGHT?
ZIP
NO! WHY WOULD I DO THAT?!
YOU COULD PUT ANESTHETIC ON THEM OR SOMETHING. YOU ARE A DOCTOR'S DAUGHTER, RIGHT?
ISN'T THIS CUTE AS IT IS? IT'S A MINI PAN-THERE.

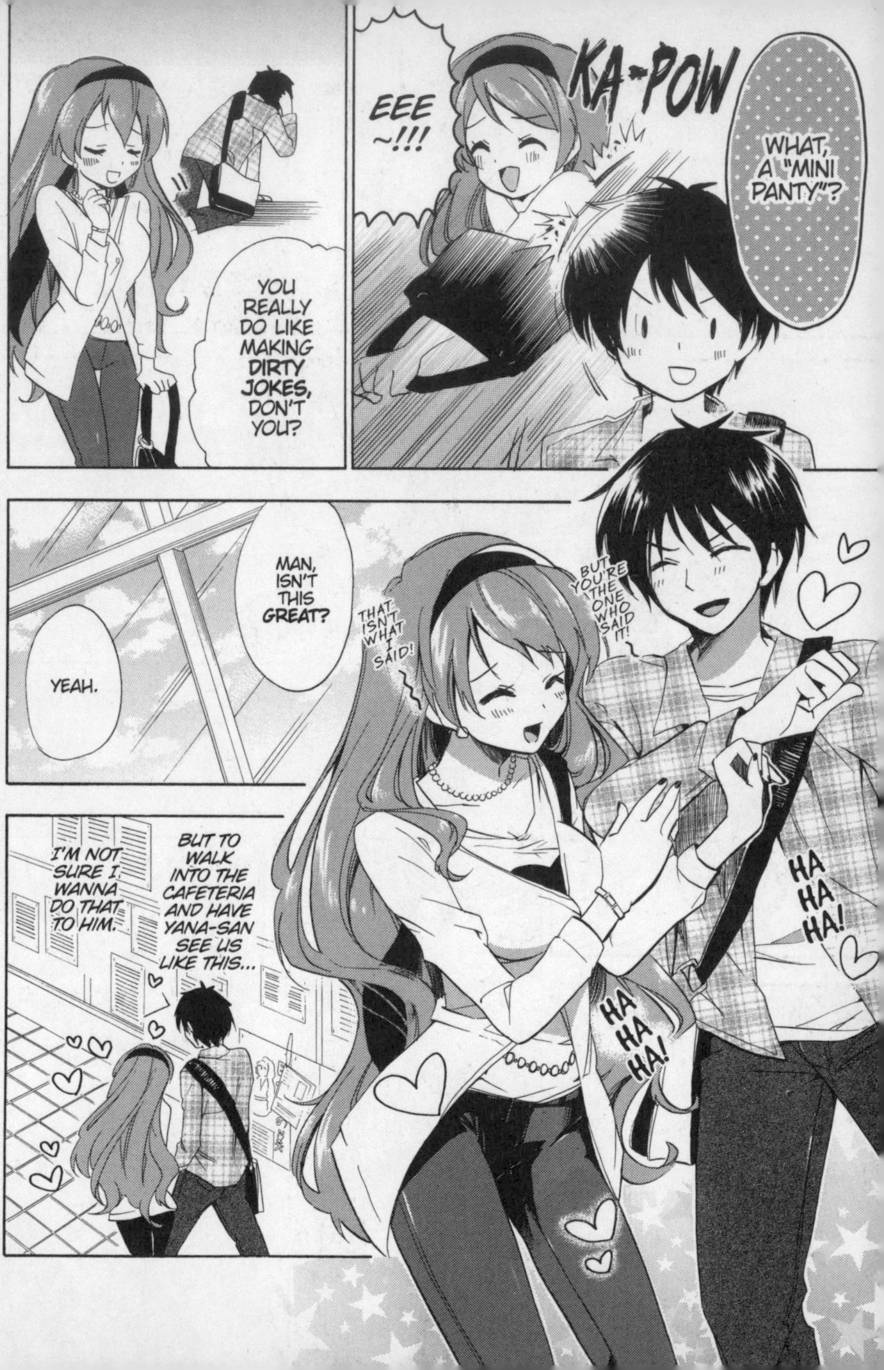
WHAT, A "MINI PANTY"?
KA-POW
EEE ~!!!
YOU REALLY DO LIKE MAKING DIRTY JOKES, DON'T YOU?
BUT YOU'RE THE ONE WHO SAID IT!
THAT ISN'T WHAT I SAID!
HA HA HA!
HA HA HA!
MAN, ISN'T THIS GREAT?
YEAH.
BUT TO WALK INTO THE CAFETERIA AND HAVE YANA-SAN SEE US LIKE THIS...
I'M NOT SURE I WANNA DO THAT TO HIM.

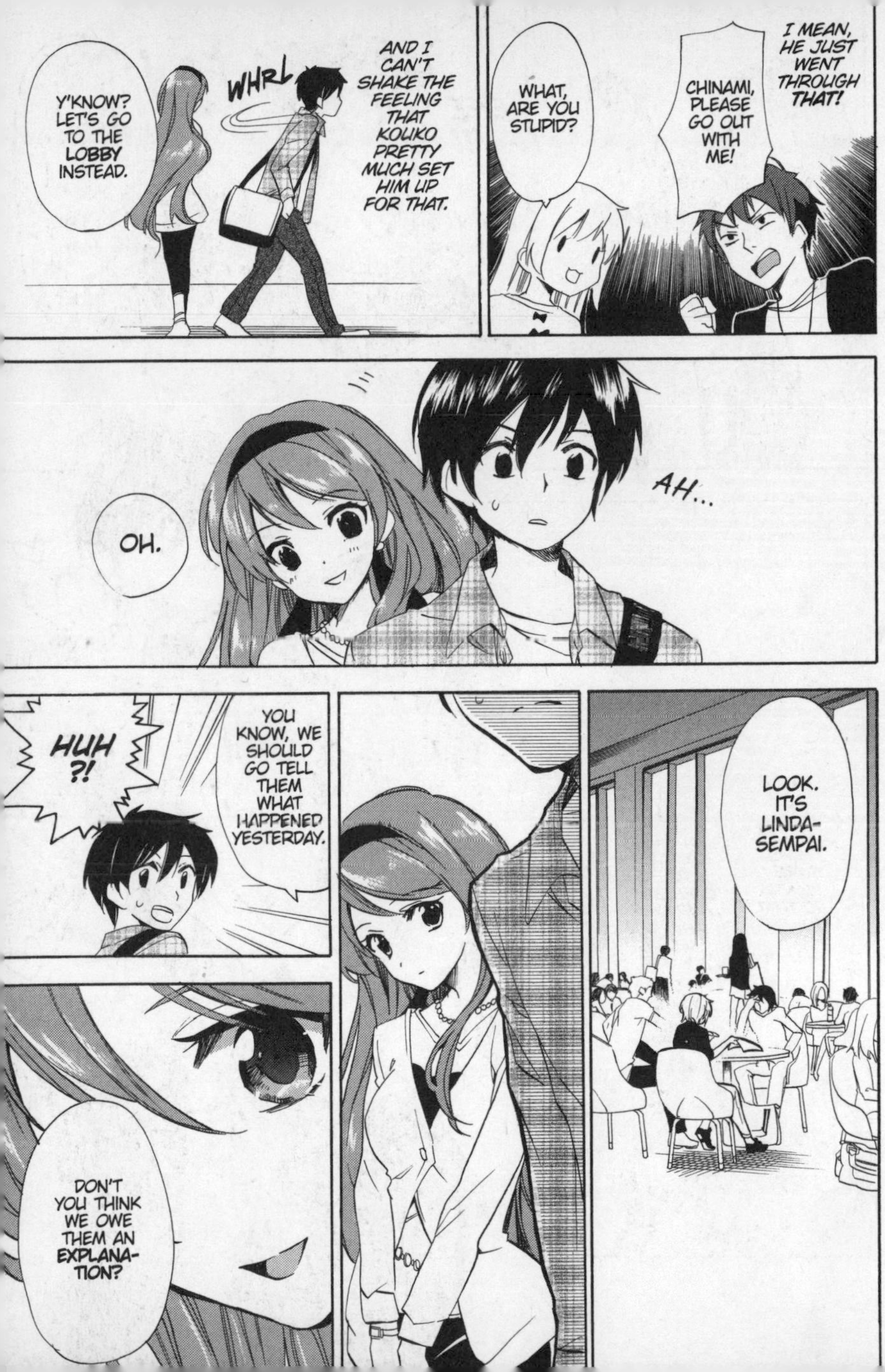
I MEAN, HE JUST WENT THROUGH THAT!
CHINAMI, PLEASE GO OUT WITH ME!
WHAT, ARE YOU STUPID?
AND I CAN'T SHAKE THE FEELING THAT KOUKO PRETTY MUCH SET HIM UP FOR THAT.
WHRL
Y'KNOW? LET'S GO TO THE LOBBY INSTEAD.
AH...
OH.
LOOK. IT'S LINDA-SEMPAI.
YOU KNOW, WE SHOULD GO TELL THEM WHAT HAPPENED YESTERDAY.
HUH?!
DON'T YOU THINK WE OWE THEM AN EXPLANATION?

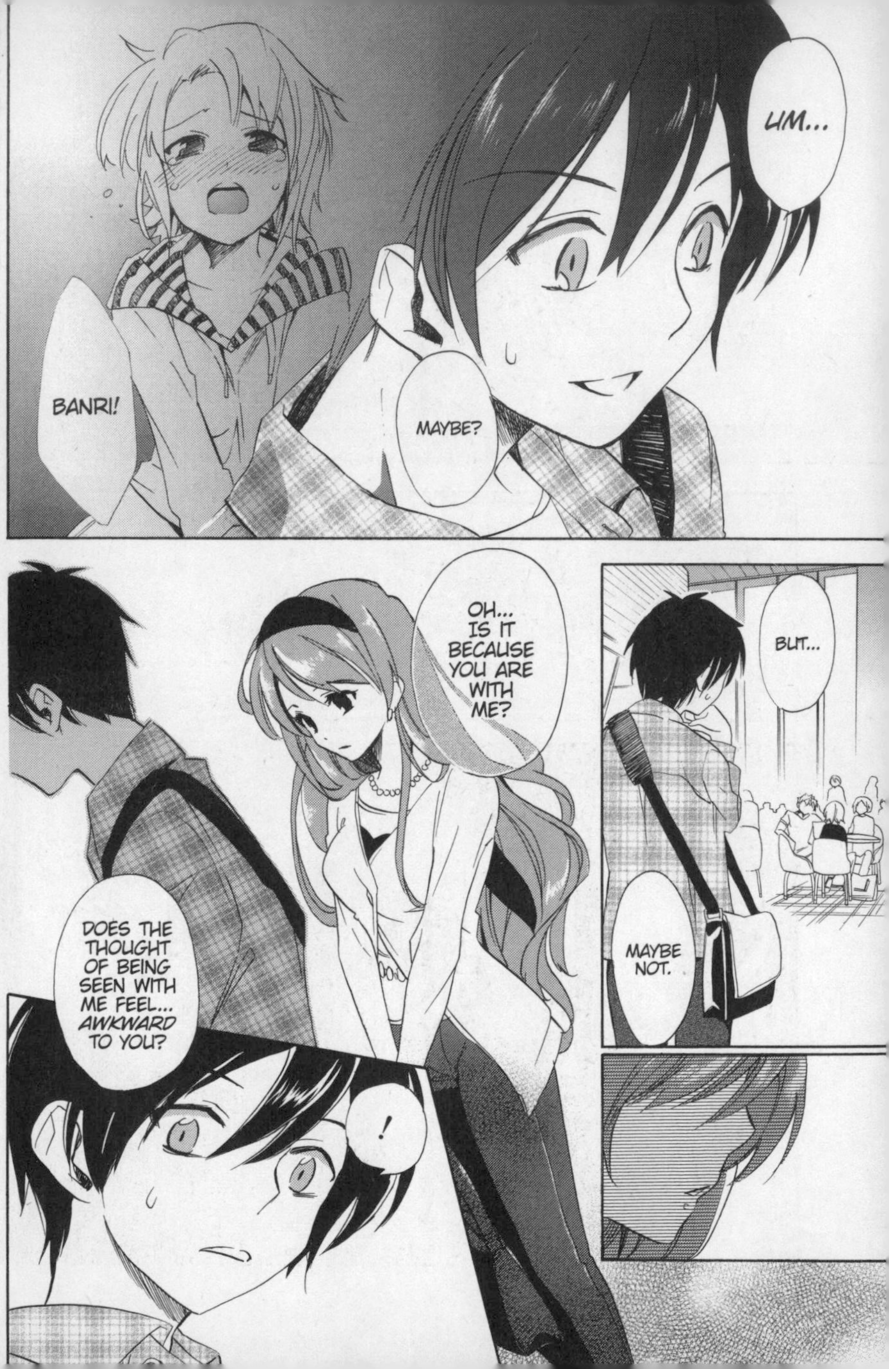
UM...
MAYBE?
BANRI!
BUT...
MAYBE NOT.
OH... IS IT BECAUSE YOU ARE WITH ME?
DOES THE THOUGHT OF BEING SEEN WITH ME FEEL... AWKWARD TO YOU?
!

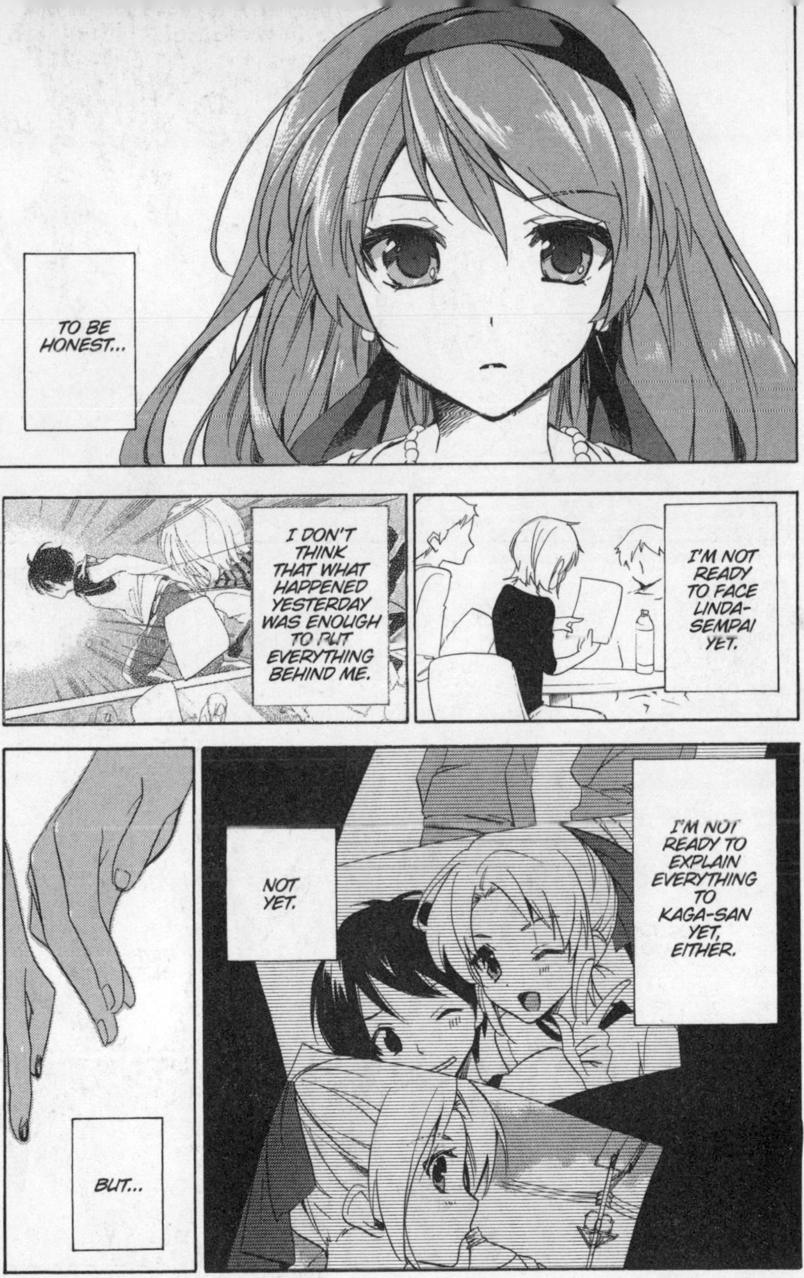
TO BE HONEST...
I'M NOT READY TO FACE LINDA-SEMPAI YET.
I DON'T THINK THAT WHAT HAPPENED YESTERDAY WAS ENOUGH TO PUT EVERYTHING BEHIND ME.
I'M NOT READY TO EXPLAIN EVERYTHING TO KAGA-SAN YET, EITHER.
NOT YET.
BUT...

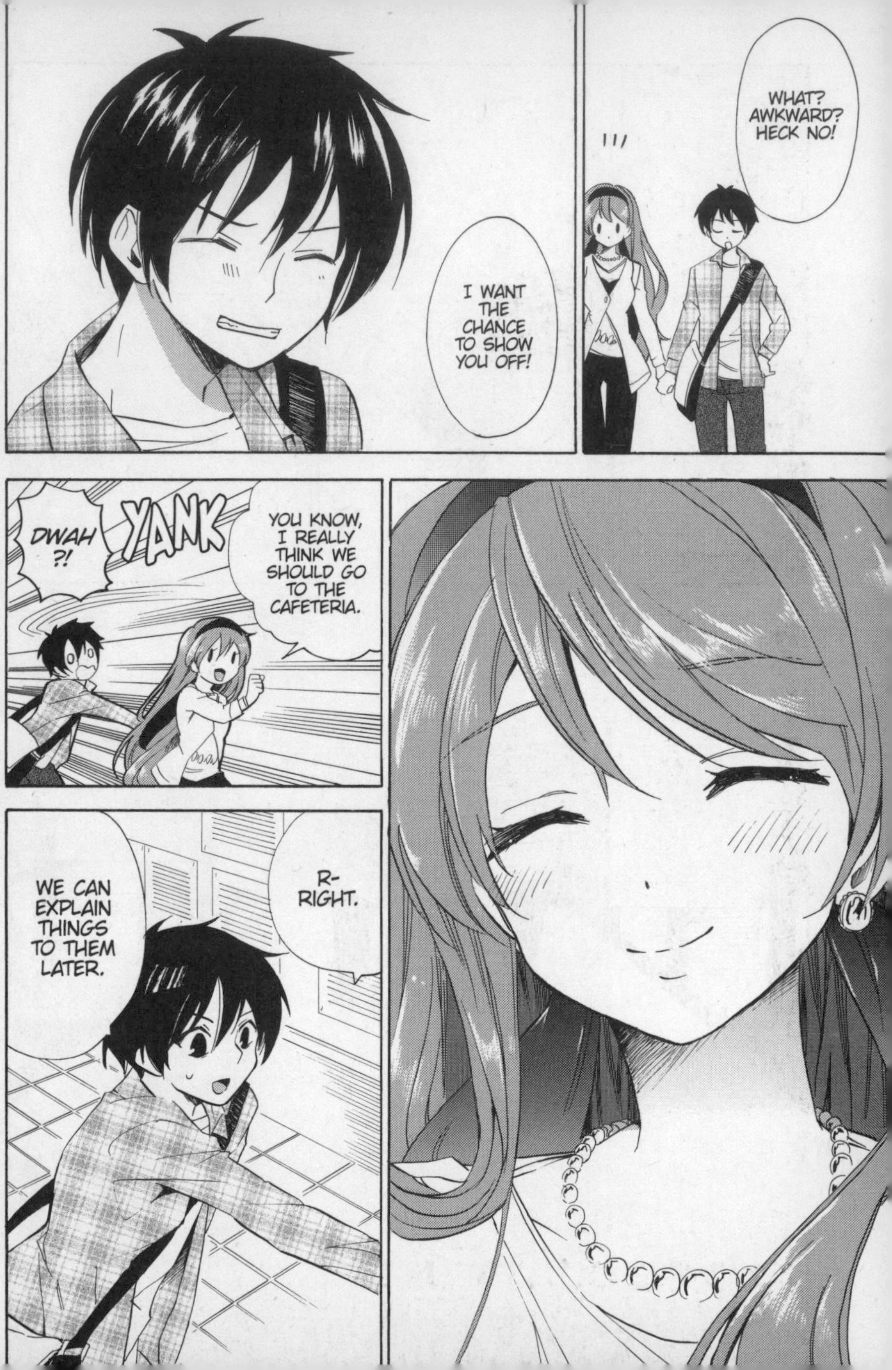
WHAT? AWKWARD? HECK NO!
I WANT THE CHANCE TO SHOW YOU OFF!
YOU KNOW, I REALLY THINK WE SHOULD GO TO THE CAFETERIA.
YANK
DWAH ?!
R- RIGHT.
WE CAN EXPLAIN THINGS TO THEM LATER.

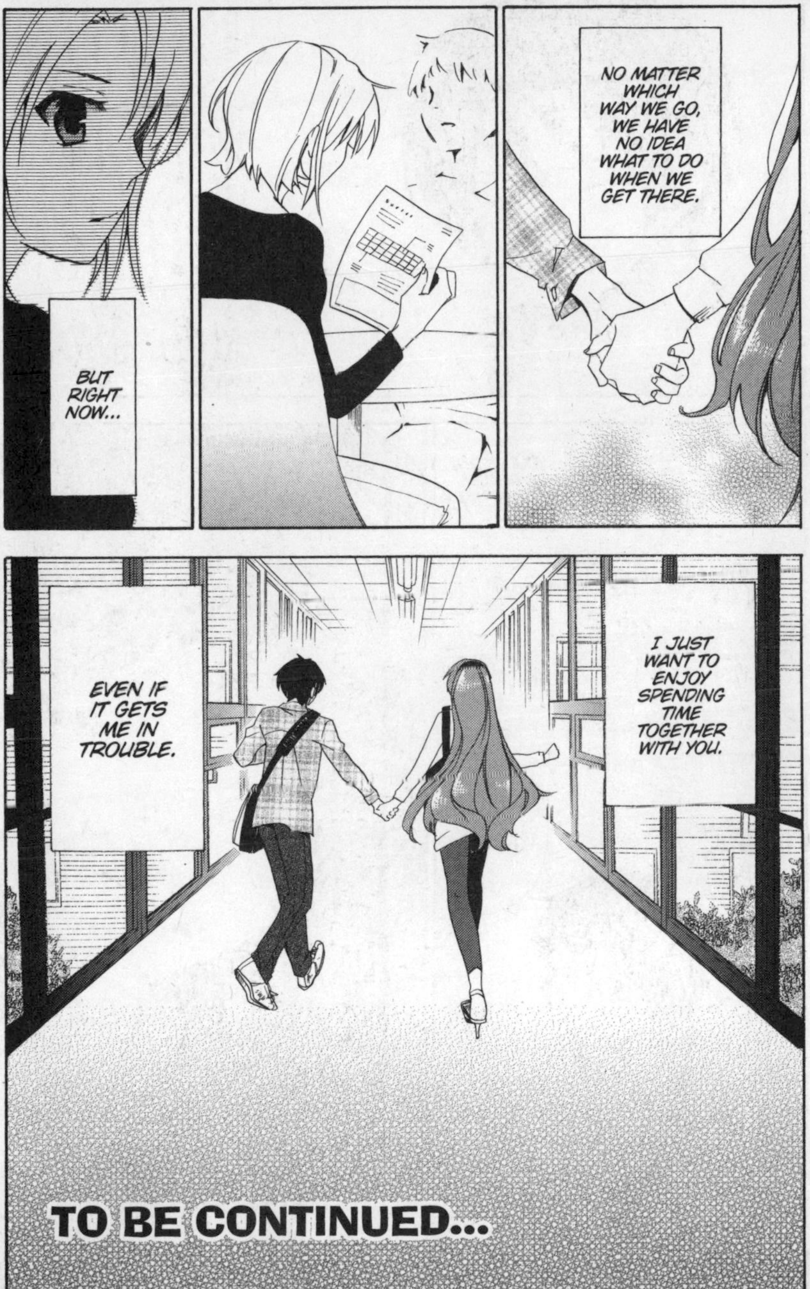
NO MATTER WHICH WAY WE GO, WE HAVE NO IDEA WHAT TO DO WHEN WE GET THERE.
BUT RIGHT NOW...
I JUST WANT TO ENJOY SPENDING TIME TOGETHER WITH YOU.
EVEN IF IT GETS ME IN TROUBLE.
TO BE CONTINUED...

SEVEN SEAS ENTERTAINMENT PRESENTS

GOLDEN TIME
ゴールデンタイム VOL. 4

based on the novel by **YUYUKO TAKEMIYA** / art by **UMECHAZUKE** / original character design by **E-JI KOMATSU**

TRANSLATION
Adrienne Beck

ADAPTATION
Bambi Eloriaga-Amago

LETTERING
Roland Amago

LAYOUT
Mheeya Wok

COVER DESIGN
Nicky Lim

PROOFREADER
Shanti Whitesides

PRODUCTION MANAGER
Lissa Pattillo

EDITOR-IN-CHIEF
Adam Arnold

PUBLISHER
Jason DeAngelis

ISBN: 978-1-626922-86-0

Printed in Canada

First Printing: July 2016

10 9 8 7 6 5 4 3 2 1

FOLLOW US ONLINE: *www.gomanga.com*

READING DIRECTIONS

This book reads from *right to left*, Japanese style. If this is your first time reading manga, you start reading from the top right panel on each page and take it from there. If you get lost, just follow the numbered diagram here. It may seem backwards at first, but you'll get the hang of it! Have fun!!

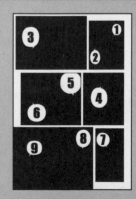